ALTERNATIVE
AMERICAS

ALTERNATIVE AMERICAS

A Reading of Antebellum Political Culture

Anne Norton

The University of Chicago Press • Chicago and London

ANNE NORTON is assistant professor of politics, Princeton University.

The University of Chicago Press, Chicago 60637
The University of Chicago Press, Ltd., London
© 1986 by The University of Chicago
All rights reserved. Published 1986
Printed in the United States of America

95 94 93 92 91 90 89 88 87 86   5 4 3 2 1

LIBRARY OF CONGRESS CATALOGING-IN-PUBLICATION DATA

Norton, Anne.
   Alternative Americas.

   Bibliography: p.
   Includes index.
   1. United States—Civilization—1783–1865.
I. Title.
E165.N87   1986   973   86-6987
ISBN 0-226-59510-2

For my family

Contents

Acknowledgments

This work was researched, and first written, in the Department of Special Collections of the University of Chicago Library. I remember with gratitude the expertise and interest of those who worked there. I am also indebted to the Department of Special Collections of the University of Pennsylvania Library, and to the Department of Special Collections of the Princeton University for wood-cuts from the Hamilton Collection reproduced in chapter 7. I should like to express my appreciation for funds received from the Princeton University Committee on Research in the Humanities and Social Sciences.

David Greenstone, Nathan Tarcov, and Aristide Zolberg saw this manuscript from its conception. I recall with pleasure conversations enriched by their dissent, scholarship, and insight. I did not follow all their counsel, but I am sure the manuscript is better for the advice I did take. Jeffrey Tulis read the manuscript in its entirety at a later stage in its gestation and performed the offices of friend and critic with particular grace.

A year at the Pembroke Center for Teaching and Research on Women at Brown University strengthened my conviction that an understanding of gender is essential to an understanding of politics, and gave me theoretical perspectives on identity that I have only begun to explore.

I am obliged to my black and Southern friends and students who have wisely and kindly helped me to an understanding of communities of which I was not a part. And in this work, where metaphors of family and friendship are so prominent, I am obliged to my own family and friends, in whose wisdom and kindness I have begun to understand those communities of which I am a part.

Introduction

In the beginning, Locke wrote, all the world was America.[1] The primeval forests of the New World, the unmeasured plains and unscaled mountains of an imagined yet unknown continent evoked in the Old World the image of a pristine and unremembered origin. This unexpected continent, standing in the way of the Old World's journey to itself, seemed to contain the secrets of a common past, the promise of a common fate.

America was "a world primal again, with visions of glory incessant and branching."[2] In this Edenic innocence men would be born to a perfect equality, and the nations of Europe would see in their relations the lineaments of a long-forgotten nature. The nations of the Old World expected in the New not the steady accretion of layer upon layer of history and hierarchy, a recapitulation of their own making. Rather they awaited

> A new race dominating previous ones, and grander far, with new
> contests,
> New politics, new literatures and religions, new inventions and arts.[3]

America's peculiar situation—unprecedented, unparalleled, unrepresentative—made it an object of universal interest. The Americans were as no other people. They were instead what all the world once was, and what all men might be. "The cause of America," Thomas Paine wrote, "is in great measure the cause of all mankind."[4] Paine's declaration echoed abroad. "'Tis a common observation here," Franklin reported from France, "that our cause is the cause of all mankind, and that we are fighting for their liberty in defending our own."[5]

The America of Europe's engendering was created in the conflicts of another continent and inherited the consequences of events and ideologies, circumstances and contradictions it had never known. America, as the outcome of European history, offered a prefiguration

1

of Europe's fate. "I did not study America just to satisfy curiosity," Tocqueville wrote, "I sought there lessons from which we might profit. I saw in America more than America; it was the shape of democracy itself which I sought . . . to know what we have to hope or fear therefrom."[6]

The America of Europe's imagining, the consequence of conflicts it would never know, appeared as an experiment in the capacities of man. When men met in battle to determine the meaning of America, Lincoln declared that their struggle would decide not merely whether that nation, but "whether any nation so conceived and so dedicated"[7] could long endure.

Not all regarded the American cause as an experiment. For some the establishment of government of the people, by the people, and for the people was America's manifest destiny, the long-foreseen fulfillment of a providential plan. Others more terrestrial saw in America the eventual culmination of the history of mankind. The Fathers of the New Israel and the Fathers of a New World Order likewise saw in the new nation's birth the advent of the millennium. The unlikely founders of unlooked-for religions saw in America Eden and Armageddon; the beginning in rebellion and the end in war.

In this many-voiced claim—to universality, to singularity, to the beginning and the end, to initiation and culmination, to comprehension and incomprehensibility, to unruliness and to imperial rule— Americans have spoken themselves into being. "Do I contradict myself?" America asked, and answered, "Very well then, I contradict myself."[8] America, ever expanding, extended from the Atlantic to the Pacific, from the tropics to the tundra, a flag planted on every pole and endlessly in orbit, embraces contradiction like a mother with child. Those who would understand America must themselves come to comprehend these contradictions.

Americans are all liberals, Louis Hartz wrote.[9] J. David Greenstone has seen in the structure of successive controversies the recurrence of a persistent bipolarity, "two opposed—although equally liberal traditions";[10] adherents of substantive standards and the inheritors of an empiricist tradition; the sons of God and the daughters of men.[11] So it is. Stephen Vincent Benet's "Invocation," preceding his epic of the Civil War, may well serve here:

> All these you are, and each is partly you
> And none is false, and none is wholly true.[12]

In America all are liberal. Republicans are democrats and Democrats republican. In America all are Puritan. Allen Ginsberg asks with

Cotton Mather, "America, when will you be angelic?"[13] In America the children of the covenant are "men and women who think lightly of the laws."[14]

Americans have ordered their understanding of themselves through contradiction. Successive party systems have opposed Federalist and Republican, Whig and Democrat, Democrat and Republican. There is a family resemblance between Federalist and Whig, Whig and Republican. There is a constancy to Democrats in their transmogrifications. Behind this series of oppositions is another, always permeating, but not always coincident with these. The twinned American inheritance of Enlightenment and Reformation reveals itself recurrently in American political culture. Shadowing these oppositions are others less formal, but no less meaningful: the English and the Indian, the Puritan and the Cavalier, white and red, white and black, East and West, North and South, man and woman. These oppositions, doubled and redoubled, have created a network of meaning through the articulation of difference.

It is fitting that this portrayal of an America enunciated in contradiction should come itself in contradiction to portrayals of America as a culture of convention, covenant, and consensus. It is fitting that the portrayals of America as a comprehensive consensus should be opposed for their partiality.

These works are partial to the political culture of the North. The meaning of America, variously conceived, invariably results in the exclusion of the South. What America cannot include the interpreters of America need not comprehend. For Hartz the South was the "alien child in the liberal family," driven in its alienation to a "fantasy life" and finally deluded by "a feudal dream."[15] This interpretation rests on categories taken from its own time rather than the time to which it ascribes them. One forgets in it that the South retained in secession the name American and that, in the midst of their enmity, the Confederate and the Unionist concurred in regarding the Southerner as American. Freedom, Hartz wrote, is the "res Americana." The Southern states were slave states. This contradiction makes it impossible for Hartz to encompass the South in America. It was not so hard for the Americans. Hartz wrote of a reconstructed South, partly persuaded of its feudal past, that had become in the years he wrote the sign for the enduring structures of slavery: black disenfranchisement, black inequality, black poverty, black exclusion, white shame. His interpretation of America expunged the South from the meaning of America. That South, however, was not the South that lost. That South was the South we won.

If, for Hartz, America belongs to Locke, then it is fitting that the South be the province of Filmer, the province of patriarchy. This interpretation ignores the language of the era. Nowhere in American political culture, North or South, does one find advocacy of monarchical institutions. Yet throughout America, throughout the antebellum period, the North was identified as masculine and the South as feminine, in an elaborate constellation of metaphors. This use of gender as a paradigm for the organization and understanding of political difference offers insights into the importance of gender as a political category. It also requires a reconsideration of the meaning and ascription of patriarchy.

Southern culture was neither feudal nor patriarchal. Yet the South was, as Hartz describes it, "alien." Southern alienation came not in consequence of a fantastic feudal revival or a regression to an imagined illiberal past, but rather in response to the North's return to the founding before the Founding, its reiteration of the paradigms, principles, and primacy of the Puritan tradition. The founding at Plymouth was recognized, no less by its adherents than by its opponents, as an alternative to the Revolution. In it the creation of America was ascribed not to the consent of men, but to the dictate of God. It marked the materialization of God's will in the world.

The Revolution was rebellion and reversal. Government was set aside in it and authority reverted from the rulers to the ruled. This advent in outlawry, this inauguration in inversion, once marked as the source of the regime's legitimacy, became the enduring sign of the people's self-engendering. The genesis of the nation in a collective act of will, however accomplished, however signified, entailed an affirmation of the latent right of insurrection.[16] It suggested the possibility of endless and varied self-determinations.

Secession seized this possibility. Thus the contradiction of founding in revolution brought forth another set of contradictions. In the South, recourse to revolution was prompted by conservative resistance to Northern progress and justified by a tradition of rebellion. In the North, radical changes in the social and political order accompanied a denial of the Revolutionary tradition and an enthusiasm for progress traced its origins back to the Pilgrim Fathers. Northern adherence to the territorial boundaries and institutional structures came with a retreat to the cultural and ideological boundaries of the dominant Northern sectional culture.

The Puritans, being great writers and wont to write about themselves, early attained an influence on national culture and national identity disproportionate to their numbers. Writing much, they have been much written about; thus they have won a disproportionate share of historiographic and literary attentions. The literature which has grown up around the Puritans is remarkable for its insight and detail as well as for its size and influence. The works of Perry Miller and Sacvan Bercovitch are the most impressive of the genre, forming from the writings of the Puritans and those who followed them an understanding of the formation and character of American national identity. This literature, however, is itself confined within the tradition it seeks to comprehend. The very features that give coherence and continuity to this reading of American mythic history and American identity from the Puritans to the present render it, of necessity, partial and defective.

Hartz excluded the South from a tradition which should properly include it. Bercovitch's work privileges as American a culture that could not embrace the South. The mythic history of this America begins in Scripture and, through the Puritans, leads inexorably to industrial capitalism. Bercovitch, like the sectional culture he describes, subscribes to the doctrine of predestination.[17]

In delineating national identity, the significant features are not those which form an objective mythic unity, but those which are subjectively recognized by persons within the culture as constituents of the national identity. While traits characteristically attributed to the Puritans remained roughly constant throughout America, the Puritans were praised in the North, derided in the South. They served, in antebellum political culture, not as the symbol of a common cultural origin, but as a shibboleth for regional disparity. Nor were the religious beliefs and familial structures derived from this tradition dominant in the South and West. The jeremiad, which Bercovitch distinguishes as a paradigm structuring American political discourse, was a form not commonly employed nor yet politically significant in Southern or Western discourse. Divorced from its cultural context the jeremiad is deprived of meaning, yet within that cultural context it is clearly the expression of a distinct regional identity. Bercovitch argues that "the Revolutionaries were agents of the pre-determined course of progress," fearful of disorder, democracy, and rebellion. This, which applies in a qualified sense to the Federalists, ignores the antiauthoritarian, democratic, and occasionally anarchic tenor of many anti-Federalist documents, and the ideological distance between the Federalists and those who would become Democratic-Republicans. The Federalists Bercovitch quotes were themselves responding to the radical threat which they believed these forces represented.[18]

The conception of American nationality and of the nation's ideological and cultural boundaries which Bercovitch describes was in fact peculiar to Northern sectional culture, and indeed confined to certain groups within that culture. The definition of American nationality promulgated by these groups became dominant first in Northern sectional culture, and later (through the North's victory in the Civil War) in national culture. It was actively resisted, however, by the South, and by groups on the periphery of Northern sectional culture. This resistance was effective in tempering the repressive policies and institutions which attended this puritanical understanding of American nationality. Because Bercovitch confines himself within the cultural boundaries of the New England Way in his studies, this dialectic appears as the result of tensions within that culture, a scheme which obscures the meaning of debates over American nationality and political legitimacy. By accepting the Puritan notion of continuity in American history from the Mayflower compact onward, Bercovitch also obscures the process whereby a narrow sectional culture rose to national primacy, and acquired an unrivaled influence over the formation of institutional structures.

It is exactly because he has confined himself within the New England Way that Bercovitch's account articulates so precisely the development of American liberal ideology within that tradition. His description of the growing importance of the jeremiad as a mode of political discourse and a model for social integration is a great contribution to the study of American political development, and an instructive example of the study of paradigmatic development. His account of the development of a conception of American nationality within the Puritan tradition reveals the emphasis on order and control within that tradition. His account of the extension of the boundaries of American nationality emphasizes the narrow ethnic and cultural boundaries of the community the Puritans delineated and illustrates the extent to which assimilation became a requisite for inclusion in the American community. Bercovitch's account of the American mission and the primacy of the word in it is subtle, rich, and thoughtful. But it is not complete.

Shadowing the exclusion of the South, indeed, contained within it, is another series of exclusions: the absence of blacks, of Indians, of women. The constriction of American identity which increased the structural exclusion, the spatial and temporal isolation of groups already only ambiguously included in American nationality, was accompanied by a reconstruction of American understanding. Following the paradigms established by the inauguration of separate spheres, and in accordance with a narrowed conception of the character and limits of politics, aspects and elements of American political culture were artificially distinguished and delegated to the scrutiny of disciplines whose professionalism ensured their continued segregation.

This disciplinary demarcation, the devaluation of domesticity, and an intolerance for ambiguity encouraged, indeed insisted upon, the academic segregation of studies concerning blacks, Indians, women, the working class, and others peripheral to the dominant cultural, political, economic, and social structures of American nationality. These studies, like their objects, were structurally devalued or excluded by the several disciplines. Within studies of political structures and of the dominant culture, the influence of the periphery on the center was little noted and still less examined. Where it was examined, it was generally as a discrete set of events or phenomena, divorced from the central concerns of the discipline.

The revaluation of values that confronted academia, and America, in the sixties began to redress this. In the immediately succeeding years, however, attention to the heretofore-neglected periphery was facilely dismissed as mere fashion. It is not. The recognition of the role of the other in the definition of identity, the role of difference in the articulation of meaning, is essential to an understanding of collective identity. The recognition of the role—and the meaning—of those groups which are peripheral and "other" to any given polity is essential to the demarcation of that polity's boundaries and to the comprehension of the content of the identity those boundaries define.

This book gives a reading of American political culture as it led to the Civil War, a period bounded by the years 1815 and 1865. Many of the changes and changing cultures examined here fall outside those years, beginning before and extending beyond the time those years demark. Nevertheless, the years themselves may serve as signs. They mark the time between the end of America's wars with England and the end of America's war with itself. The first marks the completion of American separation from England, a process that falls outside this inquiry. The second marks the inauguration of a single American identity; the establishment of the United States as a noun which would thereafter take verbs in the singular. The Revolution and the War of 1812 made manifest, and gave formal expression to, the differences that separated America from England. The Civil War was the incarnation of a wholly American contradiction, the materialization of an immanent conflict in the meaning of America.

The time between these significant years was a time of tension and division, of contending cultures and conflicting loyalties. North and South came to represent contending conceptions of America and hence alternative notions of the standards of legitimacy which the regime was required to satisfy, of the historical origins of the nation, and its eschatological significance and constraints upon its future course. This adherence to alternative Americas was manifested in regional identities which presented, in disparate constellations of traits, attributes, and associations, radically different conceptions of American individual rights and collective authority.

I am concerned here not with the facts of those institutional conflicts, nor with the existence and extent of material conditions which created the peculiar cultural configurations of North and South. These cultural configurations—the contending conceptions of national identity which expressed themselves in institutional opposition—are themselves the object of this work.

The choice of alternative cultural representations of national identity as object determines the claims and sources proper to this work. Matters of fact and material condition figure in culture through the mediation of experience and intellection. This translation from a material to an ideal dimension of politics changes a quantifiable object into one which is susceptible not of proof but of interpretation. Because I am concerned with these diffusely subjective national identities, I am interested not in what Northerners and Southerners were but in what they believed North and South to be. For this reason, partisan accounts of Northern and Southern character are preferable as evidence to verifiable accounts of the material conditions of Northern and Southern life.

The translation from a material to an ideal dimension is also necessarily an act of abstraction. In it particular events and conditions acquire general significance. This book treats particular phenomena only as they figure in the political culture, altered by experience and intellect and given general significance. The best sources for this purpose are those which are themselves artifacts of the culture—primary sources—and particularly those which had wide popular circulation or influence. In this context therefore, a hackneyed metaphor repeated time after time in newspaper poetry of no literary merit surpasses in utility a phrase of timeless originality peculiar to its author. A book review, which reveals how a work was received back into the political culture whence it came is of greater interest than the book alone. Finally, mention of certain individuals and texts (e.g., Tocqueville, Perry Miller, *Uncle Tom's Cabin*) has become expected, if not obligatory, in works on this period, both as evidence of the author's mastery of received wisdom and as a mark of the culture's continuing regard. In consequence, one may read the same passages many times. This imposes an anachronistic order on the culture and an academic consensus masquerades as a cultural one.

Individuals, like conditions and events, are altered by incorporation into cultural configurations. The creation of individual identity occurs in the tension between identification with and participation in a collective identity, and differentiation from that identity, which necessarily transcends the ideal and corporeal limits of individuals. Culture may be pictured as a grid, to use Max Weber's phrase, a "network of meaning" in which order is given to the whole by the systematic relation of intersecting lines. Individuals, then, construct themselves within the culture like buildings on a grid, flesh upon bone. They use not only the lines of the grid, but the negative space between them. Everyone is encompassed within a culture, but individuals construct themselves against it as well as according to it.

I will follow certain lines within American political culture and articulate their relation to each other. Because individuals do not coincide exactly with the cultures in which they are encompassed, I will not describe particular men. But while the examination of an individual, or individual works is a project radically different from that of this work, there is nonetheless a kinship between them. They are related as concave is to convex. In examining an individual one looks for artifacts within the culture—books and letters that he wrote, records of speeches that he gave, descriptions in the letters of others, train tickets, laundry lists, rent bills, the spoken recollections of the living, the written recollections of the dead, the patterns and influences of projects he named, ordered, or initiated—and one endeavors to see order and import in these. As the culture is amended by the inclusion of the individual, so the individual is amended by inclusion in the culture. Within the polity the individual remains distinct and separable, while within the individual distinction gives way to commonalty, and separation to participation in a collective identity. As individuals and their works leave artifacts in the culture, so cultures leave their artifacts in men. Those who study cultures look to particular men not primarily as components of a culture, but as vessels comprehending it. I use individuals in this book as carriers of culture. When I discuss an individual it will commonly be only to illustrate the aspect of the culture with which I am then concerned. When I treat an individual at length, as I do John Randolph, it will be to show how his politics and his persona showed, over time, resistance and accomodation to cultural paradigms.

The same considerations govern my interests in particular works.

I am concerned with these not as objects in their own right, but rather as they contribute to a culture and carry that culture within them. Some injustice, then, will be done to the grace and subtlety of particular works. Greater works, showing their merit in a peculiar integrity, will yield to less distinguished works which illustrate more clearly the paradigm under discussion. Other works, subtle and precise in themselves, will be presented in the debased and abbreviated form in which they influenced or expressed the culture, where an undistorted view would disguise or distort their place within it. A good case in point is the *Autobiography of Benjamin Franklin*, which seems to have entered the culture under false pretenses. Citations of this remarkable work in the generations following its publication present it as evidence of Franklin's exemplary piety, sincerity, and Christian virtue, a selection of traits not wholly consonant with the text. These traits, however, became an integral part of Franklin's mythic persona. They served to establish the mythic Franklin in relation to certain lines and paradigms in American political culture. In articulating these paradigms and their relation to others in the political culture, it is necessary to attend to the traits ascribed to Franklin and his *Autobiography* rather than to those the work itself evinces.

Individuals and cultures are not exactly coincident, nor are cultural constructions and the reality they pretend to describe. Robert Beverley, the Southern author of *The History and Present State of Virginia*, who began his work "I am an Indian," was not an Indian. Randolph was not a woman, Whitman was not a mother, Lee was not Washington, Lincoln was not Christ, the South was not a goddess, Indians were not cannibals, Northerners were not Puritans nor Southerners Cavaliers. Yet if these cultural constructs, and the myths, paradigms, and identifications to which they gave rise, are not true, they are nevertheless full of meaning. Each name—Indian, Goddess, Mother, Christ—embraces a constellation of traits, attributes, and associations separable from the material referents to which they would be most literally applied. Thus, "Indian," which speaks of Sioux, Cherokee, and Cheyenne, speaks also of violence, nature, nobility, paganism, liberty, autochthony, anarchy, and cannibalism. In saying "I am an Indian," Beverley took as his own the traits his culture ascribed to the Indian. The evidence of his ethnicity strips away the literal meaning of his statement, and "Indian" becomes the sign for a constellation of traits, a structural relation to English nationality and the American land. Had Beverley said, "I am an Englishman," the statement would have more literal veracity, but it would carry less meaning. It would be, perhaps, more true but less revealing. Through this seeming lie, Beverley was able to speak more truthfully about his identity.

It is possible to speak of the territorial boundaries of a nation, the legal requirements for residence within it, the rights the law recognizes in citizens and the obligations incumbent upon them, their language, their occupations, and their exports. These, however, do not exhaust the meaning of the statement "I am an American." National identity commonly precedes the legal definition of the state. It may survive the dissolution of the state's territories. Nationality entails not only accordance to certain objective criteria, but also subjective participation in a collective identity. This collective identity, like any other name, compasses a constellation of traits, attributes, and associations. In identifying himself with that name the national acknowledges himself to be described by these.

This subjective nationality has, however, no formal expression. Metaphors, like that employed by Robert Beverley, reveal the informal, nonquantifiable content of nationality. They provide traits in which nationals can recognize their commonalty, symbols and gestures in which they can express it. Metaphors are especially important when nationality is inchoate, nascent, or in flux. In the use of metaphors the speaker likens the unknown, unclear, or ill defined (in this case, his national identity), to an object whose traits and political significance are well established. The differentiation of North and South, the Union and the Confederacy, was accomplished in part by the liberal use of metaphor. Likening the Southerner to the Cavalier emphasized certain traits characteristic of the Cavalier as definitive of Southern national identity. The use of other metaphors for Southern identity differentiated the Southerner from the Cavalier and made clear the traits in which they were identical.

The metaphor uses the object, in this case the Cavalier, as a sign. The subject, the Southerner, is identified with the signified constellation of traits, and with the signifier, the image called up by the name of the Cavalier. The identity of traits prompts the initial metaphor. Subsequent references—in speech and gesture—to the name and image of the Cavalier then call up the traits in which they have their identity.

Certain metaphors are important for their referential as well as their significant meaning. In addition to their significant content, a constellation of abstracted traits, they carry personal associations. Familial metaphors—mother, father, brother—may prove more powerful in their personal and referential meaning than as signs. Rhetorical strategies may exploit or be undone by this importance of the referent.

The referent is important, because at this juncture politics and psychology are conjoined. For example, in the antebellum period, alterations in the referential meaning of mother and woman and regional disparities in the meaning of father and mother sped the differentiation of North and South.

Metaphors are used to clarify more than the content of nationality. In addition to ascribing, through analogy, certain traits to a yet ill-defined identity, they may identify a structural resemblance. In such cases, a group is identified with another whose structural position in a given set of relations is well known. In this rhetorical strategy, liminal groups figure prominently as objects in the definition of national and subcultural identity.

I have taken the term "liminal" from Victor Turner's study *The Ritual Process*. It corresponds roughly to the terms "marginal" and "peripheral," designating an individual or (and more often) a group, whose inclusion in the community is ambiguous.[19] Such groups are subordinated within, or excluded from, economic, social, and political structures. Their antistructural character is revealed in the traits ascribed to them. Among these are equality, poverty, community, silence, sacredness, nakedness, anonymity, madness, unconventional sexuality, spontaneity, divinity, and bestiality. The first seven of these traits are Turner's.[20] The next three are the fruit of my own observations of the liminal. The final two are taken from Aristotle's observation in the *Politics*, that the man outside the city must be either a beast or a god. I have observed that those who find themselves radically alienated from political structures claim for themselves the traits of beasts or gods, or are ascribed such traits by those who reject them. Each of these traits (this is not an exhaustive list) indicates exclusion or withdrawal from the political order.

When a group indentifies itself, through metaphor, with another group, or individual whose liminality is recognized, it expresses a subjective perception of an analogous subordination in structure. Identification with these recognized liminars then serves as an assertion, on the part of the speaker, of a subordination similar to theirs. In metaphoric strategies of this sort, identification is prompted by a formal similarity—occupying the same place in structure—rather than by identification with specific traits. This difference is blurred, however, by consequent use of the metaphor. There, the common structural position which prompted the original identification is expressed by recollection of the metaphoric object in speech and gesture. This identification through gesture often involves the momentary adoption of traits characteristic of the liminal group with which the subject wishes to identify. Thus the Sons of Liberty, for example, put on feathers, moccasins, and warpaint for the Boston Tea Party.

Metaphoric identifications, whether prompted by a coincidence of traits or an analogous structural subordination, manifest themselves in the same way. I distinguish them here because they serve different political functions. Identifications by trait serve to articulate—that is, to order and express—national identity. Structural identifications express the relation of a self-conscious collectivity, a people, to others in structure. The first process is the differentiation of one people from another. The second process is one of alienation from the prevailing structural order—from the regime, and from hierarchies of social and economic power. Each of these processes may culminate in rebellion or revolution. They are commonly interrelated. Thus the development of Southern national identity was sped by a common apprehension of exploitation and subordination among the Southern states. The propagation and elaboration of national identity was facilitated by the use of metaphoric paradigms which, while illustrating the structural subordination of the South, identified it with an object whose traits, attributes, and associations were appropriate to an emerging Southern national identity.

Metaphors identify the subject with an established sign for a certain constellation of traits, attributes, and associations. Paradigms set signs against one another in a formal relation. Paradigms provide patterns for comprehension—intellectual and institutional ordering and incorporation—within the culture. If culture resembles a grid, paradigms may be likened to sections of that grid which provide patterns for the grid's extension, ensuring its coherence and stability.

Three types of paradigms show themselves in this period of American political culture. In corporeal paradigms, a series of bodily functions provides a formal model for a political, social, or economic process. Thus the paradigm of eating, digestion, and elimination provides a formal model for manufacture and territorial expansion. In social paradigms, a social relation provides a model for a political one. Thus the understanding of the Civil War as a "war of brother against brother" likened the relation of the warring North and South to a familial relation of established significance. In historical paradigms, a past conflict or set of relations provides the model for a present one. The past conflict involves parties whose traits are established in the culture in a conflict whose ideological significance is equally well established. By likening the present to the past conflict, speakers provide accounts of both the significant characteristics of the parties and the character and significance of the conflict. The most famous of the historical paradigms for the Civil War is that provided by the English Revolution: the conflict between Puritan and Cavalier. This provided metaphors for North and South which were thought to illustrate the salient traits of each section and a model for their conflict which attributed to it the ideological significance of the English Revolution.

Corporeal and social paradigms are especially interesting because they reveal a dimension of political culture in which the political and the psychological meet. These paradigms, and the formal relations between political and psychological process which they reveal, invite the use of analytic tools from several disciplines. Social and historical paradigms indicate mechanisms whereby political cultures extend themselves institutionally and chronologically. In social paradigms an existing social institution, ordering a given set of relationships, provides a model for a new political institution, ordering previously disordered relations. This provides insight into how political cultures achieve cohesion, and an explanatory model for institutional growth. Historical paradigms serve a similar function. Here, however, the integration is historical: a model discerned in the formal resemblance of past and present conflicts provides a means for integrating the experience of the present into an understanding of the past. Through the use of this mechanism the nation is able to foster an image of itself as a continuous entity, constant in time. Examination of this mechanism reveals the relevance of myth and history to politics, for changes in the former are required by—and hence reveal—imminent alterations in the latter. Nations which remake their past remake their present selves. Such changes are not made, as some would have it, to ascribe legitimacy through primordiality, but rather to assert the synchronicity of the nation, the persistence of collective identity in time.

Part 1 treats the reformation in Northern political culture—the revival of the founding at Plymouth and the creation of a constricted American identity appropriate to the nation founded there. The existence of an admirable literature on the Puritan tradition makes it possible, indeed desirable, to foreground the conflicts attending this reconstruction of the meaning of America.

Part 2 describes the recognition by Southerners of a distinct national identity, and their attendant alienation from the Union. Southern metaphoric identification with the three most important liminal groups of the antebellum period—women, blacks, and Indians—simultaneously indicated the constellation of traits definitive of Southern nationality and made manifest the ideological content of that identity. Southern use of maternity as a paradigm for political development and as the source of standards for political right will also be explored.

Part 3 offers an interpretation of the political culture of the emerging West. The primacy of the maternal paradigm in the South and the paradigm of eating in the West permits a comparison of these two corporeal paradigms. The policies and structures associated with these as well as the disparate character of the signifying corporeal processes reveal their radically different ideological content. The differences revealed by the use of these alternative paradigms appear constant across cultures. Two of the metaphoric strategies adopted by the South will also be of more general interest: trait stripping and the appropriation of psychic drives through metaphor.

Part 4 treats the Rebellion in two chapters. The first is a deconstruction of the significance of the slavery issue in antebellum political culture. The civil rights movement radically altered American political culture and American national identity. In doing so it changed our history. To determine the significance of slavery as an issue in antebellum political culture, it is necessary to place it in its antebellum context, as the central issue in a constellation of issues important in the politics of that period. When the slavery issue is seen in relation to questions of nationality, labor, and the viability of the family as a sociopolitical institution, both political alliances in the period and the shameful course of race relations after it become more intelligible.

The second chapter of part 4 treats three metaphoric paradigms for the Rebellion. Two of these are historical, one is social. In each case, North and South employed the same paradigms. They differed in the frequency with which they employed particular paradigms, the traits they ascribed to parties in the paradigmatic conflicts, and the significance they read in the conflicts themselves. Thus, while North and South read in their conflict a reenactment of the paradigmatic struggle of Puritan and Cavalier and concurred in the ascription of metaphoric roles, they differed in their assessments of the meaning of the conflict and hence in the meaning of their respective roles. Northerners read the conflict as a decisive moment in the world historical progress toward liberty. The South read it as the momentary triumph of military dictatorship. Hence, Northerners employed the Cavalier as a sign of authoritarian repression, Southerners as a sign of the defence of legitimate right against military usurpation. The continuation in each section of the primacy of liberal ideology was thus obscured. An asymmetry in the historiographic attention devoted to the two sections has perpetuated and detailed the interpretation which prevailed among the adherents of the victorious Union, without that accompanying elaboration of the Southern interpretation which would clarify the conduct and structures of the Confederacy. Because the paradigms entail interpretations of American history and ideology, and (in at least two cases) general theories of political development, the use of one in preference to the other is highly significant with regard to both the subsequent ideology of the regime and intellectual constructs having currency in successive moments of the political culture.

The final chapters, in part 5, present three attempts to integrate the Civil War into the mythic history of the once-again-United States of America. The works of Melville, Lincoln, and Whitman on the Civil War endeavor to construct a single people from the divided ranks of the victorious and the defeated. They endeavor to cull a continuous and continuing history from the experience of enmity and division. The reformation of national identity in the wake of the war, and the altered history which attended it, led to a reinterpretation of American identity in light of the recent conflict. The reformed identity comprised an altered set of traits, attributes, and associations, some drawn from antebellum models, others from the war itself. The revised history was ordered in accord with paradigms explaining the origin and issue of the war. This altered American identity elaborated itself not only in historical accounts of the nation and the war, but also in the subsequent policies and institutional development of the United States. The firm establishment of industrial capitalism and the legitimation of an institutional military and of military conquest, rooted in paradigms and conditions antedating the war, were secured in the circumstances of the Union victory and served thereafter as powerful constraints on American politics.

In speaking as I have, and shall continue to, of North and South, I conjure up the image of two monolithic opponents. Within the separate cultures of North and South there were, of course, a multitude of subcultures. All parties, however, recognized a fundamental distinction between the political cultures of North and South. Members of subcultures were regarded by themselves and others as integrated wholly or partially in the comprehensive culture of the section which contained them. North and South became, and have remained, signs for the constellation of traits, attributes, and associations which were thought to distinguish each section. It was along this division that the war was thought.

One
THE NORTH

1   The Word Made Flesh

The Northern, like the Southern, states had been settled by English outlaws and outcasts. In the South these had included
convicts and younger sons, the ambitious, the adventurous, the impoverished and exiled. The circumstances of colonial settlement were
merely a picaresque prelude to the great events of Revolution. In the
North, however, the founding at Plymouth became the decisive moment in regional political culture. The Puritans were the Founding
Fathers of Northern sectional culture. Theirs was a scriptural community. They were governed by the Word, as Bercovitch describes them,
by a particular and privileged writing, the Scripture of the Christians
and the Jews. Yet their political culture can be described as scriptural
not merely because of the primacy of the Word in it, but because it is
characterized, and self-consciously so, by the qualities that distinguish
the written.

They were children of the covenant, of a long series of covenants
between man and God, and man and man: God and Noah, God and
Abraham, the new covenant of the New Testament, the Magna Carta,
the Mayflower Compact, the Constitution. In serving as a historical
paradigm, the scriptural covenant reiterated in the Bible unites compact and writing. These are, in any case, intrinsically allied. It is in the
nature of writing to establish covenant. The written possesses the
qualities sought in covenant; it endures and it endures unaltered. The
written preserves the author, but once written it is no longer subject to
his will. Where there are multiple authors, they are indissolubly
bound to one another in the text. Without writing, without scripture,
there is no covenant.[1] Writing creates communities removed from the
will, and enduring beyond the lives of their authors.

America, Washington Irving wrote, was governed by words: "the
simple truth of the matter is that their government is a pure, unadulte-
rated logocracy or government of words."[2] Irving's description is very

rich. It embraces not only Bercovitch's conception of America as a nation of Scripture, but also the conception of America as the creation of speech. America is at once a spoken and a written nation.[3] The authoritative act in which the people speak themselves into being is preserved by the use of the present tense in the Preamble to the Constitution, where it is revived by each reader. Speech is the proper medium of consent, individual and immediate. Written consent may bind an unwilling people to the determinations of an earlier identity. Speech makes necessary the renewal of consent, the constant regeneration of the nation in the sentiments of the people. The Revolution established consent as the determinant of the government's right to rule. The Constitution attempted to give an enduring expression to this affirmation of the authority of consent. In doing so, it wedded the consensual understanding of legitimacy to the tradition of scriptural authority privileged within the Puritan tradition.

Writing, like other acts, is an imposition of will on the material world.[4] The Puritan tradition sanctified these acts of reformation, which enabled men at once to escape from the limits of nature and to establish their authority over it. This issued not only in the reverence—and reiteration—of covenant and scripture, but also in economic modes of reformation. Max Weber's *The Protestant Ethic and the Spirit of Capitalism* is especially interesting with regard to America, where (as he observed) the spirit of capitalism attained its apex. The primacy of rational-legal authority, discipline, the assembly-line method of manufacture, capitalism as a calling, and the mass army each had a place in the complex of ideas and institutions impelled by the Reformation. In America, the historical circumstances of Puritan emigration and settlement mediated the conceptual paradigms of the Reformation.

The Puritans, on their errand in the West, were impelled by the imperative to make manifest an immanent divinity. The paradigm of the Incarnation, peculiar neither to their sect nor to Protestantism, transformed their relation to the natural environment. The figure of Christ presented the images of God in man, the soul in the body, the ideal in the material, the word in the world. The redemptive power attributed to the incarnate God suggested that the operation of God, soul, and the ideal upon their respective dichotomous partners effected a salutary transformation in the latter.

The Puritans had approached the wilderness in the West not as a refuge or a garden but as the unredeemed material, to be subdued, transformed, and overcome. They first cleared the ground for farming, an act which they and their descendants regarded as removing it from nature to civilization, from the province of the unredeemed to inclusion in the divine scheme.

> Strike! With every blow is given
> Freer sun and sky
> And the long hid earth to heaven
> Looks, with wondering eye![5]

This selection from Whittier's *Songs of Labor* illustrates this understanding of labor as an imitation of Christ. The laborers are portrayed as liberating the earth in enabling it to look upon heaven. The militant description of their assault on nature may, however, owe more to the circumstances of the Reformation in England than to the original paradigm. The Puritans, it must be remembered, were partisans of Cromwell, associated in Northern political myth with the more martial of the religious virtues. Their relation to their natural environment is thus pictured not merely as that of ruler to ruled, but as that of a conqueror:

> We make of Nature's giant powers
> The slaves of human art.[6]

Agriculture and husbandry are human orderings of natural processes whereby the production of nature is rendered predictable, and thus more useful and profitable to men. In them, the workings of nature are assimilated to the rational patterns produced by men. The attribution of omniscience to God, the identification of God and Logos, and the notion that the possession and exercise of intellect likens men to God, assign intrinsic as well as instrumental sacredness to art in its dichotomous relation to nature. Through the arts men inscribed themselves on the natural world. They remade that world in their image, as God had made them in his. The art of farming, however, obliges men to accord themselves to the workings of nature.

During the early national period, while the Northern states remained, demographically, predominantly agricultural, representatives of the states nevertheless portrayed the section as "commercial" in character.[7] This was routinely marked as a point of disparity between the Northern and Southern sections. Because the practice of commerce removed men from immediate dependence on the land and substituted a system of values and relations determined by the invisible hand of the market, and by intellect, it was an occupation more expressive of the character of a community whose integrity depended on its distance from the natural. Other traits attributed to the section reinforced this character. Northerners routinely insisted that the North was a region of greater erudition and higher culture than the South. Southerners portrayed the North as a nation of shopkeepers and peddlers, whose singular distinction lay in their capacity to make money (artifical value) by creating artful imitations of natural goods, wooden nutmegs being the usual example. Thus, a Southern congressman would say of a Northern colleague, "the gentleman comes from a section of the country where the people could see a dollar with the naked eye as far as he could see it with a telescope."[8] The *Southern Literary Messenger*, engaged in a little sectional sparring with the *North American Review*, was willing to concede the nutmegs, but asked "what of the horn flints, or the wooden hams, or the wooden clocks, and all the rest?"[9] The *North American Review*, which had prompted the controversy by publishing an especially effusive praise of the Puritans and their descendants, would quarrel with the Southerners, but Northerners were commonly ready to accept the trait of sharp dealing as their own. Thus one native of Connecticut wrote:

> What land is that whence peddlars come
> A thousand miles or so from home
> With tin, and basswood trenchers; some
> With patent nutmegs and new rum
> To gather up the coppers?—hum
> Connecticut.

That he did not find this trait irreconcilable with the piety which the Pilgrim Fathers had instilled is evinced by the next verse, which finds Connecticut a land "where parsons live" and "humble sinners seek reprieve."[10]

In his analysis of, or rather, panegyric to, the "New England character" Peleg Sprague, then senator from Maine, astutely related the repression of internal to the conquest of external nature. The Puritans, he wrote: "adopted a rigid system of education for their children, by which all outward manifestations of internal emotion were forbidden and repressed. But the fire which was not permitted to break forth only glowed with more enduring intensity within . . . From obvious causes it has generally been directed to some branch of productive industry." This "pervading zeal and ardor and energy," he continued, "has subdued the forest and spread far and wide the beams and blessings of civilization."[11]

Manufacturing represents the decisive human triumph over nature, for in it men alter the shape, and indeed the essential character, of natural resources, creating as they will. Entirely rationalized, the process of manufacturing effects both the conquest and exploitation of nature, in accordance not with natural processes but with rational objectives. "Guided by mind," E. G. Squier wrote, "man has rendered subservient to his will the conflicting elements, prisoned the air, harnessed the demon of fire, and disarmed even the hissing thunderbolt of its dread power and conducted it harmless to earth . . . These are the triumphs of mind in the material world."[12] Industry enabled men to imitate the creative power and omnipotence of God in their relations to the material world. The transcendence of the corporeal which they believed their faith granted them was thus expressed in a like triumph of mind over the material. In conquering natural forces, men "harnessed the demon," and recompensed themselves for their submission to God by making nature submissive to them.

Whittier exclaimed over Lowell, Massachusetts, "Marvellously here has Art wrought its modern miracles!" but he described the factory as a "prison house." Lowell was a city "springing up like the enchanted palaces of Arabian tales in a single night," but, he writes elsewhere, "Over the gateways of this New World Manchester glares the inscription WORK OR DIE." Within the city, rivers were "tamed and subdued to the purposes of man, and charmed into slavish subjection to the Wizard of Mechanism." The imprisoned "Genii of Mechanism," "each in his iron harness," were "raising us by wheel and pulley, steam and water power."[13]

Whittier associated natural forces with pagan magic, industry with "Gospel" and "the millennium."[14] Mind conquered nature and elevated man by likening him to God. "Mind," the Reverend Channing wrote, is "the highest force in the universe . . . This created the heavens and the earth."[15] Men were doing God's work in manufacturing, remaking the world in their image and to their purposes, as God had made man in his.

The attribution of omnipotence to God affirmed that the course of history would eventuate in the accomplishment of his will. This invested history with extraordinary importance, for in its course the pious and the interested might perceive the working out of the will of God. The Puritan settlers of New England had possessed a strong sense of their place in this sacred history. They continually recurred to the past for prophetic prefigurations of the present and intimations of the future. They saw history as a progress, linear and ultimately eventuating in the best of all possible worlds. Whig historians, imbued with this understanding of history, thus wrote as Rufus Choate did, "to withstand the pernicious sophism that the successive generations as they come to life, are but so many flights of summer flies, without relations to the past, or duties to the future."[16]

History was the materialization of the will of God. As such it partook of the nature of Scripture, revealing to man the divine will by inscribing it in the material world. In history men become participants in Scripture. This understanding of history not merely as text but as Scripture saw individual will absorbed and comprehended in the divine, but it granted to each generation an enduring significance and charged it with a mission of world historical significance. "The truth is," Dr. Sprague sermonized, "each generation is acting, not for itself only, but for all succeeding generations."[17] With immortality ascribed to the saints comprising the community, the residents of past, present, and future were compassed in a single, temporally boundless community. The maintenance of the community, and with it the collective covenant with God, was thus dependent not only on the community's survival in the present generation, but also on the renewal of collective memory. "Whigs were obsessed," J. V. Matthews observes in his study of Whig history, "with the idea that the 'track of generations' was being effaced and the individual left isolated in his own egotism and willfulness, unaware of the claims of ancestors or future progeny."[18] It was a consciousness of history, Choate affirmed, which "binds us to our fathers and to our posterity by a lengthening and golden cord."[19] Certainly this consciousness of history, which distinguished the Puritans and their Whig successors, bound them to their posterity. Their comprehensive understanding of history continues to contain historians, binding them with their exegete predecessors in a scriptural community. This intellectual hegemony makes history again the product of predestination.

The Puritans and their Whig successors endeared themselves to historians on several accounts. The rank which they assigned to history is flattering. Their attention to historical continuity, and to their development as a community and their preservation of accounts and materials relating to these are convenient. Their emphasis on the formation of cultures, and hence on history, as the primary determinant of identity enhances the political significance of history with respect to other disciplines. This preoccupation with history is, the historian Daniel Walker Howe observes, "a sign of cultural awareness or progressivism." The Whigs were America's "modernizing elite" intellectually as well as institutionally. "The realization that political life is historically conditioned led eventually to the relativism characteristic of the twentieth century."[20]

Howe notes that "to define American identity Whig spokesmen typically turned to history, Democratic ones to principle." With America bound up in a continuous history that stretched from Abraham to the Constitution in a concatenation of covenants, ideology was insufficient to express the nation's eschatological importance. Because this series was presumed to be morally as well as temporally progressive, however, both American republicanism and American culture were manifestations of the progress of mankind. Howe recognizes the Whigs as representative of one of "two distinct ideological options," which had been "rivals for Americans' loyalty, struggling . . . from the first day till now." Bushnell, whom Howe quotes, regarded this ideological divergence as the impasse under the Civil War. Howe asserts that ideology must be understood in the context of its peculiar political culture, as a system of beliefs expressed with cultural referents, in a mode of political discourse which clarifies, refines, and enhances their meaning to those within the culture. Howe's delineation of the political culture of the American Whigs emphasizes their understanding of nationality as culturally determined, and their conception of the formation of culture in time. He relates this understanding of nationality, and the Whig interest in history and culture, to a central belief that "society is sovereign."[21]

The Puritans regarded the collectivity as a community of knowledge. The saints were united by their common apprehension of the final things. This eschatological knowledge assimilated them to one another and assured their salvation by effecting their participation in divinity. This community was thus similar to the ideological communities of modern revolutions, inasmuch as the boundaries of the community corresponded to a set of common beliefs. The ideal unity of the community of saints, however, was manifest, according to the paradigm of the Incarnation, in the material world. The Puritans saw signs of sainthood in material prosperity and, more importantly, in behavioral conformity to convention.

The ideal unity of the community of saints was also thought by the Puritans to have found material expression in America. American political unity thus acquired sacred significance as the material and temporal expression of the ideal unity of the community of saints.

The influence of Protestantism on the form and content of political rhetoric in the antebellum period was without parallel. The proselytizing efforts of the Protestant Evangelicals had increased the audience and influence of the clergy. Men acquainted with German philosophy adhered to a notion of historical progress in which the Reformation was both the mark of past and the determinant of future progress. Hegel's philosophy thus served to reconcile the secular to the religious, inclining the agnostic to accord Protestantism a respect which he might otherwise have given more reluctantly. Antiauthoritarian sentiment abated after the Revolution, further securing the position of the clergy. Orators counseled in its place a reverence for law and legal authority. Community became increasingly important, for while the Founders and their official successors exhorted citizens to acquiesce to the new order, veterans of the Revolution kept alive the memory of that sentiment of immediate, subjective community which had animated the Revolutionary struggle. Collective action thus expressed an aspect of two paradigms established in the Revolution and the democratic regime.

The meaning of collective action, as the inheritors of the Puritan tradition perceived it, was encapsulated in Daniel Webster's formula "Liberty and Union, now and forever, one and inseparable." His "Reply to Hayne" remained required reading in American textbooks for generations afterward, yet it marked not the acclamation, but the dissolution of the Union. Read independently Webster's formula expressed a principle, accepted North and South, upon which America's republican institutions were bottomed. Individuals exercised their private liberty by freely uniting for the common good. The union thus formed was predicated on individual liberty and obliged to maintain it. Webster's reply was, however, a repudiation of prior sovereignties. He affirmed the sacred and inviolable character of the Union. Though his conception of the Union was legal and material rather than spiritual, it recalled the Puritan conception of America. Thus it was readily accepted in New England where it contributed to the revival of the Puritans and their articulation of the national destiny. Webster's speech, intended to preserve the Union, sped its dissolution. By evoking a particularist, sectional notion of nationality, it effectively excluded the North from political discourse with the South.

Webster's speech, though secular in content and context, was exemplary of that species of indigenous American rhetoric known as the jeremiad. Bercovitch has articulated this rhetorical form admirably in *The American Jeremiad*. In rebuking citizens for their present shortcomings, the jeremiad reminded them of the high destiny of their community and exhorted them to its accomplishment. More exact simulcra of this style were delivered by Protestant clerics throughout the North in this period. Bercovitch, himself acceding to the Whig account of the nation's origins, traces the jeremiad from America's Puritan founding through the Revolution to the Civil War. The prominence of the jeremiad as a rhetorical model is limited by its sectional character, which Bercovitch deprecates, and by the anticlericalism of the Revolutionary period. In the second quarter of the nineteenth century, the resurgence of evangelical Protestantism, the decline of anti-authoritarianism, and Whig efforts at universalizing New England's sectional culture, made it a more frequently employed rhetorical form.

The jeremiad was not an appeal to equals; it was commandment, exhortation, and rebuke. It derived its force in part from acknowledgement of the speaker's authority. As such, it reflects the Whig advocacy of a paternalistic social order, distinguished by hierarchy and authoritarian rather than democratic in its operation.

Daniel Walker Howe wrote of Whig oratory, "For the Whigs the orator performed a double service: he must not only defend the people's true interests, but show the people themselves where those interests lay." As the name suggests, the jeremiad was itself derived from a prophetic model: in revealing present sin and future glory to an erring people, the prophet prompted their reformation. The orator thus consciously addressed not the reason, sentiments, or interests of particular men, but the conscience of the community. For the Whigs, "it is society that is sovereign." It was at once the primary operative unit of political life and the source of the injunctions virtuous men conformed to. The jeremiad provided a reiteration of the character and destiny of the nation. It indicated existing elements or policies foreign to the right character of the community. It demanded that these elements and policies be put in accord with the right character and mission of the community. In its secular incarnation, it demanded the assimilation of immigrants and other groups whose character differed radically from the Whig conception of American nationality. The employment of the jeremiad in this period in support of public education, temperance, and the preservation of the Union reflected a conception of nationality which precluded cultural diversity and entailed assimilation.[22]

The Whigs had presented the Puritans as the model for social conformity. The Puritan ideal emphasized the suppression and sublimation of natural appetites, and submission to authority. Theodore Dwight Weld echoed this equation of self-improvement and self-control in his statement "Restraints are the web of civilized sociaty—warp and woof."[23] "Running through Whig political appeals," Howe notes, "was the concept of consciously arranged order."[24] The doctrine of predestination had made the ordering of temporal affairs an imitation of Christ. The efforts to increase the degree of order in the society were evidence of the proponents' willingness to assimilate themselves to a higher form of life; the example offered by the deity. Schemes to subordinate and then to assimilate foreign elements in the nation would thus improve the moral character of those who effected and those who were subjected to them.

In the years from 1815 to 1830, Americans had collectively rein-terpreted the meaning of America's national mission. The tenet that republicanism was a universally superior form of government led first to plans for the evangelical promulgation of democracy, for spreading the good news of self-government and the rights of men to heretofore-unenlightened peoples. Finally, it led to the belief that republican in-stitutions were a manifestation, in a form intelligible to all, of an innate superiority on the part of the culture distinguished by them.

Because this understanding of the sanctity of the national union grew out of the Puritan understanding of the nation's eschatological significance, it was foreign to the South, where political union was regarded as an expedient, and perhaps sentimental, measure. The South was therefore a stranger to the campaigns to encourage both institutional consolidation and subjective national allegiance, which were common in the North throughout the antebellum period. In addi-tion to legislative efforts to strengthen the relative power of the federal government with respect to that of the several states, the enthusiasts of national unity advocated such measures as linguistic assimilation and a new national name. "We want utterance for our nationality," the Com-mittee on a National Name wrote. "We want a watchword more na-tional than that of states, more powerful than that of party."[25]

By the time of the Civil War, the partisans of a historically deter-mined (rather than consensually or ideologically) determined national union had effectually established a new national name. The regular use of "Union" rather than "the United States" marked a long-standing cultural divergence. The Unionists insisted on the sacred character of the Union. They argued that it had been established in perpetuity, consummating a historical process that antedated the Revolution. They were determined to maintain its temporal continuity. They described themselves as acting on behalf of posterity.

With the Union construed as a temporally extensive community, the significance of generations and individuals—and more important-ly, their right to alter or abolish their government—was greatly diminished. Henry Clay asked, "Mr. President, what is an individual man? An atom, almost invisible without a magnifying glass—a mere speck upon the surface of an immense universe . . . Shall a being so small, so petty, so fleeting, so evanescent, oppose itself to the onward march of a great nation, to subsist for ages and ages to come—oppose itself to the long line of posterity, which, issuing from our loins, will endure during the existence of the world?"[26]

Whigs exhorted their countrymen to a consciousness of their duty to this temporally extensive community rather than to a consciousness of their individual rights. This subordination of self to the good of the community (and hence to providential dictate) was best expressed in obedience to law.[27]

Law was the objective, public expression of the will of the community. In the Puritan tradition, the community was the culmination of a providential progress and obedience to the law was readily conflated with acquiescence to the will of God. America was a covenanted nation in several senses. It served as a representation in the temporal world of the ideal community of saints, continuing a long series of God's covenants with his chosen people. Its own contractual origins, whether traced to the Constitution or the Mayflower Compact, replicated the covenant between the people and God. The position of law in the American polity was, in this scheme, analogous to the position of Scripture in the Holy Commonwealth.

The primacy of Scripture in the Judeo-Christian tradition is the source of the "religion of the law" and of rational-legal authority. The religious significance of Scripture lends to the written word an associated sanctity and enhances it as a source of authority.[28] The primacy of Scripture in the religion charges the priesthood with the function of explication, exegesis, and education, creating models for the performance of these functions in a secular context. The Puritans emphasized the importance of covenants doctrinally. This emphasis was accompanied by continued reiterations of the covenantal paradigm in their political relations. Initially, this conjoined the divergent traditions of the Enlightenment and the Holy Commonwealth, but the Puritan view insisted upon the enduring legitimacy of compacts, independent of their authors.[29]

This recognition of independent authority in contracts was of equal importance in the formation of Northern economic practices. There, the emphasis on contracts produced both a satisfactory mode of economic relations and an enduring logocentricity. This last sped the acceptance of paper currency, charters, stocks, and the practice of incorporation. Incorporation is especially significant because it was an economic practice far more common in the North than in the South during the antebellum period, and because it derived from the paradigm of the Incarnation. The first factor produced both a divergence of economic practice in the two sections and differential preferences in regard to economic legislation among their respective elites. The second is interesting because the word *incorporation*, which is virtually identical etymologically to *incarnation*, actually represents its converse: the transubstantiation of the material to the ideal and the attribution of ideal unity to a collection of persons. On the economic plane, as on the political, the corporation, like the commonwealth, acquired authority greater than that of its authors.

The Puritans had in their time, and retain in ours, an image distinguished by repression. The political tradition which seized upon them as its exemplars has perpetuated, with different emphasis, the repressive structures of the political culture engendered by the Puritans. As Peleg Sprague recognized, the Puritan system of education, which insisted on the suppression of passion and the regulation of natural functions according to strict conventions, produced individual dynamos of passion under pressure. Sprague attributed the rise of Northern manufacturing to the compensatory efforts of these repressed individuals, a conclusion which has received theoretical support from several quarters. That ethic which made every man a monk made them diligent workers also, repudiating the sin of indolence and expressing their repudiation of corporeality in their determination not to be suborned by its pleasures. The paradigm of the Incarnation made the transformation of the material according to the will and determinations of the ideal an imitation of Christ, commending to his followers not only the transformation of external nature, but the transformation of internal nature as well. This gave rise, in the antebellum period, to a legion of regimens designed for self-improvement, a goal identical to self-control in the lexicon of the political culture.

The individual practice of self-examination, temperance, education, self-control, conformity to the practices of the community, and regulation of natural functions was paralleled on the public plane by the ideal of a well-governed polity in which these goals were pursued institutionally, and where the community expressed its integrity in a universal conformity to convention and obedience to law.

The paradigm of the Incarnation commended the transformation of the natural, the ungodly, the corporeal, and the material as the imitation of Christ, an expression of the saint's already-effected assimilation to God. The covenantal model of Scripture provided a means whereby the temporal community might become an expression and imitation of the community of saints and the central covenant of God with his chosen people. Cromwell and the experience of the English Civil War provided a model for the church militant, the armed evangelism of the community of saints. There were, of course, several extant paradigms for religious conquest, from the Old Testament through the Crusades. The experience of the English Civil War was, however, a crucial moment in the formation of the identity of those Puritans who settled America. It retained its historical significance in the histories published by their successors.

The emigrant Puritans had characterized America as a wilderness which they were to conquer and transform in the name of God. Their struggles with their external environment and those who inhabited it were manifestly confrontations of nature and culture. Their conquest and transformation of that natural wilderness became an archetypal myth in American political culture.

Both Cromwell and the wars of Puritan and Indian provided legitimating paradigms for the armed conquest of the ungodly. The paradigm of the Incarnation impelled the conquest and transformation of nature, the body, and all external to that community which had been likened to God. Both the structures of industrial capitalism and the political institutions favored in the development of Northern political culture (most notably, an executive cast after the paternal model of the Puritan family and an army in the image of industry) produced men whose personal and institutional interests were advanced by war.

War, like manufacturing, gave men power over the external world. Like the organization of the factory, that of the army inculcated in men certain of the virtues central to the Protestant (more probably the Judeo-Christian) ethic. They were disciplined and self-controlled; they acted in cooperation, as a collective. They disdained their corporeality. They would sacrifice their lives for the people. They exhibited their unity in obedience to authority.

The extension of the territorial boundaries of the temporal polity provided a material manifestation of the extension of the temporal boundaries of the ideal community. More importantly, because American institutions were charged with the historically determined mission of extending the Christian religion, Anglo-Saxon culture, liberal democracy, and technological progress to heretofore-unenlightened peoples, the extension of America's territorial boundaries and political suzerainty itself advanced the progress of history and the will of God.

That political culture which developed out of the Puritans in the antebellum North was martial and capitalist, charged with the repression of internal and external nature, and persuaded of the primacy of the community. The Northern understanding of the nature and significance of the conflict with the South, and the institutional structures and modes of action which developed in that conflict, ensured the persistence and determinative power of these traits in America after the Civil War. In that war, the Union was

> . . . but drilling the new Hun
> Whose growl even now can some dismay
> Vindictive in his heart of hearts
> He schools him in your mines and marts
> A skilled destroyer.[30]

2   Man into Machine

In 1816, in Medway, Massachusetts, Walton Felch published *The Manufacturer's Pocket Piece, or The Cotton Mill Moralized*. The latter title gave the work's objective, the former its allegiance. Felch's epic advanced the cotton mill as a social model, extolling the virtues of its ordered hierarchy:

> Remark the moral order reigning there
> How every part observes its destined sphere
> Or if disorder enter the machine
> A sweeping discord interrupts the scene.
> Learn hence, whatever line of life you trace,
> In pious awe your proper sphere to grace[1]

Felch saw in industrialization the imposition of order on chaos, the triumph of mind over matter. Cotton, plucked from the bosom of nature, tumbled into the factory and emerged washed, combed, interwoven, and remade. Men were to be treated similarly. Plucked from nature, they were the raw material for a moral manufactory. Drawn into an ordered, rationalized society, they would be transformed.

Ralph Waldo Emerson's enthusiasm for industrialization was marked by an ambivalence characteristic of the literati of his age. Lauding progress, he apprehended in the ascendence of industry the reduction of man. "The railroad," he wrote "makes man a chattel, transports him by the box and ton, he waits on it." Industries are opened, factories built, and "men come in like water through a sluice way." In Emerson's articulation, this revolution, like an earlier one, might have been appropriately marked with "The World Turned Upside Down." The natural was remade by artifice, and the artificial came to rank with the natural. Men became machinery and resource, and agglomerations of resources and machinery became men. In England, already in the midst of the Industrial Revolution, Emerson had watched men become like water in a sluice way. He wrote, "Steam is almost an Englishman. I do not know but they will send him to Parliament next, to make laws." He found, he wrote home to America, "that the machine unmans the user." Man, however, had acquired new methods of creation: the natural casualties of artifice were replaced by artificial bodies as incorporation flourished. "This invasion of Nature by Trade with its Money, its Credit, its Steam, its Railroad, threatens to upset the balance of man and establish a new Universal Monarchy more tyrannical than Babylon or Rome. Very faint and few are the poets or the men of God." Balance, according to Emerson, was the work of men. Trade was a menacing behemoth, nature no kinder. "It is because Nature thus saves and uses, laboring for the general, that we poor particulars are so crushed and straitened." Man, it appears, had subdued one enemy only to rear up another. The isolated man, poet and priest, the poor particulars, flourished in neither nature nor industry. Rather each empire, animated by the common principles of exploitation and utility, swallowed up separate men.[2]

In this kinship Emerson discovered the grounds for a reconciliation of nature and artifice. "Readers of poetry see the factory village and fancy that the poetry of the landscape is being broken by these . . . but the poet sees them fall within the Great Order." Emerson's philosophy, like that of his section, was expansive, assimilative, incorporative. Order subsumed nature and industry as the Oversoul had subsumed men. Resolution was always to be found in comprehension. Factories and railroads entered the world as aliens but, Emerson affirmed, "Nature adopts them very fast into her vital circles, and the gliding train of cars she loves like her very own."[3]

The descriptions Emerson employs are themselves fraught with ambiguity. Not only is the crushing and straitening of the "poor particulars" evocative of an industrial rather than a natural process, the process is itself ambiguous. Are they, in being crushed and straitened, straightened as well? Is the "gliding train of cars" that Nature adopts so quickly into her vital circles in her stomach or her womb? Is industry conquered or nurtured by nature? If it glides to her sexual rather than to her digestive organs, does it come as child or husband, dependent or master?

The railroad, Emerson averred, "had introduced a number of picturesque traits into our pastoral scenery." His examples however, gave the lie to his enthusiasm: "The tunneling of mountains . . . the encounter of gangs of laborers . . . the character of the work itself which so violates and revolutionizes the primordial forms of nature; the villages and the shanties at the edge of beautiful lakes . . . the blowing of rocks, explosions all day, and the occasional alarm of frightening accidents."[4]

Emerson used the language of rape to describe the exploitation of nature.[5] The process he purportedly commends is marked in his description by poverty, violence, destruction, and mutilation. The railroad marred beauty, it killed men.

A similar ambivalence marks his description of the social transformations attendant upon the expansion of the railroad: "Now the locomotive and the steamboat, like enormous shuttles, shoot every day across the various threads of national descent and employment, and bind them fast in one web, an hourly assimilation goes forward and there is no danger that local particularities and hostilities should be preserved."[6] Behind this praise of the railroad as the instrument of a uniting and pacifying assimilation was the image of bonds and men unwittingly, unwillingly, transformed in a great machine.

Felch, in his panegyric to industrialization, cast the social order as machine; in Emerson's metaphor society is not the maker but the thing remade. Deliberation and morality were absent. Men were not actors, but acted upon, "bound fast in one web." The process, his words suggest, left them entrapped.

Industrialization, as Emerson recognized, "violated and revolutionized" the primordial forms of nature. Things natural entered the factory to emerge altered according to utility and the dictates of the market. Ferdinand Kürnberger, in his satirical *Picture of American Culture*, wrote "They make tallow out of cattle, and money out of men."[7] The mechanization of the process of production rendered men laborers, removing those aspects of their natural constitution which were inappropriate or irrelevant to their productive capacities. The very notion of "labor" indicated the successful inculcation of this principle, for it marks the worker's role in production as properly determinative of his identity. As the quality of personality was abstracted from humanity in incorporation, so labor was abstracted, and the status of the laborer in society determined by his role in the process of production.

Partisans of industry claimed that the regimentation of factory life improved the industrial worker by imposing order and intention on his chaotic natural constitution. Industrialization was to be the mechanism of social reform. Man, Rousseau observed, "wants nothing as nature made it, not even man . . . man must be fashioned in keeping with his fancy like a tree in his garden."[8] Industrialization promised not merely to prune but to uproot men and make their reformation entire. "Man," said Emerson, "is as made as a Birmingham button."[9]

"The final consequences," Weber wrote, "are drawn from the mechanization and discipline of the plant. The psycho-physical apparatus of man is completely adjusted to the demands of the outer world, the tools, the machines—in short, to an individual function. The individual is shorn of his natural rhythm as determined by the structure of his organism; his psycho-physical apparatus is attuned to a new rhythm."[10] That new rhythm was, according to one enamored onlooker, "the peaceful hum of an industrial population whose movements are regulated like clockwork."[11]

It was clockwork indeed for the workers. The performance of their allotted functions—natural, conventional, and industrial—was regulated by the sound of bells. These bells were singled out as especially offensive by striking workers in the 1830s and 1840s. Labor agitation then centered around the campaign for a ten-hour day. In that struggle, time was of the essence. The use of bells to divide the workday into discrete intervals, each given over to the performance of a designated activity, represented the manufacturer's authority over the worker's time. Complaints about the bells waxed with the controversy over the ten-hour day. Workers, watching the lobbying effort of factory owners, alleged that management altered the ringing of the bells to diminish the meager leisure they allotted the workers. Their time was not their own.

Lucy Larcom, recalling her tenure at a New England textile mill, remembered that when she finally left she told the paymaster "I am going to where I can have more time." "Ah yes," the paymaster replied, quoting Franklin, "time is money."[12] The factory system had incorporated time into its comprehensive scheme of world order, assigning it a calculable monetary value. The paymaster, steeped in this ideology, interpreted Larcom's flight from the system as motivated by its fundamental values.

Other mill workers wrote "morning bells I hate to hear,/ringing dolefully, loud and clear," and deplored their "obedience to the ding-dong of the bell—just as if we were so many living machines."[13] The successful inculcation of submission to this routine imposed from without ensured the development of American industry. A British manufacturer had written during the Revolution that Americans, though they had good workmen, had not yet developed personal and national habits consonant with industrialization. "The spirit of manufacturing must become the general spirit of the nation," he said, "and be incorporated as it were into the very essence."[14]

The replacement of capricious premodern work habits with the routinization requisite to industry was accomplished with singular rapidity by America's modernizing elite. The system of scientific management developed in America stood, according to Weber, at the very apex of rationality. The speed and success with which Americans embarked on industrialization did not, however, obviate the discontent of the workers. Anger over the exploitation and oppression evident in this regimentation continued. The radical Yiddish poet Morris Rosenfeld wrote in 1873:

> The tick of the clock is the boss in his anger.
> The face of the clock is the face of the foe.
> The clock—I shudder—dost see how it draws me?
> It calls me machine and it cries to me Sew![15]

The regulation of the activities of the workers through the use of bells signaled not only the ruthless rationalization of their activity, but also the subordination of their wills to the will of another.

Formerly men regulated their actions consciously. The factory system removed the worker's activities from his deliberate determination. Once responsive to his own will, he became responsive to external stimuli. His will was replaced as the cause of his activity by the will of the factory owner. He lost his freedom. His activity became a simple mechanical response rather than the result of intellect or volition.

"Too much labor," Theodore Parker told his congregation, who had no need to fear it, "makes a man a spinning-jenny or a ploughing machine, and not a being of a large discourse, who looks before and after."[16] Parker's attribution of greater virtue to those social classes blessed with greater leisure may have derived from this assessment of the debilitating effects of excessive labor. He did not recognize, however, that the regimentation of factory labor and the reduction of men to machines was particularly in the interest of those he addressed.

"The discipline of an army," John Taylor had observed, "is for the benefit of its generals."[17] The order imposed on factory workers was both a means of efficient exploitation and a system of control. This fact did not escape the operatives. Factory workers, Sarah Bagley declared, recognized owners as men who "look upon them only as inanimate machines, made to subserve their interests."[18] An agent of the mill owners demonstrated the application of this principle when he urged overseers to ensure temperate habits among the operatives, pointing out that "without any reference to feelings of philanthropy, self-interest in the preservation of our property would indicate a watchfulness on our part."[19] The Reverend Henry Miles, in his *Lowell as It Was and Is*, noted "the sagacity of self-interest, as well as a more disinterested consideration, has led to the establishment of a strict system of moral police."[20] "Sober, moral and orderly operatives" were necessary "lest profits be absorbed by cases of irregularity, carelessness, and neglect."[21]

Benjamin Franklin, whose autobiography evinces an irreverent concern for the calculable monetary returns of virtue, castigated American workmen for their continuance of profligate premodern work habits. "Saint Monday is as duly kept by our workmen as Sunday; the only difference being that instead of employing their time cheaply at church they are wasting it expensively at the alehouse."[22] The twin projects of self- and social reform that Franklin championed became the preoccupation of the American industrial age. The impulse to transform internal and external nature, to order natural processes and enlist them in the service of a rational objective, spawned a multitude of crusades, projects, and policies, and an enduring literary genre. Self-improvement manuals exhibited a passion for social and personal progress, a distrust of human nature and distaste for natural functions, an unquestioning presumption of human commonality, a commitment to routinization as a method of transformation, and the increasingly logocentric character of the society.[23]

Among the most famous of these self-improvement manuals were those authored by "self-made men:" Franklin, Carnegie, and Hilton. The standard of successful self-transformation was clearly monetary. Franklin, whose sophistication raises him above this company, provided the paradigm which his latter-day imitators altered and perpetuated. Franklin's advice noted the calculable utility of virtue; his successors would piously insist that material success was achieved only through moral rectitude. Franklin represented the transformation of Puritan to Yankee. His successors showed the persistence (and ultimately the primacy) of the Puritan in the Yankee.

Like the self-improvement manuals, those projects for social improvement which abounded in the antebellum North were primarily authored by the rich, whose economic success served as certification of their moral and intellectual worth. Like the self-improvement manuals, they affirmed that moral and intellectual improvement resulted in an improvement in material conditions. And, like the self-improvement manuals, they promised to produce a population whose industrious virtue was wholly in accord with the requirements of industrial society.

Temperance, which Franklin recommended, would improve the health, and hence the utility, of the workers. It would also lessen the observance of "Saint Monday" and those informal social gatherings which urban craftsmen had enjoyed prior to industrialization. Herbert Gutman has observed that while these activities were said to lessen the profits not only of the owner, but of the worker, workers were separated from them with difficulty.

Preindustrial craftsmen and laborers enjoyed a working style which permitted greater adaptation to individual inclination and circumstances and a greater degree of social intercourse among workers. Because many of the customary occasions for such intercourse involved drinking together or assembling in places where liquor was sold, abstention from alcohol reduced social contacts among workers. Temperance made them efficient workers. Finally, because these temperate changes in the habits and customs of the workers came at the behest of their employers rather than through their own initiative, Temperance strengthened the patterns of social relations which subordinated workers to their employers. It was one of a constellation of social reforms which were presented—and have since been regarded—as benevolent if somewhat rigid attempts to improve the condition of the lower classes, but which in practice subjected them to patterns of labor that diminished social intercourse and offered fewer opportunities for exercising individual choice. The Temperance reforms did, however, produce a more efficient, industrious, and cooperative labor force, made up of men whose newfound virtues were consonant with the requirements of industry.

The campaign for public education similarly aimed at the remaking of the working class. Like other institutions of antebellum reform, the prison and the lunatic asylum, the public school was modeled on the factory. DeWitt Clinton, governor of New York, praised the Lancastrian system of education as comparable to laborsaving machinery.[24] Horace Mann, in his "Twelfth Annual Report," wrote "our means of education are the grand machinery by which the raw material of human nature can be worked up."[25] This raw material was, Mann wrote, "so pliant and ductile as to be susceptible of assuming a greater variety of forms than any other work of the Creator."[26]

The purpose of education was thus to regulate the forms assumed by human nature, and to produce good men. "Health is a product," Mann wrote. "Health is a manufactured article,"[27] and one which the schools were capable of providing. Educational reformers also aimed at producing good citizens, instructed in the origins of American republicanism and the duties of citizens and integrated in the community, and at producing good workers: temperate, industrious, and frugal.

The educational process, which Clinton likened to laborsaving machinery, was to be characterized by order, efficiency, and rationality. By its orderliness, it habituated the young to order, predictability, and repetition. Students were habituated to regular hours of employment, and to a pattern of behavior which they would see repeated at the factory. By its subordination of students to teachers, the educational process also habituated students to extrafamilial authority. It encouraged students to regard themselves as members of a collectivity.

Through the educational system, the altered patterns of behavior characteristic of the factory were disseminated beyond the factory into the population at large. Because the literature and speeches of those advocating public education, the reports of educators, and court cases involving education were published for mass consumption and received widespread attention, the characterization of education as a manufacturing process was also widely circulated. It was, therefore, not merely a metaphor which particular individuals employed in apt description of structural characteristics of the system. Rather this metaphor itself became one of the system's attributes, delimiting policy and the popular perception of public education. The virtues of manufacture—efficiency, economy, and uniformity—became objects of the educational system and provided policy guidelines to its reformers.

Proponents of modernity saw in the factory the triumph of reason over a chaotic and capricious nature. In the factory, the natural was remade—reformed—and emerged in a more useful form. The project of remaking man was an appropriate sphere in which to apply the methods of industry.

Industrial production was praised for its superior efficiency and, obliquely, for its kinship to the ideology that contained it. Industrial methods were rational and thus universally applicable, transcending cultural diversity. The development of universally valid modes of production was particularly appropriate to an expanding, evangelical democracy. The universal validity of democratic forms was purportedly reflected in the universally valid modes of production developed by America's nascent industries. In each case, however, the extension of these universally valid forms was effected not through acclamation and adoption, but through imposition.

The family provided metaphors for an authority based on necessity, circumstance, and coercion rather than consent. Paternal metaphors abounded, first because they recalled a much-used and well-understood paradigm, and secondly because they described an authority which was conventional rather than natural in its origins.[28] The family itself, however, lost standing as a social institution. The sentimentalization of domesticity and praise for women's role in it, served as apology and disguise for the appropriation of formerly familial functions by political and economic institutions that were unambiguously the province of men. The division of space and time into discrete zones in the process of manufacturing became the pattern for the reorganization of urban life.[29] The production methods of the factory superseded those of cottage industry. In the same way, the residential arrangements and the regulation of individual activity characteristic of factory life were adopted by other social institutions—reform schools, prisons, workhouses—and praised as superior to the familial methods which had preceded them. Social functions formerly allotted to the family were increasingly assigned to institutions designed to accomplish the same ends with the efficiency characteristic of industry.

The industrialists who dominated Northern social reform movements undertook the task of remaking public institutions in the image of industry. Their perceptions of the inadequacy of the family derived in part from a commitment to rationality and community action. They were spurred, however, by the realization that the demographic composition of the lower orders was daily changing.

Families could no longer be relied upon to instill in their offspring that Calvinist constellation of values in which order and industry figured so prominently. The families of the Irish immigrants, infected with Catholicism and afflicted with a cultural propensity for riotous disorder, threatened to disrupt that process of social rationalization, which the Northern modernizing elite was determined to advance. The replacement of the family as the agent for certain family functions, especially education, would enable the state itself to assume the task of instructing the next generation, instilling in them appropriate habits, virtues, expectations, and ideals. This would confine cultural conflict to the present unassimilated generation.

As David Brion Davis noted in *Homicide in American Fiction*, fictional descriptions of urban crime increased to astonishing proportions in the 1840s.[30] This fictional efflorescence accompanied similar apprehensions in the public sphere. Novelists and legislators alike attributed the increase in urban crime to the decay of the family. Commissioners of Boston, in a public document establishing reform schools declared, "A family whose parental instructors are ignorant, inefficient and immoral is quite sure to make a disastrous failure of the education of the little ones entrusted to its care."[31] They recommended that the state remove these potentially disruptive juveniles from the care of their incompetent guardians, transferring them to institutions in which their education could be supervised by professionals.

The commission's recommendation is noteworthy not only for its confident commitment to efficiency and professionalism, but also as a manifestation of an altered view of the family with regard to the state. Here the family was no longer considered a natural institution whose primordial authority the state was obliged to acknowledge if not to emulate, but rather was seen as a steward, educating on behalf of the state. This assertion of the superiority of state to familial authority prepared the way for the promulgation of laws which enabled the state to intervene in cases of parental neglect, and to restrict the use of child labor. Such laws, however, were not immediately contemplated by the Boston commissioners. They intended rather to replace the demographically corrupted familial institution with one better calculated to instill those qualities conducive to social order.

The arrogation by the state of what had heretofore been parental authority established "the state in her true relation, that of a parent seeking out her erring children."[32] Emory Washburn praised the reform school as "the first time a state, in the character of a common parent, has undertaken the high and sacred duty of rescuing and restoring her lost children."[33]

The family, legislators argued, had failed in its charge. Judge William Sawyer wrote, "there is seldom a case of a juvenile offender in which I am not well satisfied that the parents or persons having the child in charge are most blameable." Their neglect or malfeasance, George Boutwell asserted, obliged the state to "supply the place of a lost, or what is worse, a drunken parent." The reform school, established under the aegis of the state, was "at once a home and a school," supplying not only the traditional functions of the family, but also those educative functions to which the family was inadequate.[34]

Founders of public schools intimated with increasing boldness that the best of families, though they might lay claim to better manners, could not boast the collective wisdom of the state or emulate its industrial efficiency. This official denigration of the family coincided with fervent popular sentiment on its behalf, praising its intimate natural relations. Yet this sentimentalization, by emphasizing the innocence and irrationality of women, presented a covert argument for the state's appropriation of the educative role. The state was, the modernizing elite asserted, "the true family"; thus the rioters who protested the alienation of familial functions were "raising a parricidal hand against the law."[35]

The initiation of compulsory education, already preceded by a period of stringent truancy laws, promised to extend the blessings of equality. Education, henceforth a staple rather than a delicacy, could no longer be numbered among the consequences of familial advantage. The state had become "a common parent." Acceptance of this view entailed the notion that the children of citizens, all equally children of the state, were equally entitled to parental nurture.

It was this aspect of public education which won it the enthusiastic support of Jacksonian Democrats and members of the Workingmen's Party. Their conception of education, however, differed radically from that of education's Whig proponents. While a manifesto of New York workingmen demanded public education, it accompanied this with a demand for "no ecclesiastical interference," which struck at the Whig insistence that public education include moral instruction of an explicitly religious character. Similarly, a Democratically sponsored Convention of Teachers for Popular Instruction insisted that public education forswear formal prayers, "to avoid whatever might be construed as sectarianism, or an encroachment on the religious rights of individuals." The convention, the *Workingman's Gazette* noted approvingly, had dispensed with titles of all sorts (including "Rev."). This was "an instance of practical democracy well worthy of imitation." For these people, public education promised to make equality social and economic as well as political. Citizens would then have, along with their equal rights, a capacity for their exercise which was differentiated only by nature. These proponents of public education intended to assimilate the lower orders not to the culture or religion of their betters but to their power and influence. They intended to unleash rather than restrain their political activities, to enable them to engage more effectively in politics on their own behalf.[36]

This conception prevailed in the South as well, but there it retarded rather than sped the extension of public education. Southerners, persuaded that education empowered rather than controlled the lower orders, legislated against extending it to blacks.

The ideals of efficiency, economy, and uniformity (though differently construed) were equally attractive to these advocates of public education. Democrats and Workingmen were inclined, however, to regard governmental control with suspicion, especially when it operated in concert with clerical and capitalist philanthropy, as it did in educational planning.

As the machine age progressed, it became increasingly apparent that legislation on behalf of capital—corporation and contract law— was expanding, while legislative attempts to limit the working day to ten hours were continually stymied. Tariffs on behalf of industry proliferated at the expense of farmers and consumers. These observations persuaded numerous small farmers and workers that the "controlling influence exercised in our several towns and counties, in our legislative halls, and national councils," was that of "a few purse-proud and domineering Aristocrats."[37]

This perception diminished working-class support for the performance of formerly familial functions by the states. The official denigration of the family had once been construed as an assault on familial influence, hereditary social privilege, and incipient aristocracy. It quickly became apparent, however, that neither the structure of the factory nor that of the educational system was conducive to social, economic, or political equality. Early labor agitation was thus accompanied by protests against the replacement of the family by other social institutions.

Conflict over changes in Northern society became increasingly vociferous as divergent understandings of industrialization converged. As the conception of industrialization as the conquest of nature became universal, support and opposition for it became both more enthusiastic and better differentiated. Partisans in debates over conceptually or circumstantially associated issues—education, familial authority, the denial of natural rights in industrial organization, slavery, technological development, and the tariff—ranged themselves on opposite sides of this division.

The association of affirmations of the integrity of the family, antiabolition, and natural rights in the protests of the working class formed one of these constellations of issues. Concern over the transformation of social institutions paralleled workers' apprehensions concerning the alteration of their "natural rhythms" in industrial labor. The former was the public, the latter the private dimension of a generalized resistance to that conquest of nature which industrialization advanced.

Industrialization had removed workers from their natural environment. The exchange of labor in the home for labor in the factory removed workers from direct contact with natural processes and resources in agriculture, husbandry, and provision for the immediate needs of the family. Housework and farm chores embedded men in nature. Industrialization removed workers from the countryside, substituting conventional for natural bonds, artifice for natural activity.

Domestic labor, performed haphazardly, prompted only by necessity and inclination, was replaced by labor in the factory, in which the worker's productive activity was regulated by the calculations of the industrialist. Workers were prompted to undertake or set aside a task not by need or inclination, but by the sound of the bell. Similarly, networks of personal relations based on kinship or affection were replaced by the rationalized relations of the factory town.

The exchange of home and village for residence in a factory town removed workers from the environment of personal relations created by the natural bonds of the family. The factory towns were inhabited by unrelated people; dormitories held workers of the same sex and age. The owners' boast that they provided the moral supervision and paternal care heretofore provided in the home, for which they were praised by clerics and reformers, was not entirely persuasive to those workers they pretended to protect. As Elizabeth Geffen notes, "The development of the corporate form of enterprise not only by its very nature limited individual responsibility, but added insult to injury by its inevitable depersonalization of the relationship between employer and employee."[38] The conventional impersonal paternalism of the factory owner did not satisfy the standards of paternal care entertained by the operatives. Though they accepted the paternal model as a legitimate pattern for social institutions, the personalized authority of the factory owner did not conform to their understanding of paternal care. Wage cuts and mandatory increases in productivity undermined the owners' claims that they were providing for their workers. In the early years of labor agitation, workers, accepting the paternal model, demanded that owners fulfill the obligations of paternal authority.

Protests against undemocratic arrogations of authority by "the mushroom aristocracy of New England"[39] were often expressed in endorsements of the paternalist model. "Another feature abounding in grievous wrong" one operative wrote, "is the difference in caste which the employers create between their sons and daughters and the sons and daughters they employ to increase their wealth."[40] Here social distinctions are called "creations" of the employer who properly should make no distinction between those who are equally sons and daughters. A correspondent of *The Voice of Industry* explicitly condemned the exclusion of workers from the families of their employers. "Do they find admittance into the families of the rich? Certainly not! They are factory girls—her occupation, nay her usefulness, excludes her."[41] Another factory girl angered by this exclusion wrote: "The operatives are well enough off! Indeed! Do you admit them in your parlors, are they admitted to visit your families, do you raise your hats to them in the street, in a word, are they your equals?"[42]

These criticisms accepted the abstraction and rationalization of familial relations. The consequent expectations of the workers were very similar to those of Democrats and Workingmen who saw the state as a common parent in the public school system. Citizens, or, as in this case, workers, were to be equals under the authority of a common parent charged with advancing their interests with his own. These expectations were in both cases rapidly disappointed, and embittered relations between capitalists and the working class.

David Grimsted's study of violence in the Jacksonian period notes the rioters' association of the Bank of Maryland controversy with Joseph Bossiere's alleged seduction of a young girl. Grimsted terms these "wholly separate incidents."[43] The betrayal of an orphan girl by her headmistress to a rich man was not, however, wholly foreign to the rioters' grievances. The Bossiere case enabled the workers to protest simultaneously the exploitation of labor and the displacement of the family. The orphan girl was, as the industrial workers believed themselves to be, outside the protective shelter of the family. Like them, she had trusted in surrogates—for the workers, their owners and their agents—who through greed and self-interest had failed in their trust. The rioters, in their conflation of these controversies, recognized a symmetry between economic and sexual exploitation.

Antiabolition riots, and attacks on blacks during labor riots, made similar associations. They arose from causes other than mere racism or anticipated competition for jobs. Nor were they confined to the lower orders. Leonard Richards has made a persuasive case that many were "Gentlemen of Property and Standing." These, along with some antiabolitionist workers, opposed abolition as leading to "amalgamation." Their fear of miscegenation expressed not only racism, but also their apprehensions concerning the alteration of the family as they had known it. They protested against a society in which blood, blood ties, and kinship bonds were of no significance. "For Americans who desperately feared being cut off from deep and permanent ties of class and family, clan, community and position, amalgamation touched the heart of their passion: their dread of sinking below their fathers' station and their nightmare of becoming cogs in a mass society."[44]

The loss of class and station were fears strongest among men of property and standing, but familial and communal bonds were equally important to the lower classes. All might fear incorporation in a regimented, mechanized society, but these fears will predominate among those whose lack of property, education, or influence has persuaded them of their political impotence and inability to distinguish themselves socially. Fears of becoming "cogs in a mass society" would also be reinforced by the relative anonymity felt by recent immigrants to urban areas, and by the perceptions of industrial workers that their labor was transforming them from men to machines.

Protests against industrialization and profound apprehensions concerning its cultural consequences were shared by disparate demographic groups. Farmers and urban laborers, old-style merchants and artisans, men of familial prominence and men without it had coincident fears for their identities. Richards has made an invaluable contribution by providing evidence to undermine the traditional histories of an enlightened abolitionist elite challenged by the raucous racism of the uneducated lower classes. The relative significance of class, occupation, ideology, and other factors in determining the complicated alliance systems which formed in response to early industrialization has yet to be determined.

Tocqueville, observing the relative absence of the formal structures of rank and deference which prevailed in Europe, the relative ease with which Americans changed their status or their occupations, and the relative inclusivity of the suffrage, concluded that America was an essentially classless society. This conclusion, supported in his time by the narratives of foreign travelers outraged at the presumption of their servants, and in ours by Louis Hartz, Grant McConnell, and others, has dominated writing about American politics. In studies of the antebellum period, it has obscured the character and intensity of class conflict generated by industrialization.

The absence of class conflict has been so commonly presumed that the very terms "capital" and "labor," as names of classes, are thought to have come into use considerably after the Civil War. In fact, they were well-established and oft-employed terms in antebellum political discourse. "Capital," "capitalist," and "capitalism" were used by John Taylor in 1806 and not regarded as recent coinage. His book *Arator* discussed class conflict explicitly. Because the conflicts he described were remembered or anticipated rather than experienced, they lacked the immediacy of those published a generation later. Works by those enmeshed in the process of industrialization reveal an intense awareness of class, class interest, and class conflict.

"Some say that capital will take good care of labor, but don't believe it, don't trust them," a "Lowell Factory Girl" warned in *The Voice of Industry*.[45] "Great capitalists cannot be in favor of the producer's rightful claims" said the *Workingman's Gazette*, "as without his dependence they could not command his service, and without his services their capital would be useless."[46] Present economic structures, Stephen Simpson wrote, made up an "endless chain of levers which move industry to empty her gains into the lap of CAPITAL."[47] Without an equal division of property, Simpson asserted, "we perceive our constitution of equal rights to be the merest untenanted skeleton of liberty."[48]

Simpson's *Workingman's Manual* contrasted labor and capital: "The luxurious capitalist, swelling with the overweening pride of pampered opulence, whilst the hearts that labored to produce his wealth shiver and faint with misery and want, or drag out a protracted life of endless toil."[49] Urban workingmen of the antebellum period did not subscribe to the notion that the presence of a frontier assured them of an escape from the dependent status of the industrial worker and improved their condition relative to that of European workers. Low wages restricted both their ability to relocate and their capacity for political action. "Observe how poor and dependent are the producers, and how rich and powerful the consumers of wealth"[50] the *Workingman's Gazette* urged. With "a restricted, shackled public press" and "poverty punished with a greater rigor than we punish crime," capitalists acquired the "controlling influence exercised in our several towns and counties, in our legislative halls and national councils."[51] "As long as justice is sold at the present rate," claimed the *Gazette*, "it will be purchased by the rich."[52]

Capital "buys up legislators when they are in the market; breeds them when the market is bare," the Reverend Theodore Parker wrote. "It is fairly and faithfully represented by them." Parker did not intend this as a condemnation. "Our popular legislatures are made in its image," he said of the "Mercantile Class," "and represent its wisdom, foresight, patriotism and conscience." Capitalists constituted an "aristocracy of gold . . . the best thing of its kind we have had yet, the wisest, the most human." "The saint of the nineteenth century is the good merchant," Parker concluded. "He is wisdom for the foolish, strength for the weak, warning to the wicked, and a blessing to all."[53]

William Ellery Channing agreed. The problem lay not with the rich, but with the poor who endeavored to "force themselves into what are called the upper ranks of society."[54] Channing concurred with Lyman Beecher in the dogma that disparities in wealth were "the stated policy of Heaven." "That some should be richer than others is natural, is necessary," Channing affirmed. "I would combat the disposition, too common in the labouring mass, to regard what is called the upper class with envy and admiration."[55] The rich of Channing's congregation often suffered from ennui "a misery unknown to the poor and more intolerable than the weariness of excessive toil."[56]

"Let not the condition of the poor be spoken of as necessarily wretched," Channing cautioned, "Remove from them the misery they bring on themselves from evildoing, and separate from their inevitable sufferings the aggravations which come from crime and their burden would be light."[57] The laboring classes, he wrote, were "nearer to the brute," "uncultivated, sluggish, narrow-minded." They entertained themselves with "debasing gratifications."[58] He concluded that "the prejudices and passions of multitudes among them are formidable barriers to improvement."[59] Samuel Breck, a Philadelphia merchant, denounced "the extravagance of our laboring classes," and berated the "thoughtless, vain and improvident creatures" for refusing to work for diminished wages when an increase in the prices of "all articles of first necessity" forced economy on the rich.[60]

Antebellum workers recognized that industrialization had not only widened the economic gap between the classes; it had fundamentally altered the relations of workers and owners. "We are sad," one "factory girl" wrote, "to see the interests of the employer and the employed so far removed from each other."[61] When men farmed, they attended to the vicissitudes of the weather, the depredations of birds, the price of the crop, and the existence of tariffs, despite variations in the size of their holdings. Their common interest, and hence "the common good," was readily perceptible. Industrialization removed this set of common interests from workers and owners. "Pauperism is another of the concomitants of the age of capital," the *Workingman's Manual* stated; "no man can become rich without making another poor."[62]

Travelers' accounts of Manchester and the indigenous criticisms of Dickens and Gaskell had enjoyed a ready market in America. The squalor in which the English workers lived, the tyranny of their factory owners, and the indifference of their government accorded well with the democratic doctrine that class distinctions end in exploitation. Manchester proved the superiority of American political structures and suggested that, propelled by these, America might surpass England economically as well. The Waltham system had been designed after the thought that the constraints on oppression supplied by democracy would preclude the ills produced by industry in England.

The Lowell mills were, in their first years, industrial showpieces, a series of tidy dormitories inhabited by intelligent and industrious factory girls. But, as Philip Foner noted in his study *The Factory Girls*, "the glare of the modern factory town, the showcase of the Waltham System, did little to hide the existence of exploitative wages and working conditions."[63] The English, who were to be reproached by Lowell, established the ten-hour day in 1847. Women at Lowell worked at least twelve hours a day until 1874. What was proven, *Young America* wrote, was that "the rich manufacturer, even in this great country of ours, can compell his poor operatives to work just as many hours as he pleases, or starve."[64]

The development of the American manufacturing system from 1815 to 1845 was marked by a steady increase in the dependence of workers on owners. The first factories were textile mills, the first mill workers women. These were target workers, as is still the case in countries undergoing industrialization. They retained ties to rural communities, working only long enough to acquire a dowry or support a brother's education. Wage cuts, by reducing the workers' earnings to an amount sufficient for subsistence only, made them, as John Taylor had predicted, "dependents on a master capitalist for bread."[65]

The creation of a dependent class of workers, too poor to move, facilitated the development of industry in America. With a readily available pool of labor from which to draw, manufacturers were able to open additional factories. Increases in the immigration of both white Irishmen and Southern blacks increased competition for available jobs. It fostered animosity between contending groups—male and female, native born and immigrant, Protestant and Catholic, white and black. It enabled factory owners, now that the supply of labor threatened to exceed the demand, to cut wages and demand longer hours of their workers. It permitted them to fire rebellious workers with impunity.

The interaction of these consequences had several effects. Employers were increasingly able not only to exploit the work force more effectively, but also to shape its composition. Thus the evolution of "labor" in the United States was determined in large part by its natural enemy. Capital had the dominant influence on American immigration policy, as well as on federal administrative policy and legislation, an influence which increased during and after the Civil War. The increased size of the labor pool to which the employers had access enabled them to selectively exclude certain of the groups they considered dangerous or undesirable. These selections reflect the dominant cultural tradition in the North. Blacks and women, because they possessed structural "defects" which made them evidently unassimilable, were the first to be confined to certain occupations and excluded from the greater portion of available jobs. The more assimilable Irish Catholic males were tolerated in a wider range of occupations but were regularly denied higher positions due to their presumed social and cultural inferiority.

Mill owners recognized that the disparity of interest between themselves and the workers, as well as their attempts to establish conventional social distinctions in an artificial hierarchy, would alienate those they endeavored to subordinate. The inclusion of the workers in a hierarchical social structure would require indoctrination. Another form of similarity must be substituted for the commonality of interest and experience, or for rights. Thus they endeavored to instill in their operatives the tenets of that theology which ratified their claim to authority. Huldah Stone wrote in 1847: "A man who works for the companies is little better than the machinery which he conducts. He must go to the church—which, by the way, is the Calvinist church—and vote the ticket."[66] The five dollars in pew rental that the owners extracted from their operatives for obligatory attendance at the church of their choosing and the vote cast as commanded were equally attempts to enlist the operatives in their own undoing. They illustrate the transformation of individual man from actor to instrument, not only in the factory, but in politics as well. They also associate this reduction with religiosity, and more particularly with assimilation to the religious tradition of the Puritans and the political paradigms they established.

Attendance at the church of the company's choosing (where, one suspects, the sermons were of the company's composition) was obligatory only for Protestants, and soon only for Protestant women. Catholics, whose attendance at mass was deemed more disruptive than salutary, were ordered to work on the Sabbath and fired when they refused to do so.[67] This differential regulation of religiosity reveals the owners' perception of a disparity in the requirements of these groups. The Catholics had to be divorced from their Catholicism before they could be incorporated in the polity. Until then, they remained in the province of godless nature, to be exploited and reformed.

Protestant men, predominantly native, had entered the industrial work force later than women, when competition for jobs was greater. The hazards of losing their jobs and their inability to migrate to rural areas combined with their superior socialization in the Protestant family to make them more receptive to the demands of factory owners and to the explanations for these demands.

Women, who had been the first workers in the New England textile mills, were also the first and fiercest critics of the exploitation of labor. They had undertaken strikes, work stoppages, and demonstrations in response to unilateral wage cuts and demands for increased production. Philip Foner in *The Factory Girls*, Thomas Dublin in "Women, Work and Protest in the Early Lowell Mills" and Elizabeth Geffen in "Violence in Philadelphia" provide good introductory accounts of their efforts. This aspect of labor history has been so neglected, however, that it is necessary to return to the journals and archives of the period for information as well as an understanding of the involvement of women in early labor activities. These sources are interesting because they reveal an immense, though hardly extraordinary, historical ignorance of the changing position and activities of women and, more importantly, because they reveal a considerable disparity between the ideology and rhetoric of the early labor movement, in which women were numerous, conspicuous, and active, and that after the Civil War.

By 1845, the notion that women were properly restricted to certain spheres in the exercise of their peculiar faculties had attained considerable currency, yet women still remembered that there had been a time when they were not so constrained. Feminine domesticity had not yet become primordial. Sarah Bagley, in a speech before the New England Workingman's Association, could estimate the duration: "For the last half-century, it has been deemed a violation of woman's sphere to appear before the public as a speaker; but when our rights are trampled upon, and we appeal in vain to legislators, what shall we do but appeal to the people?"[68] Bagley's words, and her chronology, suggest the revolutionary character of feminine activism.

The entrance of women into politics represented a challenge to existing authority. They, like other liminal groups, were present at the creation. Their intervention recalled that exercise of popular authority and presented the possibility of its revival and a decisive constitutional reformation.

The present laws and legislators, Bagley declared, had proved inadequate. Another rebellious woman declared "to shape her by man's law or by any other than the internal law of her nature is to do violence to her being and to subvert the prime intention of nature." Conventional and legal reformations of feminine character are here rejected in favor of the authority of nature. Nature's authority is an internal law, subjectively perceived and ineradicable, in common with the standards of legitimation. The irrefragable authority of nature is affirmed as the apology for the rebellious and unconventional conduct of the female operatives. "God made woman a living soul, and in no block lettered records of antique pages wrote the charter of her rights, but . . . inscribed it in the nature which she bears."[69]

Protests that nature had consigned the weaker sex to the protection of her natural masters were not consonant with the dictates of that internal law. Ellen Munroe wrote: "Bad as is the condition of so many women, it would be much worse if they had nothing but your boasted protection to rely on. But they have at last learned the lesson a bitter experience teaches, that not to those who style themselves their natural protectors are they to look for the needful help, but to the strong and resolute of their own sex."[70] This was much feared. Two marriage manuals of the period exhibit the prevailing fear of feminine cabals. Flint's *Art of Being Happy* asserted that "nothing is more common than this contemptible ambition of wives to govern their husbands. It is said there are coteries of wives who impart the rules in masonic conclave." Gisborne's *Duties of the Female Sex* similarly inveighed against the hazards of female conspiracy: "The love of power, congenial to the human breast, reveals itself in the two sexes under different forms, but with equal force." In women, the will to power manifested itself in "oblique machinations." Gisborne, it appears, subscribed to Nietzsche's view that "women don't rob, they steal."[71]

The most widely circulated warnings against the dangers of an amazonian uprising were conveyed in the enormously popular captivity narratives. This genre, already generations old in 1840, revealed the ease with which women assimilated themselves to the Indians. The necessary continuance of their proximity to nature in pregnancy, childbirth, and nurture likened them to the Indians in their relation to the society. They were "the voice of nature in the human family."[72]

The rebellious female workers had adhered to the god of nature, employing the rhetoric and paradigms of political action established in the Revolution. It is not surprising, therefore, that the Northern economic elite worked so assiduously to confine women within strictly delineated social and political boundaries. They had opposed themselves as workers to capital, as Democrats to Whig hierarchy, and as women to the paradigms of authority in the paternal familial model. The increased subordination of women satisfied not only the economic interest of the owners, but also the requirements of the cultural paradigm they were engaged in promulgating.

Immigration had increased the availability of labor, lowered wages, and placed men in competition with women for jobs which were suddenly more scarce and less lucrative. Factory owners, faced with rebellions on the part of their female workers, had retaliated with assertions of a fundamental female inferiority. Women, they asserted, were less rational than men; it ill suited them, therefore, to compete with men for jobs where rationality was prized. This argument provided a convenient apology for that otherwise evidently arbitrary authority owners endeavored to exercise over their operatives. A long habituation to cultural denigrations of women eased the acceptance of this notion. Thus the replacement of the less with the more rational gender coincided with increasing restrictions on the exercise of this vaunted faculty in the process of production.

Domestic labor was irregular, accomplished sporadically and idiosyncratically. The multifarious aspects of provision and nurture were not susceptible to division into discrete tasks which could then be systematically ordered and allotted. The promulgation of the industrial ideal caused a corresponding denigration of domestic labor. Thus the movement to restrict the movement of women into industry coincided with a depreciation of the labor in which they would henceforth be primarily engaged.

The degradation which women confronted in consequence was depicted by William Alcott in a contemporary compendium of instructions entitled *The Young Husband*. The prevalent view, according to Alcott, assigned the women a station of humiliating inferiority and instructed her to acquiesce. "In becoming my companion," one of Alcott's contemporaries asserted, "she consented to become my wife, and to demean herself as such." This order, he continued, was ordained by the deity; "It is not for her or others to attempt to evade the divine arrangements." The providential imperative cited by Beecher and Parker is here reproduced in the relations of husband and wife.[73]

Alcott also chose to describe the loss of liberty and the exercise of intellect with the transmogrification of man into machine. In his essay on "Conjugal Servitude," Alcott castigated husbands who regard their wives as instruments, their children as property. "Their wives are the merest slaves and drudges, their children mere automatons." A woman entrapped in such a marriage "falls completely into the jaws of the devourer of her individuality, if not of her personal identity." That arbitrary authority which the industrialist exercised over his workers, grounded neither in consent elicited by common interest nor in the claims of natural paternity, but in law, had thus become the model for a similar aggrandizement of the husband's authority in the legal family.[74]

A poem published in the Chicago *Workingman's Advocate* of 1873 reveals the success this idea achieved in less than a generation. The narrator disputes the virtues of the newly introduced sewing machine:

None of your patent machines for me
Unless Dame Nature's the patentee.
I like the sort that can laugh and talk
And take your arm for an evening walk,
And do whatever the owner may choose,
With the slightest perceptible turn of the screws.
. . . What do you think of my machine?
Ain't it the best that ever was seen?

This poem is interesting in several respects. Although it expresses continued hostility toward machinery, praising the superior creative capacity of nature and the multifarious talents of the human constitution—

T'isn't a clumsy mechanical toy
But flesh and blood. Hear that, my boy!

—it accepts, and indeed praises, the transformation of woman to machine. The narrator asserts his ownership of the woman, and in doing so reveals the coercion implicit in the relation. The machine, once man, now "does whatever the owner may choose, with the slightest perceptible turn of the screws."[75]

The transformation of man into machine, the *Workingman's Advocate* recognized, deprived the worker of intellect and volition. Yet the author, rather than condemning this alteration of nature's creation, endeavored to profit by it.

The greatness of soul which characterized women in the early labor movement, prompting them to embrace the antislavery cause, oppose the exploitation of Irish immigrants, and make common cause with their male co-workers was very rarely present in the post–Civil War labor movements. The ready acceptance of women as property and of blacks as inferior and properly excluded from labor organizations cast doubt upon the putative principle of the Union. They provide, however, a partial apology for the lassitude of labor in the years following the Civil War.

Confining women within the home, and thus enhancing the cultural association of the natural and the feminine, was not without costs. Women were then constructed as entirely apolitical, moved by private loves and hates, and by the imperatives of their natural, corporeal constitution.[76] They were without loyalty to the state. Thomas Dew associated this hazard of feminine confinement with Achilles, whose violent heroism rose out of passionate affection. John Frost, in his account of *Daring and Heroic Deeds of American Women,* while relating tales of feminine ferocity and vengeance, asserted that these came in response only to attacks on the family.

Frost's message was twofold. He suggested that the natural affections characteristic of maternity could move women to acts of extraordinary violence and heroism. He also warned that attacks on domesticity and disruptions of the home would release women from their conventional confinement and enable them to exercise their Achillean propensities freely, "sparing neither sex nor age."[77] The home, no less than the reservation, was designed in the interests of those without.

The sentimentalization of domesticity which prevailed in the North reserved domestic tasks to women.[78] The dangers occasioned by so enhancing feminine proximity to nature were obviated by increasing insistence on conventional constraints on the conduct of women. Women were exhorted to adhere more strictly to standards of morality and deportment in their narrowed social sphere, including attention to more stringent notions of propriety in feminine expression. These were especially strict with regard to speech concerning natural functions: ingestion, digestion, defecation, and procreation. Of these, women were forbidden to speak, except with the most cumbersome circumlocutions.

The Puritan view of nature undergirded the social structures confining women in Northern political culture. The community was obliged to accomodate the childbearing function of women. Women were therefore associated firmly with the persistence of nature in the community, and hence with the corporeal, the material, and the unclean. The clearest illustration of the constellation of associations which clustered about maternity in Northern political culture is the definition of "mother" given by Noah Webster in the *First American Dictionary.* Webster devoted two columns of the dictionary to an etymological exposition of maternity, associating "mother" with "dam, womb, lees, . . hysterics . . . vagina. . . mud, mold . . . matter, pus, . . . stuff, the material from which anything is made . . . cause, origin, root, spring, matrix, . . . the bed of a river, a sink or sewer, . . . purulent running . . . purulent discharge."[79]

Mothers were evidently unclean, associated with decay and decomposition. Each of these effects a return to undifferentiated nature. This is death eternal in the Puritan scheme, and Webster invests it with appropriately repugnant associations. He makes it clear, however, that this unclean matter is endlessly fertile (womb, vagina, cause, origin, root, spring) and possibly violent (hysterics). As the material from which anything, and hence all things, may be made, it cannot be dispensed with, yet it is base, and diseased. The separation and confinement of women in a narrow sphere within the community, which becomes yet more constricted while they are exercising their natural capacity for maternity, at once preserves this necessary material and prevents the contamination of the community.

Because the maternal function was at once necessary and hazardous to the community, women had to be simultaneously encouraged to perform it and prevented from realizing its significance. Sentimentalization of the home, and the mother's affective primacy within it, accomplished the first object, while repugnant associations (and physical fears) attached to procreation and parturition accomplished the second. The sentimentalization of home and mother in popular culture associated her with morality, education, refinement of manners, and taste. Conformity to this ideal reformed the maternal character according to the community's norms and its opposition to nature. Attention to this artificial maternity hid the perpetuation of the physical function. The physical function, indeed, was increasingly alienated from those who experienced it. The emergence of obstetrics and gynecology as distinct subfields of the medical profession and the earlier appropriation by physicians of the practice of midwifery removed control over childbirth from women to men.

At the same time, women's bodies became the object of study and attempted rationalization. A burgeoning literature on women's health, which devoted particular attention to the reproductive function, prescribed treatments for feminine disorders and putatively hygienic patterns of behavior. These works constructed the capacity for childbirth as a source of disease and infirmity, the act of childbirth as an illness. This literature begins among women, with authors like Catherine Beecher, Eliza Ware Farrar, Sara Josepha Hale, and Lydia Sigourney.[80] Initially, attention to health (one's own and that of the household) was commended to women as part of their peculiar duty, an obligation falling within their separate sphere. It accompanied advice on domestic economy, child raising, and morals. These works acknowledged a thoroughgoing division in the duties peculiar to each sex but treated domestic activities of all sorts as essentially conjoined. These first efforts at rationalization of women's separate sphere succeeded admirably. They were followed by increasingly specialized and technical treatments of distinct domestic functions, and by a transfer of authority in these fields from women to men.[81]

In the North the capacity for maternity was regarded with fear and loathing, in the South with fear and envy. Southerners endeavored to disguise woman's natural possession of this capacity, and appropriate it metaphorically to themselves. Northerners also endeavored to disguise the feminine capacity for maternity, but they shunned it. The ideological significance of this disparity becomes apparent when one considers the associations which attached to maternity in each section. All regarded it as a preeminently natural function. Both sections attributed primacy to maternity in the state of nature. Both regarded revolution as recurrence to nature.

For women, nature thus became the province of their rights and their rebellion. Convention deprived them of rights; convention prevented their rebellion. While men were increasingly wont to attribute their possession of rights to provisions of the civil constitution, women were obliged to discover theirs "in the nature which she bears," outside and in defiance of the law. Women who braved the association of convention with morality to claim their natural rights raised again the specter of women freed from the constraints of convention and assimilated to the Indian. Like the Indians who opposed the Puritans, they presented a challenge to the conventional, covenantal, and constitutional community.

The revolutionary recurrence to nature and affirmations of natural right were not, of course, confined to women. Indeed, the repugnant associations attached to feminine nature in Northern culture hindered its employment as a revolutionary identity, while legal and customary constraints on feminine activity made it increasingly impracticable. Male workers, whom alienation or ethnicity had rendered liminal, recognized the arbitrary and conventional character of their subordination and rightly regarded recurrence to nature as an appropriate expression of dissent.

The urban violence of 1830 through 1850 illustrates the contextual richness of the rioters' antipathy to convention. The liminal traits—insanity, intoxication, gaiety, extravagance of dress and gesture—which commonly mark the rebellious alienated express rejection of those conventions characteristic of a society from which the alienated feel themselves excluded. These were evinced by antebellum rioters. The recurrence to nature had, however, additional meaning for these victims of industrialization.

Jacksonian rhetoric had lauded the era as the "Age of the Common Man," even as the establishment and growth of industry had created unprecedented divisions between the classes. Affirmations of natural equality confirmed suspicions that increasingly evident social distinctions were arbitrary and unnatural.

Internal group violence had been confined, in the early years of the republic, to isolated instances of organized resistance to specific legislative acts. Riots, of diverse and frequently indeterminate origin, became frequent in the 1830s. David Grimsted counts twenty major riots in the five years from 1828 to 1833, followed by sixteen in 1834 and thirty-seven in 1835. John Higham, in *From Boundlessness to Consolidation*, recognizes in the riots an aspect of the boundlessness that characterized Jacksonian rhetoric. Grimsted concurs: "The psychological appeal of riot in democratic society is that the situation gives a sense of acting by a higher code, of pursuing justice and possessing power free from any structural restraint . . . this is a kind of apotheosis for democratic man."[82] This shows the survival of Jefferson's tentative admiration for anarchy in American political culture and suggests that the revolutionary tradition which Southerners appealed to in their disputes with the North survived in the North as a vehicle of dissent from the prevailing political culture.

Rousseau ascribed divinity to that assumption of sovereignty in which men realize their collective character, determine the boundaries of their polity, and ratify their laws. Grimsted termed the riots an "apotheosis." It is not surprising, therefore, that the Reverend Dr. Sprague, in a sermon in Albany, termed these riotous affirmations of popular sovereignty "a species of infidelity."[83] Whether one regarded it as "the mob forcing its way into the judgment seat" or the recollection of an earlier, constitutive, divinity, "popular turbulence" did indeed "set at nought all legal authority." It was, as the editor of the *Spirit of the Times* asserted, rebellion against "the constituted authority of the law."[84] The apotheosis of democratic man was the antithesis of selfless submission to the will of God.

Those who adhered to Nature's God held another view. "Junius," writing in the aftermath of riot, asserted that "the people had acted on the maxim that 'resistance to tyrants is obedience to God'." Jefferson, to whom this phrase is commonly attributed, would not have gainsaid him. "I hold it," he wrote Madison, "that a rebellion now and then is a good thing, and as necessary in the political world as storms in the physical."[85] Rebellions were produced, he averred, by "encroachments on the rights of the people," to which popular resistance provided an appropriate corrective. The willingness of the people to take to the streets evinced a salutary concern for the security of their rights, and tended to maintain the representative character of the government. Riots were to be regarded as an acceptable form of political action, providing a challenge to government when it became overweening or unrepresentative.

This qualified approbation of riot lingered into the Jacksonian period. Indeed, the egalitarianism espoused by Jackson's supporters, and the practice of evangelical revivals, encouraged mass expression of sentiment. The proliferation of voluntary organizations illustrated the significance and affirmed the democratic character of collective action. The experience of the Indian Wars, and of war with England, apprised men of the efficacy of violence even as it excused its exercise. "The ideological tenets and political emotions of the Age of Jackson focusing on the centrality and the sovereignty of the individual both encouraged riotous response to certain situations and made rioting hard to put down."[86] Excursions outside the law recalled that natural independence democratic theorists attributed to individuals. Collective action, marked by the same lawlessness, expressed a natural community, a common will.

John Runcie and Leonard Richards have questioned the attribution of spontaneity to the formation and action of antebellum mobs. They contend that the existence of intention in their assembly and choice of targets indicate leadership and thus (following George Rudé's analysis of European mobs) that they lacked that spontaneous community characteristic of peoples when social structures and conventions are abandoned. Runcie asks, "How, for example, can one call spontaneous mobs that assembled at church meetings with bags full of rotten eggs? The typical mob congregated intentionally and organized its action."[87]

The ascription of spontaneity to antebellum mobs was made by those who saw and those who participated in them. Mobs appear both united and disorganized. In that tremendous disorderly mass, individual participants and observers alike perceive the operation of a single will. This commonalty is produced less by the calculation of a common interest than by a sensation of emotional community. Attempts by civic officials, in Jacksonian America and in our own time, to discover leaders in mass uprisings, charge them with inciting to riot, and try, fine, or imprison them, represent attempts to deny the popular character of the dissent. It matters little whether the rioters were incited when they regard themselves as participating in a manifestation of spontaneous community.

Horace Holley, in a lecture given in honor of Lafayette's visit to America, emphasized the intimate relation between experience and meaning in the use of language. Words, he contended, signaled different things in Europe, "since words drew their strength from the vividness of the impressions for which they stood, the more energetic the experiences represented by the particular terms, the more powerful the thought to which they would give rise." American language was language "in earnest," constantly corrected and refined by "the consent of those who are deeply interested to maintain its truth and significancy." Language, according to Holley, acquired its moral and intellectual worth—its truth—from immediate experience. American professions of republicanism were vindicated by experience. "Our condition," Holley declared, "gives the force and definiteness of daily experience to the whole vocabulary of liberty, rights, reciprocal advantages, the dignity of our nature, and the common welfare."[88] Jacksonians, recognizing that the Revolutionaries had established their claim to free government directly, by their own labor, attempted to vindicate their inheritance with the argument that democratic institutions involved them in the same immediate experience of liberty that had distinguished the Revolutionary generation.

Mob action provided a similar empirical confirmation of that community which was said to undergird American democratic institutions. The immediate, personal, apprehension of democratic community vitiated individual feelings of alienation and impotence. Participation in this community acted as a sort of democratic sacrament, subsuming citizens in a single body, offering communion and confirmation at once. Grimsted's description of one mob reveals its sacramental qualities: "The mob emptied Johnson's and Glen's wine cellars and referred to the wine they abundantly drank as 'American blood' perhaps suggesting that it was squeezed from their townsmen's labors, as well as evoking older rituals of saturnalia in which the continuance of patterns of authority was made acceptable by their brief ritual cessation." He quotes a bank clerk who wrote "the mob of Cincinnati must have their annual festival, their Carnival, just as at stated periods the Romans enjoyed the Saturnalia." These moments of communal abandon were, the clerk concluded, "their practical demonstration of sovereignty."[89]

Other accounts corroborate the liminal traits displayed by the rioters. Leaders, by all accounts, were difficult to distinguish. Such as could be discerned were given Indian names "Red Jacket" or "Black Hawk" in unconcious recognition of their prepolitical community, their "savage independence." Witnesses attributed leadership to others because "he acted like a madman" or "he wore a curtain ring around his neck."[90]

The rioters, one Baltimore witness testified, " might have been insane . . . a great many passions make men insane besides liquor."[91] Madness is a form of intellectual liminality. Those who feel themselves alienated from their social order may seek self-expression in idiosyncratic acts of irrationality. When alienation is common, displays of communal madness may evince a common desire for a new order, for new paradigms intelligible in the light of altered experience. Participants in these communal displays of irrationality express their dissatisfaction with the state as representative. Their disorderly, capricious behavior manifests a comprehensive rejection of the existing social order. In recalling, for a moment, that subjective, voluntary community which the regime purports to represent, they endeavor to remind the regime of its proper function. Their irrationality demonstrates the dysjunction between the regime and the community.

In the Jacksonian case, as the testimony of the Baltimore witness indicates, passion made men mad. Whigs, and the Puritans before them, advocated the suppression of passion—temperance—in order to advance civilization. Passion belonged to nature, reason to civility. The "march of mind in the world" was characterized by increasing rationality in the social order. Passionate irrationality may then represent dissent from the process of civilization so conceived. Certainly it affirmed the desire and ability of the people to break out of the confines of objective law. Francis Grund, however, recorded that Jacksonians regarded riots and vigilantism as "not properly speaking, an opposition to the established laws of the country," but rather "a supplement to them as a species of common law." Those who held the notion that the jurisdiction of the federal government, and indeed, of government in general, should be severely limited could countenance vigilantism as an ad hoc democratic committee. In a government where, as the Westerner told Mrs. Trollope, "We makes our own laws," it was difficult to counter claims that vigilantism was merely an active expression of the will of the people. Many judges, confronted with popular abrogations of the law, preferred to look the other way. As Grimsted describes it, "mobs in that period functioned more as an accepted part of the political structure than an attack on it, largely because the authorities recognized their legitimacy." Americans condoning vigilantism and riot, Grimsted contends, were "seeing democracy less as a legal and technical system than as a psychological construct: Everyman's sense of his equality and right to decide." These illicit activities were thus the very antithesis of that deference to objective law and legal-rational authority which the Whigs were engaged in establishing.[92]

Northern political culture thus retained not only the Puritan covenental and familial paradigms, which demanded selflessness, temperance, and submission to authority, but also elements of that Revolutionary tradition which affirmed the primacy of popular authority and invested men with a conviction of their natural rights and independent worth.

In the antebellum period, however, this latter tradition was much eroded. The predominance of Whigs in the establishment and administration of the public schools, and in the composition and publication of textbooks, eased the inculcation of their moral and political precepts. The control of state and local legislatures by the Northern economic elite countered the informal efforts of workers to limit the length of the working day and resist arbitrary wage cuts. In her recollections of her years at the Lowell Mills, Harriet Robinson wrote: "It is hardly necessary to say that so far as the results were concerned the strike did no good. The dissatisfaction of the operatives subsided, or burned itself out, and the authorities did not accede to their demands, the majority returned to their work and the corporation went on cutting down the wages . . . thus the status of the factory population of New England became what we know it to be today."[93] That condition was described succinctly by Stephen Simpson, who observed, "All combinations of labor to resist the extortion of capital are illegal, and those who combine are punished as felons, conspiring against the the welfare of the state. All combinations of capital to oppress industry are legal, and receive a reward for their labors."[94] The legal subordination of labor to capital, the gradual inculcation of belief in the primacy of objective law, and the dependence of democracy on capitalism similarly moved the Democratic Party away from its early advocacy of economic and social equality toward policies more accomodating to capital.

Alterations in social institutions—the diminution of the social role of the family, the emergence of state institutions for education and for the care of the poor and the insane, and the restriction of feminine involvement in politics and society—increased psychological and political repression. The next chapter will describe how the resurgence of the Puritan tradition in response to immigration aided this repression and constricted the nation's ethnic and cultural boundaries.

3   Restraint and Reform

Economic expansion demanded two changes in America's demographic composition: the movement from Europe to America and the concentration of an enlarged population in urban areas. The encouragement of european immigration had been the conscious objective of American mercantilists from the inception of the republic. Mercantilist theory predicated economic development on the presence of a labor pool not tied to the land, but dependent on industry for employment. English and German restrictions on emigration of skilled workers further aided the maintenance of European industrial superiority by preventing the transfer of technological developments necessarily entailed in the emigration of skilled workers. The wisdom of such restrictions was revealed when an emigrant from England gifted with a particularly good memory, enabled New England mill owners to construct copies of those looms which had established England's primacy in textile manufacturing.

Americans had inserted in the Declaration a grievance charging the king with preventing the expansion of colonial populations. Legal restrictions on Atlantic crossings, occasioned by Anglo-French hostilities, precluded most immigration in the first generation of American independence. Succeeding generations witnessed a radical alteration of this state. The resolution, or at least diminishment, of hostilities on the Continent coincided with the English realization that they now possessed a considerable surplus population, most of it Irish. Unable to reduce it by employing them in war, the British Parliament resumed with enhanced vigor its ancient policy of unloading "paupers, criminals, and Celts" on its colonial offspring.[1]

In 1825, 11 percent of the American population was foreign-born. This figure rose to 35 percent in 1845 and by 1855 had reached over 50 percent. Despite attempts to deflect immigrants from the shores of the United States, immigration continued to increase steadily throughout the antebellum period. Many of those whose ships had landed in Canadian rather than American ports rapidly found their way over the border and into the expanding textile factories of New England.

American manufacturers recognized in this sudden influx the opportunity to expand industrial production, lower the wages currently given the workers, and thus to challenge English supremacy in textile manufacture. Commercial interests were equally gratified. A ship that had sailed to England full of cotton might return to America full of immigrants, thus substituting the receipts of steerage for a heretofore-unprofitable return. The trade in population, closed by war and the abolition of the slave trade, was thus renewed.

Manufacturing and commercial interests were, of course, the province of the Northern states. Western interests, however, were equally advantaged by immigration. That speculation in land which distinguished the wealthy in the West became increasingly lucrative as competition for land increased. The desire of immigrants to buy land in the West, which brought Northern industrialists and Western landed interests into conflict, thus formed the basis of their alliance in favor of immigration.

Jacksonian Democrats and workingmen's parties in the North supported the availability of cheap lands as a means of removing workers from complete dependence on their industrial employers. Agrarian romantics among the Jacksonians had derived from Jefferson the notion that the ownership of land ensured personal independence and provided the nation with that "sturdy yeomanry" upon which democracy was dependent. Workers recognized, moreover, that the possibility of alternative forms of livelihood enabled them to demand higher wages from their industrial employers. Western landed interests, conversely, welcomed increases in the demand for land. All of these parties were united by a common cultural antipathy to rich Northeasterners.

The very factors which divided the Western and Eastern rich united them on the subject of immigration. Eastern industrialists endeavored to increase competition for jobs; Westerners, competition for land. The attitudes of both these factions were complicated, however, by the predominantly Catholic composition of the immigrant population.

One New Yorker wrote, "The continued swell of increasing numbers emigrating from Europe, and making their homes amongst us, a large proportion of whom are Romanists: Irish, Germans, etc. cannot but awaken solicitude and thoughtfulness as to its bearings upon our institutions."²

Westerners, who had long been in competition with the French and Spanish on the frontier, were accustomed to regard Catholics as the enemy. Americans of the colonial period had feared the collusion of Catholics and Indians on the frontier. The English, as late as 1838, had been threatened with a Catholic rebellion uniting the French and Irish in Quebec. American expansion to the West had been accomplished in competition with the Catholic French and the Catholic Spanish. It affirmed, therefore, the temporal superiority of Protestantism and established Protestantism as a distinguishing cultural trait of the Western Americans. Manifest Destiny recalled the Puritan notion of a peculiarly American mission. In the West, the temporal extension of the Holy Commonwealth found its material expression in American spatial extension, and territorial extension acquired a sacred character. Western men of Southern antecedents and irreligious inclinations spoke of their expansionist enterprise with evangelical fervor. The territorial extension of the United States was identified with the extension of American culture, and thus with the superiority of Protestantism to Catholicism. Manifest Destiny was providential.

New Englanders had inherited their capitalism and militant religiosity from the same source. Their Calvinist antecedents had imbued them with an inclination toward capital and a particularly vociferous form of Protestantism. The Yankee and Puritan alike regarded capital accumulation and material success as evidence of personal superiority. Industry was equally a pursuit and a virtue. Catholicism was the very antithesis of this ideal.

The Catholic church was the old enemy of both the Northeast and West. Protestant industrialists, like Western expansionists, welcomed immigration while they deplored the Catholicism of the immigrant. Thus those parties most desirous of immigration were also those most fearful of cultural diversification. This distinctive tension did much to determine sectional attitudes toward social policy in the West and Northeast. The Catholicism of the immigrants sparked a recollection in each section of its cultural mission. Each had regarded itself as charged with the spread of Protestant civilization. Recollection of this providential mission encouraged efforts to acculturate and assimilate the Catholic immigrants. This was especially true in the Northeast. There, the Protestant Crusade reached its zenith, impelled by the efforts of a legion of Protestant clerics.

The traditional prominence of clerics in the political affairs of

New England gave their fulminations against Catholicism an explicitly political character. The political culture of New England located the Reformation, and more particularly the English Revolution, as the source of both civil liberties and American Protestantism. The Pilgrim Fathers had united the struggle for Protestantism with the struggle for civil liberties. Catholics, necessarily outside Protestantism, were thus regarded as the ancient enemies of liberty. Their presence and their influence in the polity were represented as a threat to republican government. Protestant proselytizing was, therefore, less a sectarian bid for primacy than a patriotic defense of the foundations of the regime. Americanization entailed the inculcation of Protestant beliefs.

The influx of Catholic immigrants had also placed an unexpected burden on the philanthropic resources of established, primarily Protestant, churches. Provision for the poor was still the province of individuals and the churches. The arrival of large numbers of impoverished immigrants had taxed the charitable resources of Protestant churches in two respects: by immediately increasing the numbers of the destitute and by lowering wages, thus impoverishing many more. They were, therefore, obliged to encourage an increase in philanthropic activity on the part of the rich in their congregations. For the wealthy industrialists to whom this appeal was addressed, philanthropic activity offered a means of assuaging personal doubts concerning the social consequences of their self-interested actions.

The first immigrants, and many of those who emigrated spontaneously, were of the class Americans purportedly welcomed: skilled mechanics and farmers with savings enough to purchase lands in the West. Hireling laborers and other largely unskilled workers were, however, recruited for factories and public works by Eastern businessmen as early as 1818.[3] The growth of industry greatly increased the pace of labor importation.

Like the archetypal capitalist of Weber's *Protestant Ethic* who amasses capital which he is forbidden to enjoy, the antebellum industrialist who imported immigrant labor felt himself obliged to render at least a portion of the profits turned by this supply of cheap labor to those philanthropic organizations which promised to improve the condition of the immigrant operatives. It was very much an investment in human capital. Labor was implicitly reduced to but one of the resources which the capitalist was obliged to replenish in the pursuit of his calling.

The association of resurgent Protestantism with the philanthropic capitalists is complex and multifaceted. Simple virtue was called forth by the tenets of an increasingly visible church. The Protestant Crusade inculcated suspicions of the Catholic immigrants and, in some industrialists, guilt over their role in encouraging immigration. At the same time, this Catholic population offered its employers the opportunity to participate in the evangelical enterprise vouchsafed by the heroes of the Reformation. They could convert the Catholic. With Protestantism so prominent a part of American nationality, conversion served as both cultural socialization and ideological indoctrination, a rudimentary catechism for infant Americans. The acculturation and assimilation of the immigrant was an act at once of patriotism and of religious zeal.

Irish and many German immigrants had been differentiated from native-born citizens by their religion. This was a significant obstacle to their integration, for religion had provided the dominant paradigms of New England's political culture. Traits associated with the Irish—violence, intoxication, poverty, gaiety, and "love of the old sod"—are liminal traits. Their journey over water and their ambiguous status as resident aliens further enhanced their liminality. As immigrants, they were on the threshold, the limen, of nationality.[4]

Religion, however, remained the primary trait which distinguished the immigrant from the native-born and placed him on the cultural periphery of the nation. Although there are multiple representations of this liminality in metaphors employed of the Catholic, the most prominent is the image of the woman. Femininity was the metaphor most frequently employed to express liminality in the antebellum period. It was consistently used in accounts of Indians, blacks, and Southerners. In literary and political treatments of the immigrant Catholic, the metaphoric ascription of femininity to immigrant and church regularly figured as a cipher for their liminality and for those foreign traits which placed them on the cultural periphery.

The metaphoric femininity of the immigrant and the immigrant's church took several related forms ranging from rape to the image of the woman armed. Authors of nativist tracts against the Catholic church commonly, indeed unanimously, recounted stories of the seduction of women by priests and Inquisitors, though these carried varying messages.

In some, the woman is portrayed as victim. Thus, in Anthony Gavin's best-selling *The Great Red Dragon, or the Master Key to Popery*, a dying priest confesses, "I have spared no woman of my parish for whom I had a fancy, and many of my brethren's parishes, but I cannot tell the number."[5] The author of *Pope or President?* asserts, "It is the same thing to put a nun's veil on a girl as to expose her to public prostitution,"[6] and recounts the sadistic treatment of nuns in convents and the torturing of women by the Inquisition. Robert Breckenridge, in *Papism in the Nineteenth Century*, treats of the confessional, where the young and lustful priests "make all sorts of shocking suggestions to the penitent." "Men," he observes, "very seldom go."[7]

This last aside is very telling. In all the nativist tracts I examined, in all the Protestant histories of the Catholic church, in all the essays on religion in the schools, there was never a mention of a male convert to Catholicism. Nor did they recount tales of men's confessions, except those of priests. They were replete, however, with detailed accounts of feminine conversion. There are several reasons for this. Women, being less educated, and presumed to be more submissive and more gullible by nature, reflected the same vulnerability to priestly domination that Protestant Crusaders attributed to the oppressed and untutored immigrants. The exploitation of the weak and ignorant, whether women or immigrants, emphasized the power and rapacity of the Catholic church.

The Catholic church had itself been personified as a woman in the earliest rhetoric of the Protestants. The "Scarlet Whore" of Revelations was universally interpreted as a metaphor for the Church of Rome. The 1856 edition of Gavin's work has as its frontispiece a representation of this woman, riding an ass, holding a cup of wine. She was, the Reverend Edward Beecher said, "drunken with the blood of saints"; Scripture had held "the inhabitants of the world are drunk with the wine of her fornication." "Rome herself," Beecher declared, was "the great whore."[8] William Hogan, author of *Popery! As It Was and As It Is*, speaks of "the Old Lady of Rome in her dishabille," and writes, "holy mother church knows full well that no honest or honorable man could see her in her native deformity without a shudder of disgust."[9] Four traits emerge in this regularly employed personification: intemperance, of both the Church and its devotees, maternity, violence, and a lascivious and seductive sexuality.

The ascription of feminity to the Catholic church and Catholic immigrants was a Northern mode of signifying people whose natural passions and appetites have been released from conventional bonds. This was made more explicit in accounts of individual Catholics and converts. The Church, Breckenridge wrote, was "the mother of harlots."[10] "Monastaries and nunneries, under control of Jesuits, were but vast Sodoms," "legalized Sodoms," in which "every confessor has a concubine and there are very few of them who do not have several."[11] Nuns commonly confessed, "I have abandoned myself to all the sins I have been capable to commit."[12]

Despite this condemnation of sinfulness, the Sodoms of the Ro-

man Church were often rendered rather attractive in the highly colored narratives of the condemnators. Anthony Gavin's story of a young
girl spirited away to the harem of a Spanish Inquisitor has the unlucky
virgin plied with chocolate and cookies, gifted with brocades and diamonds, and only sporadically subjected to the attentions of the Inquisitor, who was, in any case, "a charming lover." A chapter in *Pope
or President?* entitled "Convents Exposed" describes, in addition to
more lascivious recreations, operas and comedies performed within
convent walls.[13]

These narratives of convent and confessional, like the earlier captivity narratives, contained delicate warnings that the realm of unrestrained nature might prove attractive to women, hazardous to men
and to society. In Catholic countries, Protestant authors warned, men
became subservient to their mistresses, and even to the lovers of their
wives. "The peace of the family was banished from all Italy," they
declared, and warned ominously, "The Italians ceased to be men."
Catholicism destroyed the family by permitting wives and daughters to
evade the authority of husband and father. In a chapter warning of the
perils of Catholic education, one author related a story of two sisters
who were thereby converted: "On returning home they absolutely refused to hear the reading of the Holy Scriptures, or to unite in the
family worship of the Protestant parents. The agonized father implored
them to kneel before the Lord at the family altar, but they remained
inexorable, and preferred to kneel before the priest in the confessional
to the living and true God."[14] This passage is very rich. The significant
relation is that of the daughters and their father, who, after the Puritan
model, is acting as the agent of the Lord. Here, as throughout this
genre, women represent the Catholics, a man the dominant Protestant
community. The daughters have not exchanged one religion for another in their conversion, but have abandoned all religion. They "refused to hear the reading of the Holy Scriptures," and "to kneel before
the Lord." They preferred to "kneel before the priest," putting a man
in the place of God. Since the author had previously related the sal-
acious goings-on of the confessional, the statement that they preferred
kneeling before the priest in the confessional to worshipping "at the
family altar" amounts to an assertion that they abandoned a pious family life for pagan sensuality.[15]

Priests, nativist authors contended, claimed an authority superi-
or to that of husband and father.[16] They, however, were constantly
employed in the service of "holy mother church" and in "worship of
virgins," through whom conversions were effected. Their services as

confessor and exorcist were exploited by ambitious and rebellious women, who either pretended to visions and miracles as a vehicle for social advancement or used a pretended possession as an excuse to "talk blasphemously of God and his saints," and "beat husbands."[17]

Catholicism emerges from these accounts as a state within that province of ungoverned nature in which subordinated groups turn upon their superiors. In addition to the unfilial daughters and belligerent wives, nativists provided detailed accounts of servants seducing, poisoning, and informing on their Protestant employers at the behest of the Church.[18] This reflected the fear of violent revolution on the part of the subordinated immigrant workers. They were, the Reverend Herman Norton warned, like "the image or statue of the Virgin which Bonaparte found in the dungeons of Spain who stretched forth her arms to embrace and pressed the victim to her breast, cutting him in a thousand pieces."[19]

The Catholic church, was the realm of death and sex, of intemperate passions and unrestrained appetites. It served as a negative referent in the redefinition of Northern sectional and ultimately national identity. Toward these aliens in their own borders, the Northern elite directed a two-part policy: restraint and reform. The violent predilections and insurrectionary tendencies of men outside the religious covenant and social conventions must first be restrained to protect existing institutions and those they encompassed. The maintenance of social order thus became the principle concern of those who most valued and were best served by it. Fear of riot, insurrection, and revolution made allies of politicians, capitalists, and the clergy. As Amy Bridges has observed, "an economical form of police" was the most frequently expressed desire of a legion of moral reform movements.[20]

The second part of the twofold strategy which directed elite response to the increase in immigration was reform. The arrival of the immigrants and the prospect of their continued residence within the borders of the United States made reform as well as restraint a practical necessity. The ideological aversion of even the most interventionist Whigs to direct authoritarian rule in America made the maintenance of order through the police an untenable situation. The continued sporadic outbreak of revolution throughout the states of Europe seemed, moreover, to indicate that such a course was finally ineffectual. Elites therefore sought means of securing immigrant acceptance of the social order. For the elites who directed the majority of the reform movements, the project of integrating immigrants into the society was equivalent to increasing their utility as a labor force and decreasing their inclination to foment radical political, economic, or social reform. The reformers themselves, however, were actively and avowedly engaged in a revision of American culture and American ideology, which aimed at restricting radical democracy and popular participation.

The Temperance movement illustrates both the desire of established elites to maintain their status and a profound revision of American cultural values. The relation between status politics and the Temperance movement has been ably described in Joseph Gusfield's *Symbolic Crusade*. Although organizations of reformed alcoholics, the Washingtonians for example, became part of the movement later, the Temperance campaign was founded by clerics and prominent philanthropists who were not themselves the object of reform or reproach. Gusfield contends that their philanthropic enterprise was impelled by their desire to distance themselves from the increasingly visible and vociferous lower classes. With birth no longer an adequate inducement to deference on the part of the lower orders, those scions ambitious for continued familial prominence were obliged to discover an alternate grounding for their pretended superiority. Gusfield notes that the Temperance and antislavery movements drew their founding members from old Federalist families. "They were men who felt the demise of the traditional values of their social class, and in trying to restore those values, attempted to recoup their dwindling status . . . They were an elite without function, a displaced class in American society."[21]

Lyman Beecher's *Six Sermons on Intemperance* (1843) reveal the intimate connections between the Temperance crusade and the anxieties of an attempted aristocracy. "When the laboring classes are contaminated," he declared, "the right of suffrage becomes the engine of destruction." Attempts to maintain a limited suffrage were failing daily. It was necessary, therefore, to change the character of the lower classes. Manifestly unfit for the franchise, they must be either altered or excluded. The latter alternative had been closed by their betters. The former had not yet been effected. The intemperate and enfranchised poor were thus Beecher's "engine of destruction." "As intemperance increases the power of taxation will come more and more into the hands of men of intemperate habits and desperate fortunes; of course the laws will gradually become subservient to the debtor and less efficacious in protecting the rights of property." The old order had in some sense acceded to the values of the new. With deference increasingly the consequence of wealth rather than birth, the maintenance of the status quo depended almost entirely on the preservation of old fortunes. Beecher feared not only that old debts might be legislatively nullified, but also that "the power of taxation will come more and more" into the hands of the intemperate.[22]

Intemperate men are prone to radical measures. Beecher's language suggests that "intemperance" refers not only to the liberal use of spirits, but to the spirited use of liberal principles. Intemperate, that is to say, progressive, taxation might remove the last material indication of a putative moral superiority. Property would be divided not by some invisible and providential hand, but by law, and at the behest of the people. While the operation of the market and the consequent distribution of property remained mysterious, it might be regarded as a providential indication of divine favor. Taxes were then a profane tampering with a sacred determination. The voice of the people, and the temporal order, rather than being assimilated to the will of God, became an alternative to the sacred order.

Gusfield rejects outright the notion that the Temperance movement was Puritan in its origins. Inasmuch as the Pilgrim Fathers countenanced the use of alcohol and were moderate rather than abstinent in their use of it, he is correct. Alcohol has, however, as he himself observes, rather little to do with it. The Temperance movement was animated by the desire to establish a temporal order in accord with the will of God. In doing so, they expected to evince their providential election and secure for themselves a corresponding position in the social order.

Benevolence was not merely a guise for temporal ambition; rather, it gave sanction to that ambition. Participation in the Temperance crusade evinced the moral rigor of the participant and promised to secure his social superiority as well, for such a state, in which the chosen ruled and the people responded with an "easy and habitual obedience,"[23] was in accord with divine election. The struggle of the righteous to aggrandize their temporal status was not merely countenanced by the Protestant clergy, it was urged upon them. Those whom election had secured in the Holy Commonwealth could pursue temporal status secure in the belief that they were advancing not merely self-interest, but the interest of that community of saints in which they were comprehended.

The enterprise of manifesting the ideal in the material world went back beyond the Pilgrims to the Reformation and the Incarnation. The Pilgrims, however, were the archetypal representation of this endeavor in American political culture. The emergence of the Temperance movement coincided with a resurgence of reverence for the Pilgrim Fathers.

The Revolution represented the birth of a new world order, universally appropriate and grounded in the rights of man. The Pilgrims represented the birth of a new world order, but one in which sovereignty and the power of election rested with Providence rather than the people. The Puritans were tied to an Anglo-Saxon ethnic identification. Both the revival of Puritan history and the Temperance movement were impelled by resistance to Irish Catholic immigration. Both advanced the notion of restraint and a determined sobriety against the intemperance they feared in the immigrants.

Lacking that common ethnic history which purportedly bound Americans to one another, the immigrants could establish commonalty with the natives only on principle. The Revolution provided an ideology sufficient to embrace them. The revival of the Pilgrim Fathers at this juncture suggests that Whigs and Moral Reformers, like their Puritan and Federalist forebears, entertained some reservations regarding the ideology of the Revolution. The Revolution, moreover, recalled a period of passionate resistance to authority, the repudiation of obedience, and the affirmation of the rights of man. Established elites necessarily feared the reaffirmation of popular authority and a renewed opposition to formal government. Clerics and organized religions, already apprehensive of that popular activism awakened by revivalist methods, saw in the recollection of the Revolution the reiteration of a temporal political order wholly independent of God.

That species of nationality which the Puritans represented was cultural rather than ideological. Inclusion in the polity was contingent upon assimilation. This promised to secure the maintenance of the status quo and the continued dominance of established elites. The image of the Puritan united ethnicity and religiosity, reflecting a similar union in the Moral Reform movement. The Pilgrim Fathers presented a reflective model of what the moral reformers saw as their own ideal character. Use of the Pilgrims as a counter to the Revolution enabled established elites to maintain their nationality even as they repudiated the fundamental principles of the regime. It enabled clerics to advance religious doctrines as productive of, and thus prior to, the ideological doctrines of the Revolution. The notion of a vast world historical process of which the Reformation, and in America the Plymouth founding, were decisive movements, enabled Protestant Americans to promulgate a conception of America's boundlessness which extended through time rather than through space. Thus, while the ideal of America maintained its claimed universality, it derived this from its eschatological significance rather than its accordance with the nature and rights of man. In this scheme, the grandeur of American empire derived from its historical origins and its temporal continuance.

The partisans of this empire were charged with a duty to posterity. Territorial expansion was a manifestation of this historical progress. The expansion of the temporal boundaries of the nation to include remembered forebears and an imagined posterity was accompanied by a constriction of the cultural boundaries of the nation. American republicanism was, this articulation affirmed, the consequence of the Reformation. American nationality thus required a corresponding reformation of the immigrants. They were obliged to adopt "Anglo-Saxon" mores and the tenets of the Protestant religion prior to becoming truly American.

Intemperance and intoxication each indicate an abandonment of conventional restraints. Sermons linked this to "Sabbath breaking," "profane swearing," and a disregard for religious injunctions. Political orations likened this to disregard for the law. The immigrants, while they remained ignorant of or indifferent to the conventions of the dominant culture in America, were therefore a source of immorality and lawlessness in the republic. Piety and law, especially the law of convention and compact, were dominant values in the culture of New England. As the Protestant crusade expanded the national importance of the cultural variant, these values became important cultural indices of subjective nationality. Intemperance had long been associated with two cultural alternatives to Puritan New England: the Southerner and the Indian.

Indian alcoholism was recognized as a problem from the earliest days of the colonies. The source of the difficulty lay in the Indians' practice of customs appropriate to a hunter-gatherer economy. As Beverley noted in his *History and Present State of Virginia,* the Indians were accustomed to alternate abstinence and indulgence. When they had no food they ate nothing uncomplainingly, when food was plentiful they ate all they could. "They accustom themselves to no set meals but eat night and day when they have plenty of provisions or if they have got anything that is a rarity."[24] Restrictions on the consumption of alcohol by the Indians merely made it more of a rarity and ensured its liberal consumption when available. Colonists less observant than Beverley tended to regard Indian abuse of alcohol as but one aspect of a characteristic intemperance. Indian intemperance, like Indian anarchy, and Indian violence, manifested the absence of conventional restraints and emphasized the disparity between Indian and New England culture.

Southerners, who answered to the attributes of the Indian in other respects, were likewise credited with the intemperate use of alcohol. The hard-drinking Southerner exemplified not only anarchy but self-indulgence. Intemperance, Northern moral reformers argued, was merely one aspect of that indulgence of the appetites characteristic of Southern culture.

The association of Temperance with other forms of self-restraint silenced the movement in the South. Although many Southerners had been sympathetic to the movement in the 1820s, its association with the Protestant crusade, Whig politics, and antislavery critiques of Southern self-indulgence, had lost it a hearing by the 1830s. The association of the Temperance movement with Whig partisanship similarly alienated Jacksonian Democrats: "Despite commitment to Temperance as a doctrine, the Methodists of western Massachusetts, who were staunch Jacksonians, advised their adherents against contributing to the Society."[25] Temperance had come to entail an antiegalitarianism independent of abstention from alcohol, and antithetical to Jacksonian democracy.

Like public education, however, it was an issue of such significance to many that they supported legislators they would otherwise have opposed, by virtue of their stands on Temperance alone. This phenomenon, no less than the increase in funds available to Whig candidates through contributions from the Temperance movement, enabled the Whigs to make considerable electoral advances despite widespread recognition that Temperance was allied to New England's bid for sectional primacy.

The association of intemperance with the immigrants expressed the perception of the New England elite that they were outside the conventional boundaries of the culture. It was enhanced by reports of heavy drinking preparatory to, and during, the urban riots of the 1840s and by the sacramental use of wine in Roman Catholic masses. The transubstantiation of wine in the Mass differentiated the Catholic immigrants from the predominantly Protestant natives. Within the context of the Temperance movement, it carried several related messages. The immigrants were, by reason of their religion, culturally distinct from the dominant culture. Their distinction was manifest in the performance of mysterious and irrational rituals and in their violent, and equally irrational, behavior during the riots. Both the riots and the religious arcana presented the threat of a passionate, irrational, and ignorant populace incited by evil men to the defiance of law and convention.

The emphasis upon the role of priests in the Catholic church and unnamed leaders in the riots served to emphasize that dependence and ignorance which established elites wished to attribute to the lower classes. Thus it served to confirm their contention that immigrants were unfit for democratic institutions even as it provided reasons for denying them the exercise of democratic rights.

Raids on the alcoholic reserves of the rich are often seen in riots of the lower classes. They serve several purposes. The rioters reveal the hoarding of a universally valued good by the rich. They divest the hoarders of it, indicating their rejection of the claim of the rich to privileged status. They consume it themselves, thus indicating their equality, and—by their casual appropriation of property—their brotherhood or membership in a natural community where property is determined by use. The common consumption of whatever food and drink they find is characteristically described as sacramental by both participants and observers of such riots. The resulting intoxication further liberates participants from inhibitions and conventional constraints.[26]

It was exactly this liberation that Moral Reformers most feared. They were convinced that the maintenance of morality was dependent upon the maintenance of the legal and conventional order. The Puritan antecedents of the Temperance movement are evident in this anxiety.

The Puritan conception of America as the land of the millennium, the land prepared for the accomplishment of a providential plan, had spread, aided by Yankee emigration, throughout the nation. It became so thoroughly diffused, and so widely accepted, that contemporary scholars are wont to speak of its "secularization." This is not entirely accurate. The traditional Puritan conception of America's millennial role had become conflated with Continental notions of the "march of mind in the world." Thus Lincoln, in an early panegyric to rationalization, spoke of the Temperance "revolution" as one moment in the temporal progress of mind, one in a concatenation of revolutions, each mightier—and more economical—than the last: "Its march cannot fail to be on and on until every son of the earth shall drink in rich fruition, the sorrow-quenching draughts of perfect liberty. Happy day, when, all appetites controlled, all passions subdued, all matter subjected, mind, all-conquering mind, shall live and move the monarch of the world. Glorious consummation! Hail Fall of Fury! Reign of Reason, all hail!"[27] Nowhere, perhaps, could one find an utterance more evocative of Weber's phrase, "sensualists without heart." The Temperance movement entailed in Lincoln's estimation not only abstinence, but the suppression of all passion, the conquest of all material impulses.

The march of mind was the conquest of nature—not merely external nature, but the natural, instinctive appetites that move all men in the state of nature.

Lincoln, in youth a skeptic, in death a saint, bears witness to the determinative strength of Puritan providentialism. His early speeches praise reason unreservedly. Mind has the place the Puritans gave to God. Similarly endowed with omniscience and omnipotence, this abstracted, impersonal deity yields in Lincoln's later rhetoric to the image of the Puritan Father-God. In the American experience, rationalism and a commitment to social and political rationalization have not been hostile to piety. On the contrary, Protestant clerics, particularly in the antebellum period, were at the forefront of campaigns for rationalization in public institutions. They believed that the triumph of Protestantism and the reign of reason were objects wholly in accord.

Lyman Beecher's hostility to Catholicism in his *Plea for the West* is purportedly derived from the fear that the Catholic church would subvert free institutions in America. This arose, in part, from the Church's opposition to liberalism in Europe, in part from their belief that the doctrines and institutions of the Church were intrinsically hostile to free inquiry. Catholics, Beecher asserted, were enjoined to a perfect and unquestioning obedience; "no one may read the Bible but by permission of the priesthood, and no one permitted to understand it and worship God according to the dictates of his own conscience." He quoted Dwight's estimate of the Catholic Austrians, "slaves, slaves in body and mind, whipped and disciplined by priests to have no opinion of their own." Protestantism would surely triumph, Beecher claimed, should the doctrinal esoterica of the Catholic church be opened to public examination. "A book of well-authenticated documents, without note or comment, would nearly supersede the necessity of controversy . . . There is nothing in Catholic, more than in Protestant human nature, to demand implicit confidence, or preclude investigation and vigilance." Education, Beecher affirmed, was requisite to the continuance of free institutions; "such masses of ignorance are the material of all others most dangerous to liberty, for as a general fact, uneducated mind is educated vice."[28]

In Beecher's articulation, religiosity and enlightenment were conflated. The illiteracy which prevailed on the frontier presented an opportunity to unscrupulous demagogues and a threat to republican institutions. The situation was made much more grave, however, by the intrusion of a population unschooled in the laws and customs of a free state: "This danger from uneducated mind is augmented daily by the rapid influx of foreign immigrants unacquainted with our institutions, unaccustomed to self-government, inaccessible to education and easily accessible to prepossession, and inveterate cruelty and intrigue, and easily embodied and wielded by sinister design."[29] They were, nativist authors argued, unfit for the suffrage. Robert Breckinridge protested against those laws which permitted naturalization within five years, arguing that the franchise was "a right they never had at home, and are unfit to have anywhere." "Their priests," he asserted, "control their votes, direct their combinations, encourage their violence."[30] The ignorance attributed to the immigrants made them appear especially vulnerable to the machinations of the Vatican. "This vast number of immigrants," Gavin wrote, in his summary of the "History of the Papacy in the United States," "are headed by priests, many of them Jesuits."[31]

The trait which had set the immigrants off from the population they had joined in America also served as a basis of commonalty, uniting them. Individually ignorant, impoverished, and politically impotent, they represented a general threat only when regarded as a body, animated and directed by a malevolent force more knowledgeable than they. The hierarchical arrangement of the Catholic church and the evident subordination of the laity to the authority of the priest suggested the method whereby they might be organized and their collective power exploited. The immigrants' Catholicism thus provided them simultaneously with a goal, a grievance, and a strategy. That trait which made them evidently foreign provided them with the grounds for their own collective action. The organization of the Church suggested the tactics whereby they might be most successful. "Their physical power, and property, and vote," Lyman Beecher declared, "are as entirely as in Europe within the reach of clerical influence."[32] The subordination of the laity to the priests, and the priests to the pope, made the politics of the Vatican in Europe a matter of immediate importance to the Americans.

The antiliberal pronouncements and policies which the Vatican had recently undertaken in Europe awakened reasonable fears among Americans that the Church might contemplate an actively hostile role in opposition to the democratic institutions of the republic. Thus Leavit and Lord published *Foreign Conspiracy Against the United States* in 1835, as Lyman Beecher, in his *Plea for the West* simultaneously announced the pope's plan to take over the Mississippi Valley. *The History of the Papacy in the United States* reported that "conscious of its increasing weakness in Europe the Church of Rome has been endeavoring to plant itself in the free soil of America. It meditates the most tremendous designs against our civil and religious liberties . . . The fearful danger seemed everyday increased from the constant immigration which was being poured in upon us."[33] The pope, this History declared, was "the mere tool of Austria, the home and resting place of despotism itself."[34] Beecher saw the relation reversed, making the tyrant Metternich the servant of the Church. "That wily politician does not sleep over our prosperity, or despair of our overthrow . . . he is sowing with broad cast among us the elements of future strife."[35]

Fears of Catholic plots in the New World had a long history in the annals of the states. The Maryland colonial legislature had heard of a planned uprising of blacks, Indians, and Papists. Because each of these groups, viewed from the center, was on the cultural periphery of the nation, the possibility of combined insurrection uniting them seemed less improbable to the threatened than to the parties of the supposed threat. The fearful recognized not the disparate cultural traits of these groups, which would militate against an effective collaboration, but their common distance from the culture at the center. The spirit of democratic evangelism, with its attendant denigration of the significance of culture in favor of a universal humanity, had reduced apprehensions of rebellion among the culturally peripheral. With the increasing sentiment in favor of the primacy of culture in the determination of politics, which began to dominate the Northeast in the 1830s, apprehensions of collusion among the liminal revived. These persisted through the 1850s. In *Startling Facts for American Protestants*, the Reverend Herman Norton reported Roman Catholic attempts to incite black rebellions, and "the efforts of the Pope and the Emperor of Austria, to win the Indian tribes over to the Church of Rome."[36] These preparations, Norton averred, indicated "a fearful Indian war" engineered by the pope in the interests of the Church. The response issued by Bishop Hughes to charges that the Roman church intended to control the Mississippi Valley did little to allay these suspicions. "Everyone should know it," he declared with impolitic candor, "Everyone should know that we have for our mission to convert the world."[37] This emphasis upon the catholicism of the Roman church established it as a threat on yet another, more fundamental, level to the cultural integrity held up as ideal in Whig New England.

Like the assumption of unnamed and invisible leaders in the urban riots, the distant figures of the pope and Metternich affirmed simultaneously the ignorant dependence of the immigrants and the gravity of the danger they presented to the republic. A patriotic concern for the fate of the nation and a benevolent desire to liberate the immigrants were thus the impulses which purportedly actuated the partisans of assimilation and anti-Catholic crusades. In this articulation, restraints on the rights of immigrants and Catholics were properly construed as defenses of the democracy rather than as attacks upon it.

Notice of the un-American character of the immigrants necessarily wakened apprehensions that their European character was visceral rather than vestigial. Immigrants, John Quincy Adams insisted, "must cast off their European skin, never to resume it. They must look forward to their posterity rather than backward to their ancestors, they must be sure that whatever their feelings may be, those of their children will cling to the prejudices of their country." Horace Mann wrote, "Everyone acknowledges the justness of the declaration that a foreign people, born and bred and dwarfed under the despotisms of the Old World cannot be transformed into full stature of American citizens merely by a voyage across the Atlantic."[38]

Mann expressed the popular opinion that the experience of despotism altered the character of the immigrants. His choice of words, however, suggested that the apprehended defects were in the nature of the individual immigrants. They were "born and bred and dwarfed." Another of his comments, in a *Lecture on Education*, made this more explicit: "It is the ancestors of a people who prepare and predetermine all the great events in that people's history."[39] Ezra Gannet, a popular Protestant cleric, similarly compared the influx of immigrants to a transfusion of bad blood "tainting the blood of childhood and suffusing the cause of a subsequent debility and decay."[40] The corporeal metaphors used by Adams, Mann, and Gannet illustrate the Whig view that nationality was determined by history, culture, and irreversible evolution, rather than by volition and ideology. This understanding of "foreign" was accepted by census takers along the Eastern seaboard, who counted as "foreign" children with one foreign-born parent.

Assimilation was not to be expected in a single generation. The movement for the establishment of public schools supported by the state was animated by the notion that children removed from the undemocratic and immoral influence of their immigrant parents might be more rapidly assimilated. Stanley Schultz, in his study of antebellum Boston public schools as "culture factories" records the efforts of nineteenth-century reformers to this end.

Samuel Bates, chairman of Boston's School Visiting Committee, wrote that the object of public education was "to train up all the children within its jurisdiction to be intelligent, virtuous, patriotic American citizens." Immigrant children, the New Englander wrote, must be "liberalized, Americanized," through education. Public schools "draw in the children of alien parentage with others, and assimilate them to the native born."[41] "The education of the nation," Lyman Beecher wrote, "the culture of its intellect, the formation of its conscience, and the regulation of its affections,"[42] was a process which must embrace those children whose unenlightened, European parents would otherwise raise them in a fashion subversive of American institutions. "With the old," the *Massachusetts Teacher* wrote, "not much can be done, but with their children the great remedy is education. The rising generation must be taught as our own children are taught. We say *must be* because in many cases this can only be done through force . . . the children must be gathered up and forced into school and those who resist and impede this plan, whether parents or *priests* must be held accountable and punished."[43]

The public education which Lyman Beecher and his fellow reformers envisioned was not, despite Beecher's protestations, a community of free inquiry. Rather it was a form of deliberate indoctrination, intended to secure not free institutions merely, but the prevailing social order, and the property of the ruling class. "The safety of our republic depends," Beecher declared, "upon the intelligence, and moral principle and property of the nation." Metternich's human wave tactics had already put property in hazard by "quadrupling our taxation"[44] for the relief of pauperism, and threatening to place the power of taxation permanently in the hands of the enfranchised, foreign poor. The Boston School Visiting Committee recognized the danger, writing, "those children should be brought within the jurisdiction of the Public Schools from whom, through their vagrant habits, our property is most in danger." Writers in the *American Annals of Education* insisted that workers and immigrants in the North must be taught "to look upon the distinctions of society without envy." William Ellery Channing reproached the poor for their "recklessness, their passionateness, their jealousies of the more prosperous." A little free inquiry had undoubtedly apprised those he rebuked that, for them, in the scheme of conservative Bostonians, freedom was to be "just another word for nothing left to lose."[45]

Horace Mann more astutely observed that "the favored classes may think they occupy more favored apartments in the ship but, if it does founder the state will go down with the steerage."[46] Workers and capitalists alike recognized that this alteration in the composition of society required an appropriate amendment of social institutions. The recognition of a great gulf in the comfort and opportunities of rich and poor had made established elites fearful of popular rebellion. Rather than seeking to ameliorate the cause of popular unrest through a more equitable distribution of the profits obtained in the expansion of industry, industrialists endeavored to increase their profits and their security by establishing patterns of deference and class distinctions foreign to the ideology of the regime they were putatively designed to defend. Education offered a remedy for a natural resentment of conventional privileges and distinctions. Reformers might then proceed with the rapid promulgation of new customs and the construction of an altered social order.

Central to the effort to inculcate a spirit of emulation and submission to the children of the rebellious was Noah Webster. Schultz observes, "His famous *Elementary Spelling Book*, the Blue-backed Speller, sold over 20 million copies between 1782 and 1847, copies which undoubtedly were used by many more children than the total number sold." Replete with injunctions to industry, thrift, and acquiescence to authority, the spelling book endeavored to inculcate "American" values in the foreign and secure them in the native-born. The moral tales, exhortations, and aphorisms encouraged that very mindless submission to authority that Beecher had deprecated in the Catholics. "Poverty, he stressed, could be ennobling if the poor would only remain content with their lot . . . Webster believed that with his textbooks and through the common schools, a benevolent society could enlighten the lower classes—and render them harmless." Public education aimed not merely at the strengthening of social distinctions and patterns of deference in New England, but at their extension throughout the nation and to the foreign-born. The values with which Webster larded his texts were preeminently the values of New England's Calvinist elite.[47]

It is scarcely surprising, therefore, that the movement toward compulsory education met considerable resistance from Boston's Irish Catholics. School officials rapidly discovered that while Protestants sent their children to schools, and even to reform schools, with alacrity, Catholic parents were reluctant, and occasionally obdurate. School regulations required Catholic children to read from a Protestant Bible and recite Protestant prayers, a practice which continued throughout the United States until the 1960s.

The Boston School Visiting Committee, responding in one of its annual reports to charges that Protestant instruction in public schools was a breach of constitutional guarantees of the separation of church and state, "confirmed the worst suspicions of the Catholics." The committee declared, "The ends of governance require that religious instruction should be given in our public schools . . . the whole character of the instruction must be such and such only, as will tend to make the pupils thereof, American citizens, ardent supporters of American institutions." Like Beecher, the committee contended that Protestantism was intrinsic to American nationality.[48]

When over nine hundred of the Roman Catholic children in Boston's Eliot School rebelled against this deliberate indoctrination and refused to read the requisite Protestant version of the Bible, the courts made the city's intention still more explicit. Henry C. Durant, who represented the school committee, argued that American liberty "had always seen religion and government conjoined." Durant's argument gave the lie to Beecher's declaration that "all Protestant denominations would resist with loathing and abhorrence" any union of church and state. Beecher did observe, however, that the union of church and state had characteristically been "coveted by the state and sought for the purposes of secular ambition." Durant urged the court to "banish the vain delusion forever that our Saxon Bible can be taken away. Neither foreign tyrants nor foreign priests will ever have that power." Catholic resistance to the committee's efforts to make the public schools an arena for Protestant proselytizing was thus rendered an assault on religious liberty.[49]

Catholics, Protestant opponents declared, had "made War on God's Holy Word by its expulsion from the free and public schools of this country"[50] when they proposed the abolition of religion in the schools. "It is a question of civil and religious liberty. It is whether the Word of God shall be circulated and read by the entire community."[51] Edward Beecher praised "the free schools of this nation, consecrated to God and liberty, in which prayer daily ascends and the Word of God is read."[52]

Diane Ravitch argues in *The Great School Wars* that the use of Protestant Bibles, Protestant prayers, and the denigration of Catholicism in the public schools was an entirely innocent sectarianism. The New York Public School System, she writes, merely "failed to recognize that its version of nonsectarianism was sectless Protestantism."[53] This is nonsense. The school system itself, in its official pronouncements, was no less explicit than the Native American Party, the American Protestant Society, the American and Foreign Christian Union, and the individual advocates of Protestant instruction in the schools, in its affirmation of the opinion that Protestant religion bottomed American republican institutions and was an essential component of the national character. Ravitch's account obscures the class and cultural intolerance which characterized elite support of public education in the period.

A compromise proposed by the Archbishop of New York, which would have permitted the reading of both the King James and Douay Bibles and deleted derogatory references to Catholicism in existing school texts, was decried with equal fervor by nativists. "Even those books which praised the pilgrim fathers for their zeal in God's service, who were exiles for conscience's sake—were blackened with ink."[54] This, Herman Norton wrote, amounted to "calumniating the faith and character of our Puritan ancestors," an attempt which should "rouse the spirit of indignation in the heart of every descendant of the Pilgrims." "Oh ye spirits of the Pilgrims! Where are ye?"[55] "What true-hearted American," Edward Beecher asked, "does not love and revere the Pilgrim Fathers and all the other noble Protestant founders of this nation?" It was imperative, Beecher argued, to "demolish Popish defenses derived from the doctrine of the rights of conscience,"[56] and restore both God's Holy Word and the sacred history of the Puritan Founding to the public schools.

Having failed in their attempts to remove sectarian religion, or religion altogether, from the public schools, Catholics began to remove themselves. The establishment of Catholic parochial schools was first presented as a return to an earlier American system which had allocated state funds for education to church schools. When the state refused support to the parochial schools, citing the separation of church and state, and the presence of a public school system, many Catholics perceived the action as an attempt to force their children into schools where they would be assimilated to the Protestant majority. This increased support for the newly established parochial schools.

The establishment of a Catholic school system competitive with the public schools underscored the cultural disparity of Catholic and Protestant. It enhanced fears of the monolithic character of the Church of Rome and prompted assertions that the "main design of these institutions is to convert the children and youth of Protestants."[57] The public schools thus became firmly associated, culturally and institutionally, with the maintenance of a Protestant America. The result of the school controversy, Robert Breckinridge declared, "demonstrates that there exists in this country a real and deep-seated *religious public sentiment* which is capable of being reached, roused, and concentrated, for the safety of our faith and the advancement of our Master's cause."[58] The controversy had revealed the latent power of this religious tradition to serve as the source of political commonalty, and as a determinant of the legitimacy of political action and public policy.

The extraordinary feat of rhetorical legerdemain whereby the Boston School Visiting Committee portrayed Catholic resistance to Protestant proselytizing in the public schools as an assault on religious freedom depended for its success on the ancient association of Catholicism with persecution and Protestantism with religious liberty in Northern political culture. Catholicism was the religion of the Inquisition, everyone knew, and everyone knew that the Pilgrims had been partisans of religious liberty. The use of the term "Saxon Bible" for the text in question increased the ease with which these culturally established roles were recalled. The school committee's defense was made implicitly not only on behalf of Protestant religion, but on behalf of a mythical Anglo-Saxon ethnicity. "The American people," one author affirmed, "are not a Roman Catholic race."[59] The committee and those it represented had established themselves as the champions of an assimilative process which affirmed the cultural superiority of the established elites.

New Englanders of the antebellum period, whose cultural influence came to surpass their numbers, read in the words "religious liberty" less a guarantee of freedom of worship than a civil liberty imbued with religious principles. Politicians and private citizens asserted confidently that American democratic institutions were derived from Protestant models and depended on Protestant piety for their continuance. This reiteration of the narrow cultural norms established in the Puritan paradigm denied sanction to diversity and effectively precluded pluralism founded on equality. Though it prompted considerable social experimentation, this reiteration of the Puritan ideal was conservative of existing social distinctions.

By ascribing a primordial and providential origin to an existing social order, established elites characterized egalitarian agitation as immoral, treasonable, and antidemocratic. The successive revolutions in France, which replaced a democratic regime with military despotism and monarchy appeared to confirm conservative suspicions that revolutions, unless speedily abridged, ended in terror and tyranny. Assaults on property, men like Channing, Webster, Beecher, and Parker declared, were especially inclined to undermine free institutions. The Calvinist notion that God entrusted his elect with a greater share of temporal resources could then be regarded as a divine plan for the protection of democracy.

Nativists and advocates of a hierarchical and avowedly paternalistic social order made much of connections between the immigrants and Continental revolution. Some argued that European governments habitually exported suspected insurrectionists to the United States, hoping to foment unrest here. Although actual emigration of dissidents was never significant, most Americans regarded the increase of German immigrants as a consequence of the failure of the 1848 rebellion. Conspicuous involvement of the actual Forty-eighters in the labor movement and in agitation for political reform exacerbated anxieties over immigrants as potential insurgents. These apprehensions contributed to the denigration of the Revolution in favor of the Plymouth founding.

Although New Englanders had often depicted the Pilgrims as fugitives from persecution and monarchical tyranny, the idea of America as a haven for refugees had come to be associated with a more radical democracy.

Tom Paine had praised America as "an asylum for persecuted lovers of civil and religious liberty from every part of Europe" and Jacobin exiles from France had immigrated with the blessing of the Jeffersonians.[60] These associations were sufficient to damn the notion of America as a haven for political refugees in the minds of New England conservatives.

They preferred the founding at Plymouth to any Revolutionary founding, much as Burke had preferred the Glorious Revolution because it was neither glorious nor a revolution. Adherence to the Revolution as the determinative movement in American history, or to the Constitution as indeed constitutive, granted the American polity a universalism which they could not countenance. Divested of those ethnic and religious accretions which attached to New England's sectional culture, the American regime, impelled wholly by the force of its ideology, might become a force for radical democracy. This threatened to alter both the present preeminence of established elites, and their conception of America's world historical mission.

The labor and Bible riots, in which Irish immigrants were conspicuous participants, increased anxieties over the revolutionary propensities of the immigrants. Riots evinced a disregard for the law, and thus for the regime and the criteria which secured its legitimacy. Rioters were not merely rowdy, they were seditious.

The Jacobins who had come from France to America experienced in Revolution were—though in practice deistical or rationalist—of Catholic stock. This gave rise to an enduring American association of

Catholicism and violent revolution. The presence of Catholic missionaries on the frontier and fears of politically hazardous Indian conversion contributed to this association. The role of the Spanish clergy in inciting guerrillas against Napoleon enhanced it, the riotous Irish in America perpetuated it.

The revolutionary character of the immigrants arose in part from their position on the periphery, in part from a putative cultural disposition. Protestants were by nature "temperate, frugal and industrious," Catholics were otherwise. "As soon as he confesses to his priest, he hurrahs for democracy, by which he means anarchy, confusion, and the downfall of heretics." The priests, for their part, were said to encourage "a rabid and revolutionary press."[61] As Tocqueville had forecast, Catholicism, which was a conservative force in Europe, became associated with the forces of radical democracy in America. Priests were reported to have blessed hickory sticks at rallies in urban Catholic churches.

This report associated the Roman church with Jacksonian democracy, and both of these with popular violence. The Church "concealing its ultimate designs under the motive of affording protection to the weak, seeks to overthrow all law and order, pandering to the worst passions of an ignorant and ferocious populace."[62] Catholics and Democrats alike were animated by "passions" and opposed to "law and order." Each represented the "ignorant and ferocious populace" feared by Northeastern elites. The Catholic church was said to be behind the organization of mechanics' and workingmen's parties, encouraging egalitarianism by promoting these and by introducing domestics in Protestant households to ideas of social equality. It was during this period that the Democratic Party first came to be regarded as the party of "Rum, Romanism and Rebellion."[63]

Northeastern elites feared the insurrectionary proclivities of the immigrants more as they came to compose a substantial portion first of labor and, soon after, of the labor movement. Here the Irish ethnicity of the immigrants was the mediating trait which associated their revolutionary character with Catholicism. In most of the mines and factories of the North, the ethnicity of worker and capitalist replicated the arrangement prevalent in England. In the mines of Schuylkill County, Pennsylvania, for example, the mine bosses were Anglo-Saxon, the miners Irish. This revived patterns of interaction and enmity with which the recently emigrated Irish were extremely familiar. For the owners, and for Northern elites generally, it associated ethnicity with social status. Owners could thus fear, and workers effect, a wholesale transfer of clandestine Irish resistance organizations into American mines and factories. One historian observed that "the radical social reformer was by no means unknown to the Irish immigrant," and that "followers of Chartism were numerous among the Irish of the anthracite coal region." The organization which acquired the most notoriety in American labor history was, however, the Molly Maguires.[64]

The Molly Maguires acquired a twofold reputation for insurrection. Both before and after the Civil War they were reputed to have incited labor riots and to have engaged in arson and sabotage against the mining corporations. During the war, they were accused of resisting the draft and treasonably obstructing the war effort.

Colonel Alexander McClure, who was in charge of the Pennsylvania draft of 1862, wrote "In several mining districts there were positive indications of revolutionary disloyalty, and it was especially manifested in Schuylkill, where the Molly Macguires were in the zenith of their power." Lincoln and Stanton favored sending in the Union army to enforce the draft. As Wayne Broehl notes, "their doubts were well-founded. Labor all over the country was suspicious of the war." The recollection of the Pilgrims, the Puritan revolution and the Reformation, which played so great a part in the legitimizing rhetoric of the war, was ill calculated to appeal to the Catholic miners. The miners also shared the view, which came to prevail in the Democratic Party, that the war served to strengthen the interests of corporations at the expense of the workers.[65]

The legends which surrounded the Molly Maguires in antebellum Pennsylvania also illustrate the Irish immigrants' perception of their own liminality. The name "Molly Maguire and her children" commonly used to denominate the members, reproduced the mother-child paradigm which Southerners used to describe political union and Northerners used to describe both the South and the Catholic church. One version of the name's origin was that "Molly Maguire was a poor widow evicted from her home after the landlord's agent severely abused her and her daughter." This cast the symbolic woman as victim and emphasized the exploitation of the immigrants. Another version held that Molly was "a huge fierce Irish woman, with a pistol strapped to each thigh who led gangs of young Irishmen dressed in women's clothes on night raids." This account, with its emphasis on sexual ambiguity, is characteristic of descriptions of liminality.[66] The image of the woman armed represented the power of the rebellious. A song, circa 1845, sung by the Molly Maguires, made a similar point:

> I saw the youth and bold recruits,
> Well-headed by Molly Maguire.

> Said Molly to her darling sons,
> "Those tyrants we must tumble
> Such filthy tribe we can't abide
> We'll rule them meek and humble."[67]

This association of Irish Catholics and violent revolution contributed greatly to the restoration of Protestant clerical influence in American politics, for it provided clerics with an articulation of the ideal boundaries of the regime that immediately identified their religious authority with political authority, and enabled them to speak authoritatively on political questions.

The understanding of political culture which emerged from the fear of Catholicism held that ideology was collective rather than individual, the product not of reason or of will but of the historical experience of a commonly conditioned community. The understanding of history as progress, and particularly as a progress toward godliness and liberty, suggested the possibility of ranking nations and peoples according to their historical (as well as their putatively evolutionary) development. Theodore Parker asserted that "in the world there are inferior nations, savage, barbarous, half-civilized; some are inferior in nature, some perhaps only behind us in development; in a lower form in the Great School of Providence—negroes, Indians, Mexicans, Irish, and the like."[68] In this sermon, he follows the notion that individual capacities were the consequence of the historical experience of the community. Parker's sermon belongs in a series entitled *Social Classes in a Republic*. In this series he intended to offer an apology for the existence of social hierarchy in a democratic regime. Individuals of these "savage, barbarous, half-civilized" communities were inferior to members of the American community. Their inferiority was a hazard to the perpetuation of republican institutions. The hazard was diminished by their subordination. This scheme of legitimate domination legitimated both internal hierarchy and external conquest. Parker argued that the inferiority of members of these communities was circumstantial rather than essential. Thus he could affirm human equality even as he argued for subordination. Political relations, Parker's articulation argues, are to be determined not by human nature, but by history. History is "the Great School of Providence," a mechanism for universal assimilation. The order of the forms, he implies, is ordained by God. At this moment, men and policies properly recognize their various degrees, but in time they will complete the required course for study, and education will render them alike.

The defects ascribed to the immigrants extended to the slaves as well. Alexis de Tocqueville, in a rare mention of immigration, combined the free blacks and the immigrants, and characterized them as the greatest danger to American democracy, "a rabble more dangerous even than that of European towns."[69] Their socialization had manifestly not included the experience of free institutions, nor had they become habituated to the exercise of civil liberties. Their histories, such as they had, were not the same. They were rarely of the same religion. The argument that immigrants unused to liberty would rapidly descend to license had long been employed of the slaves as well. The arrival of the Irish immigrants, and the consequent contraction of American political culture, would seem to have foreclosed citizenship to the slave. Certainly it resulted in a strengthening of legal and customary restrictions on freed blacks and slaves. Yet it was at this moment that abolition attained the apex of its influence.

The relation of Protestant clerics to the cause of abolition has been variously portrayed. Ann Douglas writes that "most recent historians agree with the Abolitionists that the Northern Protestant clergy, with important exceptions, notably failed to protest significantly the evil of slavery." Her support for this contention, however, rests on the character rather than the absence of clerical opposition. She cites the example of Horace Bushnell as typical. Bushnell formally opposed slavery in 1839 and in 1850 urged his Northern congregation to "violate and spurn" the Fugitive Slave Law. What compromised Bushnell, for Douglas, was the nature of Bushnell's opposition. "In modern eyes, however, his attack on slavery reads suspiciously like a defense."[70]

Douglas is correct in characterizing Bushnell as "a racist." She is also correct in observing that her reading of his attack is a modern reading. She is in error, however, in characterizing Bushnell's racism as "more or less identical with the current white Southern opinion." White Southern opinion on the subject of blacks was fragmented and diverse. Few Southerners, however, very few indeed, would have agreed with Bushnell's statements that blacks were "animals and nothing else," and "not physiologically descended from the stock of Adam." Black humanity was not merely a matter of common opinion in the South; it had formal expressions in the law. Douglas gives no provenance for this Southern opinion. Hers is a modern reading.[71]

Douglas errs in ascribing Bushnell's opinions to Southerners generally. She is correct, however, in observing that racist opposition to slavery was far from atypical. It marked not only those Northern clerics who failed to join forces with radical abolitionists, but many of the abolitionists as well. Douglas admits that Charles Grandison Finney, one of the most "forthright" advocates of abolition, "kept black and white students firmly segregated."[72] The practice of segregation prevailed at most abolitionist meetings, racist opinions predominated in many abolitionist writings. Frederick Law Olmstead, like Bushnell, saw the eradication of slavery as a means of ensuring "the inevitable disappearance" of blacks from the American nation.[73] We have already seen that Theodore Parker, whom Douglas cites against Bushnell as an uncompromised abolitionist, entertained a belief not only in the innate inferiority of blacks, but in the cultural inferiority of the Indians, Mexicans, and Irish as well.

Affirmations of essential human equality are, in Parker's scheme, entirely irrelevent in temporal politics. Because the constitution of polities and the creation of a social order are processes embedded in history, political and social institutions must be formed in acknowledgment not of human equality, but of ethnic and communitarian inequality. The premise of human equality, though fraught with eschatological significance, is properly foreign to political administration. Instead, nations are advised to emulate the providential educative and assimilative process in their own institutions.

The movement to improve presently inferior but innately equal cultures through education and assimilation endeared its proponents to many blacks, but entirely alienated them from the Irish. These, who might have thought that they evinced in their similar appearance, their common language, and their similar histories a closer kinship with the "Anglo-Saxon" Protestants, were outraged by their inclusion with the "savage" and the "half-civilized."

Such ill-considered groupings by clergymen and politicians, like Parker, exacerbated immigrant hostility to blacks and encouraged racist attacks. American blacks, accustomed by generations of slavery and legal inferiority, to social degradation and disenfranchisement, generally received this arrogant benevolence with greater equanimity. Not all, however, were so acquiescent. The Amistad captives, who were conscious of their natural rights and actively engaged in demanding them, soon fell afoul of their liberators. "Most of the young men," Wyatt-Brown notes, "disliked the 'hard times' work clothes given them," outfits customarily worn by Southern slaves. "The abolitionists rigidly insisted that they should be humble and decorous both in conduct and appearance in order to comply with the white man's notion of their station in life."[74]

The explicit subjugation of those the abolitionists had purportedly freed indicated from the outset that emancipation need not entail equality. Thus Noah Webster, who had seen fit to include in his 1790 edition of *The American Dictionary* "some definitions relative to the slave trade," wrote to James Kent in 1843, "Nothing can be more obvious than that *by appointment of the Creator* in the constitution of man and human society the condition of men must be different and unequal." No one, he wrote Daniel Webster, "is born free, in general acceptance of the word 'free.'" Freedom had thus become demeaned to a sort of charity given by the greater to the less, for which they were obliged to show an appropriately deferential gratitude.[75]

Abolitionists like George Bourne were not therefore regarded as inconsistent in their simultaneous insistence on the emancipation of blacks and the subordination of Catholics. According to Parker's scheme, the emancipated blacks, though free, would still be "in a lower form" requiring, like the Irish Catholics, the Indians, and the Mexicans, a spell of assimilative education. The reduction of liberty from a natural right to a legally ascribed privilege was a necessary accompaniment to the promulgation of a hierarchical social order. In such a scheme, the community was primary.

Individual men, representative of their communities, may recapitulate the process of national development in their own educations. Their assimilation prefigures the anticipated civilization of that community they represent. This enabled men of that period to praise Frederick Douglass, and men of a later period to praise Booker T. Washington and George Washington Carver, without relinquishing their commitment to racial subordination. Rather than serving as proof of an existent equality, these men became exemplars of an equality to be achieved only eventually, and through assimilation. The assimilation of Irish immigrants and Negro slaves would prefigure the triumph of American civilization in the world.

The arrival of culturally disparate groups in growing numbers intensified concern over the character of the polity and the criteria for citizenship. The passage of the Revolutionary generation had left the nation in the hands of those who had inherited the Constitution, rather than those who had created it. Their citizenship was the gift of circumstances. Their circumstances inclined them to regard the polity and their collective national character as similarly predetermined: the work of Providence rather than particular men. This conception of the origin of the United States accorded with both the doctrines of the Puritan Fathers and the more recent doctrines of Hegel.

The idea that circumstances were constitutive of national character led, ultimately, to a requirement of twenty-one years residence prior to naturalization. Thus, proponents argued, the requirements for citizenship and suffrage were the same for the foreign- and the native-born. The stricture, legislated in 1790, that immigrants be both free and white further removed citizenship from determination by either ideology or volition.

The arrival of unprecedented numbers of Irish immigrants, their rapid incorporation into the work force, and their effective exclusion from prevailing definitions of American nationality had created a visible tension between conceptions of the worker and the citizen. Immigrants, their employers argued, were acceptable as workers, but they were at best second-class citizens. Their disparate culture alienated them from that which was decisively constitutive of the true American. The emergence of an industrial hierarchy effected a resolution of this contradiction. This resolution, seen most clearly in the formal structure of the factory town, encompassed immigrants in the society while providing for their systematic degradation. Subordination was the condition for their inclusion. This societal accomodation of simultaneous cultural rejection and economic integration is akin to Southern familial inclusion and political exclusion of the slave. The factory was (once again) substituted for the family as the dominant unit of Northern social organization.

Equality and individuality are entailed in the name "citizen." Labor, however, is collective and impersonal, a resource. The subordination of the American worker during the antebellum period was nowhere so apparent as in the emergence and alteration of the labor movement. Early efforts to resist capitalist exploitation of American workers had affirmed the natural and civil rights of the workers as individual citizens. Factory owners and agents, conversely, were confronted as individuals who had attempted to exceed their natural and civil rights as individuals. This effort was defeated so resoundingly that the right of one man, or of a small group of men, to claim authority over a mass of workers now goes not merely unchallenged, but unquestioned. Employers, legislators, the courts, and finally the workers themselves recognized that the individual as worker was denied the rights and character of the citizen. The absolute and arbitrary authority of the employer, and the subordination of the employees, were antithetical to the ideology of the regime, yet they prevailed in the work place. Industries, like foreign enclaves in the polity, maintained their own laws within their walls. Factories and businesses came to have the privileges of foreign embassies, and claimed immunity from the obligations of democracy within their gates.

Workers were finally persuaded to acknowledge the alienation of their labor and denominate it a separable, saleable commodity. Owners and their representatives negotiated not in their own name and individual character, but in the name and character of the corporation. In order to treat with them on something approaching equality, workers were obliged themselves to incorporate. The formation of unions in the late nineteenth century was predicated on the workers' acceptance of the notion that in their dealings with management their status was to be determined by their function. Within the industry they were not men with the rights of men, or citizens entitled to free assembly and free speech, but rather a tool subordinate to the intention and will of the employer, and a resource to be exploited. They were "labor." The incorporated unions that they formed were artificial bodies representative of labor. In this way, all those employed by the company were assimiliated to the one man or group of men who owned it, and the rights of labor against those of management were at best equivalent. In the antebellum period, however, all labor was denied corporate status. Workers were divested of the rights they held as men and citizens and collectively reduced to the status of an inanimate resource. Their relations with their employers were not those of one citizen to another. Rather they comprised a material resource without the status of persons before the law.

The increase in immigration decisively reduced the status of workers in two respects. Competition for available jobs lowered wages and increased the dependence of workers on their capitalist employers. The rise of the corporation, and of that legislation which effected it, altered the relation of workers and employers, making workers legally subordinate and divesting them of their civil rights in the work place.

This was the most profound social change effected in the antebellum period. From this time forward, workers have been prevented from dealing with their employers on terms of political equality. The fictive person of the corporation provided a justification for the fictive superiority of the capitalist to the worker in industrial relations. The social superiority claimed by wealthy owners over their impoverished employees received considerable support from this legislative construction of industrial relations. The collective reduction of workers from a group of individuals with the rights of citizens to an industrial resource provided a means for maintaining the social and economic superiority of the capitalists. The expansion of industry during the Civil War increased the national economic significance of industry and aggrandized the political influence of the capitalists.

The examination of national identity which followed upon this great increase in immigration had resulted in the contraction rather than the extension of America's cultural boundaries. By 1860, it had been decided that those boundaries were not only too narrow to accomodate the mad, the poor, the black, the ignorant, the Indian, and the Irish; they were too small for the South as well.

The conquest of the South and its subsequent subordination in the Union completed the work of comprehension and isolation, assimilation and segregation that characterized the spatial and temporal extension, the ideal and cultural constriction of the Union.

Two
THE SOUTH

4   The Motherland

In 1930 twelve Southerners, alienated from the prevailing industrial order, and resentful of what they took to be a false
history, promulgated by the North, published a collection of essays
entitled *I'll Take My Stand: The South and the Agrarian Tradition.*
They argued that "the fundamental and passionate ideal for which the
South stood and fell was the ideal of an agrarian society."[1] Their argument was important not only because it was an accurate characterization of antebellum Southern political culture, but because it expressed
an enduring allegiance to a distinct Southern identity, and an allied
resistance to that new industrial order which the North's triumph in
the Civil War had decisively secured.

Southern identity, as they in their allegiance construed it, was
determined primarily by the South's agrarian character, Redfield
might have said of the Southerner as he did of the peasant, "The land
and he are part of one thing, one old-established body of relationships."[2] The South, Donald Davidson wrote, was an agrarian society,
"one in which agriculture is the leading vocation, whether for wealth,
for pleasure, or for prestige—a form of labor that is pursued with
intelligence and leisure, and that becomes the model.[3] The practice of
agriculture, in this understanding, both defines the relationships that
bind men to one another and to the land, and serves as a model for
subsidiary cultural constructs and relationships.

Planters and smallholders sow and harvest their crops in the
same seasons. They plow, till, manure, reap, and thresh in the same
order, at the same times. Changes in the crops, the climate, and the
land itself forecast changes in their circumstances. Burdened by the
same concerns, performing the same tasks, seeing in their fields and
farms very much what their neighbors see, they readily recognize their
common character. This recognition of community undergirds all polities. Farmers and husbandmen are aided in the development of a

distinct political culture by that common language they possess in consequence of their common experience. Their common habituation to the techniques, customs, and demands of farming provides them with a common vocabulary of images, symbols, and metaphors. Frank Owsley, describing the genesis of this agrarian society, noted that the South was settled by farmers: "The tradition of the soil found a hospitable rootbed in the Southern colonies . . . centuries of farm lore and folkmemory. Each word, name, sound had grown from the soil . . . Thoughts, words, ideas, concepts, life itself grew from the soil."[4] Their common experience granted them a common political culture; their common language determined its content and development.

In the tradition which Owsley and his eleven compatriots represent, the South was settled by transplanted autochthons whose agricultural traditions flourished in the new world. The earliest Southern literary productions bear witness to that tradition. Robert Beverley's *History and Present State of Virginia* represents an early example of that Southern literary genre in which *I'll Take My Stand* established itself. Beverley's work offered a description of Virginia, a natural history of the colony which comprehended the political organizations and affairs of the English and the Indians. John Randolph, not of Roanoke, authored a work on gardening in the same period, which illustrated the prestige and putative virtues of the cultivation of the soil. Works of this sort recalled Cicero and Xenophon and represented a self-conscious revival of that tradition. Beverley's work provided the model for Jefferson's *Notes on the State of Virginia* in the early national period. John Taylor's *Arator*, published in the same period, provided a model for *I'll Take My Stand*.

Arator, like *I'll Take My Stand*, is episodic. Originally issued as a series of letters to a Virginia journal, the chapters of *Arator* treat of defects in the practice of agriculture and in the prevailing political order. Bottomed on the premise that agriculture and politics are inseparably allied, *Arator's* critical essays protest against the subordination of agriculture to capitalism, arguing that the latter is hostile to democratic regimes. The practice and improvement of agriculture, conversely, promotes the growth of public liberties and private virtue. Both Taylor and the Twelve Southerners who authored *I'll Take My Stand* acknowledged agriculture as the basis of Southern community. They evinced a common sense of the South as a region distinct from the remainder of the nation and marked its agricultural character as the source of its peculiar identity. Taylor looked at an emergent, the latter Southerners at a dominant, industrialism. Thus Taylor appealed to agriculturalists throughout the nation, while his successor-compatriots evinced a sense of distance and disparity between themselves and Americans of other sections. All, however, regarded the Southern political order as directly derivative from the experience of agriculture.

Southern secessionist sentiment coincided with the birth of American industry, Northern triumph with the establishment of an industrial-capitalist order in America. Thus Southern national identity developed in opposition to this economic alteration. Canonical works in the political literature of the South had, from the earliest days, emphasized agriculture as the foundation of politics in the Southern states. The archetypal political leaders—Washington, Jefferson, Madison, Monroe, the Randolphs, and Taylor—had all been farmers. Jefferson had designed a superior plow, Washington had bred a better jackass. Distinction in politics, in Southern tradition, accompanied distinction in agriculture. Randolph, when he wished to cast aspersions on Jefferson's elegant abstractions, compared them to his plow, which, though it was exhibited by the savants of Paris, plowed not half so well as the cumbersome Carey plow. Agriculture provided the region with a common political language; it provided Randolph with a metaphor intelligible to all his constituency. More importantly, his use of the metaphor implied that the farmers to whom he appealed could judge Jefferson's politics as they judged his plow. Their common experience granted tham an essential equality.

The practice of agriculture produced men, in the South and in its several states, who were evidently dependent less on each other than on the land. This imbued them at once with a common loyalty to the land and with a sense of their individual independence. Jefferson acknowledged and commended this consequence of agriculture in his praise of the democratic yeomanry. Southerners believed themselves—as others believed them—to retain a distinctive consciousness of their personal liberty. They traced this to their ability to provide for themselves. Provision for their own preservation precluded dependence on others and enabled them to retain their natural liberty in civil society.

Jefferson was speaking of citizens. In fact the primary unit in agricultural society is that of the household. The routine tasks of agriculture and husbandry were accomplished by cooperative efforts on the part of man and wife, children and slaves. The household lived and worked together, acting as an economic unit. The primacy of the household in agrarian society had several important consequences for Southern political culture. Home, household, and hearth acquired that sacred, sentimental character commonly granted them in agrarian societies. As the primary economic unit,[5] the household provided a ready model for political and economic organization, a model which was employed with increasing frequency as Southern political culture developed.

Use of the "Old Dominion" as a name for Virginia suggested both the derivation of the polity from the household and the sovereignty of domesticity to Virginians with a classical education. Like the Ciceronian writings on agriculture, this practice likened Virginia to those classical regimes which had served as models for American republicanism, further confounding an agricultural with a democratic tradition. It also evinced a self-conscious identification with a pagan tradition, decisively distancing the South from the religiosity which dominated New England's political culture.

The South's god was the God of Nature. Nature's God, Jefferson had written, endowed men "with certain inalienable rights, among them life, liberty, and the pursuit of happiness," rights which he traced to their religious practice of agriculture. These rights, whether attributed to the beneficence of Nature's God or to the independence secured by providing for oneself, came in consequence of a continued proximity to nature. They were thus analogous to the produce of the soil, and equally to be cultivated.

Because proximity to nature was thought to yield both sustenance and liberty, it appeared in Southern political culture as an especially virtuous and advantageous condition. References to the state of nature in early Southern writings characterized it more as Rousseau's heaven than as Hobbes' hell. The high status of nature in Southern culture commended the natural to men. Daniel Walker Howe has observed that Southern "cotton planters and small farmers shared a folk culture that valued flamboyance rather than restraint, hedonism rather than the work ethic."[6] Francis Gaines wrote of the planters, "No class in our history has been characterized by a greater eagerness for festivity, for gaiety."[7] Southern culture commended internal with external nature, urging the cultivation and praising the efflorescence of each. Cultivation implies control, but control with its end in aggrandizement and fecundity. Southern political culture, in commending the natural and valuing the independence of individuals, encouraged self-assertion and the exercise of will. This set Southern political culture in opposition to that Northern Puritan tradition which simultaneously urged the conquest of internal and external nature.

Nature, in this latter tradition, was a condition of savagery antithetical to civilization. Thus, though Rufus Choate might refer to the Southerners as "the peculiar friends of liberty," he could damn them for it, saying with James Birney that "the reason that savage and barbarous nations remain so—and unrighteous men too—is that they manage their affairs by passion not by reason."[8] Southern continuance of natural liberty in their cultivation of internal and external nature would, according to these latter-day Puritans, continue them in a state of natural barbarism.

With the dawning of the industrial era in the mid–nineteenth century, the contrasting images of Puritan and Cavalier would suggest that the conquest of external nature could not be accomplished without an attendant conquest of internal nature. At the opening of the century, that had merely affirmed that the enjoyment of rights and the pursuit of happiness were likewise secured by the proximity to nature which agriculture afforded.

The practice of agriculture set Southern lives in a set of common rhythms. The common experience of these cycles gave them a sense of community. The cycles themselves influenced the mores and institutions of the community. The seasonal character of agriculture afforded Southerners designated periods of leisure. These, necessarily coinciding, granted them the opportunity for assembly and encouraged communal activities. The combination of agriculture and politics thus appeared eminently natural. Legislative sessions, campaigns, and courts coincided with the season of leisure designated by nature. Politicians could thus continue as farmers, maintaining their experiential bonds with the community.

The practice of farming and husbandry requires daily attention to a multitude of tasks. It requires the household to remain on the land and in each other's company. It was thus "a way of life" rather than a series of discrete tasks. The influence of agriculture on the society, residence, and activities of the agriculturalist made farming a way of life. The primordial character of this vocation, the derivation of a common language and innumerable customs from it, encouraged its adherents to conceive of it in this way. Moving in conjunction with the natural rhythms of growth, reproduction, and decay, it appeared to them that life itself, or more importantly their own lives, had grown from the soil. These processes continued interminably, and the lives of those who worked the land continued in their rhythm. It would thus have been difficult as well as inaccurate for planters to regard their occupation as separable from the rest of their lives, or from the land. Rather they were held in a network of relationships which united the contrived and the natural, men and the land, the ideal and the material. Their labor mirrored the human condition.

Their products answered human needs. They provided for those requirements all men had by virtue of their bodies, accomplishing this through a rational ordering of natural processes, simultaneously according themselves to their environment and their environment to themselves. This elegant arrangement commended itself to mind and body, providing a model for political and social order which spoke to the fundamental features of temporal existence.

Experience more than philosophy thus instructed Southerners in the political significance of self-preservation. They secured their independence from other men by providing for themselves; they acquired power and influence proportionate to their provision for others. This formula was evident in environmental, domestic, and political relations. It followed from man's natural constitution. Provision, agrarians recognized, was the basis of natural and legitimate authority. This tenet was the most important consequence of the South's agricultural character. It provided an accessible criterion for the assessment of legitimacy. It suggested a model for social and political relations consonant with the character of the culture.

Agriculture had provided Southerners with a form of life and a common language. Thus, the most common occupation among Southerners could scarcely be described as a job. Others often said that they did not work. Frederick Law Olmsted, in his antebellum *Travels*, describing his journeys through the Southern states, frequently remarked upon the indolence, not merely of the planter class, but of the slaves and the yeomanry as well. The leisurely pace of life in the South has become a commonplace in American culture. C. Vann Woodward called it "the Leisure-Laziness myth"[9] and marked its significance in differentiating the South from that political culture dominated by the Puritan ethic.

Capitalism and industrialization depend upon the accumulation of capital reserve. Agricultural products are not easily hoarded, nor does agricultural labor often permit the accumulation of substantial capital reserves. Southerners lacked both the economic machinery and the cultural impetus appropriate to the Protestant ethic and the spirit of capitalism. Long after the war's end and the South's defeat, Southerners would contend proudly that Southern arts were "the arts of living and not of escape"[10] and affirm that the South's "ancient leisureliness—the assumption that the first end of living is living itself . . . is surely one of its greatest virtues."[11] The conception of Southerners distinguished from a Northern ethic of religious industry and pious enterprise by a willful involvement in the immediate enjoyment of existence offers a misleading but finally enlightening summation of their complex political culture.

Southern arts, as John Crowe Ransome asserted, were the arts of living, Southern culture a culture bounded by the natural limits of corporeality. They recognized their social structures and private experience, their liberties in the civil state, and their criteria for legitimation as arising from their dependence on the land, a dependence dictated by the simple but irrefragable demands of the human constitution.

The primacy of agriculture in shaping the private experience of Southerners, and thereby the public constitutions of the Southern states, inclined Southerners to regard themselves as men of the earth, autochthonous. They emerged from the land as children from the womb, bearing as children often do the marks of their maternity. It was a commonplace throughout the Union that Southerners derived the characteristic warmth of their temperament from that of their climate. Southerners were wont to make much of the connection, seizing upon the ancient metaphor of the motherland as especially descriptive of their situation.

The maternal metaphor expressed the intimate relation of the farmers to the land. They were dependent on it for nurture, they lived like fetuses in it and upon it. The maternal metaphor thus described both the relation of individuals to the land and their consequent community. It compassed both the man's dependence on the land for nurture and the farmer's care and culture of the land. This last was among the duties of maturity, arising at once from interest, affection, and gratitude. "Keep your land," Randolph's mother taught him, "and your land will keep you."[12]

Rather than regarding the political community as existing outside and in opposition to the natural environment, as the Puritans had done in the North, Southerners conflated land and nation. Political community originated in the common relation of these men to their land. The emergence of a people was thus a flowering of nature, a view entirely consonant with Southern Revolutionary doctrines of natural rights. The establishment of the polity was not, therefore, an abridgment of these rights, but rather a confirmation of natural rights in a community having its origins equally in nature.

The maternal model presented to the Southern mind the possibility of a natural corporate identity. The child in its mother's womb was encompassed by her physical boundaries; their commonalty was natural and necessary. The child at the mother's breast was nurtured through the workings of the natural processes characteristic of her physical constitution. Proximity and dependence, self-interest and self-love, gave rise to bonds of affection. This paradigm at once described the relations of mother and child, men and the land, citizens and the nation. The primacy of agriculture in Southern life enhanced the political significance of the maternal model. In this model, as in Southern life, agriculture and politics were commingled and conflated. It expressed both that agricultural relation of men to the land, from which economic and social relationships were derived, and that popular political community in which all citizens were comprehended. Perhaps most importantly for particular men, it evoked early associations of pleasure and security.

While New Englanders were rocking in the bosom of Jesus, neither fed nor coddled, but rather weaned and selfless, Southerners were suckled by nature. Raised in a balmy climate, they were accustomed to regard nature as an indulgent and beneficent mother. The experience of maternal nurture among the dominant planter class was similarly marked by indulgence and affection. Philip Greven, in his study of family structure distinguishes modes of child rearing—among Evangelicals, Moderates, and the Genteel—by class, but notes that the first was confined to the North and that the last was characteristic of the South. Puritan families were characterized by the absolute and arbitrary authority of the father. The exercise of paternal domination was directed toward the subjugation of the child's will. Southern families, conversely, were characterized by indulgent and affectionate care of children. Rather than habituating their children to the suppression of passion and subjugation of the will to authority, they encouraged self-assertion. Greven marks these conflicting attitudes toward the self as the source of the fundamental disparity between the child-raising methods of the Evangelicals and those of the Genteel. Among the former one saw "the Self-Suppressed," among the latter "the Self-Asserted."[13] Greven's account of childhood among the Puritans demonstrates that the subjugation of the child's will was a recapitulation of the community's submission to the will of God. The child's achievement of selflessness, demonstrated in his submission to paternal government, provided the infant with an introduction to the demands of his divine Father. Children were born in that sinfulness which belonged to men in the state of nature. Their salvation depended upon their departure from that state. The Evangelical manner of child raising thus emphasized the regulation and restraint of natural functions and the suppression of natural passion.

Southerners likewise regarded their children as small simulacra of the natural man. Nature, however, had figured in the theories of Southern political theorists as the source of the rights of man. Children were not therefore regarded as especially sinful or malevolent. Rather than occupying themselves with the salvation of the infant soul, Southern parents commonly praised the innocence and beauty of their offspring. Some zealous enthusiasts of nature, among them Patrick Henry, let their children run about barefoot in the manner advised by Rousseau. Throughout the South, Northern travelers observed, "children are much indulged."[14] They required, in the Southern view, not conquest but cultivation. Attitudes toward children in the two sections were directly related to their divergent attitudes toward nature.

The indulgence of children was particularly evident in maternal care. The mother's bond with the children and her authority over them was evidently natural. With nature commonly regarded as a source of comfort, provision, and liberty, and civilization the source of restraints and duties, Southerners expected "the caresses and tender fondness of an indulgent mother," and "the unwearied and unceasing watchfulness and attention of an affectionate father."[15] Daniel Blake Smith's study of familial relations in the Chesapeake Bay area planter culture, gives evidence of the exceptional intimacy and affection between mothers and children. Discipline and restraint were secondary, in early childhood, to indulgence, encouragement, and affection. They were requisite less to virtue than to civility, and were consequently regarded as primarily the responsibility of the father, whose authority was conventional rather than natural. Maternal authority was thus experienced in provision and tenderness, associated with intimacy, comfort, and security. Childhood was remembered as a period in which self-expression was encouraged rather than suppressed, and the maternal relation as one which was both pleasant and salutary in its effects.

In March of 1837, Beverley Tucker gave a lecture before the students of William and Mary College. In April the lecture was published in the *Southern Literary Messenger*. In this lecture, "On Government," Tucker distinguished maternal care as that from which society sprang. Nature, Tucker said, had ordained for each man "a season of dependent weakness, prolonged until the senses have acquired their perfection—till the affections have begun to bud—till the dawn of thought has broken up the darkness of his mind." The capacity for empirical observation, compassion, and intellect in particular men was requisite to the emergence of society. Prior to the development of these, each man was "the constant recipient of benefits which the infirmities of his nature teach him to prize, and to receive with gratitude and love. It is by this fastening process that the heart is warmed to a sense of inextinguishable obligation."[16]

Calhoun, in his *Disquisition on Government*, written between 1845 and 1850, and published in 1853, similarly regards the weakness of infants as evidence that the social state is natural to men.[17] He argues, however, that men are born enmeshed with their fellows in the formal structures of society, endowed by their Creator with the capacity for social intercourse. Social and political activity is thus the consequence, in Calhoun's scheme, of divine grace, an addendum to, rather than a consequence of, man's natural constitution. Men require neither sensual perfection, intellect, nor fellow feeling for their entrance into the social state. It is accomplished by divine edict.

Tucker's considerably more acute articulation attributes sociality to nurture. Society has its origins, then, in the protopolitical, natural community of mother and child. Nurture causes the child's heart to "put forth those filaments which cling to the breast that feeds and cherishes him with a tenacity that no time can relax and no violence can sunder. The mother thus becomes a connecting link among those who are alike the objects of her tender care."[18] In this analysis, politics continues to have its origin in the weak and dependent condition of the infant. Society, Calhoun affirmed, is necessary to the "preservation of the race." Tucker more astutely regarded society as the creation not of the race, nor of its Creator, but of individual men. They are inclined towards it, he averred, by this definitive experience of natural community. They are drawn toward their fellows by the common recollection of this common experience.

Time, Tucker declared, cannot relax the bond between the child and its first source of affectionate provision. The recollection of the mother-child relation is granted a status superior to consequent experiences and their historical recollection, not because of its temporal primacy, but because of its definitive character. The mother is the author of the child's political being. Provision is the source of her authority.

Tucker's affirmation of the fundamentally constitutive role of maternal nurture is thus accomplished by the suggestion that men realize their commonalty in the remembrance of things past. Nature, rather than history, is named the womb of politics, but history, this scheme suggests, may be the means for the realization of lesser social distinctions.

The polity originates in the recollection of the mother-child relation and the understanding that this experience is common to all. Self-knowledge, first of individual experience, and then of that common condition which defines humanity, provides the foundation of the community. Therefore, Tucker states, "no violence can sunder" this protopolitical bond. Coercion, in his scheme, is foreign to the social impulse. The polity is not a refuge from the war of man against man, but a recollection of the love between mother and child. Tucker's myth of political genesis is noteworthy, not only because it integrates, and indeed relies upon, the evident fact of sexual bimorphism, but also because it affirms the feminine: nurture, affection, and peace. This is attended by a denial of the authority of coercion. The bond between mother and child is natural, perhaps instinctive. The recognition of this experience as common to humanity, which initiates in separate men that fellow feeling upon which political life is based, is subjective and intellectual. In all this violence has no place. The alteration of circumstances which violence can effect may indeed influence successive political constructions, for these are formed in acknowledgment of those common experiences constitutive of particular communities. Violence itself, however, is alien to politics. Tucker's rejection of coercion as a source of political authority is characteristic of Southern political thought.

Maternal authority is based on provision. The mother acquires the right to rule the child and the attendant, inseparable duty of provision for it, from nature. Tucker's model suggests that natural dominion is transitory rather than enduring. Authority and the duty of provision end with the child's maturation. The perfection of the senses, the efflorescence of affection, and the dawn of thought separate the child from the mother. Independence comes in consequence of the completion of the child's being. Heretofore, it has existed as an extension of her being, nourished by her, its defects supplied by her perfection. Necessity dictates its dependence, her dominion. Development completes the child, ending its dependence on the mother.

This concept of community is extraordinarily dynamic; as formerly dependent groups, encompassed by the polity, mature, acquiring self-consciousness, fellow feeling, and the capacity to provide for themselves, they became independent. Tucker's model recalled to Southerners the memory of America's separation from England and suggested the direction of their sectional self-consciousness. Southerners, unlike their Northern compatriots, had left England without antipathy, and maintained ties to the mother country long after independence. They regarded their culture as derivative of the English. Southern literati were attentive to English literary trends; Southern political journals diligently recorded the doings of the House of Commons. Economic relations provided other forms of association even as they facilitated cultural exchange. America was the child of England.

The Revolution was thus not a repudiation of English culture, nor of the English political tradition; rather, it was an affirmation of American political maturity. The colonies had developed enough that they were no longer encompassed in the interests of the mother country. They had arrived, moreover, at a consciousness of their peculiar national characters. Independence, according to this view, should have followed upon the Declaration. England's errors were those of a too-fond mother reluctant to own her child grown. The Revolution might have been averted, one Southerner argued in 1835, if England had granted the colonies a status equivalent to the metropolitan provinces, acknowledging their development and endeavoring to maintain a community of interest. Even the English, he contended, now recognized Grenville's error in attempting to maintain the colonies in the status of dependents. This opinion, as the author knew, accorded well with Burke's famous speech on conciliation with the colonies.

England, Burke had declared, had wished "the colonists to be persuaded that their liberty is more secure when held in trust for them by us (as their guardians in a perpetual minority) than with any part of it in their own hands." The colonies, however, had proceeded to "form a government sufficient for its purposes," evincing their capacity for self government in the most irrefragable way. The Americans, Burke remarked, are "a recent people, a people who are still, as it were, but in the gristle, and not yet hardened into the bone of manhood." In their development "a generous nature has been suffered to take her own way to perfection." Having formed their own government, and "found the possibilities of enjoying the advantages of order in the midst of a struggle for liberty," the colonists revealed that they had indeed attained their majority and came forward to claim their birthright. "We cannot, I fear, falsify the pedigree of this fierce people, and persuade them that they are not sprung from a nation in whose veins the blood of freedom circulates." They should, Burke contended, be acknowledged as they wished to be, "fourteen separate governments, containing two millions and upwards of free inhabitants." "My hold of the colonies is in the close affection which grows from common names, from kindred blood, from similar privileges, and equal protection. These are ties which, though light as air, are strong as links of iron."[19]

They were strong enough to last the four generations of the South's tenure in the Union. A Southern poet, calling himself "Backwoods," left evidence of these ties in a poem entitled "America to England." He emphasized England's role as the motherland and contrasted the natural and instinctive affection of child for mother with the injunctions of a "more formal education":

> For we loved thy glories England
> Loved thy genius, felt it ours
> Shared thy fame, thy Norman spirit
> All its purposes and powers
> Loved the motherland that bore us
> And with instincts truer far
> Than the teachings of the schoolmen
> Followed still our natal star.[20]

The poem is intended as a rebuke to England for relying on her puppy aristocrats rather than her virtuous commons. America's democratic institutions are praised as English in their inspiration. In "Backwoods," as in Burke, the child has surpassed the mother in her own virtues.

This understanding of political development animated seccessionist thought. The South, it was argued, had developed—indeed had always possessed—a culture and character distinct from the remainder of the nation. A confederacy, limited in its jurisdiction and powers, might answer the requirements of sections diverse in interest and character. A national, consolidated government could not. The South, moreover, had already attained that consciousness of national identity which independence required. It gave promise of securing economic independence as well. The United States, according to this scheme, had served the South as America served England, as the womb of statehood.

The South, if it failed to follow the example of the Revolution, would find itself in that state of abject colonialism which the founders had abjured. A proponent of secession wrote in 1856 of an imagined 1950, in which the North would rule the Union: "In a commercial point of view the South may be considered as her province, with a relationship similar to that borne by the colonies of Great Britain to the mother state."[21]

Separation implied not a repudiation of the ideological principles upon which the mother nation was based, but rather the achievement of cultural and economic independence. Southerners were able, therefore, to maintain the constitutive myths of the Revolution and the

Founding despite their willful separation from the nation. Indeed in their separation they reenacted those myths, recalling Revolutionary battles as they fought at Antietam and Malvern Hill, avowedly emulating their Revolutionary forebears.

Southerners throughout the war compared their generals to the heroes of the Revolution, their conduct to the conduct of that generation. Northern writings reflect instead the popular sentiment that the cause of the present generation had been removed from that of the past in the unceasing march of history. The truth was marching on. Northern rhetoric in the sectional disputes prior to the war, and during the war itself, was marked with the conviction that the nation's historical progress was spiritual as well as temporal. They were thus faced, as Lincoln expressed it, "with a task greater than that which rested on Washington," and they expressed their enterprise as one of advancing or purifying the nation rather than defending it in its original character. Northern poets were thus able to recognize the likeness of the Southern to their fathers' cause. Melville wrote:

> Who looks at Lee must think of Washington
> In pain must think and hide the thought
> So deep with grievous meaning is it fraught.[22]

Edmund Wilson, a century later, saw the same resemblance: "Lee belongs, as does no other public figure of his generation to the Roman phase of the Republic, he prolongs it in a curious way which, irrelevant and anachronistic as it may seem to a Northerner, cannot fail to bring some sympathetic response which derives from the experience of the Revolution . . . The Lees had never really left the world of the thirteen colonies."[23] Separation from England had been a response to English usurpations of English liberties. It was in accord with English principles of political right. The South, secessionists claimed, separated from the United States when the government exceeded its charter. Secession was to serve as restoration. "The Constitution of our forefathers," Jefferson Davis claimed, "is the Constitution of these Confederate States." Copies of the Confederate Constitution were circulated by journals and newspapers and in pamphlets, side by side with copies of the Constitution of the United States, to establish the legitimacy of this claim to the public.

The maternal model, when applied to the South, suggested that those dependent individuals resident within it might in time come to attain an understanding of their common experience, feel the stirrings of mutual affection, and go out of Egypt a new-made people. Southerners acknowledged the implications of this theory to their future development. "When Moses could emulate the Egyptian priesthood he was able to embody or to represent his people and to lead them forth from bondage; for then they had acquired all the knowledge which was possessed by the Egyptian. The time will come, I doubt not, when the negro slave of Carolina will be raised to go forth out of bondage."[24] This would occur, presumably, after the slaves had absorbed the knowledge of the Carolinians, as the Carolinians had absorbed that of America, the Americans that of England, and Moses that of Egypt. The author was not less aware of the historical precedents for response to secession. "When that time comes, it may be that we, like Pharaoh, will be loth to give them up. But that that time is very far remote is sufficiently evident from the condition of free negroes in the northern states. Without restraints of any kind they have yet raised no city to themselves, raised no community of their own."[25] Their failure to build cities evinced a lack of technological expertise and economic self-sufficiency; the absence of community among them suggested that they had not yet developed fellow feeling. These qualities, which Tucker marked as requisite to political maturity, would rightly precede secession.

Some Southerners, members of the African Colonization Society, had endeavored to hasten their erstwhile dependents to a state of political maturity by sending those inchoate nationals to Liberia, where they might fight savages and malaria in an instructive imitation of the Virginia colonists.

In Virginia, the legal ascription of inferiority to the slave hindered his development. Thus one partisan of the society wrote, "man in a state of conscious inferiority cannot unfold his powers anymore than a plant in the dark . . . He must feel his equality." The society's plan was to remove these people to an environment more favorable to their future development. The North, they recognized, was not suitable. "Another alternative is to colonize them by force in the Northern states . . . But the project is impracticable; for the subtle casuists of the North make a refined distinction between free negroes and fugitive slaves. The latter, coming on the 'Underground Railroad' they welcome with open arms, while the former, coming in open day, are repelled with indignation and contempt."[26] The speaker cites the Black Laws of Indiana, Illinois, Ohio, and Delaware and that racist fervor which had stymied several Virginian efforts to settle freed slaves in the free states. Liberia, it was assumed, would be free from this racial hostility and, moreover, afforded the heathen blacks a blessing in their Christian brothers.

The plan for Liberian colonization had, however, two insurmountable defects: most masters did not want to send their slaves, and most slaves did not want to go. Those who left found a society as hierarchical as that which they had left, an execrable climate, and the expected savages and malaria. Resistance to colonization efforts revealed that while the slaves had not yet absorbed all the knowledge of Egypt, they had nevertheless been decisively removed from the customs of their African forebears. That socialization which the clergy commended for converting the African had instilled in the subject a preference for Southern society. Perhaps more importantly, the integration of particular slaves into the families of their owners formed bonds of intimacy if not affection, which both parties were loath to break. One response to colonization ran:

> What! colonize old coachman Dick!
> My foster brother Nat!
> My more than mother when I'm sick,
> Come, Hal, no more of that![27]

The black slaves had, like women, been established in a position of permanent dependence within the home. This entailed the affirmation of a fundamental and irremediable inferiority on the part of each dependent class. Those who protested that slavery was inextricably bound up with the Southern form of life, and thus incapable of eradication, accompanied this assertion with an affirmation of black inequality. As these protests became more frequent, so did accounts of an innate black inferiority.

In the Jacksonian period, the influence of those who doubted the innate inferiority of the black race remained strong, and Southerners feared the fire next time. Guilt, and the fears that attended it, prompted numerous experiments in establishing communities of freed slaves in America, and swelled the ranks of the African Colonization Society. Not a few Northerners believed then that Southerners were sincerely committed to the abolition of slavery within their borders. Some believe it now; Richard Brown writes that, in 1820, "it was generally true that no men in America were more honestly committed to the notion that the institution was wrong than those men of Jeffersonian conscience who were the Old Republicans of the Senate. Eleven years later, in 1831, some of them would mount in the Virginia Legislature the last great effort south of the line to abolish slavery."[28] These men acknowledged that blacks, if they were to attain a consciousness of their particular identity, would not be easily integrated into the American polity, in whose constitutive myths they had had no part.

The character of the mythic and martyred Lincoln eased their introduction into the reconstructed Union, but segregation secured their effective exclusion North and South. The animosities born of a long subjection were allied to those of an enforced emancipation, and blacks remained estranged, oppressed, and excluded from the political culture of the American polity. Their integration more than a century after their putative emancipation sparked a communitarian reformation of the nation they entered, and marked a change, as yet incomplete, in the content of American political culture.

5   The Republic

Agriculture provided the social structures, root paradigms, and metaphors of Southern politics. The emergence of technologically advanced, capital-intensive industry in the Northern states thus differentiated not only the economic structures, but also the conceptions of sectional culture and sectional identity which prevailed in North and South. Agriculture was the acknowledged source of the patterns and imagery of Southern political discourse, a principal component in the Southern conception of American identity, and a practice which Southern ideology marked as essential to the maintenance of liberal democracy. The introduction of industry in the United States could, therefore, radically distance the political cultures of North and South before their economic arrangements were decisively differentiated.

Northerners and Southerners, the partisans and opponents of the manufacturing system, marked the establishment of industry in America as a process which would transform the nation. All concurred in marking agriculture as an economic system characteristic of the Revolutionary era and America's infancy. In the South, the association of agriculture and the Revolution was of great ideological significance. The continued economic and cultural primacy of agriculture symbolized, and was thought to secure, the continuance of those political institutions the Revolution had established. The establishment of industry in the North, and the cultural transformation which it entailed, were thus regarded as distancing the section from the ideology and political arrangements of Revolutionary America. In the period of sectional schism which preceded the Civil War, Southerners came to regard themselves as the defenders of this Revolutionary ancien régime, and the South as the loyal province of classical republicanism. An emerging consciousness of Southern cultural peculiarity was thus coupled with a conscious adherence to America.

The alterations in ideology, in the economic and political arrangements, and in the subjectively perceived cultural boundaries of America which began in the antebellum North have, in the century following the Civil War, taken hold with more or less tenacity throughout the nation. These changes have redefined America in the political cultures of succeeding generations. In the context of this altered America, the antebellum South is indeed aberrant. It is from within this context that students of America's political culture have assessed the South's waywardness.

Recent works in the philosophic and cultural origins of American republicanism offer a different perspective. J. G. A. Pocock's work *The Machiavellian Moment* places the ideology of the American Revolution in the context of a developing English liberalism. The ideology of the American Revolutionaries, Pocock writes, was that of the "country party."

> Its values and concepts were those with which we have grown familiar— a civic and patriotic ideal in which the personality was founded in property, perfected in citizenship, but perpetually threatened by corruption, government figuring paradoxically as the principal source of corruption and operating through such means as patronage, factions, standing armies (opposed to the ideal of the militia), established churches (opposed to Puritan and deist modes of American religion), and the promotion of a monied interest—though the formulation of this last concept was somewhat hindered by the keen desire for readily available paper credit common in colonies of settlement.[1]

Pocock, along with Caroline Robbins, Richard Gummere, Bernard Bailyn, H. Trevor Colburn, and J. R. Pole, has located the American Revolution in the context of English debates over the character and location of sovereignty, institutional constraints on the executive, and the extent of legislative authority. This common anglophone republicanism had its immediately relevent historical antecedents in the English Civil War and its aftermath. The utility of this delicate and discerning analysis for students of American political culture is somewhat diminished by the assumption (here Pocock's) of the "singular cultural and intellectual homogeneity of the Founding Fathers and their generation."[2] This assumption of a monolithic American culture is surprising in light of the author's careful attention to subcultures and ideological variants in English political culture. It is especially surprising given the assertion that American subcultures had their origin in the period of English political schism which he examines so assiduously.

The assumption of a single American political tradition ignores the subjective perceptions of the Founding Fathers and their generation, who were acutely aware that American identity embraced at least two culturally as well as geographically distinct sections. More importantly, this assumption necessarily ignores the disparate relations of these divergent cultural traditions to English political culture, and, especially, to the English Civil War, in which the debates over authority, the church, and the army became fundamentally divisive.

Pocock's reprise of that constellation of issues which distinguished the classical republicanism of the country party itself suggests the fissures and fault lines in American political culture. Pocock recognizes a common antipathy to establishment, but is obliged to distinguish the two principle modes in which that antipathy was expressed: the Puritan and Deist modes of American religion. These divergent modes were themselves aspects of divergent cultural traditions. Pocock's citation of this religious disparity is felicitous, for it calls attention to the historical antecedents of these divergent cultures.

The Puritan mode of American religion, the political and cultural beliefs which accompanied it, maintained affective and institutional ties to the Cromwellian party in the English Civil Wars. This subculture was dominant in the Northern states, especially those of the Northeast. Within that section, paradigms derived from Protestant, especially Calvinist, theology, from the conduct, experiences, and mythology of the Roundheads in the English Civil War, and from the circumstances of the Pilgrims' emigration to America, influenced responses to the central issues of republicanism. The historical antecedents of the Northern states are particularly relevant to the issue of standing armies.

Opposition to standing armies, and an attendant insistence upon the militia system, were sufficiently general—in the Revolutionary era—that they were given expression in an explicit (though unsuccessful) constitutional proscription of standing armies. In the Northern states, however, opposition to standing armies declined with the passing of the Revolutionary generation, while it remained constant in the South. This divergence reflects an earlier disparity. The Puritan antecedents of Northern political culture provided a paradigm whereby the standing army might be legitimated. The first English standing army was Cromwell's New Model Army, which had the favorable associations which Northern political culture attached to the Roundhead enterprise. It was, moreover, established by the "Self-Denying Ordinance," a name and notion which would have as profound an appeal for mid–nineteenth century Americans as it had had for their Puritan progenitors. Opposition to the English royal army was common throughout the colonies, but the New Model Army and Cromwellian tradition provided a historical referent for acceptance of, indeed insistence upon, a standing army of nonmonarchical origin. It was not the form but the use and allegiance of the army which was decisive in the Puritan tradition.

Opposition to established churches in Northern political culture proceeded along similar lines. The Northern colonies, particularly Massachusetts Bay, which occupied a central position in the political culture of the region, had historically served as a refuge for dissident Protestant sects. These were broadly nonconformist but differed from one another, and from the Anglican church, on multiple points of doctrine. They were thus united in opposition to the establishment of the Anglican church, and to the establishment of any church, inasmuch as none could hope for a clear title. This was sufficient, in the Revolutionary War era, to secure disestablishment and constitutional guarantees of religious freedom.

It is incorrect, however, to equate this with a scrupulosity in the separation of church and state or a principled approbation of religious toleration. Perry Miller, Sacvan Bercovitch, and other students of the Puritan influence on American political culture have described the extent of clerical influence on politics in the Northern states. They have also observed that the root paradigms of American identity in that section were religious in origin and retained religious associations into the middle of the nineteenth century. The establishment of public school systems in the Northern states in the early nineteenth century was marked by successful efforts to integrate sectarian studies into the curriculum.

In the South the circumstances of disestablishment accorded more closely with the situation and ideals of English republicanism. "Unlike you," John Randolph (of Virginia) wrote to Josiah Quincy (of Massachusetts) "we had a church to pull down."[3]

Northern political culture was at variance with the classical republicanism of the Revolution on several fundamental ideological points. In each case, the variance was evidently owing to the disparate historical antecedents of Northern political culture, and classical republican ideology. The experience of the English Civil Wars had shaped both, but very differently.

Pocock observes that the first and formative opposition to the standing army in England arose in opposition to Cromwell's New Model Army, and had two sources. The first was the Royalists, who objected to any army of Cromwell's, but opposed in addition the mercenary character of the army. Schwoerer writes "At the beginning of the Civil War, the chivalric ideal motivated more than one man to side with Charles I. Such notions inclined the English upper classes to disdain a man who fought for pay." It was, however, "the men on the left, especially republicans" who "developed the strongest indictment in both parliamentary debates and the press of the standing army."[4] Republican opposition to the standing army, Schwoerer notes, rose out of "classical and Renaissance philosophy rather than from pacificism or Christian idealism."[5] This is an extraordinarily valuable observation in several respects. It counters the unpersuasive efforts of many writers on British and American antiwar movements to derive these from Christian sects or Christian theology. It suggests an alternative explanation of their origin that accords more with the political contexts of those movements and the affiliations of those involved in them. It accords with a consistent differentiation of classical republicanism from the militant religiosity of the partisans of Cromwell, in matters of ideology, historical antecedents, education, rhetoric, and style. Finally, it may be extended to the United States, where the political cultures of North and South perpetuated these divergent traditions and finally confronted one another over the same issues which had divided their cultural ancestors.

The English republicans evinced their Enlightenment origins in their political indifference to religion, their adoption of classical rhetoric and pen names, and their conscious attempts to emulate historical figures and reproduce the republican constitutions of a mythologized classical antiquity. The same style and objectives characterized the Founding Fathers.

In the Southern states, this style and ideology persisted long after the Revolution. Northerners increasingly employed a religious rhetoric drawn from scripture and the English and American Puritans, and cast themselves, when looking for a symbolic identity, as partisans of Cromwell, mythic figures from the Reformation, or the Pilgrim Fathers. Southerners, through the Civil War, continued the classical republican use of personae from pagan antiquity, occasionally employing English republicans (especially Sydney) in the same fashion. Cicero's Catiline Orations, and the speeches of English republican orators, rather than the Puritan jeremiad, served as their oratorical models.

Southern political culture lacked that Puritan religious tradition which had been the primary influence upon the founding and formation of Northern political culture. The central figures in American mythic history were, to them, the heroes of the Revolution and, more distantly, the central figures of English republicanism who were recognized as their ideological kindred. Oratorical characterizations of America pictured it in the likeness of the Roman Republic, with favored American political leaders in appropriately classical guise. It is difficult to determine whether Southerners were, in their private opinions, more deistical than their Northern compatriots, but their political leaders and political structures clearly followed that mode.

The insignificance of religious forms and the Puritan tradition in Southern political culture is an important point of consonance between that political culture and that of the English country party. It reveals why the Southern states, unlike the Northern, continued to adhere rigorously to the ideology of the Revolutionary era, which had insisted upon the separation of church and state, and upon the maintenance of a militia rather than a standing army.

Students of Southern history have commonly mistaken Southern militance for a cultural approbation of the military.[6] Ignoring the vigorous and prolonged insistence upon proscription of standing armies which maintained a militia system in the South through the Civil War, they read in the Southern enthusiasm for hunting, duels, military heroes, regalia, and campaigns an enthusiasm for a military establishment. This misrepresentation of Southern political culture can be corrected by distinguishing between the formal and informal, individual and collective, forms of violence and their varied political significance.

Violence, in both Northern and Southern culture, was regarded as a recurrence to nature, a momentary escape from the conventions, laws, and customs of civil, if not civilized, society. This conception of violence is, if not universal, common throughout Western culture. Psychoanalytic theory assigns this meaning to personal violence. Hobbes named violence the state of nature. Popular culture associates it with animals and primitive men. Nineteenth-century Americans made this association explicit in their characterizations of duelists, Indians, and others who were thought to employ violence informally and individually.

The same understanding of violence attached to wars between states. States were, in their integrity, construed as persons, and being united in no covenantal community and subject to no higher law, were as persons in the state of nature in their relations to one another. For citizens of a state at war, however, participation in this formal and collective employment of violence was a fulfillment of contractual obligation, an expression of political allegiance and active involvement in the structures of the state rather than recurrence to a prepolitical state of willful individuality.

Formal collective and informal individual violence express, respectively, consciousness of legality and inclusion in a community, and the exercise of individual will without the boundaries of civil society. Informal collective violence, riot, expresses a consciousness of community without objective law. Formal individual violence, dueling for example, expresses the exercise of individual will in accordance with established forms. The primacy of law and covenant in the political culture of the North caused members of that culture to regard all but formal collective violence as a recurrence to nature and a renunciation of civil society. Formal collective violence was, however, a powerful and deeply meaningful reaffirmation of community. This view of violence was buttressed by the significance of Cromwell's army, war with the Indians, and the Revolution, in the mythology of the section.

Since Northern political culture did not admit community without law, informal collective violence was also regarded as a recurrence to nature, or as an attack on the legal community clandestinely instigated by a hostile foreign power. Formal individual violence was regarded as murder. Northern political culture did not admit community without law. Neither did it admit law without community. Adherence to form in private relations, or in the willful pursuit of a private object, did not differentiate formal individual from informal individual violence in Northern political culture.

Because mythic and theoretical accounts of the existence and character of prepolitical community had had a prominent place in Southern political culture, Southerners were able to conceive of community without law and law without community. They were thus able to distinguish these four modes of violence and to formulate diverse evaluations of them and institutional responses.

Informal collective violence was recognized in Southern political culture as encompassing revolution. Employment of this species of violence evinced the popular withdrawal of "the consent of the governed" from a regime. With government thus denied, the informal community of the rebellion might prove a polity in embryo. The American Revolution had served as the model for political development in the South, making the separation of a subculture from the mother country the archetype of national genesis. Expressions, violent or pacific, of a collective consciousness within subcultures thus merited particular attention.

Where riots and rebellions were not revolutionary they nevertheless recalled the possibility of recourse to the right of revolution. Jefferson, whose influence on Southern political thought was unparalleled, wrote that such rebellious manifestations of the popular will serve as a salutary corrective to the inevitable tendency of governments to arrogations of authority and institutional corruption: "Unsuccessful rebellions generally establish the incroachments on the rights of the people which have produced them. An observation of this truth should render honest republican governors so mild in their punishment of rebellions as not to discourage them too much. It is a medicine necessary for the sound health of government."[7]

The recurrence to nature implicit in the employment of formal individual violence served a similar purpose. Like informal collective violence, it affirmed the persistence of natural rights within the constituted state. It suggested, however, that momentary excursions outside the polity and into nature could be mediated by structures prior in time or authority to those of the structured state.

Each of these modes of violence affirmed a principle central to the republican ideology of Southern political culture. Social tolerance of these modes of violence should not, however, be construed as a uniform cultural approbation of violence or an institutionally established militarism.

The central figures in Southern political thought—Washington, Jefferson, Madison, and Monroe—insisted on the subordination of military to civil authority in war as in peace, and on the maintenance of a militia system and the proscription of standing armies. The arguments against a standing army which these men, and others, established so firmly in Southern political tradition demonstrate the persistence of classical republican ideology in the South.

Like the English country party, Southern republicans feared executive use of a standing army to suppress legislative or popular opposition. Cromwell's example was a prominent proof of this danger. "The New Model Army," Schwoerer writes, "began as an instrument to win the Civil War and became an instrument to secure a revolutionary government whose base of support had grown increasingly narrow."[8] Fears that the military might be employed in this fashion were expressed by the Democratic-Republicans in their opposition to the Alien and Sedition Acts, by John Randolph in his opposition to the War of 1812, by Benjamin Watkins Leigh (writing as "Algernon Sydney") in opposition to Jackson, and by Beverley Tucker, who made it the premise of his novel *The Partisan Leader*.

Southern political culture also emphasized the connection discerned by English republican theorists between the standing army and the interests of capital. Washington's Farewell Address, in addition to warning of foreign political entanglements, cautioned that commercial involvements could also drag the nation into war. John Taylor's *Arator* described the imperial ambitions of capital and characterized "mercenary armies," in good country party style, as the expensive and hazardous tool of an enlarged state acting on behalf of a "monied interest."[9]

Southerners maintained the classical republican policy toward standing armies and the capacity to distinguish between modes of violence, because they were foreign to the Puritan tradition. This mode of American religion conflated law and covenant and elevated these to a position of primacy in the political culture. It also offered culturally sanctioned—indeed, revered—paradigms for the establishment of a standing army and religious influence upon public institutions.

Southern political culture, like the classical republicanism of the English country party, reflected the influence of the Enlightenment rather than Christian tradition. Southerners, moreover, saw their historical antecedents in the republican and Cavalier opposition to Puritan governance in the English Civil War. More attention has been paid to the influence of the Cavalier mode on Southern political culture than to their debt to English republicanism, for this latter debt was presumably the common property of all Americans.

The South's immunity to the influence of Puritanism exempted it from the changes Northerners made in the ideology of classical republicanism. With the Revolution won, and independence secured, those who attributed to law and covenant a sacred significance were less inclined to mark government as the source of public or personal corruption. That Protestant ethic worked most powerfully where Protestantism was strongest, altering the traditional republican insistence on the importance of agriculture in securing a republican ideology.

The South's perpetuation of the classical republican ideology which had guided the Founding Fathers was due in part to the common intellectual and historical antecedents of Southern political culture and the English country party. Each evinced the influence of Enlightenment philosophy rather than Puritan theology; each had its origins in the English Civil War. The continuance of classical republicanism in the South after its waning in the North was also due to the disparate economic arrangements which prevailed in the two sections. Southern political culture, like that of the English country party, was thought by its adherents to have derived its peculiar character from the primacy of agriculture.

Agriculture was assumed by Southerners, as by the country party, to cultivate certain civic virtues in its practitioners, and to establish obstacles to governmental corruption and arrogations of authority. The country party, as Pocock observes, postulated a past virtuous society of agrarian warriors, which they endeavored to reestablish in the present age. Southerners, who saw in America the revival of the Roman Republic, endeavored to maintain the virtue of that state through the continuance of the agrarian economy which had produced it.

The primacy granted to agriculture in Southern political culture was not merely a sentimentalization of the ties of blood and soil or a meaningless artifact of their English antecedents. The belief of Anglo-American republicans that the self was "founded in property" as Pocock terms it, was a concept of considerable import in the philosophy of Locke. "Every man," he wrote, "has property in his own person."[10] Those natural rights which Locke recognized in individual men were attached to their bodies and embraced within this understanding of property. Property was also construed as including what individuals required to preserve themselves in their bodies. Locke also argued that property might include those things which men produced through labor. In each of these cases, the definition of property and the determination of the boundaries of the self is made with reference to the body and the corporeal requirements and capacities of man.

This understanding of property enhanced the status of agriculture in several respects. Unlike commerce, investment, or ownership of (as opposed to labor in) a factory, agriculture gave the producer a clear title to his product. In addition, by making the body and corporeality the source of rights and obligations in political life, it enhanced the political status of those whose labor enabled not only them but others as well to preserve themselves. The recognition of the superiority of farmers and laborers to traders and capitalists moved successive generations of Southerners to advocate political alliances with artisans, mechanics, and farmers throughout the United States. The idea that political life was formed in recognition of a common corporeality ran directly counter to the Puritan view of the polity as the expression of a spiritual unity produced by common knowledge, or grace.

Locke's definition of property inclined him, as it would later republican theorists, to an endorsement of maternal authority. In refuting Filmer's argument for patriarchal authority Locke wrote: "Nobody can deny that the Woman hath an equal share, if not greater, as nourishing the child a longtime in her own Body out of her own Substance. There it is fashioned, and from her it receives Materials and Principles of its Constitution."[11] This is the very model of property, and the extension of the self in it. Following this model, Locke employed the common metaphor of nature as "the common Mother of all," to whom all things belong until labor alienates them from her.[12]

Southern concepts of maternal authority, employment of the maternal metaphor, and theories of the relation of agriculture to politics, arise from this conception of property.

The classical republicanism of the South can be discerned on several levels. It was expressed in ideology and cultural style, the doctrines which governed political action and political institutions and the form in which these were expressed. Southerners retained the Revolutionary generation's distrust of the formal structures of government as productive of corruption and prone to arrogations of authority. They opposed the standing army and the established church, advocating, as the Founding Fathers had, the militia and the separation of church and state. They retained a belief in natural rights, an approbation of agriculture, a conception of property founded in corporeality, and a suspicion that governmental structures tended to advance a monied interest. Like the Revolutionaries, they continued to identify themselves with the republics and republicans of classical antiquity, taking their pseudonyms and their oratorical style from these examples.

This ideology, and the public policies which it dictated, were supported by the economic structure of the community. The maintenance of agriculture was regarded by both the Revolutionary generation and successive generations of Southerners as requisite to the maintenance of republican institutions. It therefore occupied a position of great significance in the culture of the South from the Revolution to the Civil War.

The ideology, cultural style, and values governing the character of the economy, which were shared by these classical republicans, had a common origin in Enlightenment opposition to monarchy (whether that of Charles I or Cromwell) presented by the Republicans during England's Civil War.

The North, conversely, varied from the republicanism of the Founding Fathers on each of these three levels. This disparity was expressed ideologically in the belief that the formal structures of government—law and covenant—were productive of public and private virtue, in the belief that Protestantism undergirded the republican institutions of the regime and was not properly separable from them, in the belief that the commonwealth was constituted of men united by spiritual rather than corporeal commonalty, in a cultural emphasis on duties rather than rights, in a contingent rather than an intrinsic opposition to the standing army, and in an approbation of trade and industry as further removing men from dependence on nature. Northerners also favored a cultural style marked by the austerity and piety of the Puritans, and rejecting the paganism and pride associated with classical antiquity.

Religious tradition rather than agriculture was the basis of sectional commonalty in the North. Cultural values favored commerce and industry, and this preference was reflected in descriptions of sectional identity. Rather than supporting classical republican ideology, this religious tradition undermined it, supporting instead the concept of comprehensive nationality and the primacy of law.

Nor did Northern political culture share the origins which bound Southern political culture to the ideology of the Revolution. They recognized their culture as derived from Christian rather than from Enlightenment tradition and, historically, from the supporters of Cromwell rather than the English republicans.

The Cavalier persona adopted by later Southerners was a symbolic rejection of this cultural tradition and its associated ideology, style and values. Michael Johnson, in his book, *Toward a Patriarchal Republic*, confirms that even the most conservative Southerners never appeared to entertain the idea of a monarchy. Monarchy was an absurdity in America, and with the elimination of this issue in the constellation of issues represented in the Cavalier/Roundhead dichotomy, the Cavalier persona took on an altered meaning. It represented opposition to Cromwell, and hence to the Puritan religious tradition. To the Southerners who adopted it, it also represented opposition to the standing army, to the use of force against the people, and to military usurpations of legitimate authority.

The South's alienation and growing sectional self-consciousness was not indicative of alienation from the ideology of the Founding. The appearance of aberration in Southern political culture is due rather to the alterations in republican ideology and institutions which the dominant Puritan tradition effected in the increasingly wealthy and populous North.

Southern adherence to the classical republicanism of the Founding while the influence of the Puritan tradition altered ideology, institutions, and conceptions of America in the Northern states, is illustrated by the changing politics of John C. Calhoun. Calhoun's transformation from nationalist to sectionalist reveals the persistence and primacy of classical republican ideology in the South.

Calhoun began his congressional career as a nationalist, a proponent of tariffs, industrialization, internal improvements, expansion of the national bureaucracy, an energetic federal government, and a large, well-funded, and active military. He ended it as the representative of an alienated section. In making this change he was obliged to shuck off a good deal of his former ideology.

Calhoun's youthful nationalism expressed itself in enthusiastic approbation of the War of 1812 and ambitious forecasts of American military expansion. Southern culture, however, maintained the ideal of the militia and attendant fears of a standing army. The older, Southern Calhoun accorded himself to this view, writing in his *Disquisition on Government*, "Such indeed is the repugnance between popular governments and force—or, to be more specific, military power—that the almost necessary consequence of a resort to force by such governments to maintain their authority, is not only a change of their form, but a change into the most opposite—that of absolute monarchy."[13] This alteration in his views necessarily entailed a retreat from his early and enthusiastic espousal of an aggressive national military posture and his advocacy of foreign wars. While it might be at first supposed that Calhoun's remarks in the *Disquisition* refer solely to Jackson's Force Bill, it should be remembered that he had explicitly advocated war with England, and projected other wars, as a means of decisively establishing the authority of the American regime.

The Force Bill did, however, demonstrate simultaneously the hazards of an energetic government and the use of the military against the people. Aggrandizement of the federal government, and that national consolidation which Calhoun had originally advocated, thus threatened not only the wealth of "the laboring portion of the population" (farmers and mechanics), as the tariff had demonstrated, but their liberties as well.

Calhoun is commonly—and with some justice—pictured as an advocate of patriarchal authority, and an opponent of liberal democratic institutions. He was, however, careful to insist that "the people are the source of all power" and that government owes its creation to "the will of the people." Rather than presenting his doctrine of the concurrent majority as a desirable alternative to democratic government, Calhoun argued that government by concurrent majority is more democratic than that of a numerical majority, and, further, that the latter will have the strong tendency to slide "finally, into absolute government." Even if these affirmations and arguments are regarded as nothing more than a fabric of mystifications designed to hide his true intentions, they demonstrate that republican institutions and the primacy of popular authority remained unchallengeable in Southern political culture.[14]

Calhoun's advocacy of a concurrent majority reflects another aspect of the disparity between Northern and Southern political culture. With it, Calhoun contended, nations can embrace culturally diverse groups, without discriminating among them. In passages which recall his nationalism, Calhoun praised the capacity of the British Empire to embrace diverse cultures. "A Constitution," he wrote, "must spring from the bosom of the community and be adapted to the intelligence and character of the people and all the multifarious relations internal and external, which distinguish one people from another."[15] He believed, however, that governments originating in circumstances of cultural homogeneity would tend to become absolute and oppressive. The necessity for compromise and institutions accommodating to this need, which arise most readily where disparate cultures are embraced, tend to preserve popular government.

Most Southerners were not inclined to accept Calhoun's novel proposals for the reformation of the governmental structures of the United States. When the Constitution of the Confederate States appeared, it contained neither a plural executive nor provision for a concurrent majority. It is a mistake, therefore, to regard Calhoun's thought as representative of his section. This very idiosyncrasy is revealing, however, for the arguments Calhoun employs on behalf of his proposed reforms are drawn from the political culture. Thus Calhoun, arguing against natural rights and attributing to God "the care and superintendence of the whole," still finds the origins of government in the corporeal requirements natural to man, and arguing against absolute democracy contends only that it is ephemeral while a mixed government secures popular rule for a long duration. Thus, as the ideological and policy changes entailed in his change from nationalist to sectionalist illustrate the difference in national and sectional character, so his arguments for altering political institutions indicate the common assumptions and values which held him to his section.

This looking to nature for the origin, limits, and sanction for politics, as well as for economic and social structures, is characteristic of Southern political thought. It marks Southerners from the colonial era to the time of the Vanderbilt Agrarians. In the antebellum period this tendency separated North and South. Southerners, consciously adhering to nature, would maintain the family as the primary unit of social organization and the institution charged with the social functions of education and care of the poor and the insane, while Northerners increasingly employed public institutions as agents of the state.

Southerners continued agriculture in economic primacy and continued to praise it for maintaining a harmonious relation between men and external nature and between separate men, and for facilitating the maintenance of natural rights in civil society. The development of industry and the extension of commerce in the North, and the enthusiastic promulgation of industrial techniques and industrial organization by Northern modernizers, were thus regarded as endangering the community by eliminating a commonalty of interest and experience among the citizens, endangering liberty by creating artificial relations of dependence and patronage, and endangering the continued enjoyment of the beauty and utility of nature by altering the relation of men to the land.

In politics, Southerners continued to regard legislative, judicial, and executive intervention in noncorporeal dimensions of life—religion, ideology, speech—as outside the proper province of government. Adhering to the conception of property as an extension of the self effected through holding, cultivation, labor, or provision, they resisted attacks on property as attacks on the individual in his natural liberty. This broad construction of property complicated the issue of slavery, for while many Southerners affirmed that men could not justly have property in men, the validity of the familial model was affirmed by ideology as well as deeply embedded in social structures. The belief that provision granted authority had ramifications beyond the slavery issue, allying it to the continuation of agriculture (and hence of liberty) in the South, and with the issues of labor and the tariff. Southerners of widely varying views on black slavery were united among themselves by their agreement that nature was the proper determinant of political status. This belief, while it did nothing to resolve the issue of slavery, changing it merely to a debate over the natural rights and requirements of the two races, distinguished the South from the North, where political and personal status were determined by election and by law and where the question of rights fell before that of duties entailed on members of the divinely or temporally covenanted community.

Nature served in the South as the acknowledged source of political and economic relations. It was therefore sacred and authoritative. Signs of the continuance of natural relations in civil life legitimated the regime and the polity. Actions construed as recurrence to nature were thought to reinvigorate and reaffirm the legitimacy of the prevailing republican political order. This imbued relations, symbols, and identities marked as natural in the symbolic lexicon with exceptional political significance. It encouraged displays of personal independence and idiosyncracy, led to deliberate emulation of groups thought to be in a state prior to politics (and hence closer to nature), and granted cultural sanction to the indulgence of natural passions and natural appetites. It was on this level that Cavalier and Roundhead were differentiated. The popular image of the Roundhead, in both sections, was one of piety, austerity, discipline, and the repression of natural passion. That of the Cavalier, conversely, was irreligious, playful, indulgent in eating, drinking, and sex, passionate, and undisciplined. This dichotomy represented the deliberate effort in Northern culture to repress internal as well as external nature, and the relative laxity of this psychological repression in the South.

On several levels—in politics, social relations, economics, and psychology—the conflict between North and South was one of culture against nature. The natural rights ideology of classical republicanism in the South was accompanied by a constellation of cultural values and paradigms which affirmed that culture's desire to remain in close proximity to nature.

6   Images of Identity and Alienation

Each of the three groups which will be examined in this chapter served regularly as a metaphor for the South in literature and political discourse. They share another likeness as well; they are all, in the context of antebellum American culture, liminal groups. Turner wrote, "Liminal entities are neither here nor there, they are betwixt and between the positions assigned and arrayed by law, custom, convention, and ceremonial."[1] They are neither wholly within nor wholly without the community.

Turner was concerned with the formal rites marking social and cultural transformations. These serve, as he recognized, to reaffirm or redefine the community, usually—as is the case in initiation or puberty rites—by changing the composition of the community. Liminal entities are endowed with special significance on these occasions because they are those who will be included or excluded, accepted or rejected. They thus represent the possibility of life outside the community, and the possibility of the dissolution or alteration of political structures. They are potentially, and symbolically, revolutionary.

Social and cultural transformation are not, of course, peculiar to tribes small enough to observe the inclusion and exclusion, the political arrival and departure, of particular members. Such transitions, in larger states, are similarly marked by increased public attention, formal and informal, to those whose status in the polity is ambiguous.

The American South, in the antebellum period, was in a state of transition; increasingly alienated from the Northern, and hence from the United States, and increasingly conscious of its as-yet informal community. In this period, in this place, Indians, blacks, and women were the principal liminal groups. All were Americans; all were excluded from the formal structures of the polity. This ambiguity made these groups appropriate symbols for the ambiguous state of the South in its transition from section to Confederacy.

Southern identification with these liminal groups was expressed on two levels: in identification with the traits the culture ascribed them and in identification with their liminality.

Southern metaphoric identification with the traits ascribed to these groups, and the position and treatment accorded them in Southern social and political structure, followed a common pattern in each case. It was a rivalry. In each case, Southerners identified themselves with those on the boundary by appropriating traits culturally ascribed to them. This identification was expressed explicitly in literature and political discourse, indirectly in symbolic or evocative modes of dress or behavior. The exercise of these traits, still ascribed to both the South and the liminal group, was then alienated from the group through Southern social, political, and economic structures.

Thus, Indians, ascribed a pride and violence with which Southerners identified, were defeated, disarmed, and rendered necessarily pacific and subordinate. Blacks, ascribed an enviable sexuality, encountered legal as well as social barriers to marriage with whites and in slavery were denied both legal marriage and the free exercise of their sexuality. Women, whose capacity for maternity was of great significance in the political culture of the South, were obliged to conceal the signs of their productive sexuality and to resign provision for the child after birth to the husband or his agents.

This simultaneous ascription or acknowledgment of traits and structural alienation of the same traits from these liminal groups enabled the South to appropriate the traits and incorporate them into the structures of the polity without divesting them of their antistructural character and associations.

The significance of this pattern in the South's treatment of these liminal groups becomes apparent when one considers the meaning of these traits, and of liminality itself, in American political culture.

Turner, "rather in the fashion of Levi-Strauss" presented a long list of binary oppositions to differentiate the properties of antistructural liminars from those of the structured political system. He observed that "this list could be considerably lengthened if we were to widen the list of liminal situations considered. While *communitas*/structure and not having/having may be universal, other dichotomies—for example, childhood/adulthood, and outlawry/law-abidingness—might characterize other liminal situations."[2]

Certain of the oppositions Turner enumerated, moreover, are contingent upon particular structures. Among the Ndembu, sexuality is allied to sociality, and hence to structure. Turner therefore listed sexual continence/sexuality among his oppositions. He observed, however, that among the hippies sexuality was regarded as a "polymorphic instrument of immediate communitas rather than as the basis for an enduring social tie."[3] In the Christian tradition, sexuality was identified as carnal and hence in opposition to the constitutive spirituality of the community of saints. The institutionalization of liminality in Christianity, and particularly in the notion of monastic community which the Reformation sought to make coextensive with the congregational community, must be taken into account in efforts to separate structural and antistructural traits in Christian cultures.

Sexuality, in American political culture and particularly in Northern political culture where Protestant Christianity had its greatest influence, is explicitly associated with prepolitical, antistructural *communitas;* in the language of the Enlightenment, with the state of nature. This state is distinguished by three properties: sexuality, domesticity, and violence. Each of these is associated with a form or condition antithetical to the structured civil order. In place of spiritual unity, there is sexual unity; in place of the soul, the body; in place of a temporally infinite community, a geographically defined one; in place of eternity, land; in place of the pacific unity of a common spiritual consciousness, violent physical contention; in place of the promise of eternal life, the certainty of death.

By identifying themselves with these traits in their liminal carriers, Southerners expressed their alienation from structure and civil order. By appropriating these traits to themselves in the structures of the civil order, they expressed the conviction that certain properties of the state of nature might persist in civil society.

The traits whose continuance Southern culture endeavored to secure were intimately related to the Southern affirmation of classical republican ideology, the primacy of agriculture, and provision as a source of political authority. The family was the primary unit of economic and social organization in an agrarian economy, and a system of authority based on provision and dependence. Agriculture was historically and philosophically allied to classical republicanism. Sexual union and the often-consequent family were forms of community prior to politics. Violence, and the capacity of one man to kill another, were marked by Hobbes as a proof of human equality.

The attitudes toward these traits and the treatment of these groups in Southern political culture contrasts sharply with those in Northern political culture. There, these groups were negative referents rather than objects of identification. The qualities ascribed them remained constant, as did the association of these qualities with the state of nature. Northerners, influenced by the Puritan tradition, regarded covenanted civil society as requisite to public and private virtue, rather than as the source of public and private corruption. Here again there were multiple associations. Men without the community were outside the community's covenant with God. They were embedded in nature, and dead in sin. Sexuality was associated with spiritual death and, metaphorically, with physical death. Death was "ashes to ashes, dust to dust," the return of the body to the land, a material reunion. Both agriculture and the temporal continuance of the race reproduced physical life, and both necessitated a dangerous involvement in natural processes. Northern political culture sought to excise rather than appropriate these traits.

Southern identification with the liminality of these groups, and—in the case of John Randolph, with the liminality of this man—expressed a Southern sense of alienation from existing political structures. Identification with liminal entities symbolically expressed a sense of "not having" in the distribution of natural resources—a sentiment expressed structurally in opposition to the tariff—and "powerlessness" against the federal government and the weight of the remaining states. Because liminality is antistructural and hence, in American political culture, an affirmation of the natural, the South's identification with the liminal expressed a rejection not only of the political structure, but of the Northern conception of the *communitas* which undergirded them.

The final portion of this chapter discusses Southern recollections of John Randolph and his place in the mythology of the section. This will serve to demonstrate the interrelationships of these three liminal groups in the formation of a Southern political identity. It will also illustrate something of the interplay between personal and political identity, allegiance and legitimacy.

It will be remembered, I trust, that in examining these groups I am examining images of Southerners, and of the South. The self-conceptions of members of these groups, insofar as they saw themselves as distinct, are not immediately relevant to this inquiry, though they are of profound interest and importance in themselves. Nor are the facts of the matter immediately relevant. I am not arguing therefore, that Randolph was impotent, women amazons, Indians without government, or blacks the loving dependents of motherly masters. I argue that they were so on that plane of culture in which allegiance and identity were delineated, and that they were so symbolically, as ciphers for key relationships in Southern political culture.

INDIANS

The Indian has passed away
But creeping comes another
Deadlier far—Picket take heed:
Take heed of thy brother.[4]

The Civil War has been called a war of brothers; the American archetype of fraternal strife. The identification of Southerner and Indian in this poetic moment of the war suggests something of the history of the fraternal metaphor. Melville, in writing of the war, regarded its fraternal character as neither archetypal nor unprecedented. Rather he had recourse to an earlier fraternal conflict. The enmity of Blue and Gray had been preceded by that of red and white. In identifying the Southerner with the Indian, Melville was not merely observing that the white had won and hoping the blue would do as well. American culture had ascribed likewise to the Southerner and the Indian a constellation of traits which distinguished them from what would become the dominant cultural type in American politics.

Certain of these traits—poverty, sexual ambiguity, violence, and impotence—are expressive of alienation and liminality. Others, notably proximity to nature, willfulness, extravagance of dress, and godlessness, indicate aspects of American culture which were being excised and abjured as the cultural content of nationality was defined with increasing rigor. Southerners and Indians each came to represent a rejected but latently enduring alternative to the dominant American political culture. Southerners had identified themselves with the Indian with their first stirrings of self-consciousness. Robert Beverley's *History and Present State of Virginia* began with the declaration "I am an Indian." Beverley had undertaken this description of his native state as a corrective to the fantastic accounts of travelers to America, travelers being, as he averred, "of all Men, the most suspected of insincerity." His account would be rendered not in the style of the French, who "are fond of dressing everything up in their gay fashion," nor of the English, who "invent more within the compass of Probability," but in the plain style of the Indian, which "depends upon its own intrinsic value, and like Beauty is rather concealed than set off by ornament." In adopting the name of Indian, Beverley endeavored to take on the character of the noble savage.

The Indians, as Beverley described them, were "in the state of Nature." They had no written laws, "nor did the Constitution in which

we found them, seem to need many." In this state of natural community, "Nature and their own convenience" prescribed their conduct.
Beverley commends it. Indians are distinguished in his narrative for
their physical perfection. "They are straight and well-proportioned,
having the cleanest and most exact limbs in the world: They are so
perfect in their outward frame that I never heard of one single Indian
that was either dwarfish, crooked, bandy-legged or otherwise mis-
shapen." The endurance and beauty which they possessed in consequence excited Beverley's admiration. Their moral constitution, which
depended upon education and intrinsic virtue rather than enforced
injunctions, was equally admirable. Though they were "at their own
disposal" they were brave, temperate, proud and chaste. An "excess of
life and fire, which they never fail to have, makes them frolicsome, but
without any real imputation to their innocence." Despite their passion
for revenge, their wild games, their "Terrible Aires," and their
fondness for hunting, they were a peaceful people, "happy, I think, in
their simple State of Nature, and in their employment of Plenty, without the Curse of Labor." They, and Beverley with them, "have on
several accounts, reason to lament the arrival of the Europeans, by
whose means they seem to have lost their Felicity as well as their Innocence."[5]

The Indians, in Beverley's archetypal account, represented man
in a state of virtue and gaiety, enjoying natural plenty without an effort
and without the corruption attendant upon luxury, residents of Plato's
City of Pigs. In this condition, their physical and moral constitutions
developed unhindered and unharmed, endowing them with unparalleled virtue. The English, rather than diminishing and debilitating them, might have embraced them to their own advantage. "Intermarriage," Beverley wrote, "had indeed been the method proposed
very often by the Indians in the Beginning, urging it as a certain rule
that the English were not their friends if they refused it. And I can't
but think it would have been happy for that country had they embraced this Proposal." Other Virginians, taken with the beauty and
strength of the Indians, or perhaps with that gaiety which Beverley
found "not to be resisted," proposed intermarriage as a means of preserving the Indian nation as they improved their own.[6]

The land hunger characteristic of the Virginians, Beverley among
them, moved the colonists to displacement and annihilation, rather
than to the espousal of the Indians. Constant intercourse, of the sort
occasioned by war, continued nevertheless to acquaint the colonists
with the Indians.

When early schemes of eugenic miscegenation gave way to campaigns of conquest and removal, the Southern and Southwestern soldiers adopted elements of the attire and customs of their prey. The Indian habit of relying upon "surprise and ambuscade" proved admirably suited to wars in the wilderness.[7] The Revolution made Indians of the Americans, divorcing them from England and from England's government, and throwing them back upon their yet inchoate nationality. Certain of their distinction and obliged to rely upon tactical innovations rather than superior resources, they were inclined to resort to methods characteristically employed by those who were, like themselves, American.

In this way, Beverley's picture of the Indian as representative of a lost state of virtuous prepolitical community became conflated with the memory of ruthless and unconventional violence. The Revolutionaries, in preferring to violate the written law in favor of their own undocumented community, had already likened themselves to the Indians. Their adoption of Indian tactics marked their rejection of convention and their exchange of an English for an American character—in addition to advancing the progress of their arms. The Sons of Liberty, wearing war paint to the Boston Tea Party, were not the only Revolutionaries to emulate the Indian. Francis Marion, the "South Carolinian Swamp Fox," employed their tactics, and Lafayette, fighting Cornwallis in Virginia, was aided by a band of imported Algonquin.

The success of the Revolution, and that determination—especially marked among the Virginians—to establish a government at once less onerous and more virtuous than that they had abjured, recalled and romanticized Beverley's Indian Eden. Indians lived in the bosom of nature; the Revolutionaries would recur to nature for confirmation of their rights. In returning to nature, the Revolutionaries revived the legendary protopolitical idyll of the Indian.

This mythic community had been established in political culture as that in which life in accord with nature produced fewer public burdens and greater private virtue. The notions of noble savagery purveyed by Rousseau and by Beverley and others of his stripe, colored American expectations of post-Revolutionary government. In New England, where the Indian state of incivility was regarded as more like Hell than Paradise, the association of private virtue and felicity with the absence or restraint of government was untenable. Virtue followed the propagation of the law. In Southern political culture, however, the Indian had long stood as a cipher for this very notion.

The wars against the Creeks, the Cherokee, and the Seminole succeeded in removing the Indian from the South. The image of the

Indians remained prominent. Although they warred against the Indians, Southerners retained the Indian as a symbol of a constellation of culturally endorsed values. Those most thoroughly engaged in the actual annihilation of the Indians were frequently their most flagrant imitators. Andrew Jackson, with his adoption of an Indian, and Sam Houston, with his adoption by one, may serve as illustrations. The Southerner, and the early Westerner of Southern antecedents, endeavored to replace rather than to eliminate the Indian. They were not enemies but rivals.

The historically derived association of Indians with revolutionaries endowed this rivalry with yet another aspect. As the settlers had envied the Indians' title to the land, so the successors of the Revolutionaries, doubtful of their own deserts, envied the deeds which had won the land for their fathers. In taking the guise of Indians, post-Revolutionary generations pretended to a perfect title.

Southern violence recalled both the Indians and the Revolutionary imitators of the Indian style. It offered immediate subjective experience of that natural liberty which was thought to be the active exercise of the rights of man. This momentary recourse to man's natural condition at once likened men to the Indians—and thus to all men in their primordial liberty—and enabled them to experience the state in which their fathers had consummated the Revolution. They were thus able to experience, if not to participate in, the actions of the Revolution which bottomed the regime.

The wars against the Indians further enabled them to transfer their rivalry with their fathers onto a more acceptable and accessible object. The Indian provided the means for their replacement of their fathers. In killing Indians, they symbolically eliminated the Revolutionaries identified with them, even as they imitated the violence of those Revolutionaries. In emulating the Indian, and thus identifying themselves with him, they both pretended to a title superior to that of their fathers and identified themselves with their fathers by association. Thus their replacement of both Indians and Revolutionaries consisted in a simultaneous emulation and annihilation of these.

The association of violence with the Indian became prominent in Revolutionary rhetoric and increased with the extent and intensity of the Indian wars. Continued emulation of Indian practices in the South, and Southern employment of the Indian as representative of desirable traits, associated the South in the popular imagination with that lawless personal violence characteristic of the Indians. This was the violence of the state of nature.

The Indian figured as a symbol of pacific nobility in a natural

Eden in the rhetoric of Southerners advocating the abandonment of convention in secession, both from England and from the United States. Rhetorical employment of the Indian as a symbol of violence was less frequent at such times. Independence and continued advocacy of the Constitution, and thus of written law, tempered the enthusiasn of post-Revolutionary orators for the state of nature and inclined them to attach an implicit caveat to their emulation of the Indian.

The Indian served in the South as the concrete expression of prepolitical, and thus protopolitical, community. This was the central trait in that constellation of traits which they represented. Attached to it were both qualities ideally ascribed to the state of nature—innocence, simplicity, lawlessness, violence, sensual gratification, happiness, and poverty—and other qualities historically associated with the Indians and consonant with this putatively natural character: impotence, unletteredness, and tragic decline. Qualities historically associated with the notion of a state of nature and the philosophy of the Enlightenment—democratic revolution for example—were also frequently conjoined with the image of the Indian. Southern emulation, employment, and advocacy of that which was Indian thus served as a means for the ordering and expression of intrinsically alien but phenomenally related aspects of their political culture.

Southern articulation of Southern culture coincided with the growth of secessionist sentiment in the South. This was due in part to circumstance, in much greater part to that desire for independence which invariably accompanies the achievement of collective self-consciousness. As the South came to a realization of its peculiar character, it began increasingly to manifest the desire to express this perceived peculiarity in objective law. The symbolic function of the Indian in the antebellum period reflects this developing nationality.

The importance of the Indian to Southern political culture in the antebellum period is derived from his usefulness as a symbol of alienation and prepolitical community. Thus, identification with the Indian expressed both alienation and involvement in an undocumented but nonetheless authentic community. Use of the Indian as a symbolic expression of the South's alienation was not confined to Southerners. Preeminent among the traits likewise attributed to Southerners and Indians was a proclivity for forms of apolitical and extrapolitical violence especially expressive of alienation.

Recourse to vigilantism may serve notice that a community contained within a larger polity regards itself as properly governed by its own laws, rather than those of the larger whole. Vigilantism may express the perception of inadequacy in the existing laws, or in their laggard enforcement. In the South, the federal government, and the governments of the states as well, were not charged with the regulation of the daily affairs of the citizenry. Indeed, Southern ideologues had long insisted on the need to fence in government, limiting the intervention of officials in social relations. This political scheme prescribed a large area of independence to the states and local authorities, and a still larger area to the citizenry. Men accustomed to voluntary organizations and enamored of collective action find in vigilantism an expression of their allegiance to democratic forms. They are able to assert the authority of the regime even as they move beyond it. Under such a government, men make their own laws. Vigilantism and lynch law served in the South as affirmations of the authority of the community. Like Nullification, they acquired their legitimacy from the notion that authority derived from popular acclamation, and that this force could at any time amend laws promulgated by a lesser author. Moreover, Southerners enmeshed in the myth of Restoration, protested in these acts the amendment and abridgment of the Constitution.

Each Southern generation had repeated the charge that the federal government, in fealty to the North, had exceeded its constitutional mandate. The proscriptions contained in the Constitution had been disregarded. If the legislative and judicial branches were unable or unwilling to prevent encroachments on the jurisdiction and authority of the states, the states themselves might restore the vigor of constitutional proscriptions through a determined defense of the boundaries of their authority. That this might be accomplished through the concerted but spontaneous action of an alarmed citizenry rather than through the formal structures of the state's authority was, though unfortunate, only to be expected.

This sequence of events provides the plot of Beverley Tucker's novel, *The Partisan Leader*. Tucker's essay in predictive social science posits Van Buren at the end of his fourth term, at the head of "a consolidated government, with the forms of a republic and the powers of a monarchy."[8] The Southern states, with the exception of Virginia, have seceded and confederated. The Old Dominion has remained loyal to the Union, and Washington, in order that it may remain so, has quartered troops there, in expectation of a conflict with the new Confederacy. Tucker, whose opinion of contemporary politicians was diminished by his unsuccessful attempts to number himself among them, has state officials buckle. Their acquiescence derived not from "the loyal and generous spirit" characteristic of Virginians, but from an unstately servility. Redemption comes not from the government, but from the household.

Recourse to natural community and to guerrilla warfare would effect the independence of the South as it had that of the United States. Tucker's title *The Partisan Leader* recalls both the Revolutionary and the Indian. Apart from explicit references within the work, the name "partisan" was applied to that form of warfare which we call "guerrilla," and which has remained the special province of the revolutionary. In Tucker's time the tactics of "surprise and ambuscade" kept their ancient association with the Indian. The importance of familial community in his story further recalls the Indians, for it was the mode on which their society was believed to be organized. Recourse to these tactics and this mode of social organization affirmed the independence of the community.

Private violence, similarly, affirmed the independence of the individual. John Lyde Wilson, writing a manual for duelists in 1858, argued that "a tame submission to insult and disgrace" was contrary to the "history of all animated nature," and to that pride characteristic, if not of America, at least of the Southern states.[9]

Pride among citizens was to maintain in them a proper regard for one another's rights, in much the same way as the insistence of the states was to restrain the arrogations of the federal government. Not rights only, but manners, were to be maintained by this salutary pride. Wilson, answering accusations that the prevalence of dueling in the South evinced a sectional barbarity, wrote:

> I am very sure that the citizens of the states so disrespectfully spoken of, would feel a deep humiliation to be compelled to exchange their urbanity of deportment for the uncouth incivility of the people of Massachusetts. Look at their public journals and you will find them generally teeming with abuse of private character which would not be countenanced here. The idea of New England becoming a school for manners is about as fanciful as Bolingbroke's idea of a patriot king.[10]

The proscription of personal violence, Wilson contends, has persuaded men that they may abuse one another with impunity, so long as they do not transgress the laws. Thus the affirmation of the primacy of law results in personal humiliation, publicly in the denigration of popular authority and privately in denying private recourse to those who are privately offended. The forebearance demanded by these laws is, Wilson argues, contrary to nature:

If a man be smote upon one cheek in public, and he turns the other which is also smitten, and he offers no resistance, I am aware he is in the exercise of great Christian forebearance, highly recommended and enjoined by many good men, but utterly repugnant to those feelings which nature and education have implanted in the human character. If it was possible to enact laws so severe and impossible to be avoided as to enforce such a rule of behavior, all that is honorable in the community would quit the country and inhabit the wilderness with the Indians.[11]

This passage is noteworthy for its rejection of Christian in favor of natural virtues.

The South's resemblance to the Indian was advanced by many Northerners as evidence of its godless character. While Southerners since Beverley had associated the retreat from civilization to nature as effecting a return rather than a departure from virtue, this view had never prevailed in the North.

Timothy Dwight, in his influential *Sermon on Dueling*, also argued of the duelist that he, in "claiming and sharing all the blessings of civilized society, arrogates also the savage independence of wild and brutal nature." This, however, Dwight regarded as neither virtuous nor desirable. "To him" he declared "government is annihilated."[12]

For both Wilson and Dwight, private violence recalled the independence of the Indians. These in turn represented that natural state prior to politics, in which each man answered for himself. The emulation of the Indians did indeed threaten the annihilation of government. As Dwight recognized, the refusal to acknowledge the law's authority to govern personal conduct not only expressed the desire to limit the law's extent, but also affirmed the superiority of men to the laws they make. This threatened anarchy.

In the North, where membership in the Holy Commonwealth was requisite to private virtue, political conventions were ascribed a similarly decisive role in the maintenance of human virtue. Law was sacred and civility "blessed." In the South, however, men still entertained doubts of the sort which troubled Jefferson.

In a letter written to Madison in 1787, Jefferson had enumerated three forms in which societies exist. The first, he said, was "without government, as among our Indians." Though he proceeded to advocate representative government, he acknowledged "It is a problem, not clear in my mind, that the first condition is not the best."[13] Indians boasted residence in the state of nature where men, according to Jefferson's doctrine, enjoyed the perfect possession of their natural rights. They were tied together by the natural bonds of interest and affection. And they were happy.

Beverley's account of the Indians marked their pacific playfulness as evidence of their natural state. They manifested their enjoyment of liberty in a frolicsome spirit and "boisterous play." They were "happy in the State of Nature." Mary Jemison's account of her captivity among the Indians similarly emphasizes their prepolitical character. Jemison, however, marks their violence and the preeminence of familial ties as evidence of their natural condition.

Membership in the Indian community was, according to Jemison, determined by families. Prisoners were presented to families deprived of members, and the family was left to dispose of them as they chose. "They generally save him and treat him kindly. But if their mental wound is fresh, their loss so great that they would deem it irremediable, or if their prisoners do not meet with their approbation, no torture, let it be ever so cruel, seems sufficient to make them satisfaction." These sacrifices, Jemison concludes were "family and not national." Her rendering of Indian practices allies violence to that intensity of feeling which creates familial bonds.[14]

Both violence and this passion productive of revenge were politically subversive. Beverley's Indians were protopolitical, enjoying a natural community free from structural restraints. Political life was not merely alien but antithetical to the practices of Jemison's Indians.

Jemison's narrative was characteristic of a genre that, though circulated nationally, had its origin and greatest circulation in the North and West. Captivity narratives spoke to Puritan fears of declension, to their suspicion that unrestrained nature would prove irresistibly seductive to the purported partisans of civility and that their efforts to bring order to the wilderness would fall victim to the disorderly instincts they had endeavored to subdue in themselves. The conflict between white and Indian thus manifested an interior conflict. The Indian was the incarnation of instinct: natural and passionate, uncivilized and disorderly. The white man brought order and civility, subduing nature. In America, as in man, the Indian was the original proprietor of the now common ground.

Michael Rogin's study *Fathers and Children* has articulated the relation between Americans and Indians with extraordinary insight. The Indian was the older brother of the race. Like whites, members "of the great American family" and "descendants of Adam," Indians were preeminently "children of nature." The fraternal metaphor expressed a fundamental commonalty even as it differentiated red and

white. The Indian's primogeniture expressed a primacy that was derived both from his historic precedence on the land and from the supposed developmental precedence of his race. All men were once as the
Indians are now. Thus Francis Parkman wrote, "Barbarism is to civilization as childhood is to maturity." Parkman's formula suggests an
inarticulate recognition of the principle that men in their personal development recapitulate the progress of the race. For the Puritans and
their descendants, the conquest of the Indians and the wilderness represented the collective achievement of what each individual was enjoined to achieve in himself: the subordination of nature to civilization.[15]

The fraternal metaphor also recalled the replacement of the elder
by the younger sibling. In recounting the history of Plymouth Colony,
John Quincy Adams argued that the displacement of the Indians was
not a cause for blame. The savage Indians had been, he thought, too
long indulged in their unchallenged enjoyment of the sweets of nature.
They must be torn from the breast to make room for the encroaching
whites. The Indian would be removed because he blocked the forward
march of progress, a process both inevitable and right. His birthright,
therefore, was imperfect. "What is the right of a huntsman to the forests of a thousand miles over which he has traversed in search of
prey . . . Shall the exuberant bosom of the common mother amply
adequate to the nourishment of millions, be claimed exclusively by a
few hundred of her offspring?"[16] Unwillingness to relinquish the
breast marked the Indians as both immature and voluptuous.

The Indian, Beverley noted, scarcely needed to labor, while he
lacked the appetite for luxury. Nature provided liberally for the needs
she occasioned. Those who, like the Puritans, regarded labor as productive not merely of necessities but of virtue were thus obliged to
deplore the indolent condition in which they found the Indian. Culling
metaphors from Scripture, as was their wont, they seized upon Jacob
and Esau, rather than Cain and Abel, as emblematic of this fraternal
strife. Like the legendary Indian who signed away Manhattan for a few
blue beads, Esau had consigned his birthright for a mess of pottage.
The legend of Jacob and Esau, Rogin notes, "hardly provided secure
grounding for the justice of white claims." Jacob, however, had the
sanction of God, which was thought to supersede all claims to natural
precedence. "The elder," God had said, "shall serve the younger."
"Jacob," Congressman Richard Wilde echoed, "will forever obtain the
inheritance of Esau." The imputation of duplicity was a small matter
when there was empire in the offing. Jacob had been blessed with the

sovereignty of nations, a trait which made comparison with him in his fraternal dealings even more attractive.[17]

As the parties in the fraternal conflict changed from white and Indian to North and South, North and South alike cast the South in the role of the Indian. The South had been preeminent in the Revolution and the Founding; Southerners retained the agricultural economy which was being altered in the North with the growth of commerce and industry. Thus they appeared to belong to the earlier nation. Southerners argued in the years preceding secession that they had adhered to the ideology of the Revolution and the provisions of the Constitution, while the North had not. They were the legitimate heirs of the Founding. The fraternal relation of white and Indian thus had its constitutional corollary in the relations of North and South.

As God sanctioned the act of Jacob who usurped the right of his elder brother, and Adams the act of the Puritans in their removal of the Indian, so Northern clerics of the Civil War impressed their imprimatur on this latest fratricide, confident that the same Providence which had advanced the annihilation of the Indian would suffer them to deal similarly with the Indian South. Southerners, conscious, perhaps, that they had received not even some poor pottage for the loss of their primacy, recurred to an earlier fratricide:

> Ah, the blood of Abel crieth
> For vengeance from the sod
> 'Tis the brother's hand that's lifted
> In the face of an angry God.[18]

The story of Cain and Abel, like that of Jacob and Esau, records a fratricidal conflict. Southerners, in preferring this conflict as metaphor, likened themselves to Abel, the victim of an unjust and unlooked-for attack.

Unwillingness to relinquish the breast had marked the Indian as at once immature and voluptuous. Similarly, Southerners were pictured as a pampered lot, waited upon by legions of retainers and, more importantly, clinging luxuriously to an indulgent mother.

The conviction that climate influenced the constitutions, and hence the behavior, of a region's inhabitants, had a history at least as ancient as Plato. More recently, Rousseau in his *Social Contract*, Montaigne in his *Essays*, Sprague in his history of New England, and Beverley and Jefferson in their accounts of Virginia had marked the effects of climate on the mores and laws of nations. Voltaire had distinguished between countries where one thought and those where one sweated. Jefferson had placed Virginia in a zone not unfriendly to the former activity. Detractors, picturing the South as immured in the steamy luxuriance of the tropics, could look to his declaration "I feel like an orang-utan"[19] and argue for the latter. All acknowledged that the prevailing temperatures were sufficient to heat the blood. Thus the passionate excess considered characteristic of the Southern temperament was laid to long residence in a balmy climate.

Northerners in antebellum writings and orations seized with alacrity upon Southern descriptions of their section as composed entirely of granite and ice and totally devoid of natural plenty. From such a land, Northerners maintained, life is sustained with difficulty; arduous labor and ingenious contrivance supplant natural plenty as the support of men. Nature smiles on the Southerner, giving him an easy subsistence and precluding the need for labor; she is less indulgent to the North. There, her niggardly provision obliged men to reject dependence on Nature and turn to their own invention and ingenuity. In this way, South and North were demarcated as the provinces of nature and contrivance.

The consequences of maternal cossetting, whether actual or metaphoric, were well established in the literature of the period. In *Guy Rivers, A Tale of Georgia,* the murderer is marked out by his Southern origins. His propensity for mayhem is the result of an indulgent upbringing, replete with maternal caresses. His mother "provoked my passions . . . Did my father reprove my improprieties she petted me and denounced him . . . she made my passions too strong for my government."[20]

Suspicion that the Southern family structure lacked the discipline and order attendant on the institution of active and inviolable paternal authority provided the plot for this antebellum novel. As the title suggests, the dangers attendant on the indulgence of individuals were equally to be found in states. Guy Rivers' tale was a tale of Georgia.

Maternal primacy, in this scheme, fostered passion and violence. This derived from the idea that while maternal authority was natural, the conventional authority of the father was requisite to civilization. The role of the scriptural patriarchs in removing men from the chaotic and immoral obedience to instinct cast further doubt on the desirability of maternal authority.

Guy Rivers, the Indian living in voluptuous proximity to Nature, and the Southerner similarly situated were associated in antebellum political culture with extraordinary acts of private violence. The Indian was a hunter, and in Northern myth a fierce warrior and a cannibal. Daniel Adams' *Geography*, published in Boston in 1820, described Southerners as sharing the Indian's taste for violent entertainment, "dancing, horse-racing, cockfighting and chiefly hunting."[21] They were renowned for dueling. They had perpetuated several infamous assaults on prominent abolitionists and offered rewards for the heads of several more. These lawless acts of violence likened the Southerners to the Indian and invested them with a character thought similarly alien to political life.

The association of this subversive violence with maternal primacy is multifaceted. One aspect derived from the supposedly seditious accounts of the origin of government offered by Tucker, whose secessionist sympathies were well known. In this praise of maternal authority as the origin of political life, Tucker himself had invoked the memory of Pocahontas, "the foster mother" of Virginia.[22]

The story of Pocahontas provided an actual familial connection between living Southerners and the Indians who had preceded them. Elemire Zolla, in his book *The Writer and the Shaman*, remarks upon the appeal of the Pocahontas legend, "The entire Pocahontas episode provided first rate material for the making of a myth . . . It had everything; the element of chivalry, the missionary, the savage, and, given the protagonist's rank of princess, the continuity of royal rule."[23] The Virginian aristocracy had seized on Pocahontas as a vindication of that natural nobility they ascribed to themselves. Proud boasts of descent "from that excellent Princess" Pocahontas distinguished the Blands and Randolphs, and these, through unnumbered intermarriages, had diffused this thin stream of aboriginal blood so thoroughly among their kind that even Thomas Bouldin, who confessed to the House that "I have myself none of their blood,"[24] could nevertheless boast of a cousin named Powhatan.

The legend and the aboriginal ancestry that accompanied it found a place in the mythology of the antebellum South for several reasons. Southerners, especially Virginians, had long desired for themselves certain of the qualities they commonly attributed to the Indians: the beauty and charm Beverley ascribed them, and their unsurpassed fierceness in battle. Captain John Smith had commended "their Magistrates for good commanding, and their people for due subjection and obeying."[25] Pocahontas, in her marriage to John Rolfe, enhanced the claim of the interloping colonists to the land they settled. Herself embedded in nature, she provided the sanction of natural, maternal authority to the descendants of those settlers.

Tucker, who called her "unfortunate," did not regard Pocahontas' escape from her pagan polity as a blessing. Rather, it represented
that declension which followed upon the aggrandizement of government. As sectional divergence increased, and, with it, Southern resentment of their loss of standing in the Union, the history of the
Indians appeared to presage their own. Tucker's suggestion that
Pocahontas was the "guardian angel" and "foster mother" of the colony, evoked sentiments of kinship as well as gratitude.

Antebellum Southerners, particularly secessionists of Tucker's
stripe, likened the history of the Indians to their own. They had lived
with New England, as the Indians had with the English, and they had
suffered from the connection. Pretensions on the part of the North to
moral and technological superiority enhanced the analogy. Southerners on the eve of the war observed their declining population as numbers waxed in the Northern states, and recalled the decimation of the
Indian. The Indians had been a great nation, nourished by the earth's
plenty, wandering where they pleased. Now their neighbors endeavored to expand, confining them by treaty to an increasingly limited
space. They had lost their accustomed primacy.

Nor were Northerners loath to admit the resemblance. Indians
exhibited that quality which they marked as most characteristic of the
South: overweening pride. Southerners, a Connecticut Geography informed Northern children, were "haughty and imperious."[26] The Pilgrims had noted of the Indian, "He will not stick it to say he is all one
with King Charles. He thinks he can blow down castles with his breath
and conquer kingdoms with his conceit."[27]

In the writings of Captain John Smith and his followers, Powhatan is invariably styled "The Great King" or "Emperor." He held
court "with a Majestie I cannot express, nor yet have often seen, either
in Pagan or Christian."[28] This aristocratic hauteur and habit of command was seized by Southerners as appropriate to themselves. Randolph, chastising Northerners for their lack of gumption, exclaimed:
"There was not a man that ever wore a string of wampum, even if he
were the last of his tribe, who would not feel disgraced by such submission . . . There was not an Indian tribe, however reduced, that would
unresistingly suffer what we had endured."[29] An anecdote, perhaps
apocryphal, but current in the antebellum period, illustrates the desire
of Northerners to see both Southerners and Indians put in their place:
Randolph haughtily inquired of a shoemaker-turned-congressman
what he had done with his leather apron. The ingenious tradesman
replied that he had "cut it into moccasins for the barefoot descendants
of Pocahontas." John Quincy Adams's diary is replete with entries in

which he vents his spleen on the arrogant Southerners, deriding their pretensions and wishing for their humiliation, individually and collectively. The early Puritan settlers saw in the Indians all that they had endeavored to repress in themselves. Inhabitants of that disordered nature from which they had endeavored to distinguish themselves, the Indians were ascribed all the ferocity, pride, indolence, and lusty playfulness which the Puritans thought characteristic of man's natural state. To many Americans, however, these attributes were not unattractive.

Southerners delighted in ridiculing the dour religiosity and dry erudition of the "land of steady habits." The values of order and conformity which this epithet suggested were foreign to the South. Rather than envying the epithet, they joined with their Northern critics in recording their fondness for parties and dancing. "No class in our history," one of their descendants proudly affirmed, "has been characterized by a greater eagerness for festivity, for gaiety."[30]

The single remembered Puritan who, like the South, emulated the playfulness of the Indians, celebrated them, and married with them was Thomas Morton. The infamous exemplar of natural apostasy abjured the Puritan ideal of a new Israel carved out of the American wilderness and championed instead the wilderness they endeavored to subdue, seeing in it the promise of a New Arcadia. Consonant with this heretical view he abandoned the Puritan usage, "New Israel," for the milk and honey implicit in his preference for "New Canaan."[31] Like many of the seventeenth- and eighteenth-century Virginians, Morton hoped to effect the regeneration of the human race through the union of pagan Indians and Christian Englishmen. His own descriptions suggest that he had discovered in the New World the very things that the Puritans had fled in the old: pagan philosophy, erotic energy, natural virtue, and physical and intellectual fecundity.

The community at Marrymount offered a place for intercourse among the English and Indians. The infamous "Revells" provided the occasion for a resurrection of the Dionysia of the English countryside, pagan celebrations characterized by the same abandon attributed by the Puritans to the Indians. As Bradford wrote, "They also set up a Maypole, drinking and dancing about it like so many fairies, or furies, rather, and worse practices, as if they had anew revived the feasts of the Roman goddess Flora, or the beastly practices of the mad Bacchanalians."[32] The expulsion of Thomas Morton from Plymouth Colony represents that rejection of sexuality and disorder which continued to distinguish New England. The Revells were particularly threatening to the Puritans.

The momentary escape from convention was anathema to men who believed that obedience to their God, whence came the private and the common weal, entailed the repudiation of man's natural character. Moreover, Morton's Revells were recognized by all parties as a continuation in the New World of the pagan celebrations which had enlivened the English court. This fear of reunion with the culture they had willfully separated themselves from invested the Cavalier and Yankee dialectic with portentous significance.

Ancestors of the Cavaliers had come to the promised land with the notion of improving their circumstances rather than themselves. Unlike the Puritan refugees, they retained an affection for their native land, which they bequeathed to their descendants. They aspired to, rather than disdained, the amorous abandon of the English court. The Virginia aristocracy, formed, as the Blands, Bollings, Randolphs, and Bouldins were, from the intermarriage of English and Indian, presented to the New England mind the possibility of the establishment of the New Canaan rather than the New Israel. American would be not the City on the Hill, but the Merry Mount, offspring of a pagan union. The propagation of the Cavalier type awakened at once fears of an aristocratic feudal order and self-indulgent sexuality.

The South stood in the same relation to the Northern abolitionists as Marrymount had to their Puritan progenitors, and the court of Charles I to the Roundheads. The temporary suspension of law, order, and convention in favor of riotous frolicking, indiscriminate sex, dancing, drinking, and destruction imperiled the covenants on which Puritan society was based. The fragile compacts binding God and man, and men with their compatriots, had succeeded a state characterized by violence and disorder. The practices of Southerners, as New England saw it, threatened a return to that perilous, indeterminate state in which sexes and races mingled unashamedly.

The Cavalier type had an origin more ancient and more interesting than a Southern fondness for the romances of Walter Scott and Bulwer Lytton. It reminded Americans that the cultural disparity of North and South was—in American terms—primordial. It had begun in England. The two sections had been settled by men who differed in class, character, and circumstances, in their manners and in their political allegiance. Both believed that the Northern settlers had been distinguished by an austere religiosity, the Southern settlers by flamboyance in their actions and their dress.

The Cavalier and Yankee dichotomy represented a set of enduring alternatives. The latter entailed the repression of natural desires, the reform of human nature, the transformation and exploitation of external nature, and through these the assimilation of nature to God. The former alternative involved the exercise of will, the cultivation of internal and external nature, and the affirmation of the self. God figured not at all. Cavalier and Indian each represented affirmations of nature, the self, and the subjective, in opposition to convention and objectivity.

BLACKS

The relation of Southern whites to blacks was considerably more complex than that of whites to Indians. Early Southern democratic theorists, among them Jefferson and Randolph, had regarded the blacks as a foreign body within the polity. Thus Jefferson wrote a condemnation of the English king into the Declaration, first for permitting the importation of slaves, then for inciting them to insurrection. Those who acknowledged in the slave the possession of those natural rights common to man feared the time when they would tumble to this self-evident truth and reveal that "manly spirit" which had marked the rebellious Americans of the Revolution. Slaves, resident in the state not in consequence of consent, but rather through force, and without civil rights, could not be regarded as included within the ideological boundaries of the nation while those were determined by consent. Those convinced that all men were endowed with natural rights feared the moment when that might invite their exercise. As Jefferson wrote, "We have the wolf by the ears, and can neither hold him nor let him go."[33]

John Randolph, whose elder brother had manumitted his slaves upon his early death, had been apprised by experience of the difficulties attendant upon emancipation without equality. Richard Randolph's slaves had been adequately provided for by the terms of his will, yet once separated from his governance, and thus from their designated niche in the social order, they had been unable to integrate themselves securely in Virginian society.[34] The settlement which Richard Randolph had left as an instructive example to his fellow planters became a byword for thievery.

Chastened by the example of Israel Hill, John Randolph provided for the emigration of his slaves. His executor diligently purchased land in Western Ohio to provide the freemen with farms. Accounts given by men once slaves in Charlotte County mention the multifarious emotions roused by the departure of this vast procession.

The citizens of Mercer County, Ohio, however, would not let them leave the ferry. John White, Randolph's manservant, whose freedom he had been especially intent on securing, promptly petitioned the Virginia legislature for permission to return, making in addition the novel but entirely appropriate request that he be considered a ward of the state.[35] Certainly the constitutional provision which made a slave, for representational purposes, three-fifths of a man, and granted on that basis additional representation to his state of residence, suggested that the slave belonged not only to his owner but to the state as well.

This provision may have had considerable influence on Calhoun and other theorists of his stripe. In treating population as a measure of representation rather than as regarding the representative as responsible to those constituents who elected him and determined his district, the three-fifths rule granted constitutional sanction to the view that interests rather than individuals were to be represented. The slaves were thus thought to be included within the interests of their white masters.

Efforts to integrate the black slave into the legal and social environment of the South progressed markedly during the first two decades of the nineteenth century. Thomas Hart Benton, who had been instrumental in securing to Missouri slaves the right to a jury trial, contended that Northern pressure for emancipation had abridged this progress. He termed Northern antislavery agitation "fatal outside interference which has checked this progress of Southern slave policy amelioration, and turned back the current which was setting so strongly in favor of mitigating the condition of the slave."[36] The legal status of slaves did not improve during the four years prior to the war. Indeed several Southern states issued strictures governing the purchase and removal of slaves and requiring legislative permission for their emancipation.

In New People, Williams writes that miscegenation followed much the same pattern, tolerated and increasing in frequency until about 1850, when it became anathema.[37] Other methods of social integration increased in extent and intensity. The establishment of domesticity as the paradigm for Southern political life relegated the slaves to inclusion in the plantation household. This method, though it made a troublesome anomaly of free blacks, secured the slaves firmly within Southern society.

Calhoun, in describing sectional divergence, wrote that the North was an aggregate of individuals, the South of communities. The first of these communities was that of the family. The industrialization and urbanization of the Northern states had lent additional political significance to the notion of family in the South. Each of these developments had been distinguished by orators in both sections as contributing to the independence of the individual and the decay of the family.

Antebellum Southerners, Clement Eaton wrote, evinced "an intense local attachment or patriotism that was supported by a strong feeling for family (including blacks and whites.)"[38] Since provision for the slave represented the master's claim to authority over them, their inclusion in his family effected a political vindication of his right, according to the standards of the South. More importantly, regional mores and state law had forged bonds of emotional and economic interdependence between master and slave. "In the Old South," a New Southerner observed, "slaves often considered themselves and were thought of by their owners as part of the latter's family."[39] The forms of address—"Auntie," "Uncle," and "Mammy"—commonly used with slaves were themselves indicative of the extended family concept.

This mode of social integration had, of course, profound ramifications. Southerners extolled the benefits of associations with Christians on the morals and manners of the African. They were more reticent concerning the slaves' effect upon their masters. The cultural exchange was indeed reciprocal. White children raised by blacks imbibed at least as many religious beliefs as they imparted. The effect of an early inculcation in the rudiments of an altered but still alien magic could alter the structures of plantation authority. Slave narratives record the existence of several shaman-figures who exercised an unquestioned authority over white and black. Slave religion influenced Southern Christianity as well.[40]

The familial model also affirmed implicitly the common humanity of slave and free. "The 'traditional' or 'family' view," C. G. Sellers wrote in *The Southerner as American*, "regarded the slave as more person than property."[41] The Louisiana Supreme Court delivered itself of the opinion that "slaves being men, they are to be identified by their proper names."[42] A writer in the *Southern Literary Messenger* went further, affirming in 1856 the "fundamental equality and common humanity of black and white."[43]

Those who held views less extreme were nevertheless inclined to diminish the distinction between slave and freeman in the familial context. Genovese notes that in the plantation of one H. C. Anderson, the word "slave" never found its way into the record.[44] Rather, Anderson referred to slaves as "hands" and called them by name. Slavery was a frequent subject in Southern magazines, but the word "slave" seldom appeared.

The daily relations of free whites and enslaved blacks, though they entailed deference and subordination on the part of the latter, were intensely personal, constrained by local custom and individual preference, and tempered by the bonds born of long acquaintance and the necessity of daily intercourse. Frederick Law Olmsted saw "among the dark gentry the finest French clothes, embroidered waistcoats, patent leather shoes, resplendent brooches, silk hats, kid gloves, and eau de mille fleurs." They were dressed, he reports, "not only expensively, but with good taste."[45]

This was not entirely to Olmsted's taste. Though he advocated abolition with considerable enthusiasm, he favored the argument that it would reduce the "unnatural" intercourse between black and white and provide labor more cheaply for the development of industry. He noted that there was in the demeanor of blacks on Southern streets "no indication of their belonging to a subject race except that they invariably gave way to the white people they met."[46] Southern slaveholders, particularly those of the planter class, did not trouble to distinguish the dress of their household slaves from that which they themselves affected. Contemporary evidence suggests that planters commonly dressed favored slaves as richly as they dressed themselves, reserving distinctions for those who worked in the fields. This enhanced the appearance of a communal identity between the planter class and those slaves with whom they were most intimately associated.

Olmsted's reportage is colored by his inability to attribute any virtue but docility to the slaves he saw. (He does not appear to have met any.) Seeing a black man berate white men in the street for shoving him aside, he assumes that his own presence has emboldened him, and does not hesitate to declare a paragraph later that he has not seen the "slightest evidence of any independent manliness on the part of the negroes."[47]

Southerners noted, with no small puzzlement, the tendency of Northern and foreign travelers, most often abolitionist, to denigrate the capacities of blacks. The reviewer of A. M. Murray's *Letters from the United States, Cuba and Canada* wrote: "It is strange that murdered English is so perversely thrust into a colored gentleman's mouth. . . Negroes, unless babies, use better language than that and are generally ambitiously correct in that respect."[48] There were other qualities, however, which foreigners were quick to mark in the blacks. Black women, Olmsted observed, had "a good deal of that voluptuousness of expression which characterizes many of the women of the South of Europe."[49]

In the Puritan cosmology, tyranny and sexuality were inextricably entangled. This opinion, with its attendant fears, had been passed to the Northerners of the antebellum period. Ronald Walters has described the abolitionists' perception of the South as a hotbed of sexuality. According to Walters, "virtually all abolitionists grounded their objections to the institution in this relationship of utter submission and total dominance between bondsman and master." Theodore Dwight Weld believed arbitrary power to be "the strongest human passion, and the more absolute the power the stronger the desire for it." According to Walters, "The concept of power was coming, by the 1830s, to fit into a new web of association which ensnared some of the deepest and most mysterious forces abolitionists believed to be operating in all men. . . . This included the deepest and the most fearful force of all, human sexuality. For abolitionists the distance was not great from lust to lust for power in which men could indulge their erotic impulses with impunity."[50]

"If blacks are about sex," Leslie Fiedler once asserted, "then Indians are about madness." The first proposition was, he assumed, undeniable. Each of these qualities present an aspect of the natural man, moved not by reason but by instinct, passionate and irrational. Civility, it appears, rises out of the capacity to make distinctions. In reasoning, one categorizes and codifies, distinguishing like and unlike. In civil sex, one is obliged to be discriminate in one's choice of sexual partners. As with dietary restrictions, the occasion and manner in which this natural function is performed enables men to distinguish themselves from their natural environment, and from other nations. The regulation of sexuality is characteristic of political life. It is not surprising, therefore, that a character of unrestrained sexuality was attributed to the black race, which was, Americans insisted, uncivilized and apolitical. Black sexuality, like the madness and violence of the Indian, was a manifestation of their embeddedness in nature, a condition which was not unattractive to many Southerners.

The family has its origin in sexuality. Like the sexual union, it is a form of immediate, natural community. The preeminence of the family in the South appeared in the North as a challenge to the primacy of legal or contractual community. The daily intercourse of black and white in the Southern family suggested the possibility of a more intimate and fundamental union. Each of these possibilities represented a regression from civilization back to nature. Attention to Southern sexuality thus increased with the possibility of rebellion, though increased religiosity and a campaign against particular sexual practices—masturbation, sodomy, miscegenation—which extended below the Mason-

Dixon Line, probably diminished tolerance of sexual deviance in the South. Walters, examining this aspect of abolitionist rhetoric states "At work was a more generalized sense that the South represented a society in which eroticism had no checks put upon it."[51] Walters believes that Northerners' antipathy to perceived Southern sexuality came in consequence of their own internal anxieties. They feared that the unshackled sexual impulses of the South would, like fugitive slaves, find their way northward. In the period from 1830 to 1860, however, evidence of sensuality declined markedly North and South. The *Southern Literary Messenger* began in this period to inveigh against indelicate language and immodest metaphors with at least a modicum of the enthusiasm evinced by Northern journals. The increase in social repression and legal regulation of sexual practices, which is now considered the distinguishing feature of the Victorian period, had produced legislation, a literature, and a change in mores by 1830. Advocates of these increasingly exacting standards of personal purity saw them as a sign of the progress of civilization.

The progress of civilization was, however, associated in the North with the primacy of civility. Thus, in the marriage of Theodore Dwight Weld and Angela Grimké, abstention from sexual intercourse accompanied a common devotion to political activism and social good. This is the culmination of the view, expressed by Freud in *Civilization and Its Discontents,* that sexual union is politically subversive: "The conflict between civilization and sexuality is caused by the circumstance that sexual love is a relationship between two people, in which a third party can only be superfluous or disturbing, whereas civilization is founded on relations between larger groups of persons."[52]

The South had, through the family, broached the alternative notion that sexuality could serve as the animating principle of political life, the source of social cohesion. For all parties, sexuality represented man's immersion in external nature and affirmed man's natural constitution. This, in the Puritan ethic, was tantamount to spiritual suicide. The willful self-excommunication attendant on such forays into nature rendered the person dead in sin. That passionate participation in natural processes and relationships which men experience in sex was anathema to moral reformers as well as to their Puritan forebears.

The ascription of unrestrained sexuality to Southerners by the abolitionists suggested the separation of the South from the Holy Commonwealth. Southerners were undeserving of that great role which God had ordained for the nation. They were thus marked as both disparate and unrighteous. Miscegenation was particularly evocative of the South's alienation from the nation's assigned role in the progress of civilization, for in it both the act and the object indicated the South's desire to embrace the natural. The accusation that miscegenation was rampant in the South was more than merely literal. It implied that the South in its evident desire to leave the Union, leaving its laws and its authority, was likening itself to those blacks within its own borders who were in a similarly prepolitical state. It suggested that the South's alienation was regressive. Thus the accusation increased in frequency in the years immediately prior to 1861, when actual instances of miscegenation declined dramatically. This was not due to ignorance and misinformation in the North. The accusation increased in meaning as its literal truth diminished.

Proximity to the black race, with its unrestrained character of natural sexuality, was certain to corrupt. Articles on the deleterious effects of association with slaves upon the morals, manners, and physical consitutions of young Southerners proliferated. Black women, Louisa Barker wrote, "lured young slaveholders into illicit attachments." Planters so seduced "exemplified the wreck of young manhood always resulting from self-indulgence." Henry Wright, another abolitionist author, declared, "There is not a nation or a tribe of men so steeped in sexual pollution as this." Another wrote, "The Southern States are ONE GREAT SODOM!" Nor could white women escape this "impetuous fountain of pollution"; John Rankin declared: "I could refer you to several instances of slaves actually seducing the daughters of their masters."[53]

Absolute authority, for all its charms, was apparently unable to shackle all the sensuality of "the black race in our bosom." "Not only in taverns," 'Puritan' recounted, "but in boarding houses and the dwellings of individuals, boys and girls on the verge of maturity altogether unclothed wait upon ladies and gentlemen without even exciting even the suffusion of a blush on the faces of young females, who thus become habituated to scenes which delicate and refined Northern women cannot adequately conceive." These household servants, moreover, served not merely to seduce, but to instruct. Among slaves and their mistresses, "the courtesan feats of the overnight are whispered into the ear of the unsuspecting white girl and poison her youthful mind."[54]

Slaveholders, William Lloyd Garrison declared, "seem enamored of amalgamation." George Bourne, in an antislavery tract utilizing a calculation thought more prevalent among Yankees than among its purported practitioners, wrote that the temptation to amalgamation must prove irresistible to Southern planters, for "the vice is a profit-able one." Bourne marked avarice as the fundamental drive of human nature, law the only effective constraint. Other abolitionists argued that amalgamation would "experience, in all probability, a tenfold diminution with emancipation."[55]

Manumission would separate white from black rather than joining them in a single fraternity. Elijah Lovejoy endeavored to enhance the appeal of abolition to racist antiamalgamationists by arguing that "one reason the abolitionists urge the abolition of slavery is that they fully believe that it will put a stop in a great and almost entire measure to that wretched, shameful, and polluted intercourse now so common, it may be said, so universal, in slave states."[56]

War poetry continued the accusation of miscegenation. One author wrote of the "South Carolina Gentleman":

> You trace his genealogy and not far back you'll see
> A most undoubted octoroon, or maybe a mustee
> And if you note the shaggy locks that cluster on his brow
> You'll find that every other hair is varied with a kink that seldom
>   denotes pure Caucasian blood, but on the contrary, betrays an
>   admixture with a race not particularly popular now.[57]

Another poetic offering ran:

> 'Round the matron and the daughters ring chivalric voices high
> Not the meanest soul among them but is sworn to do or die!
> "Never to the Yankee Vandal, foul and hornèd thing of mud,
> Will they leave their maids and matrons while a single vein holds
>   blood
> Perish every Southron sooner! Death? They crave it as a boon!"
> Then each desperate knight retires—to his favorite quadroon[58]

Southerners took a different view of the matter. The editor of the *Southern Literary Messenger*, attending to Harriet Martineau's account of rampant miscegenation in a review of her book, took the writer to task for her naiveté. Acknowledging the justice of the claim that planters occasionally took their slaves as concubines, he noted that "the negro and the colored woman in the South supply the place which in the North is usually filled with factory and serving girls." He advanced the proposition, common among workers, that sexual exploitation accompanies economic exploitation. The objects of lustful exploitation varied sectionally in their color, but not in their condition.

The evil is a dreadful one in both places, but having its good more particularly in the South. The result of illicit intercourse between the differing races is the production of a fine specimen of physical manhood and a better mental organization in the mulatto; and in the progress of a few generations that which would otherwise forever prove a separating wall between white and black—the color of the latter—will be effectually removed, and when the eye ceases to be offended, the mind of the white will no longer be jealous.[59]

He looked to miscegenation as a means for overcoming racial discrimination. Miscegenation figured in the North as yet another "unnatural act" in the repertoire of the decadent Southerner. It was employed, alike by abolitionists and their opponents, as a means for exacerbating rather than assuaging racial hostility. Olmsted, observing white children in the arms of black women, and adults of both races mingling daily in their homes, wrote that constant contact removed a "natural" revulsion to blacks. The Southerner quoted above would certainly have concurred, yet he regarded this as a blessing.

Assimilation of habits, Northern writers intimated, accompanied racial amalgamation. Southerners were enticed into emulation of the manners and morals of those with whom they shared their homes. Both sections attributed to the South a sensuality proportional to the warmth of their climate and their tempers. From the first, Southerners had preferred the ascription of this character to that of "cool calculators," which they fastened on the Yankee. This likened them to the image of the black race, shaped in the warmth of the tropics and colored by the sun. In the antebellum period, however, it suggested in addition a political subjection which the South itself apprehended and deplored.

The familial unity of black and white was enhanced, Endris Thorpe argues, by the political subjection of the South. "In addition to the roles that were played by all, perhaps the slaveowner could view his bondsmen as his adopted children because like them he came to be an 'ugly duckling' who held less than full status where the 'national family' was concerned . . . Did the affection which the owners felt for their bondsmen increase in proportion as their affection for the North and Union declined?"[60]

Certainly rhetorical employment of the family as descriptive of the biracial South increased with alienation from the North. Apprehensions of imminent fraternal strife and separation diminished the perceived integrity of the Union, and the applicability of the familial metaphor in that quarter. The separate character of the South became increasingly evident as debate over the question of slavery intensified. Thus, Southern consciousness of national identity was accompanied by a heightened awareness of the sectional coexistence of two separate races. This encouraged the application of the familial metaphor to the separated South.

This confusion, conjunction, and collision of familial metaphor enriches Southern accounts of family life on the eve of the Civil War. The latter half of the 1850s saw the creation of a small Southern literary genre: recollections of the deaths of slaves. Presented primarily as accounts of the authors' first childish encounter with death, they describe the individual sense of loss at the death of a beloved slave.

A particularly evocative example of this genre is "The Child On Fire," from "Sketches of Southern Life." Here the child's grief at the loss of his black (and female) companion is subordinated to a larger account of the black child's accidental death. The story begins with a praise of the Negroes in the form of a dialogue between several white women seated outside the house. The blacks are praised, not, as might be expected, for their docility, utility, or obedience, but for their innocence and their love of beauty. The central portion of the story describes how a young black girl's clothing catches on fire. Her master, described as a Revolutionary War veteran, comes to her aid, extinguishing the fire by enfolding her in his arms and clasping her against his bosom. His efforts are insufficient. The child dies after revealing her grace and fortitude, very much after the fashion of Little Eva. The final portion of the story concerns the grief of the white child who was her charge. He is introduced to Christianity through parental assurances that he will be reunited with her in heaven.[61]

The Southern preoccupation with the death of slaves on the eve of secession evinces both an apprehension of the demise of the institution and—through the identification of the South with the slave—of the South itself. It would, they feared, go up in flames. The unsuccessful efforts of the master to save the child by embracing it intimates a fear that the constitutional provisions and institutions of the Revolutionary generation had, after a short period of hope (as the child too had in the story) failed. The black race was often described, by North and South alike, as a race in its childhood. Slavery was consequently pictured as a period of temporary dependence, in which the race would develop. The

South was to be mother to the nascent race. The untimely death of the child suggests an abridgment of this development.

The final portion of the story concerns the emotionally charged and morally ambiguous relation of master and slave. It is the black child's death and departure which brings the white to a full understanding of Christianity. The possibility that the abolition of slavery might prove a blessing to the South had long been recognized. The structure of the story also suggests, however, that slavery was morally salutary, teaching children to love something foreign to themselves and thus opening their hearts to the tenets of religion and establishing the basis for political life. In another of these stories, "A Memory of My Childhood," slavery is explicitly credited with teaching love of something outside oneself and thus providing the social impulse requisite to political life.[62]

The pacific virtues of family life, which were thought to describe the relations of black and white in Southern society, were ill suited to war, though they aided in the rhetorical evocation of a peculiarly Southern community. The character of the Indian, like the black, subject but rebellious, offered a mythic persona more suitable to the Rebellion.

There were few Indians remaining in the Southern states. There were many blacks. The recollection of Santo Domingo by John Taylor and his age cohort, and of Gabriel's Rebellion and Nat Turner's uprising by successive generations, had apprised Southerners that blacks were not intrinsically submissive. Nevertheless, they steadfastly refused to ascribe to blacks the savagery which they granted the Indians. The entanglement of particular Southerners in the web of domestic relations with the slaves undoubtedly contributed to their determined protestations of the Negro's pacific character. Planters preferred to attribute the harmony of their households to natural ties of affection and dependence rather than to force.

This explanation of the relative infrequency of slave uprisings was equally attractive to the abolitionists. It enabled them to assuage fears among many Northerners that yet another wave of immigrants—this time black—to the urban North would result in revolution among the laboring classes. The introduction of blacks among the workers would introduce a tractable element into the laboring population. "The Negro race" Theodore Tilton wrote, "is the feminine race of the world." Lydia Maria Child agreed. "The comparison between women and the colored race is striking. Both are characterized by affection more than by intellect, both have a strong development of the religious sentiment; both are exceedingly adhesive in their attachments; both, comparatively speaking, have a tendency to submission, and hence both have been kept in subjection by physical force and regarded rather in the light of property than as individuals."[63] Blacks and women were, like Indians, outside the circle of civil society. The attribution of conventional status to individuals in these two groups, and efforts toward their individual socialization had removed them from the state of nature. Yet they lacked a share in sovereignty, and the law did not recognize them as complete persons. Lydia Maria Child's statement that they were considered "rather in the light of property than as individuals" marks this distinction.

Both of these groups, however, were essential to the Southern family. Their prepolitical character, no less than that of the Indian, was allied to this institution. They were emblematic of the survival of natural community in civil society.

In the South, belief in a natural tendency to submission vitiated rather than invited the use of force. Where subordination was tendered willingly, consent ratified the relation. Thus, the assumption of a tender, yielding nature in women and slaves permitted Southerners to maintain a democratic ideology alongside a hierarchically arranged social order.

The emphasis on development, maturation, and change in the Southern familial model permitted Southerners to employ women and slaves, femininity and blackness, as emblems of nascent nationality as well as present subjection. It colored Northern comparisons of Southerners and women, Southerners and slaves—intended to be wholly derogatory—by suggesting that this present subjection might be followed by maturity and independence. The conjunction of the symbol and the symbolized enervated the oppressed and troubled the oppressor. One man formerly a slave, when asked why he had not rebelled, responded that he had been sure that his people would eventually be free and that his life had been sufficiently comfortable that he had not thought it worth the trouble for himself.[64]

Southern slaveholders, as they likened their condition to that of their slaves, and considered the possibility of rebellion, became fearful of a similar reasoning on the part of those whose condition had been the metaphor for their own.

The relation between black and white, slave and freeman, in Southern life and Southern rhetoric indicates the complex intermingling of institutions and metaphors in political culture. These permitted manifold permutations in the cultural meaning and political behavior of groups within the community.

Slavery was indeed the central issue of the Civil War. Its primacy derived, however, not from the simple opposition of master and slave, liberty and freedom, but from the position of the institution in a larger cultural context. The importance of slavery to the Southern way of life was due less to its economic significance than to that familial form of social organization in which it played so important a role.

WOMEN

The primacy of the maternal metaphor in the political culture of the South, and Southerners' consequent conscious ascription of femininity to themselves, colored prevailing conceptions of woman's natural character, and of her place in society. Motherhood, Thomas Dew affirmed, was the fundamental drive in the constitution of women. Motherhood was the primary political paradigm in the South. In adopting a maternal character, Southerners arrogated certain traits proper to women and made the latter a symbol for themselves.

People characteristically ascribe to their namesakes and surrogates attributes they recognize or desire in themselves. Daniel Hundley, in *Social Relations*, wrote of maternal authority:

> In this her proper sphere, woman wields a power compared to which the lever of Archimedes was nothing more than a flexible blade of grass. It is she who rules the destinies of the world, not man. The raging tornado treads with the tramp of armies along the mountain's sides, uprooting the loftiest cedars in its fury, but there its power ends; while the silent night dews stealing without noise or bluster into the heart of the solidest rock, rend the very mountain itself asunder. So man, though he march with banners flying and the music of fife and drum to the world's end, will always find that there is a power behind the throne greater than the throne itself.[65]

To read this simply as an endorsement of female subordination is to accede unnecessarily to the notion that masculinity is everywhere prized, femininity universally disdained. In the South, femininity was envied. Hundley's panegyric associates man with technology and coercion, "the tramp of armies"; women, with the irresistible authority of nature. The power of woman moved, Thomas Nelson Page wrote, "as unseen, yet as unmistakably, as the power of gravity controls the particles that constitute the earth."[66]

Maternal authority created, as Page's image suggests, a harmonious whole, ordered in accordance with the laws of nature. This mode of authority, and the image of the woman which nature itself had inseparably bound to it, were placed in opposition to formal, constituted authority—that of the throne—and that coercive, military power which inevitably accompanies it. The former, Southern doctrine held, must ultimately prove superior to the latter. The prevailing view of the dichotomy was expressed in a Virginian's poem:

> Who talks of coercion, who dares to deny
> A resolute people the right to be free?
> Let him blot out forever one star from the sky,
> Or curb with his fetter the wave of the sea.[67]

Thomas Dew, in his essay "On the Characteristic Differences between the Sexes and on their Position and Influence in Society" advanced an alternative interpretation of femininity. Retaining, in common with Page and Hundley, the notion that woman is embedded in nature, he abandons the association of woman and order. Woman, for Page, was "all the harmonies."[68] Dew describes her as a creature of caprice, whimsy, and unpredictable destruction. Femininity, he thought, was antithetical not merely to formal, coercive power, but to politics absolutely. "The very intensity of her domestic and social virtues makes her less patriotic than man."[69] Undeniably devoted to community, her allegiance was denied the state. She belonged emphatically to those informal, subjective alliances formed by kinship and volition.

Dew associated woman with informal, natural community. In this concept two views of women meet. The first contended that women derived their dependence, and thus their sociality, from the experience of maternity. Social beings themselves, they were also the means for the introduction of men to community and the prototype for political life. The second view regarded women as irrational in their thought and in their behavior, imperiling politics by the primacy of their domestic concerns and personal allegiances.

This latter view was exemplified by the captivity narratives popular in the antebellum period. These recounted the adventures of settlers captured by Indians. David Haberly writes, "The chief characters in many of the most popular captivity narratives—Eunice Williams, Mary Jemison, Frances Slocum, and Cynthia Ann Parker, for example—were Indianized white women who declined to be redeemed."[70] Women and Indians were similarly embedded in nature. Women, this view held, readily abandoned their conventional restraints for the wild freedom and ferocity of the Indian. Cora, in James Fenimore Cooper's *Last of the Mohicans*, belongs to this species. Her willingness to join with the Indians and abandon the white world to which she belongs only in part imperils the conventions on which that world is based and endangers her associates.

In Cooper's view, and in that of Thomas Dew, women imperil customary relations. They are moved by private loves and hates. Like the Indians, they honor the bonds of kinship and volition. When their kinsmen are harmed they seek revenge mercilessly. The collection of captivity narratives made by John Frost is prefaced with the observation that "affection prompts her daring."[71] This, according to Dew's analysis, made women "like the knight of the twelfth and thirteenth centuries . . . And, strange as it may seem, the political character of women in general bears a close and striking analogy to that of Achilles." Indifferent to the commands of authority, she would inevitably prefer her own to others. "Her individuality," Dew asserts, "is much too strong for the feeling of patriotism." Rather she is moved like Achilles by private loves and hates, pride and vengeance.[72]

This conception of femininity links individuality, domesticity, and a perilous savagery: natural community with natural ferocity. Later Southerners would associate the protection of hearth and home with the demands of an emerging and rebellious patriotism. In 1835, however, patriotism was evinced in obedience to established authority. Dew nevertheless recognized the appeal of this Achillean image for his fellow Southerners and, fascinated, could not forebear elaborating on this aspect of womanhood. Rather than persuading his compatriots to emulate Hector, he contributed to that constellation of attractive associations which encouraged the Southern embrace of femininity.

Dew's delineation of woman affirms her inferiority, yet asserts her superior capacity for religious and familial activities. Thus, though purportedly incapable of statesmanship, women dominated two areas which were thought to be prior in time and authority to political life. In Dew's work as in Hundley's, woman became "the power behind the throne greater than the throne itself." Associated with all the sources of legitimacy—nature, religion, and domestic authority—she became emblematic of legitimation. Dew declared that although (or rather, because) her "inferior strength and sedentary habits confine her within the domestic circle," woman possessed a power which "subdues without effort, and almost creates by mere volition."[73] She possessed this power by virtue of her ability to persuade contending parties and her characteristic willingness to sacrifice herself for her family.

Southerners had long conceived of their role in the Union as exactly this. They had argued for the War of 1812, they recalled, although they were unlikely to profit by it, and they had supported the Compromise of 1820—which Benton called "a Southern measure" and which, he averred, "gave all to the North."[74] Throughout the debates on these and other subjects, Southern representatives had professed their freedom from calculative avarice and their desire to emulate the spirit of self-sacrifice evinced by their fathers.

The identification of these traits simultaneously with the woman and with the Revolutionary generation underscores the communitarian content of the image of the woman. It was the image of the Founders as Mothers which prompted Lincoln to say, in a phrase usually reserved for childbirth, "our fathers brought forth." The old revolutionary of "The Child on Fire" who attempted to save the burning child by clasping it maternally to his bosom was manifesting his Revolutionary spirit. The act was compared to those in which he had faced the cannons of the enemy, not because it was likewise an act of courage, but because the man's assumption of a maternal character recalled his participation in the Revolutionary community.

When Southerners of the secession likened themselves to their rebellious forefathers, they too claimed involvement in a protopolitical community. Maternity provided the definitive paradigm for that species of informal, subjective community. The image of the woman, degraded and disenfranchised, outside the boundaries of formal political life, has commended itself to revolutionaries of disparate cultures as a symbolic apology for their rebellion.[75] The image of the woman thus provided an apt symbol of rebellious community.

It had been a commonplace, prior to secession, to liken the Union to a marriage. The Southern states were regularly ascribed a feminine character, and their names—Virginia, Carolina, Georgia— were commonly given to girl-children. Randolph in an implicit rejection of this metaphoric marital relation, declared that "asking a state to surrender part of her rights is like asking a woman to surrender part of her chastity."[76] John Quincy Adams complained of the "poisoning" of the Union by the inclusion of the South. "The Constitution is a menstruous rag."[77] Adams' disgust suggests that, to men of his tradition, the feminine symbol was at least as despised as the states it symbolized.

In contrast to their Northern counterparts, who characteristically referred to their "fathers," Southern writers referred to their native states as "she" and personified them as mothers. Incidence of this terminology is ubiquitous. A fair notion of the extent of this metaphoric disparity may be arrived at by comparing *War Poetry of the South,* edited by W. Gilmore Simms, with *Poetry Lyrical, Satirical and Narrative of the Civil War*, a collection of Union poetry published in the same year, 1866. Uses of mothers as personifications of community are entirely absent in the latter, while they abound in the former, especially in the most popular songs. Women appear very rarely in any role in Northern poetry. The sole metaphoric uses of women in this volume are the figures of Columbia (in four poems) and Liberty (in one).[78]

Southern personifications of their states as women are most often derived from the maternal metaphor. In this usage—as when Governor Wise of Virginia, dedicating a statue of Washington, called it a memorial raised "by the Mother State to the Father Son"[79]—the image of the mother symbolizes the subjective informal community of the people distinct from the formal machinery of government. This community is prior in authority to constituted government and hence is marked by the absence of legal constraints. Thus Southerners, in addition to personifying liberty as feminine—something of a commonplace in Western revolutionary rhetoric—spoke of her as "Our Mother, Liberty."[80] In this articulation, suited to rebellious and emergent communities, the sentimental and voluntary character of allegiance is emphasized.

The fifth song of a cycle called "Areytos, or Songs of the South," collapses the metaphors of fratricidal conflict and the mother state:

> Sons have forgotten their mothers
> Traitors with foes have allied
> And those that we cherished as brothers
> Shrink in dismay from our side.[81]

This verse follows Tucker's articulation of political genesis, in which the awakening of fraternal sentiment follows the recognition of a common maternity.

Indifference or opposition to the rebellious community of the Confederacy was represented as infidelity to the Mother. Southerners were exhorted to

> Then gird your brave Empress, O heroes with flame
> Flashed up from the sword points that cover her breast
> She is guarded by love and enhaloed by fame
> And never, base foe, shall your footsteps be pressed
> Where her dead martyrs rest.[82]

In this passage the land and the mother are one. The Southern cause is marked as protection of the nurturing mother, especially indeed, of the breast. In undertaking the defense of the mother, the child takes the place of the absent, apotheosized fathers of the Revolutionary generation. The mother-child relation is, like the Christian archetype, characterized by the greatness and absence of the father, and by the mother's virginity.

The passing of the Revolutionary generation left its legitimate heirs in innocent and unchallenged enjoyment of the mother. They, like the Indians John Quincy Adams wished to displace, enjoyed sole possession of "the exuberant bosom of the common mother." They represented the possibility of Oedipus guiltless and satisfied. The third song of the Areytos cycle exemplifies this erotic allegiance:

> Land of true feeling, land forever mine!
> I drink the kisses of her rosy mouth
> And my heart swells as with a draught of wine!
> She brings me blessings of maternal love
> She's mine, forever mine
> Nor will I aught resign.[83]

Invasion threatened to displace the Southerners, depriving them of the mother's breast. It provided them, however, with an opportunity for the active emulation of the Revolutionaries, an assumption of their father's role. Southerners were thus pledged to protect the honor of the motherland. This recapitulated Randolph's likening of feminine chastity to states' rights. The name "Virginia" invited the metaphor. The South's claim that it preserved an ideological purity which Northern exploitation would sully made the rape metaphor particularly apt. Invasion was violation, a metaphor borne out by the vocabulary of military action in which the army thrusts forward to penetrate enemy lines. One Southern poet described the defense of Charleston thus:

> She seizes your deathbolts yet hot from their path
> And hurls back your lightenings and mocks at the fire
> Of your fruitless desire.[84]

The Southern mother was "a thing of passion, strength, and pride," "our Mother, Liberty."[85] Rape was equivalent to coercion, the antithesis of consent. Metaphorically, it suggested the violation of the

South's original, ideological purity, the abridgment of its independence, and the invasion of the land.

Northern states had asserted, in arguments consonant with Southern imagery, that the South, having received a disproportionate share of Mother Nature's bounty should be forced to rectify the imbalance by consenting to the tariff. They recognized, and endeavored to hasten, the erosion of the independence of the several states. Some contended that the nation brought forth by the maternal founders had been marred by the sin of slavery, others that the Constitution of the original regime gave too great a weight to the South in the national councils.

The personification of the South as a threatened virgin mother cast the North in an emphatically masculine and menacing role. Southern poets frequently employed the image of the serpent as descriptive of the Union. John Phelan wrote, "Around your lower limbs and waist / Her deadly coils I see"[86]; Jane Cross wrote "Their poisonous coils around her limbs are cast / She cast them off in pure and holy ire"[87]; and another insisted, "They'll never bear one fatal hour / The Northern serpent's coil."[88]

The symbol of the serpent seemed especially fitting, for it evoked not only the imperiled woman, but also the disruption of the Garden and its fratricidal aftermath. Thus, St. George Tucker wrote:

> How peaceful and blessed was America's soil
> Till betrayed by the guile of the Puritan demon
> That lurks under virtue and springs from its coil
> To fasten its fangs in the lifeblood of freemen.[89]

An anonymous author in the Charleston Mercury employed the serpent image similarly:

> A serpent lie from every mouth
> Coils outward, ever sworn to bless
> Yet through the gardens of the South
> Still spreading evils numberless.[90]

The Union, one Southerner declared, had become "the anaconda's coil." Another wrote:

> The flag which they bear
> Is a snare
> Its stripes writhe like snakes upon the air.[91]

William Gilmore Simms, in a zoologically astonishing metaphor, assured Southerners that they need never fear "the boa's frown."[92]

The serpent, in the biblical account, disrupted the Garden of Eden. The employment of the serpent as a metaphor of the North emphasized the South's agricultural character, contrasted with the industrial cities of the North. Melville, for one, regarded the Northern cause as "the fight for the city," implying "the City on the Hill."[93] Southerners saw instead the urbanization and industrialization of the North, developments which hazarded the South's agricultural economy. The phallic referent of the serpent as sign accords with the fear of conquest and industrialization as the rape of the land, and with the pervasive identification of the North as masculine, the South as feminine.

The Southern veneration of Woman, for all its sincerity, did not then extend to women. As Julie Roy Jeffrey observed: "The Southern veneration of domesticity ran the risk of becoming nothing more than a glorification of female charm and gentility, leaving woman as merely 'the most fascinating being in creation . . . The delight and charm of every circle she moves in.'"[94] The usurpation by Southern planters of feminine qualities and feminine roles reduced woman to mere ornament. Consciousness of her intrinsic merit was indeed too dangerous to be permitted her.

As Randolph had once argued that the education of blacks would necessarily acquaint them with a knowledge of their natural rights, and thus imperil their oppressors, so his imitative half brother, Beverley Tucker, argued that, once educated, a woman "will struggle for supremacy and contend for distinction with her husband."[95] Like blacks, women were a body of resident aliens, foreign to the polity, to be kept in ignorance if they were to be held in peace.

Women existed, like blacks and Indians, outside the formal structures of politics and citizenship. Their status was determined by their natural constitution and their familial roles. Robert Beverley and later writers had declared the Indian to be in the state of nature, and consequently the bearer of qualities associated with that state: violence, indiscriminate sexuality, and the primacy of the family. Women and blacks were similarly described as in a condition prior to politics. Unlike the Indians, however, they had been removed from the state of nature and endowed with all the blessings of civilization. This civilizing process, by removing them from nature, divested them of certain of those traits characteristic of men in their natural state. The first trait to be taken from them was that tendency to private violence which had secured the Indian in independence and pride.

A considerable literature has been devoted to the question of why the slaves did not rebel. It has not yet been deemed appropriate to ask the same of women. Both groups, however, were hampered by isolation from others of their kind. The average slave owner held but two or three slaves. These, working on farms no small distance from each other, and employed in tasks performed independently, had few occasions to foment rebellion. They lacked, moreover, that consciousness of collective grievance and common identity which animates rebellions. Ibn Khaldun, in his study of the North African Bedouin, marked *asabiyya*, ("fellow feeling") as the source of martial spirit among the rebellious disenfranchised.[96] Women and blacks, though conscious of their physical difference, tended to identify themselves and their interests with those of the family with which they were associated. They were slow therefore, to combine with others similarly dependent and disenfranchised.

Civilization thus entailed the loss of a capacity for private vengeance, or violence, one of the three traits associated with the state of nature. The guardianship which purportedly provided shelter and socialization to these individuals of limited capacity undertook the management of all such matters. Of the remaining traits, blacks retained two and women one. Americans continued to ascribe indiscriminate sexuality to the black race. Women, who were more closely circumscribed by social institutions, were divested (insofar as they might be) of this irregular sexuality. Chastity, indeed, was the woman's greatest virtue in civilized society. Rousseau argued that feminine chastity was requisite to the recognition of paternity, and thus to the paternal assumption of parental authority which bottomed the patriarchal family. Certainly the insistence on feminine chastity appears proportionate to the restriction of women to the maternal role and to the dominance of the patriarchal family.[97]

Confining women to the home strengthened the symbolic association of women and domestic institutions. It added a personal and experiential dimension to the feminine metaphor, increasing its intelligibility. Thus alongside the paeans to the woman armed and the all-conquering motherland grew up a forest of domestic symbols in which women were neither armed nor free, but rather protected and dependent.

Both parties to the conflict asserted that the South fought in defense of its "household gods." In the North this recalled the paganism and anticlericalism associated with the Southern Founders. In the South, it suggested the primacy of domestic arrangements in the

Southern social order and the natural sanctity of those institutions. Southern poets declared, "For homes and altars we contend," "For Southern homes we'll fight and die," and appealed, "Your hearth-stones are looking to you for protection." The charms of domestic life are invoked with regularity as an inducement to victory, and expectations of those at home as inducements to valor.[98]

These constant reiterations of Southern domesticity characterized the Union forces as offensive and invasive. Southerners, conversely, were engaged in the obligatory defense of their homes, a duty incumbent on the most pacific.

> Tis not the love of bloody strife
> The horrid sacrifice of life
> But thoughts of mother, sister, wife,
> That stir their manly hearts.[99]

These descriptions of domestic defense also suggested that allegiance to a regime should be insufficient to oblige men to take up arms in its defense. Warfare required a personal grievance; for the Southerner, as for Achilles and the Indian, it had the character of a personal vendetta.

John Frost, in the preface to his collection of *Daring and Heroic Deeds of American Women*, declared, "The heroism of woman is the heroism of the heart. Her deeds of daring and endurance are prompted by affection. While her husband, her children, and other objects of affection are safe, her heroic qualities repose in peace . . . but when the life of husband or child is threatened she throws herself beneath the threatening tomohawk."[100] Just so, Southerners contended, would they rally to the defense of their household gods. Henry Timrod, in "A Cry to Arms," exhorted Southerners appropriately:

> Could you but as your women feel
> And in their spirit march
> A day might see your lines of steel
> Beneath the Victor's arch.[101]

A rebellious spitfire attitude was considered proper for Southern women in the face of the enemy and, according to newspaper accounts on both sides, was frequently exhibited in the closing months of the war.

Prior to the war, William Taylor has observed, Northern and Southern literati had contrasted the character of the effeminate Southern planter with that of the plantation mistress as "Amazon Queen"

attended "by her incipiently Amazonish daughters." Here the portrayal
of Southern impotence in the person of the indolent and dispirited
planter is coupled with an instructive illustration of the force of maternal
authority.[102]

As the South became increasingly alienated from the North and
from the putatively comprehensive boundaries of the Union, the image
of the strong-willed, nurturing woman and the lethargic, disillusioned
man became increasingly frequent. The symbolic effeminacy attributed
to the planter class expressed their sense of effective exclusion from
political power in the Union. They felt themselves to be like women,
disenfranchised and subordinated in the prevailing social and political
order. This image occurs in literature above as well as below the Mason-
Dixon line.

Familiarity with the maternal metaphor as a model for legitimate
authority had added an additional dimension to the meaning of the
planter's effeminacy for Southerners. The figure of the woman recalled
the capacity for maternity, and thus that collective identity on which the
polity was based. Femininity was emblematic of *communitas*. The exhortation of Southern men to rise in defense of the Woman and the
ascription of feminine traits to the Southern male shared a common
derivation. The defense of the Woman represented the Southerner as a
citizen, and it served as an exhortation to the individual to defend the
mother state. The ascription of feminine traits to the Southerner expressed his participation in a common national character, as well as
symbolizing his alienation. With secession in the offing, alienation became the very matter of community. The ascription of feminine traits to
men indicated their proximity to revolution, for it simultaneously indicated their alienation and threatened a return to that natural, antistructural form of community which preceded the establishment of the state.
It affirmed a decisive constitutional difference between themselves and
the men of the North, and it suggested the basis of that disparity.

The abstraction of womanhood and maternity from women and
mothers enabled Southern planters to take these attributes and functions as their own. They had assumed the duties of provision for the
young and dependent—making mothers of themselves—even as they
transferred the simpler daily functions of maternal care from the mother
to surrogates and servants. The apotheosis of maternity was attended by
an equally fervent praise of feminine modesty, which hindered the
demonstration, and even the exercise, of the functions of maternity by
those women whose natural right they were.[103]

Previous decades had seen similar treatment of the Indian. Those who were most ardent in their emulation of Indian violence had endeavored assiduously to remove them. The affirmation of womanhood and maternity was attended by a removal of those qualities Southern planters wished to ascribe to themselves from their natural carriers. The separation of the womanly and the maternal from women and mothers freed these traits to other claimants.

Antebellum apologies for the planter's authority over his slaves depended primarily on the derivation of authority from provision. The slaveholder provided food, shelter, family, and—decisively for some— the blessings of Christian civilization to the dependent African. He acted as a mother to them. Slaves were, like children, deemed as yet unready either to provide for themselves or to assume the duties of citizenship. This supposed racial immaturity subordinated them to the slaveholders. The slaveholders, according to this maternal model, were obliged to provide them with food, shelter, and their other requirements. Ownership, in this scheme, represented the slaveholder's subsumption of the slave. The slave became his property in the Lockean sense, as his body was. The slave became a part of his master. Thus, as the courts did not ask men to testify against themselves, nor wives against their husbands, neither did they ask slaves to testify against their masters. The master's person, as recognized by the polity, included his dependents. The rectitude of this relation was evinced in his provision for them, as if he were indeed satisfying the first law of nature, that of self-preservation.

The maternal model of political relations thus provided an apology for slavery which was consonant with primary social constructs, and which was derived from that agricultural relation on which the constructs themselves were based. The notion that provision is the basis of authority is readily accepted by agriculturalists, for it simultaneously confirms the political value of their profession and their individual independence. It was also in accord with that strain of political philosophy which would confine government to the governance of the corporeal. Like most theories of liberal government, it recognized individual corporeal limits as the primary fact of temporal life and thus as determining the proper limits of political authority.

"The experience of motherhood," Dew had affirmed, "is the fundamental drive in the psychology of all women."[104] In taking on the provident, domestic functions of maternity, the Southern planter acquired the feminine soul. This extended beyond his relations to his slaves to define his role in the larger plantation household. Thus Beverley Tucker could write to his half brother John that though he deeply regretted the loss of their mother, "I have been most gratefully sensible that it has been your study to supplant her loss."[105] The adoption of feminine and maternal traits by the planter class enabled them to annex and liberate the ferocity attributed to women in nature and in defense of the homes from the restrictions imposed upon women themselves in Southern society. It profoundly distanced them from the developing capitalist-industrial society of the North, in which the functions, work places, and characteristics of men and women were being demarcated with unprecedented rigor.

The conquest of the South in the Civil War reduced this metaphoric femininity once again to a symbol of social and political subordination. The Union was restored, this time very much after the fashion of contemporary marriage, with one party in an explicitly inferior role. The image of the woman retained, however, certain residually rebellious associations long after the defeat.

The restoration of the Union gave rise in the postwar popular press to stories and reports of marriages across the contending sides. These, symbolizing the character of the restored House, invariably cast the Southern party in the woman's role. The conduct of the Southern women in the occupied territories had, however, so impressed their kinsmen and their enemies that these stories of national amity were accompanied by an equal number recounting the rejection of Union suitors by the rebellious objects of their affection. These suggested a certain doubt as to the prospects for a union in sentiment and allegiance as well as in law. They may also have reflected the sentiment, commonly expressed among Confederate women after the war, that they were not involved in the surrender, and having never taken up arms, could continue to prosecute their enmities as they had heretofore, without them. From this model sprang postwar literary portrayals of aging Southern matriarchs who maintained an intractable hostility to the Yankees, and the rebellious, entirely unconventional individualism of Scarlett O'Hara.

APPREHENSIONS OF IMPOTENCE:
THE ANTEBELLUM SOUTH REMEMBERS
JOHN RANDOLPH

Obituaries are commonly occasions for recapitulating the life and determining the public significance of the deceased. The author of John Randolph's obituary in the *Taunton Sun* was more tentative. "He was inexplicable in life," he wrote, "and who shall explain him in death?" Heedless of this warning, Southerners in the years following

Randolph's death continued to attempt explanations of his character and circumstances. Moved by the conviction that "no man was ever more truly Southern in feeling than Mr. Randolph,"[106] Southerners produced numerous recollections of Randolph. They were endeavoring to discover in his peculiarity the animating principle of their own.

In recollection, history is re-edited, refined, remade. Each author, and, in time, each generation, determines the salient features of the event or person they recall. In doing so, they indicate the culturally significant features of those phenomena and reconsider their own history.

Recollection is thus recognition, the disguised rethinking of a collective identity. Southern recollections of Randolph, in the twenty-seven years between his death and the South's secession, reveal the changing political culture of the South. As the South became increasingly alienated from the remaining United States, Southerners revised the mythic persona they had created of Randolph to fit their altered image of themselves.

As the South became increasingly conscious of its collective alienation and common sectional culture, Southerners assigned their section, their representatives, and themselves those attributes of liminality which seemed most evocative of their common character and circumstances. Randolph, standing surrogate for the South in its self-examinations, was a particularly apt exemplar of Southern liminality. He was born on the eve of the Revolution. He was descended from Indians. He was orphaned young. He was mad and prophetic, idiosyncratic and a Representative. He was extraordinarily rich, yet he lived in a cabin in the woods. He was not—to look at him—clearly male or female, old or young. He was impotent.

As Southerners became conscious of Southern nationality, they increasingly identified peculiarities of their political constitution with those of Randolph's personal constitution. There was a considerable congruence between those circumstances which seem to have formed him, and those which had formed the South. As Southerners became conscious of their alienation from the Union, they came to fear that political impotence which would necessarily accompany it.

The largest and most influential recollection of Randolph was Garland's immense biography, published in 1850. Garland's work is particularly deserving of the term "recollection," for it was culled in large part from the conversational reminiscences of those who knew Randolph. Garland himself was, as he is careful to note, "educated in Mr. Randolph's district, familiar with all the local associations of that devoted son of the Old Dominion." In his youth, he "often saw him under the most favorable circumstances, both on the hustings and in the Virginia Convention."[107]

In describing Randolph's maiden speech, in opposition to Patrick Henry, Garland is obliged to admit that the speech of nine pages which he has just given as Randolph's was not Randolph's speech at all. "We do not pretend, reader, to give you the language of John Randolph on this occasion; nor are we certain even that the thoughts are his. We have nothing but the faint tradition of fifty years to go upon." Randolph's speech is thus a small reprise not of what Randolph said then but of what he said later, to Virginians fifty years distant. "A prophet was among them," Garland wrote, "and they knew it not."[108]

Garland's Randolph is made to speak of efforts to "awe you, the people, into submission, and to force upon you, by a display of military power, the destructive measures of this vaulting and ambitious administration." He is said to have condemned the harassment of immigrants, the diminution of the rights of the states, and efforts to oblige Americans to accept "a change of masters—New England for Old England—for which I cannot find it in my heart to thank them."[109]

These were volatile issues in Virginia, but more so in 1850 than in 1798. Garland's report distinguished those animosities of Randolph's for which his Southern successors honored him: opposition to the arrogations of the federal government, a jealous defense of the rights of the states and the people, and an old antipathy to governmental coercion and the military as an instrument of official violence. Randolph's opposition was made a pattern for a later generation in similar circumstances.

The mention of New England's bid for sectional primacy reveals the depth of historical recollection in Garland's account of Randolph's speech against Henry. Garland's Randolph is made to profess, as the real Randolph undoubtedly did, a seemly reluctance to debate so venerable a hero of the Revolution. He presents as his apology the tenets of that Revolutionary regime which Henry was so actively engaged in founding: "Has the gentleman forgotten that we owe to him those 'obnoxious principles' as he would now have them? . . . He is alarmed at the rapid growth of the seed which he himself sowed—and he seems disappointed that they fell not by the wayside, but into vigorous and fruitful soil."[110] Randolph was the true defender of the faith. Born into Revolution, and educated in the democratic catechism, he had an ideological purity denied the Founders themselves, hampered by their antecedents. Randolph, Garland thus asserts, was more democratic, more American, than Henry. His dissent came not as innovation, but as a continuance of the Revolution.

In reminding his readers that the dispute between New England and Virginia was not after all a new one, Garland questioned the wisdom of the Founders in uniting them. In placing this in the context of Randolph's reproach to Henry he endeavored to reassure his readers. Dissent was not tantamount to treason. They might contemplate the dissolution of the Union secure in the knowledge that they remained the purest exponents of that ideology on which it was bottomed. Garland completes the project of making Randolph Henry's successor by making him the prophet of secession. "How long are we to wait? Till the chains are fastened upon us and we can no longer help ourselves? But the gentleman says that your course may lead to civil war and where are your resources? I answer him in his own words handed down by tradition of the past generation . . . 'Sir we are not weak if we make use of those means which the God of Nature hath placed in our power.'"[111] Or, as Henry had also said, "If this be treason, make the most of it!" Garland, through Randolph, emphasized that dissent—indeed, rebellion—was within the compass of tradition. In opposing the Alien and Sedition Acts, Virginia had been threatened with invasion. Randolph had recalled an earlier invasion and an earlier resistance. Now the South was menaced again. Garland, in recalling Randolph, recalled the legitimacy of each resistance and—perhaps most importantly—their success. He thus delineated in tradition a pattern of legitimate political action which would permit, or, more precisely, encourage, rebellion.

Garland was thus simultaneously occupied with giving credence to Randolph as an exemplary Southerner, and with establishing through Randolph a recognizable image of the contemporary South. In accordance with the work's polemical intention, Garland began his biography with the South's decline. The initial paragraph recalls the former greatness of the Virginian aristocracy. The second pictures its decline: "At Cawsons scarcely a vestige remained of former magnificence." The decline of Cawsons was the decline of the South. Once one could see "the residences of men of ample fortunes, liberal education, polished manners, refined hospitality, and devoted patriotism. They have all since passed into other hands, some have gone down entirely, and the wild pine and the broom sedge have made such encroachments that a wilderness has grown up in the place of fertile fields."[112] The perception of a lost grandeur was, Garland asserted, an important influence on Randolph and on contemporary Southerners.

There are two kinds of history, Garland observed, "the outward acted history, which is false, and the inner secret history of causes and influences; this alone is true and worth knowing." In order to divide this inner history, he argued, one must look to the psychological constitutions of men and peoples. The meaning of the war was not discoverable from the line of march. Rather, the astute historian looked to "the conditions and circumstances of the people that make war necessary." In endeavoring to discover the character of the Southern people, Garland looked to their landscape.[113]

The natural environment was, he asserted, the source of those "circumstances that gave the first impulse; the influences that first stamp their impress on the plastic clay."[114] Like modern psychoanalytic theorists, Garland regarded childhood experiences as of unparalleled importance in the formation of the individual's psychic constitution. He concerned himself, however, with patterns of behavior derived from climate, political economy, and topography as well as those created in interpersonal relations. Men raised in similar natural environments would, in Garland's understanding, share patterns of behavior developed in response to these. Commonalty was the consequence of common experience. He therefore advanced Randolph's relation to his surroundings as representative of all Southerners.

As Cawsons exemplified the decline of the South, so Randolph's experience reflected that of his fellow Southerners similarly situated. Randolph, however, was self-conscious. Garland quotes his account of a journey to his birthplace forty-one years later. During the trip across the James River, "the days of my boyhood seemed to be renewed; but at the end of my journey I found desolation and the stillness of death."[115] Randolph makes a temporal journey of his spatial one. Distance is transmuted into time, and he observes in the material world the decay he laments in the region's spiritual constitution.

Randolph thus becomes the expositor of Garland's method. "A little insight into the private life of the humblest Roman," Garland wrote, "would be worth all we know of the Punic Wars."[116] His examination of Randolph would supply that to the South. Randolph's capacity for independent self-examination, however, rendered him prophetic. In the self-conscious examination of subjective experience he divined the character and condition of that region in which he was embedded. The region had formed him with his compatriots. His psyche, like that of the humblest Roman, held the template of a common regional constitution. Garland's work was exhortation as well as inquiry. Randolph was not only a man representative of his time and kind; he was a spur to collective self-consciousness. From the examination of subjective experience, Garland affirmed, came the consciousness of regional identity.

Randolph's biography was thus to serve as an articulation of his time. In that time the astute reader could discover, like the man in the child, the lineaments of Southern maturity. Garland did not subscribe to the "great men" theory of history. Rather, his method resembles a primitive form of the notion that ontogeny recapitulates phylogeny. Insight into the character and customs of a citizen reveals the spirit and constitution of the state. He is primarily concerned, therefore, with the temperament, circumstances, education, affections, affinities, antipathies, inheritance, and ancestry—with the private constitution rather than the public doings—of his John Randolph.

Metaphor is thus made the animus of Garland's study. Each ascription of a trait to John Randolph, each articulation of his character, is a conscious act of political identification, the deliberate delineation of a nascent Southern national character.

Randolph's ancestry was that of his native state: the marriage of the English and the Indian. William Randolph, the founder of the line, was an Englishman. He bequeathed to his descendants great wealth and an attachment to things English, with one notable exception. Randolph brought his horses and his books from England; he referred to "Dillworth's Spelling Book . . . not the American edition, but the Royal English Spelling Book."[117] His godsons and nephews were continually exhorted to study the letters of the elder to the younger Pitt, and it was upon this model that Randolph fashioned his politics and his penmanship. In the latter, the *Southern Literary Messenger* observed, "one might see in the characters the admiration of the old country which Mr. Randolph always cherished."[118]

Southerners in the years prior to the war commonly put forward their attachment to things English. The continuance of economic ties to England in the wake of the Revolution had ensured the continuance of cultural exchange. Southerners with interests in England remained apprised of English political and literary developments. Debates in the House of Commons were reprinted in Southern journals alongside installments of English novels. The agrarian South experienced secondhand the problems of industrial Manchester and the trials of the Irish. They did not, however, identify wholly with the English.

The South's relations with the mother country were defined by a well-established cultural paradigm: the putative tradition of loyalist rebellion. Virginia, one Virginian noted in 1837, had been settled by partisans of the English monarchy. Resisting Cromwell to the king's defeat, they had refused to yield, fleeing to "where the spirit of loyalty was strongest," the Old Dominion.[119] This enduring epithet for Virginia itself expressed the paradigm. Virginia, settled by unyielding loyalists, had been the vanguard of the Revolution, but the Revolution, Virginians declared, was a defense of English liberties. America was the child of England, the Americans a people distinguished by the fierce pride and native freedom of the British. Burke had declared "We cannot falsify the pedigree of this fierce people, and persuade them that they are not sprung from a nation in whose veins the blood of freedom circulates."[120]

Extensive Southern interest in Burke during the antebellum period has often been cited as an indication of growing Southern conservatism. Burke, however, had been prominently associated with support for the American Revolution. In speeches for that cause he had liberally employed the rhetoric of rights, characterizing Americans in general, and Southerners in particular, as zealous defenders of the rights of Englishmen.

Complaints against assaults of the integrity of the Constitution, and against arrogations by the federal government of rights reserved to the states and the people, were recollections of this tradition. Southern constitutionalism recalled the Revolutionaries as well as the Cavaliers of the Restoration. The coupled images of Continental and Cavalier, Revolutionary and Restorationist, conflated reaction and rebellion in Southern political culture. The archetypal rebellion which had brought forth the American regime had been advanced as a restoration of English liberties. The Revolutionaries were loyal partisans of legitimate governance.

Southern secessionist sentiment was thus not properly reaction, but reenactment. The image of the Cavalier called up the associated image of the Revolutionary. Strict constructionists of Randolph's stripe were apt examples of this paradigm. They united that loyalty which was ascribed to the Cavalier with an avowed adherence to the fundamental principles of the American regime. Randolph's affectation of English manners and English accoutrements in no way detracted from his American character. That character was secured, however, less by his English than by his Indian ancestry.

The first families of Virginia derived their aristocratic pretensions less from their English than from their Indian blood. William Randolph was a gentleman, but Pocahontas (or Matoacks, as the Blands, in their preservation of her native tongue, preferred) was a princess and a noble savage. John Randolph, in common with his kinsmen, prided himself in his Indian ancestry. He wrote Josiah Quincy, "Like you I feel a veneration for the place of my residence because it never belonged to any but the aboriginal proprietors and my ancestors."[121] Randolph's sympathy contained no small reproach, for in him these two groups were allied. His inheritance, unlike Quincy's, was untainted by guile and coercion. His Indian descent invested him with a semblance of autochthony. His affectation of the suffix "of Roanoke" likewise suggested a derivation from the land.

Like his Indian ancestors, Randolph could claim title to the original boundaries of the nation. He was the elder brother, vested with the birthright, but unwilling to be cheated out of it. Randolph thus represented a legitimacy more ancient than the Cavaliers' and more appropriate to a democratic regime, a natural and irrefragable title.

"The entire Pocahontas episode provided first-rate material for the making of a myth," Elemire Zolla has observed, "The foundations of American empire created a mythological vacuum that Pocahontas's amorous adventure could well have filled." It had "the element of chivalry . . . the savage, not to mention, given the protagonist's rank of princess, the continuity of royal rule."[122] These features, so attractive to the South, had less appeal for Northerners whose culture emphasized Cromwellian Protestantism and antipathy to the violence and frolicsome sexuality which they ascribed to both the Indian and the Southerner. In the South the Pocahontas myth became increasingly expressive of a peculiar sectional culture. The chivalrous conduct in the myth recalled the Cavalier, the rank and marriage of Pocahontas assured the legitimacy of the present residents. As an Indian princess, Pocahontas united a natural, Indian, character of noble savagery and natural virtue with conventional preeminence, reconciling the conflicting demands of Jefferson and an ideology derived from the Enlightenment, with the Cavalier model.

As Southern sentiment for rebellion, which Hobbes called a recurrence to nature, increased, Pocahontas was evoked with increasing frequency. These evocations associated Pocahontas as a sectional symbol with the violent independence considered characteristic of Indians in general. An 1858 edition of the *Southern Literary Messenger* provided an abbreviated catalogue of those traits, in a description of Randolph as "the fiery, impetuous, sarcastic, proud, nobleminded, yet most unhappy descendent of Pocahontas."[123] Randolph, like his section, appeared to James Kirke Paulding "the Englishman and the Indian mixed, the latter assuming the outer, the former the larger part of the inner, man."[124] The Indian symbolized ungoverned nature—violence, irrationality, and independence. Randolph's resemblance to the Indian came in his willful independence, his alienation, and his rage, traits that became increasingly descriptive of the alienated and rebellious South.

Randolph's preeminence in an age which valued oratory illuminates his significance for his contemporaries. His was not mere oratory, it was oral rage. He hunted (Randolph came to Congress dressed for the chase), flayed, and roasted his enemies in the manner characteristic of his aboriginal ancestors. He was Indian, but, more importantly, he evinced the attributes of the Indian: uncontrolled passion, perfect liberty, and immersion in nature.

Randolph's speeches had all the marks of unrestrained idiocy; they were disordered, idiosyncratic, and subjective. It was in moments of undoubted insanity that Randolph spoke best. Thomas Hart Benton recalled these in his reminiscences of thirty years in Congress. "During such periods, he would do and say strange things, but always in his own way, not only method but genius in his fantasies; nothing to bespeak a bad heart, but only exaltation and excitement. The most brilliant talk I ever heard came forth on such occasions—a flow for hours, at one time seven hours—of copious wit and classical allusion, a perfect scattering of diamonds of the mind."[125]

Randolph rarely prepared speeches for Congress. Those he delivered were replete with references to English politics and literature, yet they were thought to derive the felicity of their illustrations from spontaneity, as when Randolph, speaking of the inevitability of gravity, pointed to a leaf as it fell. They had the immediacy which is characteristic of the subjective and the liminal. James Kirke Paulding, recalling Randolph's oratorical employment of Blifil and Black George saw not the Englishman but the Indian: "He makes war like his Indian ancestors, sparing neither sex nor age."[126] Like the Indian, Randolph appeared to be indifferent to conventional distinctions. His loyalties and enmities were his own rather than those of party. He remained like the Indian outside the formal structures of authority. His contemporaries acknowledged it. Calhoun, while president of the Senate, and charged with maintaining order in that body, was reproached for letting Randolph do as he pleased, regardless of the rules. Calhoun responded that those rules had never been applied to Randolph and that he had disregarded them with impunity for over a quarter of a century.

The records of the debates in Congress indicate that in fact Randolph rarely violated parliamentary rules of order. Rather he appears to have been an astute manipulator of these rules, a necessary talent for a man perpetually in opposition. It was nevertheless his disregard for conventional regulation which impressed itself on the memories of his colleagues and their constituents.

Randolph cultivated his eccentricities with his intellect, desiring to preserve himself in his natural singularity, in visible dissent from the prevailing conventions.[127] His affectations were not merely whimsical, however. Rather they revealed a deft, though perhaps unconscious, manipulation of symbolic language. In this way he spoke to his constituency in terms significant to them as men, and in terms derived from their peculiar culture. But despite his conversance with them, he and they alike acknowledged his distinction. In the most comprehensive sense, he represented an individuality which they had abjured.

In an era distinguished, as Tocqueville observed, by mass politics, and a plethora of voluntary associations covering all aspects of political life, Randolph disdained electioneering and professed to consider himself above capricious changes in the sentiments of his constituency. Benton, who boasted that he "detested office-seeking, and office-hunting, and all changes in politics followed by demand for office,"[128] nevertheless managed to control the entire Missouri State Legislature. Randolph held his small band of adherents by personal loyalty and ideological rigor, contracting alliances without regard for considerations beyond the issue at hand. He was, as the Whigs professed but finally failed to be, above politics.

Randolph's alienation was, however, less a consequence of choice than of political development. He had been majority leader in Jefferson's first term and continued to profess allegiance to that Old Republican ideology. The principles of the Revolution of 1800 had, however, fallen like the Seminoles to Andrew Jackson.

Jacksonians, eager to establish an unchallenged title to the nation, determinedly annihilated all that had come before them. The Revolutionaries, no less than the Indians, represented a challenge to their ambition. In Randolph the image of the Indian and the Revolutionary were conjoined. He was, as Dawidoff has described him, a "Child of the Founding."[129] He kept the look of a youth into old age, until he appeared to his contemporaries as "a boy preserved in amber." This made manifest the fate of the Founding.

The principles which Randolph represented were likewise thought incapable of growth or reproduction. His proper nation was that of the Anti-Federalists, small, without a standing army, isolated from the imbroglios of Europe, untaxed, unprotected, unimproved, all but ungoverned and ungovernable. Americans had abandoned that conception of their nationality for one far less iconoclastic, setting their sights on European recognition, national expansion, foreign wars, and internal improvements. Impelled, as emerging nations often are, by the instincts of a burgeoning bureaucracy, and endeavoring to satisfy the aims of office seekers as a buttress to the regime's legitimacy, incumbents expanded the patronage system, increasing the regime's clientele and their personal bases of support. Randolph's ideology was antithetical to rationalization and expansion.

Territorial expansion, the South soon discovered, meant expansion of the powers and machinery of government. The interest of Western states and statesmen in the continued expansion of American territory at once threatened to diminish the influence of the Southern states in national councils and exacerbated sectional conflicts over the slavery issue. The acquisition of territories administered by the federal government and the attendant expansion of the military had strengthened the coercive forces available to the government. As the South found itself increasingly at odds with the federal government, and desirous of resisting further encroachments on state sovereignty, Southern statesmen came increasingly to resent the interests and influence of the West. The West, moreover, had provided the archetype of the coercive executive in Andrew Jackson. The Force Bill established Jackson as a strong executive and set the pattern for the South's apprehension of the use of executive force against them. In Beverley Tucker's predictive novel about the invasion of the South, it is Andrew Jackson's anointed heir who accomplishes the act.

Randolph, it was said, had been buried looking to the West, that he might keep an eye on Henry Clay. Certainly he had seen danger there. In a letter to Josiah Quincy during the War of 1812, Randolph contrasted Western profits from the war with the disinterested patriotism of the South. "Remember," he wrote, "that our daughter Kentucky has been selling her whiskey and meat and meal and horses, and enjoying the chase of her favorite red game, while our only source of supply has been a little stale patriotism."[130] Randolph's reference to red game contains an implicit accusation of cannibalism entirely appropriate to the West, whose inhabitants prided themselves on their extraordinary powers of consumption.

Crockett himself had boasted, "I'll eat any man opposed to Jackson." Randolph's Indian ancestry identified him with those consumed by the West. His ideological ancestors and the manner of living he endeavored to preserve were, like the Indian, doomed to extinction. The Indians represented the childhood of the race, Randolph that of the democracy.

Randolph, now the darling of Libertarians and neo-conservatives, was a notorious radical in his youth. The Federalist press numbered him among the Jacobins. He dated his letters by the French

Revolutionary calendar, retaining an admiration for that endeavor until the efforts of Robespierre and Napoleon had brought it to a disreputable close. In the best revolutionary spirit, he refused, as chairman of the Committee on Foreign Relations, to hold meetings not open to the people, to countenance secret treaties, or to grant blind appropriations. His fall from power was occasioned by anger over the administration's involvement in secret dealings with European governments and Jefferson's reluctance to dismiss cabinet members who had enriched themselves through political corruption. He retained throughout his life a contempt for merchants and capitalists. His adherence to the ideal of the yeoman farmer combined with his haughty demeanor and aristocratic pretensions to bridge the gulf between Jefferson and the Southern planter aristocracy. Each of these successive political generations, and Randolph most emphatically among them, would have scorned the boisterous big business boosterism of their latter-day conservative heirs.

Kirk and contemporary conservatives have attempted to enshrine Randolph among the apostles of order. "He can no more keep order than he can keep silent,"[131] wrote John Quincy Adams. Unrepentantly idiosyncratic in his manners and his habits, Randolph was an appropriately intractable opponent of rationalization. Certain of his own particularity, he defended private right and state sovereignty. A Southerner of a later generation, recalling Randolph's speech "On the Cumberland Road," wrote, "An element of interest in many of his speeches was the singular habit he had of talking about himself, his state, his friends, his private opinions . . . it was egotism, but the wittiest, the most striking of all egotisms." In the next paragraph, the writer praises "the speaker's jealous state-love and pride."[132] The private and political exercise of particularity were intimately associated in antebellum Southern political culture.

"O the orator's joys!" Walt Whitman exclaimed a generation later, "to make the people rage, weep, hate, desire with yourself."[133] The orator embodied the people's passion and inspired them with his own. Randolph, so self-consciously a prefiguration of his state's consumption and decline, represented its rage. When Randolph's repudiation of national policy was first heard in the House, he was regarded as representative not of his state—or his section, whose present mood was better caught by Giles, Troop, Crawford, and Calhoun—but of an ideology whose day had past. His ability to influence national policy derived from the continued legitimacy of that defunct ideology.

Latent rather than extinct, that resistance to formal government first represented by the Anti-Federalists remained a constituent element of American ideology. Whitman recognized it.

> Still though the One I sing
> (One yet of contradictions made), I dedicate to Nationality
> I leave him in revolt, (O latent right of insurrection
> O, quenchless, indispensible fire!)[134]

The latent, minority status of this component prevented it from forming national policy, yet it shaped policy, appropriately, by negation.

As the South became increasingly alienated from the Union and from the North's successfully promulgated national ideology, that resistance represented by Randolph was adopted, albeit belatedly, by his section. Thus while early writings on Randolph emphasized his idiosyncracy, later recollections integrated this very idiosyncracy into a presentation of Randolph as "truly Southern." Alienation, by that time, had become collective rather than particular.

Despite its evident and avowed alienation, the South never regarded itself as wholly without the idea of America, insisting, at the very moment of separation that it upheld the true Constitution. Nor had the South repudiated Randolph in the years between his functions as exception and exemplar. Democracy, in its apotheosis of the individual, allowed for the retention of an anarchic and antipolitical individualism. In America, the images of Patrick Henry challenging the British, of Paul Revere riding alone through the streets of Boston, of Daniel Boone in the wilderness, and all the associated images of rebels and pioneers had established the loner as preeminently American. He evinced the self-conscious enjoyment of a perfect liberty. Randolph's evident irrationality thus enhanced rather than compromised his image as a democratic zealot. His disordered brilliance permitted the operations of Congress to retain the antirational spontaneity characteristic of prepolitical community.

Calhoun, in later years, represented himself as having heard Randolph's speeches as prophecy. Certainly the South Carolinian could have culled from Randolph's Indian visage the remembrance of how easily he and his compatriots had fallen into fratricide. Randolph prefigured both the circumstances of the impending schism and the irrationality which inevitably accompanies national dissolution and regeneration. Thus his self-confessed madness acquired political meaning and lent cultural import to the question of insanity in the disposition of his will.

The extensive journalistic attention to the trial and the willingness of eminent senators and representatives to testify in public hearings to the madness of their deceased colleague were indicative of neither public curiosity nor the deceased's celebrity. Rather they denoted the increasing proximity of that polity to a similarly disordered state and a preoccupation with their impending recurrence to irrationality.

Wrangling over the will was followed by the *Richmond Enquirer*, *Niles' Weekly Register*, and other prominent journals. The first hearings occupied some months. Public interest was renewed in 1845, when the will was again brought into question, and the old depositions recalled. That the central point at issue in the will was the disposition of Randolph's slaves made the trial a still more poignant prefiguration of the conflict his countrymen anticipated. The editor of the *Southern Literary Messenger* recalled in 1858 the establishment of the legal will by the Virginian court as a "triumphant vindication of the Northern slander that no adjudication in favor of freedom is ever made in the South."[135] Randolph's contemporaries, recognizing his liminality, described him with the discordant epithets of divinity and bestiality. His voice was as "the cry of the eagle" or "the music of the celestial spheres."[136] Henry Adams called him "a Virginian St. Michael."[137] His grandfather, John Quincy Adams, had confided to his diary "his constituents are as enamoured of him as Titania was with the asses head of Bottom."[138] He represented to conventional society the possibility of anarchy, that element of spontaneous, subjective insight on which democracy is dependent.

Men outside the polity, Aristotle wrote, are "either beasts or gods." A correspondent for the *Richmond Enquirer*, writing of the Virginia Convention of 1829–30 to the uncertain, inchoate South of 1851, again assigned to Randolph an inhuman and supernatural character. He had an "unearthly appearance." Hearing him, men had "believed he was inspired." "The man was literally petrified who encountered his glance, like him who fixed his eyes on the head of the Gorgon." It was his "magical influence" the correspondent recalled, that enabled him to make the convention the template for a united Virginia.[139]

In the years preceding secession, this remembered affirmation of Virginian nationality acquired a reassuring significance. Randolph's role in it thus offered a pattern for legitimate leadership appropriate to an independent Virginia.

It must be remembered that the persons over whom he exercised such undistinguished control were not mere sycophants or tools in his hand, they were high spirited gentlemen—men of talents and acquirements— the very flower of the Old Dominion. They yielded the supremacy not of any selfish fear or puerile admiration but, as it appeared to us, from the same impulse that enables men in time of difficulty to discover and place at their head the master spirit among them.[140]

Intrinsic to the mythic appeal of Randolph was the fact that prior to the convention Randolph had served in Congress, seen by few Virginians but his own constituents. There he had struggled to maintain the rights of the states and the people. He thus followed the common mythic pattern of the hero laboring in a foreign land, of the leader hidden until the time of need. Moreover, his career, as must be the case where charismatic authority is ascribed, represented a collective experience. His tenure in the federal legislature mirrored that of the state itself in the service of the Union: dedicated to the common interest but not forgetful of the source of foreign authority.

Randolph's mythic persona expressed the emergent Southern nationalism on two planes. His personal attributes indicated the cultural antecedents and parameters of the nascent Southern national character: the Indian, the Revolutionary, the Cavalier, agriculture, politics, and nature. His political thought profoundly influenced the doctrines and adherents of secession. On both planes Randolph represented a challenge to the established order, the spirit of opposition and insurgency.

The employment of Randolph's character by later writers utilized both dimensions. Randolph's private character provided a focus for collective identification, a symbol for that sentiment of subjective commonalty which provides the foundations of nationality. Randolph's irrationality also represented an alternative to the entrepreneurial, ordering spirit of Calhoun and Henry Clay. Consonant as Calhoun and Clay were not, with the romanticism of the secessionist literature, Randolph at once confirmed and assuaged fears that the triumph of materialism stifled the imagination.

Clay, the proponent of the American System, and Calhoun, an early proponent of aggressive nationalism, were, though Southern, tainted by their common roles as champions of capitalism and industry. Clay's reputation in the South was firmly attached to his efforts to maintain the Union and thus could not provide a pattern for leadership in secession. Calhoun, though he abandoned his early advocacy of tariffs and internal improvements, was foreign to that continuous strand in Southern political culture which emphasized the moral and political primacy of agriculture.

Opposition to capitalism had been a commonplace in Southern political culture since the publication of John Taylor's *Arator* in 1806. Capitalists, Taylor wrote, were parasites on the body politic, sponging a luxurious living from the hardworking majority of farmers and mechanics. Industry, he asserted, created "a class of poor and ignorant"[141] dependent on their employers and subject to their will. It invariably culminated in aristocracy, exploitation, and inequality. Jefferson's ideal nation of yeoman farmers was another attempt to avoid the ills of industrialization and urban growth. At the advent of the nineteenth century there had been warnings of peril ahead, but not yet imminent. Southerners a half century later felt the forecast storm upon them. Continued cultural association with England apprised them of the conditions of industrial Manchester and caused them to see in Northern industrialization an immediate threat to the common good and a challenge to that Southern way of life in which agriculture occupied the central place. The Southern response at midcentury to the industrialization of the North drew heavily on earlier sectional disputes. The most important of these was the Yazoo land scandals, which united criticisms of avaricious Northern capitalists with a defense of state and popular sovereignty.

The Yazoo scandals, which dominated Southern politics for over half a century, had provided the adolescent Randolph with an introduction to sectional politics. The controversy arose when a group of speculators, centered in Philadelphia and Boston, obtained title to lands in Western Georgia by the enterprising expedient of buying a majority in the legislature. The Georgians, ignorant of Spinoza's dictum that legislatures, to be honest, must be beyond the means of even the richest men, booted their erstwhile servants out and nullified the contracts. The people had had their revenge. Legislative integrity was demonstrably the result of the vigorous exercise of popular authority.

In the North, however, the issue was represented as endangering the sanctity of contracts, a principle essential to the conduct of business and the Puritan tradition, to the security of the polity and the salvation of separate men. The dispute thus touched first principles in the political cultures of both sections, indicating the cultural origins of that disparity which would culminate in division.[142]

The South saw in Northern objections to the nullification the machinations of capitalism, the inevitably corrupting influence of the avaricious few. The North regarded the Georgian reaction as equally interested, animated not by antipathy to a corruption they refused to acknowledge, but rather by a desire to retain control over expansion to the West.

The effect of this issue in exacerbating the ancestral, now ideological, divergence of North and South has not been adequately noticed. In each section, the land scandals challenged the perceived basis of legitimate authority. The South located legitimacy, as did the North, in popular consent. In the South, however, that popular authority remained active after the establishment of legitimate government. Indeed, the right of the regime to rule, as well as the rectitude of its actions, remained subject to popular scrutiny and vulnerable to popular correction.

This, then, was the seed of Nullification. The word itself recalled the land scandals, for the Georgians had described the annulment of those contracts obtained by bribery in this way. Nullification thus carried the association of popular resistance to Northern avaricious exploitation, in addition to recalling this active exercise of popular authority. It represented not contempt for law but adherence to democratic principles.

Randolph had agitated for early Congressional inquiries into the land scandals. His finest—and most scathing—speeches were given in opposition to those who appeared to have profited from the legal imbroglio surrounding the controversy, or from the original scam.[143] It was in this issue that Randolph distanced himself from Jefferson's administration. Yazoo at once ended his tenure as a national leader and gave a political dimension to his private integrity. His political independence, occasioned by the controversy, expressed the political independence claimed by the state of Georgia, and later by the Southern Confederacy.

Garland's account of "the Yazoo business" closed with a quotation from a contemporary journal, which presented Randolph's political alienation as a prefiguration of the dissolution of American republican government: "It is vain to pretend that republican government can stand if such corruption, and such corrupt men, are suffered to retain all the power which they prostitute, and if men of virtue, honor, talents and integrity are to be made victims of intrigue bottomed on such corruption."[144]

The Yazoo land scandals associated big business with the self-interested manipulation of the federal machinery. They linked state sovereignty with the primacy of popular authority and the maintenance of republican government. In light of the land scandals, Calhoun may rightly be regarded as Randolph's political heir. The Nullification controversy recalled the issues and associations of the land scandals. The tariff appeared as yet another effort on the part of Northern capitalists to use the national government to enrich themselves. Jackson's Force Bill evidently threatened both state sovereignty and republican liberty. Randolph's role provided the paradigm for legitimate political action employed by Calhoun in Nullification.

Calhoun's nullification, and that of the Georgia legislature, had recalled the principles of the Revolution in their rhetorical apologies. The legitimacy of each resistance to the federal government was purportedly derived from the recurrence to a prior authority: that of the people in the states. Secession was based upon a similar recurrence, and similarly recalled the Revolution as the paradigm for legitimate rebellion against constituted authority.

The Yazoo and Nullification controversies added additional dimensions to the Revolutionary paradigm for rebellion. In each case, the controversy was a manifestation of sectional divergence, and the outcome exacerbated doctrinal divergence in the political culture of each section. In the South, these successive assertions of state sovereignty had established the capitalist-industrial character of the North as central to the sectional conflict, and—in light of these sectional disputes—as decisive evidence for the North's corruption. The interested manipulation of governmental machinery by capitalists in the North was increasingly a source of antagonism in sectional disputes.

The capitalist connections of prominent Northern politicians and abolitionists associated them in Southern political culture with personal and political corruption. These connections, moreover, suggested to Southerners that their opponents were moved by economic self-interest rather than by a disinterested concern for the common good. The abolition of slavery would, for example, provide nascent Northern industries with a supply of cheap labor. The much-circulated *Travels* of Frederick Law Olmsted enhanced these suspicions by constantly affirming that workers were more cheaply maintained as freemen than as slaves. Rather than inclining Southern planters to abolition, Olmsted's calculations assured them of their high-minded disdain for calculative avarice and generous provision for their dependents. This enabled Southerners to dismiss Northern arguments for emancipation as instrumental and insincere.

The historical development of the Southern cultural paradigm for the defense of state and popular sovereignty hid the contradictions inherent in the continuance of slavery under a democratic regime. The Yazoo and Nullification controversies had cast the North, and Northern industrialists in particular, as moved entirely by economic self-interest. Tradition dictated that they would play the same role in the present controversy, agitating for abolition merely as a means for securing a weak and dependent labor force.

Northern acceptance, even acclamation, of an industrial economy was tantamount in Southern political culture to acceptance of relations of dependence within an artificial hierarchy. It was not, as far as freedom went, so very different from the peculiar institution. The English experience suggested, moreover, that the depersonalization attendant on industrialization absolved the employer from the obligation to provide for the welfare of the workers. Southern examinations of the slavery question contrasted slavery with the condition of labor in industrial society. The evident exploitation of workers in Northern industrial towns enabled slaveowners to argue that their provision for the slave was superior to the industrialist's provision for the worker. The long-standing association of capitalism with political corruption enabled them to argue that the social consequences of industrialization were worse than those occasioned by slavery. In this way a tradition of political action which had originated in the defense of popular sovereignty and natural rights was transmogrified into a defense of slavery. It went from a "cancer" to a "positive good."[145]

The transformation of Southern attitudes towards slavery simultaneously found expression in Randolph's life and necessitated revisions in his mythic persona. He had been raised, as he himself describes it as "an ardent ami des noirs." His early congressional career had been marked by efforts to eliminate the slave trade. He had said of the institution to his fellow Southerners, "It is a cancer in your face."[146]

Randolph's personal situation reflected the efforts of society at large to integrate the slaves into the community. The family was the model for that integration. Randolph, who had, like Natty Bumppo, "neither wife, nor daughter, nor sister, nor mother to love," had fashioned a makeshift household from his godsons, his nephews, and his slaves. His account books attest to his scrupulous provision for the latter; they are confirmed by the recollections of men formerly slaves in Charlotte County. What was more telling was Randolph's epistolary relations with his slaves. He regarded them as members of his household, knowledgeable in familial lore, to be inquired after and relied upon, not merely for labor, but for information, and companionship.[147]

Randolph's role in this makeshift household was derived from the maternal model. His provision for his slaves was a duty imposed by their relation rather than an act of benevolence, or a shrewd investment. His opposition to the tariffs was based in part on the realization that it would endanger the fragile and entirely artificial structure of the plantation household. The tariffs, Randolph argued, were not merely destructive of the Southern economy, they made advantageous the abandonment of those domestic and natural relations on which that economy was based. The slaveholder, already obliged to increase his cash outlay for purchases on his own behalf, was obliged in addition to pay a higher price for the wool and the salt with which he provisioned his slaves. With the price of keeping slaves thus increased, and the price they fetched in the cotton lands of the Deep South rising steadily, Randolph was under no illusions as to the course which would prove most attractive to an indebted farmer. Slaves, who had been integrated increasingly into the legal and social life of the family and the community, would be reduced in many minds to the status of a commodity.

For Randolph, the sale of slaves was unthinkable. He held to the view that "men cannot have property in men." His antipathy for slave traders was known in all parts of the Union. Whittier, a prominent abolitionist, wrote of Randolph on his death:

> He kept his slaves, yet kept the while
> His reverence for the human
> In the dark vassals of his will
> He saw but man and woman.
>
> No hunter of God's outraged poor
> His Roanoke valley entered
> No trader in the souls of men
> Across his threshold ventured.[148]

The *Southern Literary Messenger,* which gave much press and no small praise to this poem, observed somewhat acerbically, but with undoubted accuracy that "there were others who did not dare enter his Roanoke valley."[149]

By 1858, Southerners had become uncomfortable with the most radical of Randolph's pronouncements. Though they seized upon his will as vindicating Southern slaveholders to the North, they had already felt obliged to revise his historical persona. It was more politic to refer to Randolph's use of the honorific "my fellow slaveholder" than to make much of his manumissions. Accounts of Randolph in late numbers of the *Southern Literary Messenger* and in Garland's biography reveal, however, that the South on the eve of war had not acceded entirely to the "positive good" argument. Rather they read in Randolph sympathy for their present dilemma.

Garland closed his account of Randolph's will with the counsel "Let the reader pause and reflect on these things." Randolph was "a man who would cavil for the nineteenth part of a hair in a matter of sheer right—who would admit no compromise in the Missouri question, and was ready to put everything in hazard in vindication of the rights of the South." His opposition was not a defense of slavery, Garland insisted. "In December following the same man made free and provided for the comfortable maintenance of 300 negro slaves. Is there a man of that majority who voted against him, with all their professed sympathy, who would have done likewise?"[150]

Randolph was a symbol for the South. Secession was "a matter of sheer right." The slavery question had been "commenced and fomented by men who could have no other motive but political ambition and a spirit of aggression." Randolph's liberation of his slaves thus suggested the South's future course, one which, had she been left to "the Constitution and the laws of God and conscience," she would have taken earlier. Thousands, then, Garland averred, "would have followed the example of John Randolph." But "the event had again been put off for another generation." Randolph was nevertheless a prefiguration; the South would see the slaves freed only upon her death.[151]

The South, in recalling Randolph, became increasingly preoccupied with Randolph's own presentiments of the region's decline. It is tempting to see in this a sort of cultural mea culpa. It is more likely, however, that these despondent recollections served simultaneously as caveat and catharsis. Randolph was to be emulated, but his failure was to be avoided. Garland wrote, "He failed to fulfill his destiny and was wretched."[152]

William Taylor's study of sectional stereotypes in antebellum literature traces several Southern types to the recollection of Randolph. First among these were the "Southern Hothead" and the "Southern Hamlet." The former was defined by George Bagby as "a red Indian imprisoned in the fragile body of a consumptive Old Roman," a definition, Taylor notes, which was particularly evocative of Randolph. The Hothead was "an instrument of pure insurgency." Bagby's description suggests that this spiritedness was the result of unrestrained internal nature. This was the symbol of rebellious alienation.[153]

The second of Taylor's Randolph-types was "made to bear the full weight of remembered greatness and suffering . . . They are the consciousness and conscience of the South."[154] Taylor likens this type to Hamlet by reason of its brooding intellect and irresolution. The parallel went further for Southerners.

Hamlet alone sees his father's ghost. The Danish prince, deprived of the succession, is reluctant to take with dispatch the course which would restore, if not the old regime, at least the relationship between mother and child which the usurper of his father's place had disrupted. Southerners similarly acknowledged the passage of the old regime but balked at its replacement by the paternalists of the North. They contended that they alone remained faithful to the Constitution as the Fathers had composed it. For the South, as for Hamlet, the vengeance urged by their fathers' ghosts directs the effort to dislodge the usurper and seize what each regards as his own.

The Southern Hamlet then is the legitimate heir, the symbol of loyalty. The two literary types which Taylor marks as directly derivative of Randolph personify aspects of that paradigm of loyal rebellion which was central to Southern political culture.

The "indolent, conscience-stricken and emasculated"[155] planter is contrasted, in Taylor's articulation, with the amazonian figure of the plantation matriarch. This is not, as Taylor thought, a denigration of the plantation economy, but rather an exhortation to it. While the father's authority was maintained by law, the mother's was evidently natural. Her provision for those dependent upon her granted her authority over them. This provided an apology for the planter's authority over his slaves. Garland's emphasis on Randolph's femininity, coupled with his accounts of Randolph's care for his slaves, makes Randolph an exemplar of the maternal ideal.

Drew Faust has noted in *A Sacred Circle* the prominence of motherless children among the literati of the secession. Tucker and William Gilmore Simms both employed the image of the motherless child in their political discourse. The image of motherlessness symbolized for both men the likely situation of the South, least favored child in a family marked by paternal domination. Secession, recourse to the natural authority of the "Mother States" was the remedy their fears suggested. The victory of "Father Abraham," as a Union recruiting song called Lincoln, made their fears reality.

Political cartoons of the Civil War period illustrate the regularity with which this conflict was represented as a sexual schism. Lincoln was "Father Abraham" in poetry and song, the South was invariably feminine. Graphic representations cast the North—often personified by Lincoln—as masculine, the South as feminine and a mother. This reflected in part the metaphoric representation of invasion as rape, a commonplace in Southern war poetry. The maternal image recalled Southern defenses of the plantation system as legitimated by its provision of nurture to dependents. The image of the woman was contrasted with that character of aggressive, worldly, acquisitiveness entailed in nineteenth-century conceptions of masculinity. It suggested both a natural alienation from formal political organization and the primacy of domesticity in Southern community.

Randolph's sexual ambiguity was thus politically significant in 1851. Garland describes in detail his "rich soprano voice," his "delicacy or effeminacy of complexion," his slender hands, and his resemblance to his mother.[156] Contemporary definitions of effeminacy were not then, as they are now, entirely pejorative, nor did they entail notions of submissiveness. Women, particularly women of Randolph's line, were frequently identified with Indians, like them disenfranchised and capable of forming natural anarchic communities. They exhibited the tenacious personal attachments and the capacity for violence that Dew regarded as likening women to Achilles. They exhibited the Amazonian character Taylor saw in the plantation matriarch. Randolph's earliest memories were of his mother armed.

Randolph's sexual ambiguity, and its attendant suggestion of sterility, was seized upon by his congressional opponents as metaphoric of his ideological obsolescence. When Tristram Burges of Rhode Island taunted Randolph with the assertion that "moral monsters cannot propogate,"[157] it was an attack on his then heterodox, but once fundamentalist, doctrinal principles.

As the South became increasingly disenchanted with the alteration of the Constitution and ideologically distant from the Northern states, Randolph's impotence, with its attendant association of loyalty to the original national ideology, became an ever more evocative representation of his section's loss of political power. He was, it appears, materially barren, ideally fecund.

Impotence has traditionally been regarded, in Western cultures, as a species of effeminacy, a categorization, I believe, which owes less to a misunderstanding of female sexuality than it does to an implicit recognition of the political subjugation of women. Women are indeed impotent, and impotent men, when they come to serve as political symbols, may acquire a correspondingly androgynous character.

The association of recognizably feminine characteristics with the literary types derived from Randolph, and with Randolph himself, emphasizes the South's increasing liminality. Acceptance of this symbolism North and South of the line confirms the extent to which the South had become distanced from the ideological center of the Union. Acceptance of the feminine image in the South indicates acceptance of the ascribed characteristics, and of androgyny.

Rapidly proceeding alterations in the status and circumstances of women throughout American society affected the interpretation and response to the feminine character ascribed to the South. As the social structures of the two sections continued to diverge, the place of women altered as well. Thus the meaning of the metaphor divided North and South.

Three
THE WEST

7 Eater and Eaten in the Primordial West

If we are to see in North and South (as they saw in themselves) thesis and antithesis in apocalyptic struggle, then it is not surprising to see the culturally synthetic West rise with Hegelian inevitability out of their collision.

Westerners did indeed see their section as an amalgam of qualities variously attributed to North and South. This reflects not only the crude demographic observation that the West was settled by immigrants from both sections, but also an early and enduring conception of the West as absorbing all.

This is the period of the West's advent, the overture to its ascendancy. Yet the West will not loom large in these pages. The Civil War was, and remains, the war of North and South. Westerners fought in that war. One might say with justice that Westerners, and the West, won it. Yet the West enters, like America into the First World War, little and late into the narrative.

The Civil War was the culmination of a cultural divergence that long preceded the settlement and acquisition of the West. North and South drew their identities, ideologies, and allegiances from a historical consciousness which extended from the Reformation. Only a portion of this historical narrative figured in the sectional consciousness and the regional identity of the Westerner. Western participation in the cultural conflicts which the war expressed was similarly abbreviated. This disparate involvement in the matter of the war is reflected in the war's mythology, in which the West figures only slightly, and conversely, in Western mythology, where the war is an undiscussed preliminary, or an insignificant adjunct to, the affairs of Daniel Boone, Davy Crockett, Andrew Jackson, the cowboy, the Indian, the Mormon, the pioneer, Buffalo Bill, and the giant giassicus.

This then, is my apology for what I regard as an appropriately abbreviated account of Western political culture. Now, I will offer an

apology for what I do treat. Eating, which may appear as an extraordinarily frivolous inclusion in an abbreviated account, comprises a collection of metaphors and concepts which form the principal cultural
constructs of Western political culture. In it, union and incorporation,
conquest and commerce, meet. It thus elucidates the interdependence
of political economy and political culture. Eating provides an archetypal expression of the mythic process of regeneration through violence,
which Richard Slotkin's admirable study has distinguished as the principal paradigm in the mythology of the frontier.[1] Prominent features of
Western politics—the importance of charismatic authority, the significance of territorial expansion, and the legitimacy of authority obtained
through conquest—also become more intelligible in the context of the
Western preoccupation with consumption, digestion, and elimination.

Analytically, the constellation of eating metaphors provides an
archetypal equivalent to the maternal metaphors employed in the
South. This permits an examination of the political significance of divergent metaphoric strategies.

The comparison of Western with Southern metaphoric strategies
is of particular interest, because both the Southern and Western states
were regarded, and regarded themselves, as liminal to the United
States. Both were only ambiguously included in the Union. Both were
engaged in the conscious and enthusiastic creation and enunciation of
regional identity. Similarities between the two political cultures thus
indicate traits which may be tentatively considered characteristic of
liminality in America.

Western liminality was material rather than abstract, derived
from a physical rather than an ideological distance from the perceived
political center. The West of antebellum America was the nation's outer limit—untutored, uncultured, unbounded; on the make, in the
know, and on the run. The Westerners were a nation of virtuous outlaws, a society of the antisocial.

The West was, manifestly, the nation's frontier, yet, conscious of
the nation's Manifest Destiny, Westerners pushed that frontier ever
outward, constantly extending the Western boundaries of the nation.
As the easternmost states became incorporated in the formal Union,
the territories farther west were settled by Americans, and the region
remained both within and without the formal boundaries of the United
States. Regional ambiguity was further enhanced by continuous disputes over title to the territories. Spain, France, England, and the
Indians disputed with the United States over the boundaries and the
extent of their respective claims.

The cultural status of the region was equally ambiguous. While the inhabitants of some areas hurried with all the resources at their disposal to bring the schools, churches, libraries, lectures, recitals, and reform movements of the settled East to the newly opened West, others fled from the approach of civilization, or endeavored to preserve in their demeanor the uncivil exuberance of the frontier. Many endeavored to do both. Thus Benton, Houston, and Jackson would speak of extending the light of civilization across the Pacific while disdaining a pacific civility in the conduct of state politics or the resolution of personal disputes.[2]

The legendary Westerner was half horse, half alligator, unbounded in his appetites and wanderings, without culture, status, or currency. He possessed in plentitude the attributes which Turner has marked as characteristic of those who stand on the borders of their society. The Westerner in American myth was and remains the frontiersman. He stands between civilization and savagery, sometimes within the law, sometimes outside it, sometimes killing Indians, sometimes becoming one. The one constant in his mythic persona was grandeur. The typical frontiersman boasts of his extraordinary capacity for food and drink, the acreage he has claimed, trapped or traversed, his strength and vocational versatility.

The ambiguous amalgam of animal spirits and divine omnipotence is most marvelously manifest in their extraordinary feats of oral prowess. The Westerner had a "cannibal grin," a grin "like a red hot tommyhawk," an "alligator grin . . . that made em all hold on to their hair for fear it would all fly out." He could "grin down hickory nuts," "grin a hailstorm into sunshine," "grin a wildcat out of countenance." Men and women could "laugh all the bark off a pinetree," and "laugh a horse blind." They had "teeth like nails"; "with his third crop of teeth," one could "do all the family grindin'," and another could "crack walnuts for her grandchildren with her front teeth." One woman had "one of the most universally useful mouths in her face that ever fell to the head of humanity; she could eat victuals with one corner, whistle with the other, and scream with the middle; she could grin with her upper lip and frown all sorts of temptation with the under one."[3]

The mythic Western mouth was modelled on this eternally useful instrument. Grinning, screaming, biting, laughing, and eating, were formidable weapons in the Western arsenal. Grinning and screaming threatened to discommode and outcountenance every enemy from General Louis Papineau to Pukes, congressmen, wildcats, and "bars" (see figure 1). They supplied the Westerners, as the above examples indicate, with sustenance and defense, and preserved them from the vagaries of the weather. It was in eating, however, that the Westerner was the most "astonishin' to all natur."

Davy Crockett boasted that he could "yell like an Indian, fight like a devil, spout like an earthquake, make love like a mad bull, and swallow an Indian whole without choking, if you butter his head and pin his ears back." Skippoweth Branch "lived on the mountains and ate thunder," but Crockett made his breakfast on "stewed Yankee and pork steak, and by way of digestion rinse them down with spike nails and epsom salts." As might be expected, his digestive capacities were equally remarkable; he had "a gizzard like a wasps' nest."[4]

Prodigious feats of consumption are a central feature of Western mythology from Crockett to Paul Bunyan and John Henry. Frontier life, as presented in the *Crockett Almanacs*, was one long meal. The herculean hunting trips of Boone and Crockett were undertaken in search of food; their adventures gained spice from the fact that the hunter was the hunted and might himself provide a meal for bar or Injun. The Westerner could "out-hunt . . . anything in the shape of man or beast from Maine to Louisiana"; when he had the food home he indulged in feasts of Rabelaisian grandeur. Crockett (I include, in figure 2, a picture of this voracious infant) was weaned on whiskey, but as soon as he was weaned he "took to bar's meat in the most rantankerous manner and made it fly without wings." His aunt's pap "war made of rattlesnake brains and maple sap," Judy Coon "sucked forty rattlesnake eggs to give her a sweet breath," and Crockett had a nightly snack of "half a bar's ham, two spare ribs, a load of bread and a quart of whiskey." As if to underline the importance of these oral capacities, Crockett avers that his talent for voracious consumption "war one reason I got to be so good a speechifier and war sent to Congress." Indeed, his relations "when they seed me swaller they declared that I war the flower of the hull family." Several of Crockett's speeches appear in the pages of the *Almanacs*.[5] Crockett also illustrated the oratorical prowess of others (see figure 3).

The preoccupation with oratory was by no means peculiar to the West. Educated men were schooled in elocution and rhetoric through college, and the speeches of Demosthenes, Cicero, Pitt, Burke, and Henry formed an important part of their substantive instruction. There were biographical dictionaries of famous American orators, and speeches on issues of the day were printed in their entirety and circulated in pamphlet form. The length as well as the matter of the speeches acquired importance, as the filibuster became a popular Congressional tactic. The filibuster, then as now, was often associated with Southerners, but it was Thomas Hart Benton, whose speech, as a Westerner, Randolph observed, lasted a day longer than the French Revolution.

The aggressive character of eating, already evident in Crockett's professed consumption of "stewed Yankee and pork steak," is affirmed by accounts of Western fighting (see figures 4 and 5). Menaced by a rival, the Westerner wonders "whether I should eat him with salt or take him in his boots." He announces the challenge, "if you ain't off in no time I'll take off my neckcloth and swallow you whole." Accepted, "I took his knee pan in my mouth and bit clear through to the bone," "caught the slack of his britches in my teeth," or "kept my thumb in his eye and was just about to give it a twist and bring the peeper out like a gooseberry in a spoon," until his opponent confessed "he war chawed up." For those the Westerner couldn't stomach—"I can't condescend to chaw you up for you're no gentleman"—eating provided another mode of punishment: "Do you see what that cow has just let drop? It ar not honey or apple sauce ar it? Now if you don't sit down and eat every atom of it I'll make daylight shine through you."6

In the West, you were what you ate. The Westerner claimed kinship with the cousins he consumed—the alligator, the "bar," the Injun, and the snapping turtle—and obliged those whose intrinsic worth he doubted to consume a substance more appropriate to their constitution. This consumption of commonly uneaten or inedible foods expressed the Westerner's pervasive involvement with nature. All nature fed him. Similarly, his unwillingness to make distinctions in what he consumed distinguished him from civilized men, who evinced their culture and their civility in the selectivity of their diets and the elaborate procedures involved in cooking and consuming them. It is noteworthy that Crockett asserted "I am a gentleman" on the only occasion on which he refused to consume something (someone).

Michael Rogin, in his book *Fathers and Children,* has described the importance of oral aggression in the relations of Jacksonian Americans to the Indians they displaced. Indians were pictured as cannibals. In the *Crockett Almanacs,* an Indian attacks an elderly woman "determined to have a drink of her vital revolutionary sap." Repelled, he "drinks a little warm blood as a renovator." Human flesh is "injun rations." Nor is this view of the Indian peculiar to the *Almanacs.* Madison, in his inaugural speech of 1813, spoke of the eagerness of the Indians to "glut their savage thirst in the blood of the vanquished."7 Thomas McKenney spoke of the Indians' legendary "appetite for blood"; Lewis Cass wrote of a "man-eating society" among the Indians. "One Indian was said to claim at the outbreak of the Creek War that he had got fat eating white people's flesh." Rogin writes succinctly, "Indian rage was oral."[8]

Southerners, who had already secured the Indians in structures which prevented the exercise of the characteristics for which they admired them, identified themselves with the Indians and with Indian traits. In the West, where white primacy was not yet wholly secure, and white title dubious in its novelty, the relation between white and Indian was one of rivalry rather than emulation. Both sections flaunted Indian manners on occasion; both employed Indian tactics. The Southerner claim "I am an Indian," was, however, foreign to the Western genius. The Westerner contested with the Indian for the oral bliss—in the unchallenged enjoyment of the motherland—and the oral rage which he attributed to the Indian character.

Figure 1. "One of Crockett's Infant Children, Grinning Lightning at a Bear." From the Almanac for 1845 (Sinclair Hamilton Collection, no. 1001, Princeton University Library).

Figure 2. "Infant Crockett at the Dinner Table." From Richard Dorson, Davy Crockett: American Comic Legend *(1939).*

Figure 3. "Picture of Harding's Voice." From the Almanac *for 1839 (in* The Oddest of All Odd Volumes, *Sinclair Hamilton Collection, no. 1004, Princeton University Library).*

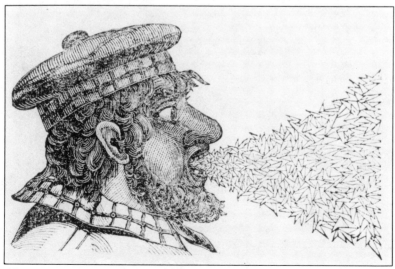

The oral prowess of the Westerner identified him not only with the Indian but with the nation. America, orators claimed, was "a young and growing country,"9 a "great land animal"10 which "expanded through 'swallowing territory' just as an animal eats to grow." Indians, Thomas Hart Benton predicted, would be "swallowed up" in an expanding America. Seen thus, the destruction of the Indians was part of an elegant economy. Jacksonian America, consuming, incorporating,

Figure 4. From the Almanac *for 1840 (in* The Oddest of All Odd Volumes, *Sinclair Hamilton Collection, no. 1004, Princeton University Library).*

growing as it devoured the Indians, ascribed to those defeated the excesses it feared in itself, butchering them for a feast of self-denial. This economy was replicated in policy. The revenue obtained from the sale of public land in the West served to finance the necessary measures for Indian removal from the lands.

Eating metaphors provided a means whereby Westerners expressed their rivalry with the Indians, their identification with the na-

Figure 5. From the Almanac *for 1840 (in* The Oddest of All Odd Volumes, *Sinclair Hamilton Collection, no. 1004, Princeton University Library.)*

tion, the vicissitudes of their condition, and their sense of their own power. The corporeal process which begins with eating provided a paradigm identical in form to the maternal paradigm employed in the South. The sequence of eating/digestion/elimination replaces that of conception/gestation/parturition. The first term in each case is one of containment and incorporation, the second one of transformation, and the third one of creation. The two processes may, however, be readily differentiated. The maternal paradigm expresses containment and nurture, development and individuation. Applied to political development, it represented schematically the maturation, emergence, and independence of a subculture from a position of political subordination.

The paradigm offered by eating, however, maintains the singularity of the eater. Eating is an aggressive act. Whether one looks to psychological interpretations of the sadism of the infant at the breast, or to descriptions in Western culture, the hostility of the act is evident. It is, Rogin writes, "the most primitive form of object relations, absorption by introjection."[11] It is characterized by violence against the incorporated and the consequent growth of the incorporating entity. It is, I believe, the corporeal paradigm which underlies the Western myth of "regeneration through violence" that Richard Slotkin describes. Because the corporeal paradigm is universally accessible, it has been much used, and by the time of the nineteenth-century West, it entailed, or facilitated, a number of additional associations. "Regeneration through violence" recalled, in the Christian context, the Crucifixion and Resurrection of Christ, which was itself a myth (along with the Eleusinian Mysteries) derived from the paradigm of eating and expressed by rituals of consumption.

Eating offered a descriptive paradigm for two of the most important features of Western culture: conquest and commerce. The conjunction of eating metaphors, of eating as a metaphoric activity, and the predominance of commerce in the economy and conquest in the foreign policy of the polity appears in two other political cultures which thus provide comparative examples of the use of this paradigm: the Aztecs and the British. The former case is especially interesting because among the Aztecs conscious elaboration of the paradigm resulted in an elaborate mythic and political structure which was both highly cohesive and self-conscious.[12]

The eater consumes. What he consumes is itself destroyed but contributes in its destruction to the aggrandizement, the growth, of the eater. Western expansion, aggressive and assimilative, followed this pattern. Consumption, in the application of this paradigm, is the model for conquest. Eating also provided a paradigm expressive of industry and commerce. The taking in of external nature, its transformation through man, and its emergence as artificial value, expressed the process operative in the factory, and more broadly, in commercial ventures. The utility of the corporeal model becomes yet more apparent when one considers the terms "incorporation" and "consumption." Corporate law, and the practice of incorporation in America were, in this period, still in their infancy. The creation of fictive corporate bodies and the attribution to them of rights and privileges was a much-questioned, and oft-contested process. Democrats, particularly agrarian democrats, were reluctant to accept the notion of fictive personality and the possession of rights by corporations. Men who adhered to a philosophy of natural rights were particularly incensed at the notion that fictive persons might have contractual rights equal (and, as it happened, ultimately superior) to those of persons by nature. This argument was related, though not identical, to that of persons like Horace Holley, who contended that language in America was "language in earnest,"[13] intimately connected to a material and experiential reality. Both parties contended against the creation of artificial value, arguing that the acceptance of the power of government to accomplish this would result in the creation of an artificial system of valuation which superseded the natural rights, and natural equality, of all men. Several of the most prominent issues in the antebellum period (and for some time thereafter) are compassed within the question of the extent of admissible artificial value.

In the early years of Jacksonian democracy this was expressed in a rigorous opposition to all artificial distinctions, titles, and rank, as precursors of aristocracy. Fears of this sort had actuated the Founders. They were continued in the opposition of early labor movements to arrogations of rank by factory owners and legal privileging of management in fictive corporations.

Monetary issues are relevant here as well. Jacksonian Democrats were distinguished in part by their insistence on "hard money," "a stable, metallic currency," as Jackson and "Old Bullion" Benton advocated. Rogin's study contains an account of Jackson's unconscious association of money and excrement, paper money and diarrhea, eliminating the bank and "cleaning the augean stables."[14] This is quite an elaborate constellation of metaphors. Rogin notes the psychoanalytic view that containment of the feces may represent the child's effort to "keep food, his original link to the mother, inside him." More importantly, the excretory process may represent an imitation of maternal creative power.[15] It is indeed, the inferiority of the product that Jackson attacks in his attacks on "Mother Bank." The bank, then, in its debased imitation of maternity through the creation of artificial value, represented another challenge of the artificial to the natural.

The Jacksonians, in their enthusiasm for eating and excretion, did not however wholly oppose the creation of artificial value. Their position here represents a retreat from their unqualified opposition to artificiality in the definition of persons and the acknowledgment of rights, which had heretofore been marred only by the approbation of a military hierarchy and the artificial devaluation of women and slaves. On the monetary issue, rather than opposing money altogether, Jackson argued for "a material product" rather than the paper money which the banks "spewed forth."[16] This suggests that their opposition to the bank in its creation of artificial value and to the fictive creation of persons and the emergence of a commercial aristocracy was a consistent opposition to the creation of artificial value as an imitation of maternity; that is, in the creation of persons, and not the creation of artificial value as such. This would account for the term "Mother Bank," for their taste for eating metaphors and the transformation of external nature which those metaphors expressed, and for their simultaneous approbation of commercial enterprises and opposition to credit. The paradigm presented in eating enhanced the status of the individual, by making him the conqueror of external nature. When it was used to create fictive persons, however, in imitation of the maternal paradigm (which it formally replicated), it reduced men to the status of their own conquered creations.

The conceptual links between commerce and conquest in the eating paradigm are especially interesting because the connection between the two in political economy is equally well developed: trading expeditions, settlement, or speculation in land locate new sources for raw materials and markets. These discoveries may make conquest of the territories desirable. They will commonly enhance military involvement in the area, through the provision of protection to expedition and/or settlement. Adversarial commercial relations enhance international hostility and increase the likelihood of war. It is interesting to observe, in this connection, that the debates in Congress prior to the War of 1812 and the Mexican War most often revolved around commercial issues: the attempted restriction of American trade by Britain and France, the expected effects of war on commerce and industry, and disputes over the size and manner of recompense for private claims against Mexico. These issues—conquest, commerce, manufacturing, hard money, and incorporation—were by no means confined to the West. Sectional divergence on these issues was reflected in the divergent use of metaphors of consumption.

New Englanders were ambivalent, rejoicing daily in the fruits of their industry and enterprise, but anxious that an accompanying materialism would divest New England of that spiritual and intellectual heritage which it regarded as equally constitutive of its sectional identity. Priding themselves on the virtues of their thrift, industry, and productiveness, New Englanders deprecated consumption, apparently attempting to excrete without eating.

Yankees went into the wilderness with the enthusiasm of evangelists, encouraging consumption (of their products), and spurring that infant leviathan which eats land to grow. They recalled, however, the apprehensions of their ancestors. Migrant Yankees came not as a community to carve out a refuge in the wilderness but as individuals to be, many feared, swallowed up within it. This fears stands proxy for another. New England, lacking the fantasies of individual omnipotence which emboldened the West, saw in individuation the dangers of alienation and impotence. Apprehensions over territorial expansion expressed fears that the attendant political and social expansion would result in the diminution, and, eventually, the dissolution, of the culturally distinct New England character. This fear was twofold. It reflected a simple fear that the large and perhaps ultimately more populous West would come to outweigh the Northeast in national councils. Because the Western democracy, and Andrew Jackson in particular, were associated with the extension of the suffrage, this fear came to be associated with that of being outweighed in their own section, by demographic sectors likely to be sympathetic to the political tenets popular in the West. Both of these apprehensions were accurate. Their prevalence in New England, particularly among the literati, give them considerable cultural currency.

Robert Bone's interpretation of Irving's "Headless Horseman" illuminates New England's ambivalence toward consumption. The legend pits Ichabod Crane against Brom Bones for the hand of Katrina van Tassel. Bone writes, "Brom is the embodiment of the Hessian spirit of mercenary values that threaten to engulf the imagination." Ichabod represents old New England, characterized by intellect, imagination and indecision; he is "overwhelmed by materialism, but at an awesome price to society, for in order to conquer, the Hessian must throw away his head." The discovery of the pumpkin the next day is, Bone declares, the final blow. "The organ of thought, intellect and imagination has become an edible. The forces of thought have yielded to the forces of digestion." Irving's story illustrates "a central theme in our national letters, the pressure of commodities on the American imagination."[17]

In the antebellum era, consumption was indulgence, aggrandizement, and disease. The nineteenth-century "white plague" of tuberculosis was colloquially referred to as "consumption." It spread with the rapidity of industrialization and the developing capitalist economy, afflicting those most hostile to the spirit of the Gilded Age: artists, intellectuals, poets, and the poor. The elaborate constellation of myths and metaphors which grew up around literary treatments of the disease reflects the continuing American ambivalence toward consumption. In the Jacksonian period, the use of individual infirmities to represent societal decline commonly took an earthier form. Letters and speeches of prominent politicians (among them John Quincy Adams, Jackson, Randolph, Clay, and Crockett) describe the defective workings of their bowels in a detail astonishing to the contemporary eye. Frequently the symptoms described coincide with the author's political position. Thus Jackson, combatting the retention of funds by the bank, reports his inability to contain the Freudian equivalent, having "upwards of twenty passages in twelve hours."[18] Randolph, opposing the increase of manufacturing, reports that whatever he consumes emerges unaltered.

Southerners disdained New England's culture of consumption and production, frequently intimating that this vulgar preoccupation with the material indicated a lack of innate nobility. These intimations, expressing what New Englanders most feared in themselves, annoyed them prodigiously. Southerners preferred to express their ambitions in other metaphors. though all sections employed food metaphors equally in debate. Josiah Quincy (of Massachusetts) referred to one measure as "the cold meat of the palace . . . hashed and served up to us piping hot from our committee room." Randolph (of Virginia) referred to the same measure as "a dose of chicken soup, to be taken six months hence." Quincy appears to have been the master of the congressional food metaphor predicting, in appropriate terms, a bill's passage through Congress "falling soon to native oblivion in the jakes."[19] A cartoon published in 1835 shows Andrew Jackson as the entrée, "roasting, as they say in Massachusetts." "In South Carolina," another onlooker observes, "we call it barbecue, only he wants a little more basting."[20]

The Westerner has been pictured in American national mythology as a man scornful of conventional status, a loner. It is a mistake to regard these attributes as entailing a repudiation of commerce, or of money. Rather, one should recall the significance of cattle drives, enormous ranches, and the gold rush in Western myth. Slotkin presents an analysis of the careers of 446 mountain men which shows that, of those who survived, all adopted civilized careers. From this Slotkin concludes that "the Mountain Man was not an alternative to the money and status religion of Jacksonian America, but an extreme expression of its values." He would have done better to demonstrate not that the mountain men returned to a community they had momentarily abandoned, but that the occupation manifested, as his conclusion asserts, the central values of Jacksonian America.[21]

The mountain men were attempting to wring money from the exploitation of nature. Like the nation, they moved steadily westward, everywhere endeavoring to convert natural resources into cold cash. Westerners distinguished themselves from their compatriots by preferring to aggrandize themselves in "quantifiable indicators," material goods, particularly objects not too far removed from nature. Slotkin's examination of the Crockett myth focuses on Crockett's passion for accumulation—of lands, votes, bears, wives; "Sheer quantity comes to delight the Colonel."[22] The Westerner, like the Yankee, preferred objective, material proofs of merit to the elusive satisfactions of honor.

The eating paradigm provided for accommodation with the Northeast in several ways. The endorsement of commerce and industry was perhaps the most important. This cultural rapprochement was expressed in several strategic alliances. The increase in European immigration, which will be discussed in greater detail later, was received by Yankee industrialists and Western speculators in land with enthusiasm, for each saw in it opportunities for profit. New England, initially wary of national expansion, came to endorse enthusiastically the internal improvements which made it possible. Westerners, regarding the nation as a "great land animal," a single organic entity, held an opinion of the nation, which like the covenantal model that had primacy in New England, emphasized its unity and mandated its extension. The same conception of unity made both sections advocates of the rapid assimilation of culturally diverse groups. Though they employed types of violence (informal individual, formal individual, and informal collective) abhorrent to New Englanders, the desirability of conquest and this unitary conception of the nation made Westerners enthusiastic advocates of formal collective violence and a standing army, that unparalleled sign of order. The conquest of nature through transformation, especially transformation through men into money, similarly united the Yankee and the Westerner. Both sections held the wilderness to be not an idyllic state of nature, but a realm of primitive cruelty in which individuals might be swallowed up. Both regarded it as a resource to be exploited rather than cultivated, something to be itself consumed. Each endeavored to convert the matter of the wilderness into something given its shape and value by man. Thus, while Westerners rightly regarded their sectional culture as an amalgam of Northern and Southern traits, the political and economic positions which accompanied their root paradigm finally inclined the West to the North in an affirmation of Union, an advocacy of capitalism, and an approbation of that military discipline which is the basis of routinization.[23]

Four
THE REBELLION

8 The Meaning of Slavery in Antebellum American Culture

Lincoln, in that reconsideration of the war which constituted the greater part of the Second Inaugural Address, asserted of slavery, "All knew that this interest was somehow the cause of the war." Jefferson Davis said, "We are not fighting for slavery, we are fighting for independence."[1]

Certain Southern politicians, journalists and literati did affirm that slavery was a positive good, yet mentions of the preservation of slavery as an object of the Rebellion are conspicuously absent from the writings and pronouncements of the Southern leadership.[2] The two most prominent of the Southern leaders, Lee and Davis, had freed their slaves prior to secession and confederation. Each affirmed that slavery, while it might have been the occasion, was not the cause of the war. Davis, in his account of the *Rise and Fall of the Confederate Government*, argued that "the dominant idea" which impelled the North to war was "sectional aggrandizement" rather than opposition to slavery.[3] Popular writings echo this assertion. Mentions of blacks are themselves rare in Southern war poetry. When they occur it is as incidental mentions of family retainers, without evidence of either rancor or apology. The 36th and 60th Regiments of the Army of the Valley of Virginia, when news of Lee's surrender came, issued a proclamation proclaiming that they had fought "for the sovereign right of self-government,"[4] not for slavery. A generation later one of the surviving veterans would recall, "We did not go to war for slavery," but "to save the Constitution as we read it, and to save ourselves and our form of government." He recognized, however, that "slavery was interwoven with the causes and intensified the bitterness of the war."[5]

If, as Lincoln argued, the North opposed and the South supported slavery, one might expect that the popular press in the North would reflect this, securing to themselves and their army the legitimacy which naturally attaches to "fighting for liberty" in an American context. They did not. Mentions of blacks, rare in the Southern press, appear with regularity in that of the North. They appear in radically different contexts, with contradictory polemical intentions. On this issue, in the war years, Northern society was divided into clearly demarcated parties. In the abolitionist press the black man was "a man and a brother," lower perhaps in the "Great School of Providence," requiring paternal care and missionary attentions, but nonetheless comprehended in an emerging consciousness of universal humanity. Certain of the more radical productions of the abolitionists had portrayed themselves as united with blacks in a common struggle for freedom.[6] The majority however, portrayed blacks as victims, and themselves as practitioners of an unusually militant form of philanthropy. This reflected both the paternal mode of political organization familiar to Northern political culture and the importance of philanthropy as a form of social activism and a method of channeling and restraining popular participation. This, the dominant strain in the abolition movement, was also free from the imputation of free love and leveling which attached to certain of the utopian communities that supported the more radical abolitionists. It prospered because it was congenial both to traditional paradigms for political action extant in the political culture and to that already-organized elite of capitalists, clerics, and social activists who were endeavoring to reform and restructure public policy and social institutions. Thus, the antislavery movement was able to profit from existing organizational arrangements, greatly increasing its capacity to influence party politics and legislative policy.

This capacity for efficient political action was, however, not without cost for the culture as a whole. That narrowing of the abolitionist movement's partisan appeal—which won it the critical support of philanthropic capitalists and capitalist clerics—alienated workers, the Irish, and Democrats in large numbers. During the course of the war, as Lincoln moved steadily toward abolition, the narrow base of the abolition movement provided a source of increasing tension between already-alienated classes.

The publication of the Emancipation Proclamation produced a fierce racist response throughout the North and East. Draft riots throughout the loyal states, which had as their primary animus the growing apprehension that the war was to be borne by workers and Democrats in the interest of capital and a Republican administration, were debased by fierce attacks on blacks. During the New York draft riots, a "colored orphan's asylum" was burned along with the offices of provost marshals; blacks were beaten, shot, and hung, and their corpses mutilated. Many others were beaten, harassed, and driven from their homes. *The Report of the Committee of Merchants for the Relief of Colored People Suffering from the Race Riots* told of over 5,000 blacks who had fled the city, taking refuge in the swamps, woods, and farms surrounding it.[7] This report gave an extensive account of atrocities committed against blacks, supported by eyewitness testimony. This testimony exhibits aspects of that complex of factors which affected racial relations and white support of the war effort.

Witnesses reported that street railroads refused blacks permission to ride and that black men were prevented by workers in certain occupations from entering their precincts. "So determined and bitter is the feeling of longshoremen against negroes that none of the latter dare show themselves upon the docks."[8] One black man was beaten though "his persecutors did not know him or entertain any animosity against him beyond the fact that he was a black man and a laborer on the docks, which they consider their own peculiar field of labor."[9]

This animosity was an expression not, as the report implies, of unalloyed racism, but rather of racism fueled by class conflict. The merchants who had formed the committee had some weeks earlier employed the blacks they now aided as strikebreakers. Thus the railroad conductors and longshoremen who refused blacks entry into areas under their immediate control expressed not merely racism, but also sympathy and solidarity with their fellow workers.

The abolitionist and nativist movements of the antebellum period had done considerable damage to relations between black and white workers. The black communities of New York and Philadelphia were substantial even in the first quarter of the century and had lived in these cities relatively unmolested, though they were subject to extensive social and legal discrimination. Early labor movements, notably those of women in the textile mills, had expressed support for abolition. After 1830, however, labor became increasingly unsympathetic to blacks, and blacks became frequent victims of violence in labor riots. There were numerous reasons for this. Increasing black and white immigration to Northern urban areas had increased competition for jobs. Patterns of segregation in housing, established early, had been maintained. These, and the increased cultural disparity between black and white workers (as the latter group came to be dominated by Irish immigrants), created substantial obstacles to interracial labor activism.

The intimate relation between abolition and nativism further alienated white from black workers. The presence of prominent capitalists in the abolition movement and the outspoken support of the movement's leaders for capital might have been sufficient to repel many workers, but their animosities were greatly exacerbated by the alliance between nativists and abolition. Some, like the Beechers and George Bourne, were leaders in both movements. Nearly all (for example, Parker, Channing, Emerson, and Weld) voiced nativist sentiments in the course of their careers. The movements shared members, leadership, and the forum provided by the churches. Thus, philanthropy of the sort represented by the Committee of Merchants for the Relief of Colored People appeared to Irish immigrants merely as an opportune alliance between a group in competition with them and their capitalist employers. They recognized that the social subjection of blacks was well established, and belief in black inferiority so widespread, that philanthropic aid to blacks remained a species of charity which would do little to improve either the circumstances or status of blacks. It would, however, enable economic elites to resist pressure from predominantly white labor organizations. In addition, by nominally championing blacks, capitalists could successfully counter political challenges which charged them with aristocratic ambition.

The Democratic Party of the first half of the nineteenth century had employed a rhetoric in economic matters which modern partisans would find uncomfortably revolutionary. Recognizing the inherent enmity between capital and labor, it declared the Democratic Party to be the party "of the masses," and pledged to eradicate radical disparities in both status and wealth. The workingmen's parties of the period pursued these ends with still greater alacrity. Equality was the shibboleth of those parties which sought and obtained the bulk of working-class support, and natural rights the justification of their claims. During these years, Democratic attacks on capitalists emphasized their efforts to obtain "special privileges"—political, social and economic—and castigated them as having evidently abandoned the necessary American commitment to liberty and "inalienable rights" which would properly eventuate in economic equality. Because this charge placed their fundamental conformity to American standards for political legitimacy very much in question, it was extremely damaging to the Whigs, and for a time held capitalist domination of American political institutions in check.[10]

The rise of the abolition movement and the involvement of the capitalist class in projects to aid blacks made this charge much less effective. Through these activities, those who were evidently engaged in promoting a social hierarchy derived from industrial relations and from wealth could nevertheless claim a profound commitment to equality and freedom and active involvement in extending these. As the Civil War was transformed from a war over the Union to a war over slavery, Democratic opposition to the war became increasingly destructive of the party's claimed commitment to freedom and equality. The attrition of their legitimacy had begun with the party's strength in the South, and among slaveholders. It was a just and damaging attack. Unfortunately, the consequent rise of the Republican party, and the establishment of capitalism as an essential part of American ideology, was not conducive to the extension of equality.

The report issued by the committee of merchants portrayed the rioters as maniac racists. The detailed accounts of the atrocities committed against blacks demonstrates that racial hostility had indeed reached unprecedented levels. They obscure, however, the stated grievances of the rioters and the character of the riot. Rather than a collective attack of the larger class of white, heavily Irish Catholic workers on a smaller, peaceful population of poor blacks, the riots were a massive and violent rejection of the war—especially of the draft and commutation—as the ultimate example of the exploitation of labor in the service of capital. The rioters were met by well-armed and well-organized troops, and the casualties they suffered were by all accounts ten times greater than those they inflicted. More importantly, the statements issued and pamphlets circulated in support of the riots mention blacks not at all, indicating that the attacks on them were not compassed in the objects of the riots. The inexcusable cruelties inflicted on blacks were used by those who put down the riots to distract the eye from their own malfeasance. Thus the merchants' report attributes the flight of hundreds of blacks from the city solely to the depredations of the rioters, without mentioning the terror caused by large bodies of troops firing at random down crowded streets. The draft and the war continued to serve the interests of capital against labor, while Lincoln and the merchants of the city enhanced their claim to act as the champions of liberty and equality despite their continued, institutionalized oppression of blacks and lower-class whites.

The commitment to blacks evinced by the Republicans was, like that of the Whigs, tenuous and incomplete. Both parties accepted the idea of a society characterized by economic inequality and an attendant social hierarchy. Daniel Walker Howe has observed in his study of the Whigs that "Whigs could help blacks without having to acknowledge their equality. On the other hand, the Democrats' egalitarianism seemed to force them to deny the very humanity of non-whites lest they have to confront them as equals."[11] Howe assumes, quite correctly, that antebellum society, in the North no less than the South, was pervasively racist. Conscious and continual attention to this fact is essential to any examination of the slavery issue in the antebellum period and the years of the Civil War. Without it, one is unable to account, not only for the racism prevalent in the Northern popular press and the institutionalization of racism in the Union army, but for the continuance of black inequality after the supposed Day of Jubilee.

The Emancipation Proclamation had been received with mixed enthusiasm in the North. One reaction, placed poetically (and probably accurately) in the mouth of an immigrant soldier, ran:

> May me hand lave me body whin I pull the thrigger
> In battle again." "Why Larry?" "Because
> The Goddess of Liberty's turned to a nigger
> An ould Father Abram's forgotten the laws.[12]

Opposition to slavery, as well as to emancipation, had also been colored by racism, as two examples from the *Republican Songbook* will attest:

> No more shall slavery's deadly blight
> Spread over our fair lands
> We want our soil for free white men
> With strong and willing hands.[13]

> I looked to the South and I looked to the West
> And I saw Black Slavery a comin'
> With Democratic doughfaces harnessed up in front
> Driving niggers to the other side of Jordan[14]

More common, at least in the early years of the war, was a pro-Union sentiment which was indifferent or hostile to abolition. One account of the Civil War which exhibits these characteristics explained the origins of the conflict thusly:

> Politicians in the sunny South the Planters did deceive
> And in the North bad men went forth, made Northern folk believe
> In language strict a great conflict must rage twixt slaves and labor
> And now amazed our swords are raised against both friend and neighbor.[15]

In this articulation, the crime was the dissolution of the Union, a heinous act committed by the South, but instigated in part by Northern agitators: "Horace Greely and other 'ism' teachers."

> We'd oughter take Massa Mealy and his abolition crew
> And make them fight for Union
> For it was these self-same fellows
> That first kicked up the fuss.
> And I think we'd oughter make them
> Help settle up the muss.[16]

This party was openly critical of abolition. One characterization of "The Wide Awakes" had them sing:

> For this we march with the torchlight
> To show our holy mission
> And worship nigger with delight
> And pray for abolition.[17]

Another observed:

> If cotton is now king of Southern people
> Nigger is God on every Northern steeple.[18]

For men of these sentiments, the proper attitude was:

> We'll fight for the Union, but just as it was
> Nor care what Secesh or Abe-o-lition does[19]

and:

> The negro—free or slave—
> We can no pin about
> But for the flag our fathers gave
> We mean to have it out.[20]

As Edgar McManus observed in his study of *Black Bondage in the North,* "concern for racial justice played only a minor role in the politics of abolition." Emancipation was often a legal condition characterized by few liberties in fact. New Jersey, for example, had abolished slavery by reclassifying its slaves as "apprentices for life." Moreover,

McManus notes, "that blacks were free did not prevent Massachusetts, Rhode Island and Maine from prohibiting them to intermarry with whites." The free states took stringent efforts to reduce their black populations. New Jersey prohibited blacks from entering the state with the intention of settling, and Massachusetts prescribed flogging for nonresident blacks who stayed longer than two months. Once in these states, and those adjoining them, blacks were either denied suffrage (New Jersey, Pennsylvania, Rhode Island) or subject to higher property qualifications than whites. Ohio passed a law expelling its entire black population.[21]

Informal obstacles to black equality in the free states were still greater than those presented by law. Connecticut had required an established period of residency for blacks who wished to attend public schools, but when Prudence Crandall attempted to teach black children in Connecticut "public antipathy forced her to shut down her school."[22] A wealthy Philadelphia merchant wrote in 1822: "Notwithstanding the laws of Pennsylvania do not forbid it, no blacks vote at elections . . . By our constitution this degraded, and I am sorry to say in the region of Pennsylvania dissipated race are allowed to give their suffrages at all elections, provided they pay the legal taxes, yet owing to custom, prejudice or design, they never presume to approach the hustings."[23]

As this account indicates, antebellum Northerners commonly held blacks in low regard. One Bostonian cleric, disinclined to abolition, averred of slavery, "As far as I have seen the fault was that the blacks had too little rather than too much to do. In the cities this is certainly the case, for they have too much time left over for dissipation and bad company."[24]

Nor were abolitionist writings free from these denigrations of black character. Frederick Low Olmsted wrote that "the great mass" of blacks "appear very dull, idiotic and brute-like; and it requires an effort to appreciate that they are, very much more than the beasts they drive, our brethren, a part of ourselves."[25] (The same, it appears, could not be said of everyone. He found blacks a "very decent, civil people" when compared to "very dirty German Jews.")[26] Olmsted noted, with some distaste, that "when the negro is definitely a slave, it would seem that the alleged natural antipathy of the white race to associate with him is lost." Throughout the South he reported "Negro women are carrying black and white children together in their arms, black and white children are playing together." Black and white Southerners exhibited a familiarity "and closeness in intimacy that would have been noticed with astonishment, if not manifest displeasure, in almost any chance company in the North."[27] Thomas Goodwin's *Natural History of Secession* (1864) marked this intimacy as the source of the South's decay. Southerners had "African playmates . . . African attendants . . . African recreations . . . African voices . . . African minds." Their retarded progress and defective freedom were the result of "the direct influence of so large a population of half-barbarous Africans interspersed among them" who had instructed them, he asserted, in the structures and principles of African despotism.[28]

One humorous account entitled "The Yank's Escape from Secesh," had the fictional Yank exclaim "May I be goll-darned if I ain't most superlatively happy to git back into a Christian white man community."[29] The Union represented a community which was—transcendentally if not phenomenally—white, male, and Christian. Northern culture, throughout the antebellum period, had been characterized by an increasingly pervasive intolerance for ethnic and cultural heterogeneity. This impulse, strengthened by the cultural responses to the great increase in Irish Catholic immigration, was most evident in the violent reaction among both abolitionists and anti-abolitionists to miscegenation. It was, one abolitionist declared, "the sum of all villainies."[30] It represented, in material terms, a feared alteration of the culture of the covenanted community.

Recognition of the pervasive character of racism in antebellum American political culture obliges analysts to come to a more exact understanding of the meaning of slavery and the slavery controversy in the culture which experienced them.

The meaning of slavery in antebellum political culture, and the source of its significance as an issue came from its pivotal position with regard to three central issues of antebellum politics: the determination of nationality, the role of the family, and the character of labor. The first was, of course, a question of fundamental importance for Southerners in the debate over secession and Southern nationalism. It was very nearly as important in Northern politics, where it pertained not only to the question of secession, but to the status of the immigrants as well. The debate over labor wracked both sections. It was expressed not only in the controversy over the moral or utilitarian superiority of free to slave labor, but also in controversies over the developing industrial economy. The period was marked by a continually heated, and often violent, debate over the relation of labor to capital, of agriculture to industry, of worker to man and citizen, of corporation to person, and of man to machine. The social transformation which attended the alteration of the American economy altered established relationships in addition to creating new ones.

FAMILY

Under the influence of industry, the significance of the family as a social unit, and relationships within the family, had been redefined. These changes in an institution so emotionally laden naturally met with considerable resistance. In the South the family had long been acknowledged as the primary social unit and as a paradigm for political relations. The family was thus a subject of controversy both between and within sections.

Enthusiasts of industrial organization in the North had conducted a campaign which resulted in the denigration of the family as a social institution. Functions formerly allotted to the family—childcare, education, provision for the poor and the insane—were assigned with increasing frequency to specialized agencies, staffed by professionals and supervised by the state. The ignorance and vice of lower-class parents and the alien customs of immigrant parents were marked out as obstacles to collective progress, as the source of juvenile delinquency and social fragmentation.

The status of the family in Southern political culture was, however, enhanced rather than diminished in this period. It expressed two fundamental principles in the ideology and culture of the South: that the act of provision conferred political authority and that there were political communities prior in time and authority to the state, toward which the state was expected to show due reverence. In each of these principles the South diverged from the North. The notion of prior sovereignties was distasteful or irrelevant to most Northerners, whose primary allegiance was increasingly national. Among the more learned, it was rejected as the antithesis of both the religious ideal of a covenanted community and the secular conception of the incorporative progress of civilization. Prior trials of this issue had consistently ranged North against South. The status of provision as a source for political authority was similarly deprecated in the North, for it tended to denigrate both the regional status of the industrializing and commercial North against the predominantly agricultural South and the status of the capitalists, who comprised a large portion of the Northern political elite. The derivation of the principle from the maternal model of political development was similarly alien to Northern cultural and religious traditions of patriarchal family structure.

Within the Southern cultural context, slavery was a domestic institution, which meant not only that it fell within the jurisdiction of the several states, but, more importantly, that it was a concern of the household. The household was a social preservation of the model of natural community that the Southerners had praised in the Indians. It was both a sanctuary of ungoverned community—and hence associated with the preservation of natural rights in society—and the proper environment for education and the achievement of political maturity. Because slaves were commonly accorded the political status of either women or children, they were, like these, confined to the family.

Slaves, and the institution of slavery, had been integrated into Southern society through the family. The issue of slavery was therefore intimately entangled with debates over sovereignty, the status of provision as a source of political authority, and the status of the family as a political model. Part of the reluctance to interfere with the institution arose from the belief that the family was properly exempt from governmental intervention. Northern attacks on slavery, because they were coincident with criticisms of the family as a functional unit of social organization, were perceived as merely one aspect of an attempt to increase the coercive authority of the state by permitting it to assume rights, functions, and responsibilities formerly allotted to the family.

This perception gained credence because the perceived attempt to consolidate familial functions in the state paralleled the federal government's attempted consolidation of states' rights. Support for both national consolidation and that model of social reform which assigned an increasingly active role to the state came, moreover, from the industrializing North, and within the North had the prominent support of capitalists and the enthusiasts of industry. This awakened an enduring Southern suspicion of self-serving alliances between capital and the state, current in Southern political discourse at least as early as Taylor's *Arator* in 1800. The classes marked by Taylor and later Southern political theorists as especially inclined to the arrogation of popular authority were capitalists, clerics, bureaucrats, and the military. The first three were well represented in the social reform movements which were conceived as destructive of the family. Because these classes were regarded in Southern political culture as the enemies of natural right and democratic government, opposition to social reform and abolition tended to express itself in affirmations of popular authority and the family.

This response, which seems to contemporary Americans to have been either an embarrassed reluctance to respond directly to the charge of oppression, or evident hypocrisy, was a direct and appropriate response in the context of antebellum Southern culture. They responded not to the issue as we presently perceive it, with the interests and associations of our own period, but to the issue within the network of meanings, associations, and political paradigms which comprised the political context at the time.

NATIONALITY

The characteristic Southern insistence on rights was also expressed in their understanding of citizenship. For Southerners, nationality was determined by consent. This principle, which animated both the Declaration of Independence and the Acts of Secession, made citizenship primarily a consequence of subjective allegiance. Thus Southerners and Democrats who held to the same view tended to favor the rapid naturalization and enfranchisement of immigrants whose migration was evidence of their consent. Blacks, however, were legally and circumstantially prevented from residing where they pleased. Their ancestors had been brought to America by force, against their own wishes. This involuntary emigration was evidence of the absence of consent. Blacks were then outside the boundaries of the polity.

The integration of blacks into Southern society was effected through the family, which was regarded as prior to the polity. Those who believed in the innate inferiority of blacks could regard this as an essentially just and stable relation, analogous to that of women, in which the only cause for concern was the slave's well-being. Those who believed in the present or eventual quality of black and white were, however, in a quandary. Advocates of colonization saw their crude and arrogant solution as a method whereby the original injustice of the slaves' kidnapping and the problem of their continued residence might be simultaneously resolved. The disinclination of many blacks to emigrate placed the justice as well as the practicality of the scheme in doubt. Both the advocates and opponents of black equality in the South believed, however, that if blacks were recognized as free citizens they must be granted the rights proper to that state.

In Northern political culture, the determination of citizenship had traditionally been beyond the capacity of the individual. In the Puritan polity, membership was the consequence of divine election. In the antebellum North this doctrine of predestined nationality held sway in an amended form. History, Providence to the pious, was the proper determinant of citizenship. This view reflected the influence of both the Puritan paradigm and prevailing responses to recent social developments. It could be easily accorded with the prejudices of the nativists and the object of those philanthropists who endeavored to assimilate immigrants and their offspring as they educated them. For the former, ethnicity was inalterable, the predestined consequence of one's unintended ancestry. For the latter, assimilation offered a means whereby individuals might alter the effects of their ancestry and education and assume the manners, customs, and values which history had matured in America. Both groups, however, regarded that culture produced by historical development as the determinant of nationality.

Throughout the North and West, history was conceived as a great progress in which civilization and industry advanced, national boundaries dissolved into ever more extensive and finally universal community, and political relations were increasingly characterized by liberty. In this vague and millennial articulation, America had its genesis in a decisive moment in the progress of liberty and was itself destined to advance the progress of liberty throughout the world.

This romantic conception of America's historical mission as the evangelist of liberty was, like the South's affirmation of natural rights, wedded to a paradoxical insistence on the subordination of certain readily distinguished ethnic groups. The presumption of America's historically determined superiority was attended by a hierarchy of development in which disparate nationalities and peoples were assigned rankings expressive of their cultural and historical proximity to the American ideal.

Thus those who affirmed that slavery was "against destiny," an obstacle to the continued progress of liberty, looked for the inclusion of blacks in the American, ultimately universal, community, but in a state of continued subordination. In an 1865 pamphlet entitled *What Ought to be Done with the Freedmen and the Rebels*, the author wrote of the newly freed blacks that Americans should "respect, honor and love them, in their appropriate place, just as we do our Irish and German citizens in their place." They must, he wrote, "be paternally cared for and aided in their new life . . . these adult children will be the better for some proper fatherly supervision."[31]

This paternal care was largely to be expressed in coercion and control, for both the blacks and the Irish. Of the blacks Dexter advised, "Let the government lay down the Scriptural rule, 'If any will not work, neither shall he eat.'"[32] John Kasson reports that Emerson acknowledged the exploitation of the Irish, "but urged as compensatory factors the unlimited opportunities America offered Irishmen. He submitted besides that the Irish possessed a vivacity and good humor that exceeded the spirits of native Americans and let them bear their burdens lightly. In any case, he concluded, the harsh regimen imposed by the railroad had distinct advantages as a means of social control."[33] Emerson expected gratitude from the Irish for their inclusion in the American mission, feared their rebellion, acknowledged their exploitation, and excused it as a burden they did not feel. This common, if contradictory, constellation of opinions came to characterize American treatment of ethnic minorities—a category which increased as the cultural boundaries of the nation constricted. It was marked by a beneficent paternalistic philanthropy, and by interested exploitation. These traits were most evident in that group which was to have the greatest influence in America after the Civil War: the industrial elite. In a prefiguration of this era, the chairman of the Committee of Merchants for the Relief of Colored People Suffering from the Late Riots responded to the thanks of black representatives with the news, "The ordeal before you is a fearful one. You will go forth without any claims upon society beyond those conceded to every man—you will meet at the outset a haughty, powerful and energetic race—a race which today rules and controls all others. Can you stand before the Anglo-Saxon and Celtic tribes?"[34] Coupled with his philanthropy was an arrogant affirmation of ethnic superiority and a conception of society as a battle between contending "tribes." Blacks, though acknowledged inferiors of "the Anglo-Saxon and Celtic tribes" were to have no "claims upon society," or that race which "rules and controls all others." This statement thus gives a succinct summary of the policies and attitudes which governed American race relations in the century which followed. Its incipient social Darwinism came into full flower in the years following the Civil War.

The emancipation and enfranchisement of blacks came within the context of this debate over nationality. The question, therefore, was one of inclusion rather than equality. Opponents of each argued for a strict constructionist interpretation of the doctrine that the United States was "a Christian white man's community" but were satisfied with the assurance that emancipation need not entail equality.

LABOR

This altered view of citizenship was attended, as I argued at the end of Chapter 3, by an altered conception of labor. There is indeed, a disturbing congruence between this understanding of the American nation and the organization of the factory. Both were highly stratified, with each stratum allotted a specific role. All profited, supposedly, by the arrangement, but the elite profited most, and they did so through the exploitation of those below them in the hierarchy. Each arrangement was purportedly predestined, whether by God or by history, and hence morally and effectually unassailable. Each was seen as a partial realization of the materialization of mind and was appropriately characterized by a high degree of rationalization.

The relation between the organization of the factory and this conception of nationality illustrates how cultures are characterized by recurrent patterns, dominant paradigms which provide individuals within the culture with an organizing principle. These may be employed, as the examples indicate, both as models for institutional organization and as paradigms for understanding the relation of ideas to one another. They enable the culture to exhibit a high degree of consistency and coherence, which serves both to express the subjective community of the members and to preserve that community by facilitating intelligible communication among them.

Immigrant workers were readily integrated into the emerging industrial system. Though they disparaged their morals, manners, and intellect, employers found it advantageous to hire immigrants in large numbers. The organization of the factory, and of industrial relations, assigned immigrants to a structurally subordinate position. This enabled employers to employ them while continuing to deprecate their culture. The integration of the immigrant into the larger community followed the same model. They were included, but law and custom increasingly assured their subordination. The factory was gradually replacing the family as the model from which social and political relations were structured. It was, however, consonant with the dominant paradigms of traditional Northern political culture, following both the organization of the patriarchal family and the model of historical progress.

As yet, however, there was no consensus that what was good for General Motors was good for America. On the contrary, labor activists from the first quarter of the century had protested that the hierarchical character of industrial organization was inappropriate to a democratic regime and had argued that democratic procedures and egalitarian relations ought to prevail in factories as well as outside them. The cultural disparity of the immigrants, and a consequent hostility or apprehension toward them, undermined this effort to democratize industrial relations. Belief in the historically produced superiority of American culture, and in America as the vanguard of industrial progress, permeated Northern sectional culture. It provided an apology both for the inclusion of the immigrant worker in the factory (where culture was irrelevant) and for his inclusion and subordination in society.

The radical distinction between the worker and the citizen thus presented a great obstacle to the democratization of industrial relations. It abstracted the worker's capacity to labor from his individual character, rights, and faculties, enabling both him and his employer to regard it as a separable, saleable resource, rather than as an aspect of an indivisible individuality.

The procapitalist abolitionism that constituted the bulk of the movement adhered to this understanding of labor. Their condemnations of slavery were not, therefore, condemnations of the exploitation of labor. On the contrary, many abolitionists argued that slavery gave excessive leisure to the slave as well as the master, encouraging idleness and dissipation in both parties and retarding the American advance of material progress. Estimates of the increased hours which freed slaves would be obliged to work—and the consequent rise in national productivity—abounded in antislavery works. For these men, the evil in slavery did not lie in the exploitation of labor which it entailed.[35]

For Southerners, however, the question of the exploitation of labor was of central importance. Because the authority of the master over slaves was purportedly derived from his provision for them, mistreatment was destructive not only of personal morality, but also of political legitimacy. Nothing in Southern culture, neither religion nor recent developments, had prepared Southerners to accept the notion that labor might be separable from the man, and the citizen remain free while the worker was exploited. On the contrary, theorists from Jefferson, Taylor, and Randolph to Fitzhugh and Calhoun had argued that political independence was secured by economic independence, while economic dependence threatened or destroyed it. Northern enthusiasm for industrial organization with its evident exploitation and attendant hierarchies, made their adherence to abolitionism seem blatant hypocrisy. Thus, Northern opposition to slavery was consistently met with an opposition to industry, which contained vociferous denunciations of the exploitation of (what Southerners regarded as only nominally) free labor. "The Senator from New York said yesterday that the whole world has abolished slavery. Ay, the name, but not the thing . . . for the man who lives by daily labor and scarcely lives at that, and who has to put out his labor in the market and take the best he can get for it, in short, your whole hireling class of manual laborers and operatives as you call them, are essentially slaves." The sole difference, Hammond concluded, "is that our slaves are hired for life and well-compensated . . . Yours are hired by the day, not cared for, and most scantily compensated."[36]

What is perhaps most interesting is the acceptance of this assessment by Northern workers and the changing effect it had on their attitudes toward abolition. Sarah Bagley wrote, "To my mind it is slavery quite as real as any in Turkey or Carolina. It matters little as to the fact of slavery whether the slave be compelled to his task by the whip of the overseer or the wages of the Lowell Corporation. In either case it is not free will leading the laborer to work but outward necessity that puts free will out of the question."[37]

Early workers' movements, animated by a natural rights ideology, had supported the abolition of slavery, deeming it an exploitation of labor like that which they opposed on their own behalf and a violation of those natural rights which they unqualifiedly affirmed. From 1820 to 1840, however, both the composition of the working class and the position which prevailed among workers on the subject of abolition changed dramatically.

The increases in immigration which had granted employers an unprecedented power over the composition of the work force (by enabling them to hire selectively), initially divided workers on the subject of abolition. Competition for jobs increased existing animosities between ethnically distinct groups, a development exacerbated by nativist tracts which included the Irish with blacks in lists of properly subordinate peoples. It also enabled employers to fire rebellious workers and those involved in labor activities. This may have reduced the number of workers who actively affirmed a liberal and egalitarian ideology.

The wage cuts and longer hours which employers were able to exact from their employees also contributed to the alienation of the working class from abolition. The abolition of slavery would exacerbate competition for jobs, resulting in further wage cuts. Unemployment would increase. The expanded labor force would be obliged to work longer hours to hold their jobs. Continuance of slavery prevented this feared competition for jobs. The evidently exploitative practices of the Northern industrialists gave credence to the Southern critique of industrialization. Southerners had claimed that their authority over the slaves, unlike that of capital over labor, was legitimate because of the inferiority or political immaturity of the blacks and from their care for them: an authority derived from provision. The hardships occasioned by the wage cuts, and the employers' refusal to provide for the sick, disabled, and aged workers, gave the lie to those who had advanced their paternal care for the operatives as an apology for the authority they maintained over them. Despite the irrefragable humiliation and oppression to which the slave was subject, many workers began to doubt whether they were materially better off than the slaves.

The *Workingman's Gazette* of May 3, 1831, asked "Who Are Slaves?" and answered that both black and white were enslaved to the rich for "might makes right, and money makes power." The operatives, one wrote, "are in fact nothing more nor less than slaves in every sense of the word." They felt they wore, the *Manchester Democrat* of September 1, 1847, reported, "fetters worse than the manacles worn by the Southern slave."[38]

In asserting that they were "slaves in every sense of the word," workers were not merely indulging in a species of extraordinarily extravagant rhetoric. They argued that they were subject not only to the same—or more onerous—material privations, but also to the continued humiliation and exploitation attendant on acknowledged social inferiority. Workers' protests against the assumption of social superiority in the manners and customs of the Northern capitalists testify to their belief that the likeness of their condition to that of the slave extended beyond a common material privation. They recognized moreover, that certain modes of social exploitation which had been especially condemned by the abolitionists were by no means confined to the slave states. "I defy the most vehement ranters against slavery to produce a section of the black code of any state which makes more of a slave . . . the female negro who has a master and owner to protect her than . . . are the thousands of unprotected white females of Lowell slaves to the overseers of a dozen or two of cotton mills."[39]

The operatives, together with the slaves, constituted, as Daniel Walker Howe states, "an unacknowledged American proletariat."[41] The refusal of Northern abolitionists to acknowledge this common oppression caused many workers to regard them with contempt and resentment. The *Fall River Mechanic* castigated "men who stand and dole out pity for the southern slave but would crush with an iron hand the white laborer of the north."[42] *The Man* had equally caustic animadversions on abolitionism among upper-class women:

> Their tender hearts were sighing
> As the negro's wrongs were told
> While the white slave was dying
> Who gained their father's gold.[43]

Successful appeals for working-class support for abolition and the war effort were made in some quarters. Concern for the preservation of familial bonds produced considerable responsiveness among the working class to the observation that slavery broke up families. This was especially true among women, in whom the altered culture encouraged an increased rather than diminished allegiance to the domestic sphere. The altered manners of the emerging industrial era had also drastically limited opportunities for feminine political activism. The abolition movement remained at least partially open to them.

Resentment against Southerners was increased as they were regularly portrayed as would-be aristocrats, the partisans of a reactionary feudalism, committed, like Northern capitalists, to the establishment of a rigid hierarchy of classes. Finally, Northern workers shared in the dissolution of sectional in a putatively national allegiance, in an emotional commitment to "the Union" rather than one of the several United States.

As the war proceeded, however, with apprehensions that the struggle for the preservation of the Union was to be attended by increased social stratification, that the burden of the war was to be borne by the poor in the interest of the rich, and that abolition would increase the power of owners and the government to suppress labor activities, working-class Democrats in the cities became increasingly restive and finally had recourse to violent opposition to the war.

If one understands the debate over slavery in its cultural context, at the conjunction of concurrent debate over labor, the family, and nationality, the alliances and enmities of the antebellum period—which at first seem capricious or contradictory—become intelligible. Anti-abolitionist sentiment prevailed among the working-class constituency of the Northern Democratic Party as an expression of opposition not only to black equality but also to associated alterations of previous social arrangements. They distinguished themselves ideologically from the economic elite not by reason of a vociferous racism, which was in fact equally prevalent among the latter group, but by reason of a complex of opinions on the interrelated issues of nationality, labor, and the family in which they radically and consistently opposed the sentiments and interests of capitalists, abolitionists, and Southerners.

9   Paradigms in Conflict

STYLES OF WARFARE

When the South seceded, declaring its independence of the Union, those who disputed the legality of the act, Lincoln among them, named their independence mere rebellion. But Lincoln knew, as much as any other man, that there could no longer be mere rebellion in America. The nation's revolutionary origins had granted all such popular upheavals a kinship with creative authority. The Rebellion had at least a family resemblance to the Revolution.

> Rebel! 'Tis our family name
> Our father, Washington,
> Was the arch-rebel in the fight
> And gave the name to us—a right
> Of father unto son.[1]

This verse of a rebellious apologia affirms the South's inheritance of the Revolutionary tradition. In "Seventy-six and Sixty-one" John Overall makes explicit the South's revival of the Revolutionary experience.[2] Poets and journalists throughout the South made this a frequent theme, writing of Revolutionary veterans again assuming arms and, more plausibly, of sons shouldering their fathers' weapons in a similar cause. Hammond in 1858 had likened the North's treatment of the South to British exploitation of the American colonies: "It was this that brought on the American Revolution. We threw off a government not adapted to our social system and made one for ourselves."[3] Confederates engaged in the active emulation of that enterprise recognized that this aspect of reenactment brought not merely legitimacy, but grandeur and sanctity to their cause.

240

> Yes call them Rebels! 'tis the name
> Their patriot fathers bore
> And by such deeds they'll hallow it
> As they have done before.[4]

Men reported that when invasion came, and Southern cities were threatened, "dignified old citizens appeared on the streets, armed and equipped with weapons that upheld the cause of the colonies against the invasion of the British in the Revolutionary War."[5] Engaged in the same endeavor, pledged to a similar valor, Southerners trusted to a like outcome.

> Rebel is a sacred name
> Traitor too is glorious
> By such names our fathers fought
> By them were victorious.[6]

The truth of that assertion, and the necessity of fighting the Southerners in the shadow of Mount Vernon and Monticello, where Washington, Jefferson, Madison, and Monroe had lived, farmed, and campaigned, in the very precincts where Henry had declared "Give me liberty or give me death," troubled the North's campaigns in the Southeast.[7] It troubled their consciences long after.

Adams—Henry Adams, that intolerant, Southern-baiting scion of Massachusetts—made a Confederate war veteran the hero of his postwar novel *Democracy*. John Carrington, Virginian, with familial ties to Washington and the Lees, was General Washington restored to us in his prime."[8] Melville's *Clarel* would praise another Confederate veteran similarly:

> Brave soldier and stout thinker both
> In this regard and in degree
> An Ethan Allen, by my troth
> Or Herbert, Lord of Cherbury.[9]

Contending or conquering, Northerners could not dismiss the likeness of the Rebel to the Revolutionary. Rebellion retained its sanctity even in defeat. Adams wrote of Carrington, "He gained dignity in his rebel isolation."[10] Rebellion, in the American experience, was that state of liminality outside and over politics, in which "our fathers brought forth" the American regime.

The resemblance of the Rebellion and the Revolution went beyond the contrived and the circumstantial. In an essay entitled, "Died of Democracy," David Donald argues that "the Confederacy, not the Union, represented the democratic forces in American life."[11] He recognized that with the conquest of the Confederacy the nation became a revolution abridged, abandoning, sometimes deliberately, sometimes unwittingly, aspects of that ideology which had preserved elements of revolution—that is to say, of active popular sovereignty—in the formally constituted nation.

"The democratic tendencies of the Confederacy," Donald remarks, "were all too plainly reflected in its army."[12] Armies in the Confederacy remained forces of the separate states, constituted of their residents, and subject to their legislatures. This was, however, less a nod to the doctrine of states' rights than adherence to the old militia system and the ideal of the citizen soldiery. Sentiment against a standing army had remained strong in the South despite the region's putatively martial character.[13] The Confederate Constitution had retained those provisions of the United States' Constitution which had been intended to prevent the establishment of a standing army. Recognizing the ease with which they had been, and continued to be, circumvented, they strengthened both the language and the machinery of the proscription.

The militia system had been designed to preserve citizen participation in the defense of the nation, and to prevent the growth of a military establishment different from the people in composition and interests. Any army the nation might require was to express the ideology of the regime in its constitution: its character was to be popular, its primary purpose protection against invasion. In theory such an army would merely express an aspect of the people in the exercise of active sovereignty.

The merit, and military deficiencies, of the militia system lay in its structural recognition of the superiority of civil to military authority. This ranking was reflected throughout the workings of the Confederacy. Davis was consequently reluctant to ask the Congress for permission to impose martial law. When he did ask, he was denied. The Congress maintained the conviction that the imposition of martial law was necessarily foreign to democratic regimes. He was permitted the suspension of habeas corpus for a limited period, and in prescribed areas. When he applied for a renewal of this authority, he was again denied.

Lincoln, on the contrary, readily assumed the character and functions of commander in chief. He declared martial law and suspended habeas corpus without consulting Congress, and without troubling to deny the illegality of his actions. "These measures," he later said, "whether strictly legal or not, were ventured under what appeared to be a popular demand."[14] They facilitated the imprisonment of over 15,000 civilians.

The Confederacy continued the inviolability of those freedoms guaranteed in the Bill of Rights. Donald noted the accomplishment of the "ardent wish" of Confederate Secretary of War Randolph that "this revolution may be closed without the suppression of one single newspaper in the Confederate States."[15] Secretary of War Stanton, on the Union side, does not appear to have held similar sentiments. More than 300 newspapers were suppressed in the Northern states during the war, and certain of their editors imprisoned. The disparity becomes particularly marked when one considers that the greater part of the war was fought on Southern territory and that the papers published troop movements with impunity. In Southern political culture, the enumerated liberties of the Bill of Rights retained their inviolability. Lincoln's "Union in liberty" was an object for which his contemporaries were obliged to surrender the present enjoyment of their liberties. His adherence to the Constitution, similarly, was expressed in an expedient indifference to its provisions. Sherman, marching South, urged Southerners to abandon "that political nonsense of slaves' rights, states' rights, freedom of conscience, freedom of the press, and other such trash."[16]

That popular ideology which prevented the abridgment of civil liberties in the Confederacy pervaded the Confederate army. Southern soldiers in the ranks elected their own officers, an old Revolutionary practice quickly dispensed with in the Union army. They remained "heartily opposed to undemocratic exercise of authority" by those officers they elected. Here, the soldiers reflected attitudes of the political culture, implicitly recognizing that popular authority remains latent, but nonetheless sovereign, even after it has delegated authority to formal representatives. This was the same doctrine which undergirded Nullification and Secession. Southern soldiers, Donald writes, "obeyed orders on the battlefield but they saw no reason why officers should give themselves special airs in camp." As one of their congressmen expressed it, "they have not lost the identity of the citizen in the soldier."[17]

The appearance of the Confederate army manifested the character of its partisans. Uniforms varied by state, locality, and personal inclination, expressing culturally endorsed values of particularism and individuality. Donald contends that "their appearance showed that they considered themselves individualistic citizens who were temporarily assisting their country,"[18] after the model of John Taylor of Caroline, who, Benton wrote, "was a skillful and practical farmer, giving his time to his books when not called by an emergency to the public service, and returning to his books and his farm when the emergency was over."[19] Southern soldiers were wont to do the same, leaving the ranks to attend the farm or when they believed the threat had passed. "Even the idea of marching at a regular rate in tidy lines offended their sense of individuality."[20] Most importantly, Southern soldiers never regarded themselves as subject to the authorities they had created; "they simply disobeyed orders they deemed unreasonable."[21]

It should be evident that I am indifferent to the tactical deficiencies, or merits, if such there be, of the lack of military discipline in the Confederate army. These organizational peculiarities are interesting insofar as they elucidate politically significant features of Southern culture. They are interesting because they distinguish that culture from its rival, and because they represent aspects of a rejected, but enduring, alternative to the prevailing American culture.

Many of the traits which distinguished the Confederate ranks were equally evident among their officers. The civilian governments strictly defined the powers they assigned their officers. The appearance of the generals, no less than of the troops, recalled significant mythic models in Southern political culture. Stuart, Beauregard, and Pickett affected the flamboyant dress, the plumes, and the long ringlets of the Cavaliers, while Lee and Jackson were marked out by their austerity. Melville records an anecdote of Jackson:

> A cap we sent him, bestarred to replace
> The sun-scorched helm of war.
> A fillet he made of the shining lace
> Childhood's laughing brow to grace
> Not his was a goldsmith's star.[22]

Northerners before the war had made much of the Southerner's high opinion of himself, his seeming self-consciousness of greatness. Southerners appear to have had at least an inclination for the grand gesture.

As is often the case, the preeminent practitioners of this—the noble gesture, the great escape, fearlessness, gaiety, and wit—were guerrillas. The most popular in the literature of the war were Mosby's Raiders. One of these entitled his memoirs *Reminiscences of a Mosby Guerrilla* and prefaced it with an apology for using a term which earlier had been considered pejorative. This form of clandestine warfare is favored by invaded, rebellious, and colonized peoples—of necessity, since it permits a greater use of popular support and may offset the superior resources of a more powerful opponent. It therefore emphasizes the liminality of the rebellious people. Set battles between Union and Confederate forces, when recounted, enhanced the image of the Confederacy as a sovereign and independent state. Mosby's raids on larger forces expressed the South's sense of itself as an underdog. They recalled especially attractive myths of the Revolution—Francis Marion in the swamps of South Carolina, the undisciplined and unerring sharp-shooters picking off the British from the trees, and the multiple accounts of small Revolutionary bands specializing in "surprise and ambuscade." Some of the most publicized exploits of the Raiders recalled like episodes in the Revolution. Mosby's capture of General Stoughton repeated Ethan Allen's famous capture of Fort Ticonderoga, in which he roused the commander out of bed to surrender in the buff. History has favored these accounts of the Revolution over those of pitched battles because they emphasize the popular character of the struggle. They also serve to throw into sharp relief the accomplishment of victory.

Mosby's men operated in this historically hallowed fashion in the mythically rich precincts of Northern Virginia, recalling in their circumstances and their conduct the events of the Revolution. Their tactics, gestures, and organization, or rather their lack thereof, expressed that kinship to the Revolution which the Confederates wished to mark in their cause. Their style of warfare was, as partisan warfare necessarily is, antistructural. One of the raiders described it this way:

> As a command we had no knowledge of the first principles of cavalry drill and could not have formed in a straight line had there ever been any need for doing so. We did not know the bugle calls and very rarely had roll call. Our dress was not uniform in make or color; we did not address our officers, except Mosby, by their titles; in fact we did not practice anything usually required of a soldier, and yet withal there was not another body of men under better or more willing control.[23]

Mosby's Raiders and other guerrilla groups acquire political significance beyond their military effectiveness because of these very traits. They illustrate in their structure that principle most important to dissident and rebellious populations: that subjective allegiance, rather than objective law, is the true determinant of authority. They deny not only the legitimacy but also the efficacy of formal rules. Munson recognized and was careful to note that their indifference to conventional regulation and military drill increased rather than diminished the discipline of the force. Unlike conventional armies, they were under "willing control." The partisans were governed by the same authority that animated the formation of the Confederacy. Both were formed and directed by the principle that the presence or absence of subjective allegiance rather than obedience to prevailing conventions determined legitimate authority. The partisans thus became an apt exemplar of the nation as a whole. Certain of these features—their lack of uniforms, and ignorance of drill—were illustrative of other aspects of the political culture they represented.

The dependence of the raiders on voluntary discipline rather than order or drill was visible to a lesser extent throughout the Confederate army. It indicates, as Donald observes, an unwillingness to surrender the privilege of self-direction. The same resistance bottoms both democracy and egalitarianism.

In place of order the raiders exhibited a more ferocious side of the playfulness associated with Southern culture. Their attacks were marked by the wild violence associated with the Indians. Accounts of these emphasize their spontaneity and suggest the liminality of both the cause and its partisans. One participant is described as follows: "All he knew about war was what he gathered in each mad dash through the ranks of the enemy, with his long black hair flying in the wind . . . He rode his horse like a Centaur." Between battles the same spontaneity was expressed in what the guerillas themselves recognized as play: "When they weren't fighting they were generally playing. While on a raid they were as light-hearted as schoolboys at recess and I have seen them chasing each other up and down the line of march oblivious of any discipline or any approximation of danger." This account draws attention to the playfulness of the guerrillas as exactly antithetical to discipline. It thus symbolized their rejection of assimilative order and their retention of individuality.[24]

Their lack of uniforms was similarly motivated. Recollections of the raiders note that they could and did obtain what passed for uniforms when they desired them. Most raiders possessed one which they usually resorted to on visits to the main force. These, in addition to indicating the unity of the irregulars with the army, offered them the opportunity for putting on the dog. Munson recalled that a uniform was "something gray." They were distinguished from one another, and from what is commonly considered a uniform, by their varied extravagance; employing such accoutrements as red silk-lined caps and ostrich plumes. These were thought to enhance the prestige of both the owner and the force. They provided an opportunity for the self-display which was encouraged in Southern culture, and hence an outward manifestation of the culture's tolerance for individuality. Assimilation was not regarded as desirable. The most conspicuous elements of these costumes-cum-uniforms were often worn into raids to distinguish their wearer. In addition to drawing attention to the wearer's exploits, they illustrated the retention of particularity in collective action.

The practice of routinely preferring civilian clothes to uniforms minimized the distinction between civilian and military, as did the practice of dispensing with military titles. This had had an institutional expression in the retention of the militia system. Here it was more than usually apt. Civilians in the area with Confederate sympathies, in addition to collaborating with Mosby's men, frequently joined them for short periods, or for single raids. Convalescent soldiers would slip out of the hospitals at night and return in the morning, becoming what Mosby's men called "guerrillas pro tem."[25] This elastic force is characteristic of guerrilla warfare. It manifests organizationally the guerrilla claim that they are a "people's army."

The tactics employed by Mosby and by guerrillas in general also emphasized that they were fighting on their own turf. These were designed to exploit to the fullest the advantages of the homeground, using knowledge of the terrain and the assistance of civilians to evade, ambush, and entrap. This resistence to invasion followed Frances Randolph's dictum "Keep your land and your land will keep you." The tactics of "surprise and ambuscade" which the guerrillas specialized in likened them to the image of the Indian in Southern political culture. They invested the guerrillas with the mythic Indian character of noble savagery while calling up associated historic imitations of the Indians' style.

The mode of warfare waged by Mosby's Raiders was a martial variant of the hunter-gatherer model. They provisioned themselves, and harassed the enemy, in that primordial fashion. They constantly changed their camp, had no fixed place of residence, and—as they were operating behind enemy lines—they were evidently indifferent to artificial boundaries. They were distinct from the main body of the army, and from formal contact or extended intercourse with civilians in the area. They resembled a tribe. George Forgie, speaking of the Southern fondness for guerrilla warfare, traces it first to the paradigm established by the Revolution. Then observing its "domestic" character, he writes, "Now we are closer to the point: partisan warfare was more interesting than any other kind because it involved the family and enveloped the

248
THE REBELLION

home."[26] Hunting down guerrillas, who have the aid and sympathy of area households, invariably entails the harassment of civilians. This further distances the invading force from civilian sympathies and enables their opponents to construe them as violators of the home's sanctity. The issues of the Civil War and the mythic personae of the contending sides made this charge both credible and onerous when directed against the Union forces. The guerrillas, in addition to relying upon—and thus allying themselves with—the household, had in their own organization something of domesticity. The absence of military titles and accoutrements among them, the extreme youth of many of the partisans, and the intimacy created by their circumstances lent them a familiar character. Not many in either army could say of their commanders as one of Mosby's men did, "It was my happy privilege frequently to snuggle up to him."[27]

The dependence of the partisans on popular support obliged them to avoid those arrogations and indiscretions which incline civilians to look harshly on soldiers. "Mosby would not permit any man to commit a crime, or even a misdemeanor, in his command."[28] Those who failed to keep to this exacting standard were required to make reparations to the offended civilian and were quickly packed off. This policy enhanced the standing of the partisans relative to the less well regulated Union force, increasing the strength of their claim that they represented a popular struggle. This was essential to the Confederacy, for its legitimacy rested solely upon the claim that the people in the states had withdrawn their allegiance from the Union and transferred it to the Confederacy. The hostility of occupied areas to federal troops, and popular aid to Mosby, underscored the Confederate charge of invasion.

Jefferson's counsel on rebellions had not been a policy much emulated by his successors. Jackson had entered the threat of force early in the game. Lincoln, in choosing to regard secession as rebellion, believed that the decision entailed another to suppress it militarily. Sherman, in a dispatch sent to Southern civilians "so as to prepare them for my coming," noted that while European wars were customarily "confined to the armies engaged," rebellions had another rule. The people were in rebellion; hence it was the people who must be fought. This dictated a policy of total war. Sheridan, describing to Bismarck the conduct of the war in the South, asserted that Union policy had been to leave them "nothing but their eyes to weep with."[29]

Sherman had forbidden pillaging at the outset of the war, only to observe in later years "I was a poor innocent then."[30] He first modified the policy, permitting foraging and confiscation, but obliging soldiers to give in return a promise to pay "at the pleasure of the United States on proof of loyalty at the time."[31] The directive reflected Sherman's growing recognition of pillage as a tactical device. Its provisions indicate that the idea of the community as sovereign had pervaded the Union in its operation as well as its ideology.

The disruption of the Union was, Sherman contended in a phrase which would be echoed by Whitman, "the foulest crime that ever disgraced any time or any people."[32] Rebellion was unconscionable because it was the state and not the people which was sovereign. Provision within the claimed boundaries of the United States was the rightful property of the army which represented it. A disputing claim could be made, and restitution asked, only if the deprived party could prove a like inclusion in that state. The same reasoning prompted similar provisions in the Emancipation Proclamation.

Sherman's policy toward pillage underwent its final and decisive transformation prior to his seige of Atlanta. He informed Hood that because Atlanta was a fortified city, that city and all it contained might legitimately be leveled. There were no noncombatants in rebellion. The punitive campaigns which Sherman launched across Mississippi and Georgia were directed primarily at private property and thus at the resolution of the supporting secessionist population. Sherman warned, "A people who persevere beyond a certain limit ought to know the consequences. Many, many peoples, with less pertinacity, have been wiped out of national existence."[33] Support to guerrillas, he wrote to General Canby, invited genocide. Grant's demand for unconditional surrender, urged on him by Lincoln, who reminded him of it when he seemed to waver, was wholly appropriate to this total war.

In the Union as in the Confederate army, the order and appearance of the troops manifested significant features of the sectional political culture which each represented. Northern soldiers readily accepted the uniforms and drill which Southern troops resisted. Some have attributed this to a higher proportion of foreign-born among the Union soldiers. This explanation, which was offered at the time, rested on the assumption that foreigners, being unaccustomed to democratic institutions, would acquiesce to discipline and render unquestioning obedience. The troops of the Northeast, which did indeed include a greater number of foreign-born, were believed by Northern commanders to be better disciplined than those of the West. Sherman, conceding this, argued that they were less effective for it. The orderliness of the troops reflected more, however, than the influence of their foreign contingent.

The process of rationalization in the North had far outpaced the South and West. There, where rural occupations predominated, the regulation of time and human activity necessary to manufacture was still unknown. Industrialization required, Weber contended, a variety of military discipline. Workers, like soldiers, were assigned particular tasks to be performed at designated times. Days were ordered like drill, and cooperative obedience became a cardinal virtue. For many in the Northern camp, the factories had been a long and thorough tenure at boot camp, accustoming them to the essential features of military discipline. The rigid hierarchy of authority, drill, and the duty of obedience were as much features of factory as of army life.

Their tenure in the factories had also accustomed workers to think of themselves as a collectivity, in which each individual had been assimilated to the mass. They had been operatives; now they were soldiers. In each case, their private identity had social and political significance only as part of a collectivity: the factory or the army. The idea of the mass army pervaded the rhetoric, poetry, and songs of the Union in the Civil War. In it, several aspects of Northern political culture conjoined.

The idea of the sovereignty of society had its American origins at Plymouth with the Puritans and their community of saints. This understanding of America is evident in the "Battle Hymn of the Republic," where the soldiers are assimilated not only to the nation but to God. Here the loss of self in community was portrayed as participation in epiphany, a collective apotheosis. The Puritan influence was also evinced in the conception of the community as temporally inclusive, and Lincoln's consequent concern for posterity. More than any other feature, the preference for "Union" rather than "United States" expressed the dissolution of particularity in community. This choice reflected the reverence for law and contract which accompanies rationalization.

Although it was a feature of Puritan political culture, the cult of the law had become secularized and the law's sanctity variously attributed to its democratic rather than divine origin. This variant prevailed in the West. In that section, the Union's claim to primacy was buttressed by its territorial and numerical superiority. Size was development in Western culture. American grandeur depended on aggrandizement; division was diminution. In this culture, the numerical superiority of North to South, while it might excite some sympathy for the underdog, was equally likely to be regarded as evidence of the North's moral superiority. That understanding of the war which contended that the South represented a minority unwilling to abide by majority rule saw the Confederates as proponents of aristocracy. This accorded well with Northern myths of Southern arrogance, and with the slavery issue, drawing attention from institutionalized hierarchies in the North and diverting the barely submerged resentments of Northern workers.

Union soldiers were thus wont to express their egalitarianism through assimilation and collective action rather than through displays of individuality. Uniforms and drill were, in this political culture, emblematic of equality. This conception also influenced the Union strategy, which preferred infantry to cavalry and movements by mass armies to raids by smaller parties.

The North's industrialization and the South's enduring agrarianism present the dominant disparity in the political culture of the two sections. Industrialization provided the North with a population accustomed to hard labor, regularity, obedience, and assimilation. It also gave the North a substantial advantage in the provisioning and arming of that force. Men accustomed to manufacturing, who credited themselves with a keen eye for profit, could readily accommodate an increased demand for firearms, wagons, ammunition, and artillery. Fighting on the home turf has occasionally been named an advantage; for agriculturalists it is doubly onerous. Each battle removes land from cultivation and hampers the provisioning of the army. Industry is doubly advantaged by war. As Richard Current has observed, "Once the financial crisis of late 1861 was passed, the Union entered an economic boom."[34] The proliferation of war industries had several fortunate consequences for the Union. It reconciled to the war some who expected to profit by it. It enabled the army to provision itself rapidly, and with less expense. It sped the development of better arms and more sophisticated manufacturing techniques. As the war continued, the industrial advantages increased. Southern politicians had decried "the military-industrial complex" (in these very words) since the War of 1812. Its establishment and aggrandizement in the Civil War confirmed the traditional Southern association of capitalist avarice with the abuse of federal, and especially executive, authority. In the North, however, it enhanced the image of America as engaged in a great progressive work, in which freedom, civilization, and industry were simultaneously advanced. Industrial development in this view was—like the cause of the war itself—merely a material manifestation of the nation's moral progress. Southerners, conversely, looked at the conduct and interests of particular men, rather than the grandeur of the emerging industrial system. Union soldiers and the Northern press compared ragged Confederates with their better-clad, better-armed, and better-fed Union troops. Rebels published accounts of partisan raids on Union sutlers' wagons, netting hauls of champagne and other luxuries intended for Union generals.

Confederate poetry commonly drew the lineaments of the Union soldier in the ranks from Hammond's famous "mudsill speech." Accustomed to exploitation, these laborers-cum-soldiers were supposed to lack both pride and valor. Their lack of independence made them an object of contempt in a culture where independence was preeminently valued. Southerners wrote of "Northern hirelings"[35] and contended "these hirelings they'll never stand."[36] The implied assertion that they were fighting, as they had worked, in another's interest, and for pay, recognized a congruence in the military and industrial systems. In the Southern mythology of the war, Union soldiers were cast as the "poor, miserable, *hired* outcasts whose / principles were bought."[37] The culture dictated pity for their dependence, contempt for their regard for money: "For gold let Northern legions fight."[38] This, when conjoined with the Southern contention that they remained loyal to the original Constitution and regime, produced the assertion that Lincoln had "bought allegiance," that they were his "armed hirelings."[39]

The large foreign contingent which came to comprise 20% to 25% of the Union Army, attached additional cultural associations to the characterization of Yankees as mercenary. The historical model for mercenaries had been that of the Hessians in the Revolution. Southern writers recalled this in referring to "the Hessian horde" and "the Northern Hessians."[40] A satiric verse asserted of Lincoln:

> He scarce can chase up quoins to pay
> The hired scum, the foreign foe
> Who comes to steal our rights away.[41]

Another Southerner wrote:

> O'er our Southern sunny strand
> Vandal feet are treading
> And the Hessians on our land
> Devastation spreading.[42]

This image was enhanced by the presence of substantial numbers of Germans among the immigrants.

Attention to foreigners in the Union ranks carried several messages. The Hessian image associated the Union with England in the Revolution. It suggested that the North had more of Europe in it than the South, that it had been corrupted. Finally, it affirmed that the Union army was an army not of brothers, but of foreigners, easing the dissolution of sentimental bonds consequent to a common history and enabling Southerners to regard Union troops as a foreign and invading force.

This perception of Union troops was not, however, confined to the South. Soldiers, in the last years of the war were known as "Lincoln dogs" and "hireling" in putatively loyal Northern states.[43] Hostility to the constitutional arrogations of Lincoln's administration, and to the military charged with their enforcement, had reproduced in the Union the schism which divided the United States.

Received wisdom, scholarly and popular, has held that the strict subordination of military to civil authority in the Confederacy, its attendant maintenance of civil liberties, and the paucity of military discipline in the Confederate ranks proved detrimental to the Southern war effort. I hold a contrary view. With the preponderance of men and resources and the advantages of an industrial economy firmly upon the side of the Union, Confederate victory depended upon the demoralization of the North. The abridgment of civil liberties under Lincoln's administration ended popular support for the war effort and resulted in widespread disaffection. As the Union military and commander in chief became increasingly heavy-handed in their dealings with dissident Northerners, support for appeasement and even for the Confederacy increased.

Prior to the war, some Southerners—among them a future general who swore he would drink the blood spilled in such a conflict—believed that ideological scruples and familial bonds would preclude martial opposition to Southern secession. When this expectation proved ill founded, more conservative predictions came to the fore. Edmund Ruffin forecast growing alienation among Northern urban masses and predicted that rioting and rampant dissaffection would cripple the Northern war effort.[44] The extent of evident urban alienation would provoke a crisis of legitimacy within the Union, undermining Lincoln's regime and obliging him to abandon the war.

By the summer of 1862, Ruffin's prophecy seemed on the verge of fulfillment. New York had been seized by an unprecedented, and as yet unequaled, display of urban violence. Rioters, outraged by the draft, had taken to the streets, attacking police and provost marshals, looting and lynching. Lincoln responded with the army. Federal troops met the rioters with "grape and canister," bayonet charges, rifle volleys, and howitzers.[45] At the end of the week, the riots had been put down.

Nineteen people had been killed by the rioters.[46] Estimates of those killed by the army range from 199 to over a thousand. Contemporary sources concurred in the statement that large numbers of corpses were smuggled from the city. Modern scholars have tended to dismiss this out of hand. Adrian Cook argues that the secret smuggling out of bodies would have proved too expensive and too difficult to be readily accomplished by citizens in a city closed by riot. The clandestine transport of bodies was charged, however, not to the citizens, but to the army, which had an evident interest in obscuring the number of casualties, and the means to do it.

The magnitude of popular disaffection was not evinced solely by the number of casualties in the New York riots. A year later, provost marshals reported that draft registers in New Hampshire, New York, Pennsylvania, Indiana, Kentucky, New Jersey, and Minnesota were amassing stores of arms. In Minnesota, reports to the War Department stated, "whole counties have been taken over." The provost marshal wrote to the head of the Draft Board, "Milwaukee is thoroughly disloyal and controlled by mobs, and has been for years." Milwaukee had followed New York with draft riots in May of 1863. Enrollment officers in Wisconsin had been forced to take armed parties of soldiers merely to secure names for the enrollment lists. Provost marshals in Indiana had declared martial law in the face of popular resistance to their authority.[47]

The impetus for the riots and resistance was succinctly expressed in the slogan "a rich man's war but a poor man's fight." The Union's policy of permitting commutation on a payment of a $300 fee offered tangible evidence that the working classes were to bear the burden of the war. Eugene Murdock writes, "The evidence appears conclusive that commutation supplies the principal provocation for the 1863 draft riots."[48] Laborers during the New York riots had drafted a protest, stating commutation as their principal grievance: "A great portion of the poor working men of the community will necessarily be compelled, under the provisions of the draft, if enforced, to leave their families in abject poverty in consequence of the odious provision exempting from military duty any citizen having $300.[39]

Opposition to the draft itself, independent of its provisions, had been extensive since its inception. Those who could, commuted. Of the 133,000 drafted in Ashtabula County, Ohio, 85,000—nearly two-thirds—commuted. Those who were unable to commute became increasingly resentful, a sentiment expressed in sporadic violence. Some took refuge first in communal strategies for concealing eligible men from the enrolling officers and later in Canada. The popularity of commuting among the more affluent classes placed a disproportionate burden on workers.

Workers, especially immigrants, provided much of the support for the Democratic Party in the North. Never enthusiastic supporters of the war, they received their share of the war's hardships with anger. Not only the draft, but the burdens of inflation and scarcity weighed less heavily on the wealthy. Workers in New York were further angered when dock strikes were broken by industry and government. The use of free black labor to replace striking workers alienated white workers from one of the war's supposed ends, and made blacks the target of extraordinary violence in the draft riots.

Successive generations of analysts have seized on these racist attacks as evidence that the riots were motivated primarily by racial hostility. The depredations of the rioters were, however, directed primarily against agents of the government and the affluent.[50] Contemporary sources observed that the rioters' animosity toward blacks was directed particularly at dock workers. These, due to their role in the strike, were made the scapegoat, as they had been the cat's-paw, of the wealthy. One black worker, more clear-sighted than his white compatriots asked, "Why should they hurt me or my colored brethren? We are poor workingmen like them; we work hard and get but little for it."[51] White workers, though unable to recognize their proper allies, discerned their enemies with ease. Rioters would spot the well dressed, cry, "There goes a $300 man!" and proceed to the attack. It had become, as Cook observes, a class war. The war had revealed, as Ruffin had predicted, a host of divisions within the Union ranks.

Those populations from which the soldiers were to be predominantly drawn, were unsympathetic to the war. They were reluctant to engage in it. Although they were unwilling to confront the Confederacy, whose offenses had failed to do perceptible damage to the interests of the working classes, they were ready and willing to confront federal troops. Popular hostilities were directed not toward the Confederacy, but toward the Union. The war had been a costly one for workers, in casualties and income. The unwillingness of antislavery manufacturers to negotiate with workers, and the use of black strikebreakers in the New York dock strike, persuaded many workers that abolition was intended to secure a larger pool of labor, and hence cheaper workers whose fear of replacement would render them submissive. The practice of giving black soldiers less pay and lower bounties in the Union army lent credence to the suspicion that antislavery activities of prominent capitalists were prompted not by a concern for justice, but by a desire for profit.

The Union army was marked by great inequality. Its organization was hierarchical, and reforms increased rather than diminished that hierarchical character. Workers bore the burden of military service, and blacks continued to be officially and methodically discriminated against. The injustices which prevailed in the society at large were not merely reproduced, but reinforced, by the changes in the organization of the army in the war years.

The abridgment of civil liberties, and the expansion of executive authority were also viewed with alarm by workers in the North. Both the urban laborers and the Western farmers were heavily Democratic. They therefore reacted with special indignation to unconstitutional arrogations by a president whom they had opposed. Their opposition derived strength from both their ideological and their partisan loyalties, factors which do not always operate in concert.

Lincoln's use of the military to suppress opposition to military policy and the abridgment of civil liberties implied a disregard for popular opinion and, hence, popular authority. Acquiescence to these alterations in the regime, whether secured by force or by persuasion suggested that they might remain indefinitely. The nation did emerge from the war radically altered. Class divisions were intensified, as workers had feared, and the labor movement was entirely defunct. The powers of the executive had been enhanced and expanded to the detriment of civil liberties, and an altered and hazardous relation had emerged between government—especially the executive branch—and the military. Industry and the military had forged a profitable alliance, and military coercion, even against citizens, had been established as a legitimate form of political action.

The Civil War had divided the nation deceptively. The parties to the conflict were not distinguished by section, nor by support or opposition to slavery. When the smoke cleared, blacks were still oppressed and unequal, a position they retained until they seized equality for themselves. The egalitarian social values and the democratic ideology of the Revolutionary era had, however, been irreparably damaged.

THE REFORMATION: HISTORIC PATTERNS FOR SECTIONAL CONFLICT

David Brion Davis remarks in *The Slave Power Conspiracy and the Paranoid Style*, "We have not sufficiently appreciated that for many American Protestants, the Reformation even more than the Revolution was the model for a timeless archetypal experience that had to be re-enacted, in almost ritualistic fashion, if freedom was to be preserved."[52] The great influx of Catholic immigrants prior to the Civil War had prompted a reactionary revival of American Protestantism, and invested it with something of its old militance. The paradigm of the Reformation was present to the minds of those who witnessed sectional division and Civil War. Recalling the mythical-historic origins of the two sections, observers—especially in the North, where militant Protestantism was strongest—saw in the Rebellion the lineaments of the Reformation. An editor of Northern war poetry after the war characterized "John Brown's Body" as "this senseless farrago—as senseless as the equally popular 'Lillibulero' of the times of the great civil commotion in England."[53] He recognized that while the content was evidently meaningless, the place of the song in the war satisfied a long-established pattern and elucidated the meaning of the conflict by likening it to its historical precursor.

The association of the North with the Puritans, the South with the Cavaliers, was held in American political culture long before the outbreak of the war. This source of sectional divergence was presented as a historical fact, and each section accepted its place in the paradigm. A Virginian, writing of sectional divergence in a review of Bancroft's *History of the United States*, observed:

> We might trace it more truly, though more remotely, to the very fact in which he glories so justly, that the people of New England are the descendants of those ancient Puritans . . . We too of the South, and especially we of Virginia, are the descendants, for the most part, of the old cavaliers—the enemies and persecutors of those old Puritans—and entertain, perhaps unwittingly, something of a hereditary and historical antipathy against the children for their fathers' sakes.[54]

Beverley Tucker called his Southerners "the descendants of the men who had defied Cromwell in the plentitude of his power."[55] A Northern observer of "the New England character" found the origin of the New Englanders' industry and their piety in their Puritan descent.

With Whig attempts to make New England's sectional culture the culture of America came efforts to make New England's Puritan ancestors those of the South as well. One author asserted, "The Puritan blood flows everywhere, swelling every vein of this great republic, diluted perhaps by intermixture, enfeebled perhaps, but still imparting something of its pristine strength and vigor."[56] This putative genealogy reflects the terms on which New England would embrace the South. They retained the Puritan blood in its purest form. In the South it had been enfeebled by admixture. The cultural constitutions of the two regions were contrasted in terms of a putative physical constitution, and culture symbolized by genetic ancestry. This species of metaphor, in which a physical is substituted for a cultural disparity, was also evident in accusations of Southern miscegenation. Even in their language, Northerners strove for the materialization of mind. This metaphor implied the superiority of North to South even as it affirmed their kinship. It was not, therefore, well received in the South. Bancroft's Virginian reviewer evinces the zeal with which Southerners repudiated any imputation of kinship with the Roundheads. The reviewer faults Bancroft for ranking Virginians among the supporters of Cromwell, holding Tucker's view that they had "withstood the usurpation of Cromwell" while it was practicable, and "fled to where the spirit of loyalty was strongest" when it was so no longer. He asks: "What is the meaning of this strange attempt to pervert the truth of history and to represent Virginia as being as far gone in devotion to the Parliament as Massachusetts herself? Why does it come to us, sweetened with the language of panegyric, from those who love us not and habitually scoff at and deride us?"[57]

Bancroft's intention, he concludes, is "to dispose us to acquiesce in the new notion that the people of the colonies, all together, formed one body politic before the Revolution."[58] The Virginian was in good company when he recognized this as an innovation. Josiah Quincy, of Massachusetts, had been swift to declare, a generation before, that "the first love of my heart is the Commonwealth of Massachusetts."[59] Harmanus Bleeker, of New York, advanced sectionalism as a self-evident truth: "We cannot help it that the country is made up of sections. We are legislating for such a country and it is our business and duty to regard the circumstances, the interests, and feelings of the people of different parts of the Union."[60] As the South had become increasingly conscious of its distinct sectional character, the North had been in the grip of ardent nationalism. The sectionalist sentiments expressed by Randolph and Calhoun appeared as doctrine to their successors, while those of their Northern colleagues appeared to their constituents as artifacts of an earlier era.

The Virginian's disinclination to accept the notion of a primordial American Union rose out of a reluctance to own the South in such a union. In this review, ancient and imminent enmity coincide. The association of Virginian history with the present as well as the past constitution of the state evinces considerable acuity. Bancroft was indeed engaged in promulgating a history consonant with the ideological primacy of New England. The reviewer, therefore, justly employed sentiment rather than document in disputing Bancroft's account. History, he recognized, is most significant not as a record of past events, for no history could compass these, but rather as an explication of their import. It discerns the significance and interprets the meaning of events, individuals, and policies according to the character of the people it endeavors to delineate. For a people fearful of diversity, it may indeed become, as Lincoln wished, a "sacred text," supplying conventional liens where natural ones are absent or attenuated.

Southerners were not such a people. Priding themselves on their distinction, and excepted from the fears which immigration had raised in the North, they preferred histories of ancient conflict to those of a primordial union. The Virginian's dissent was, he confessed, culled from oral rather than documentary history. "It accords with the hereditary prejudices and prepossessions of the present day."[61] He differs from Bancroft not only concerning the content of Bancroft's *History*, but also in regard to the claims which history may credibly make. Bancroft pretends to possession of objective fact, his reviewer to the privilege of subjective dissent.

Southern refusal to accept Whig history and the Puritan Founding accompanied the efflorescence of Southern nationalism. That particularly militant strain of reactionary Protestantism which had risen in response to Catholic immigration had been the engine of assimilation. Assimilative efforts originally directed solely toward the immigrants soon embraced the South and West as well. Southerners rejected not only the content but the very notion of a culture comprehensive of North and South.

Northern efforts toward an inclusive definition of American nationality were opposed on three planes. Southerners rejected the concept of "Union" as ideal, contending that development, rather than resulting in the assimilation of hitherto-disparate groups, was expressed in differentiation. The force of development, as they perceived it, was centrifugal rather than centripetal. On the institutional plane, they endeavored to preserve particularity through the doctrine of states' rights. Finally, they rejected the content of that rigorously delineated culture which the Whigs sought to make universal. The dissolution of the Whig party coincides with the end of these assimilative overtures to the South. Thereafter, North and South cleaved increasingly to their disparate identities, and the cultural conflict presented in the Reformation became increasingly expressive of sectional divergence.

The association of Puritan and Cavalier with North and South became more frequent after 1850. In the early years of the republic, though residents of the two sections recognized their ancestry in this ancient conflict, it was only rarely referred to. In sectional disputes, prevailing differences in occupation and manners, rather than ancestral antagonism, were marked out as the source of the rupture. As sectional schism became imminent, allusions to this archetypal conflict and the self-conscious assumption of the roles of Puritan and Cavalier became common in each section.

The conflict of Puritan and Cavalier in the English Revolution, Reformation, and Restoration, provided a paradigm which Americans found expressive of their sectional schism. Their rhetorical recourse to this model served to elucidate the disparity of North and South by likening them to well-delineated partisans in an earlier conflict. The Cavaliers were flamboyant and pleasure loving, the Puritans restrained and austere, a disparity of style and taste which Americans found equally descriptive of the South and North, respectively. The Puritans were religious; religion had remained dominant in the social and political culture of the North. The Cavaliers were ascribed a sinful and pagan character. Their associations with Catholicism carried the imputation of paganism—idols, incense, and ritual—from the sixteenth to the nineteenth century.

Writers in both sections associated Catholics with the South. One Southern journal of January 1860 referred in passing to "the Puritans of the North and the Catholics of the South."[62] A modern scholar asserts that "Southern perceptions of an ancestral antagonism between the Puritan and Cavalier were intensified by, but not confined to, the peculiar concerns of the Romantic imagination. They were, above all, responses to the divergent religious histories of the North and South."[63] The difference appears to be that of Church and Chapel in the English tradition, a dichotomy which attaches to the church a more intimate association with Catholicism than Puritans could stomach. The intensity with which Northern Protestants confronted immigrant Catholicism in the antebellum period made this imputation especially condemnatory. It was strengthened by the coincidence of traits ascribed likewise to immigrants and the South: intemperance, violence, indolence, and rebelliousness. Southern paganism had been decisively established by the Founders.

The sinfulness of Cavaliers and Southerners, in the Northern interpretation of the archetype, was revealed in their violence, their intemperance, and their unrestrained and irregular sexuality. These traits, in antebellum American political culture, were those which had likened the Southerners to blacks and Indians, as well as to the immigrants. They are characteristic of the state of nature and thus politically expressive of alienation and liminality. In Puritan culture, the state of nature was that condition prior to covenant, and thus the province of both rebellion and paganism.

Rhetorical attention to this aspect of the paradigm reached its zenith in the midst of the war. Melville, Whittier, Lowell, and less distinguished Northern poets freely associated the South with Hell, Lucifer, and the entire daemonium of sinfulness. Some examples of this extravagant species of rhetoric were marked by a little depreciatory levity.

> This Southern climate's quare, Biddy,
> A quare and bastely thing
> Wid winter absent all the year
> And summer in the spring.
> Ye mind the hot place down below?
> And may ye never fear
> I'd draw comparisons—but thin,
> It's awful warrum here.[64]

Others were not. Sherman, in a dispatch directed to Southern civilians, declared, "Satan and the rebellous saints of heaven were allowed a continuous existence in Hell merely to swell their just punishment. To such as would rebel against a Government so mild and just as ours was in peace a punishment equal would not be unjust."[65]

The memory of Cromwell and the Roundheads had firmly associated the specter of military dictatorship with the stern evangelism of the Puritans in Southern political culture. Southern fears that New England Federalists intended to undermine the democracy and establish in its place a despotic regime, through the Alien and Sedition Acts, had been exacerbated by Southern recollections of the Puritan ancestry of the New England Yankees. The role of New England in the alteration of the Constitution, the usurpation of the rights of states and people, and finally the invasion of the South, confirmed Yankees in the character of their Roundhead ancestors. The Alien and Sedition Acts had represented, in Southern history, an attempt to enforce uniformity of belief, after the Puritan model. The use of force against seceding Southern states, under the claimed protection of the deity, was similarly evocative of the Roundheads.

A Southern account of the Alien and Sedition Acts controversy, written in 1858, characterized Adams' actions as those of "a Cromwell."[66] Another article of the same year described the Cromwellian character: "Cromwell was formed to delude the minds of men. His hypocrisy, a thing far removed from what is ordinarily known by that name, was fervent, and excited sympathy, and created awe in the beholders."[67] This characterization (note the date) spoke to Southern perceptions of the antislavery and Moral Reform movements. These had taken many of their partisans from the militant Protestantism of the Protestant Crusade. They were directed explicitly to the "reformation" of the nation.

Lincoln, in his Temperance Address, spoke of this effort as a "moral revolution" which, if it were successful, would surpass the political revolution effected by the Founding Fathers. The refounding which he himself was to accomplish was thus to have in America the status of the Reformation in Christianity. The heirs of the Revolution, like the Roman Catholic church, were untrue to the spirit of their cause. Morally bankrupt—a phrase entirely expressive of the Protestant ethic—they must be rejected, and the nation purified.

Southerners who were not entirely persuaded of their perfidy regarded the religiosity professed by Northerners as a front for baser objects. Hypocrisy was their besetting sin. It was a congenital defect. Southerners spoke of a similar hypocrisy in that Reformation which their opponents put forth as their model, and complained of "the guile of the Puritan demon."[68]

Northern poets, endeavoring to describe, as their soldiers endeavored to effect, a national Reformation, took their titles and imagery from Protestant authors: Melville from Milton, Whittier from Luther.[69] Conquest of the arrogant Southerner was associated, in Northern rhetoric, with defense of the covenanted order, a phrase which united "Higher Law" abolitionists with Constitutional Unionists. The poetry of the war drew from the former rather than the latter source. Horatio Woodman wrote of the North:

> The mind of Cromwell claimed his own.
> The blood of Naseby streamed
> Through hearts unconscious of the fire
> Til that torn banner gleamed.
> God's Gospel cheered the sacred cause
> In stern prophetic strain
> Which makes his right our covenant
> His psalms our deep refrain.[70]

A Southern poem similarly recognized the kinship of the Union army to Cromwell's force, but took a rather jaded view of archetype and avatar:

> The Northern rabble arms for greed
> The hireling parson goads the train
> In that foul crop from bigot seed
> Old Praise-God Barebones howls again.[71]

The invocation of Cromwell by Northern poets merely confirmed Southern suspicions that there was conquest in the offing. North and South had long referred to this common episode in their common past, concurred in their common object, and again ranged themselves on opposing sides. Freedom was the end for both. It is, as Hartz affirmed, the "res Americana." Northern historians were accustomed to see its seedtime at Naseby, in the defeat of royal authority. The affirmation of the primacy of Parliament contained, for them, the germ of American democracy. The depredations of Cromwell's troops had merely spread a little blood meal on a fertile field.

The "Battle Hymn of the Republic" became, and remains, the foremost example of that militant religiosity in which the Northerners likened themselves to their Puritan ancestors. Howe wrote:

> Mine eyes have seen the glory of the coming of the Lord
> He is trampling out the vintage where the
> grapes of wrath are stored
> He has loosed the fateful lightning
> of his terrible swift sword
> His truth is marching on.

Southerners responded with a parody entitled "The War Christians' Thanksgiving":

> We know that plains and cities waste
> Are pleasant in thine eyes—
> Thou lov'st a hearthstone desolate
> Thou lov'st a mourner's cries
> Let not our weakness fall below
> The measure of thy will
> And while the press hath wine to bleed
> Oh, tread it with us still.[72]

The Northern contention that God was working through the Union army as He had through the army of Cromwell owed nearly as much to German philosophy as it did to Puritan religion. The Reformation had served the German philosophers as a decisive way station in the march of mind. The Germans, like their Protestant protagonists, regarded the process in which they were engaged as providential. Each moment in this process itself was distinguished by its rationality. Universally intelligible, it was sanctioned by the irrefragable authority of reason. The imposition of order upon an unruly world became in this articulation the end common to reason and revelation, the common cause of religion and philosophy.

New England's enunciation of this process leaned heavily, however, upon the inevitability of the outcome, an obeisance to divine omnipotence. Emphasis on the historical evolution of the American state removed from its formation the vagaries of individual preference. Proponents of this historicist Americanism were thus radically distanced from the Lockeanism which Hartz saw as comprehensive of American political culture.

The Puritan Revolution and the Civil War represented successive moments in the progress of history. Each had advanced the work of God in the world. The Puritan Revolution was also construed as a war of masses against the elite—a feature which made it a more attractive paradigm to those elements of Northern and Western culture which found Puritan religiosity offensive or foreign. The stereotypical Southern pride and aristocratic affectations suited this interpretation of the historical paradigm. The slavery issue had also enhanced its applicability. Employment of this interpretation marshaled support for the antislavery movement among those not initially inclined to such a course, by advancing slavery as evidence of antidemocratic tendencies in the South. The South's defeat—and the defeat of slavery—would, like the defeat of the Cavaliers and English monarchy, simultaneously advance freedom and equality. In this interpretation of the paradigm, progress was measured by the increase of liberty rather than by the progress of true religion.

The predestination of the outcome of such decisive moments in history gave the resort to arms the name and character of an Appeal to Heaven. The role of prominent New England clerics in the Revolution provided a proximate model for that clerical agitation for war which Southerners found so damning. In the West, the American title to rule had been secured by the army. Most of its heroes were military men. The significance of violence in Western political culture inclined Westerners to support rather than condemn invasion of the South. As Slotkin argues, violence was there the means of regeneration and purification, a fitting beginning for a new birth of freedom.

Military despotism had been the favorite bogey of Southern statesmen from the earliest years of the republic. The image of the Roundhead, and more particularly the figure of Cromwell, associated the Northern war effort with the military usurpation of civil authority. Lincoln's explicit exercise of the powers of commander in chief in issuing the Emancipation Proclamation, and more importantly in the suppression of newspapers, the suspension of habeas corpus, and the trial of civilians by military tribunals all seemed to confirm the Southern interpretation of the Roundhead image when applied to the North.

The constellation of values and traits represented by the Roundheads is evident in a play printed in the *Southern Literary Messenger* of September 1836. The play was *Cromwell*. Its climax comes when the hero, disillusioned rather than inspired by the events at Naseby, repudiates Cromwell to join the forces of the Restoration. He says of his tenure with the Lord Protector:

> Boy that I was I pinned my faith to Cromwell,
> For him forsook my kin, renounced my home,
> My father's blessing and my mother's love,
> Gave up my heart to him, my thoughts, my deeds,
> Reduced the fire and freedom of my youth
> Into a mere machine—a thing to act
> Or to be passive, as its master wills.[73]

Adherence to Cromwell turns a natural man into "a mere machine." The Protestant cause removed the protagonist from the home and subjected him to the will of another. Here Cromwell represents the specter of industrialization, and the fear that men, loosened from their natural bonds of kinship and affection, would become the instruments of the will of their employers. Industrialization, religious zeal, and military coercion had become so entangled in the New England character that Cromwell, who stood as a cipher for two of these, could call up that which remained.

In this play's presentation of the English Revolutionary paradigm, the connection between the repression of internal and external nature is explicitly recognized. It provides a literary reprise of the Southern judgment upon the Protestant ethic. The action of the play turns upon the protagonist's rejection of the role of Roundhead for that of Cavalier. He is brought to this by the recognition that his involvement in the Puritan Revolution has altered his natural character and relations and thereby removed from him the capacity for intellect and volition. This accords with the Southern perception that the possession of natural rights and the experience of natural relations were interdependent. The play recalled the traditional Southern suspicions of military dictatorship. The protagonist's decision to desert the Roundhead cause for that of the Restoration is presented as a return to legitimate government. His actions and speeches in the play present the prevailing Southern interpretation of the political significance of the Cavalier model.

The confrontation of Puritan and Cavalier offered a historical pattern for the cultural divergence of North and South. The willingness of North and South to identify themselves with the opposing parties in the conflict indicates some agreement as to the terms of the past and present conflict, while the disparity in interpretation of the opposing roles indicates the peculiar points at which American culture diverged.

THE HOUSE DIVIDED: FAMILIAL METAPHORS FOR SECTIONAL CONFLICT

Lincoln's metaphor for the sectional divergence which would sever the Union has become a sign for the war, as well as the cultural divergence which preceded it. Lincoln had coupled the metaphor of a house divided with the assertion that the nation could not continue half slave and half free. In fact the only households so divided were those of the South. It was their seeming permanence rather than their imminent collapse which troubled him. The metaphor, however, was seized immediately and ceaselessly employed. It remains the most common metaphor for the nation in this period.

Acceptance of this metaphor by Lincoln's generation and those following was accompanied by frequent use of familial metaphors for the conflict. These, which rarely appear to be directly derivative from the "house divided," nevertheless elucidate the meaning of that metaphor. They suggest, on first glance, what may easily be discerned by other means: that Americans of the antebellum period were preoccupied by the revision of traditional familial roles and by the perceived decay of the family. The familial conflicts metaphorically employed to describe the national conflict are fraternal, oedipal, sexual, and intergenerational. Each of these contains a variant interpretation of the meaning and character of the conflict.

Certain of these metaphors have been touched upon earlier. Here they will be examined in conjunction, with a twofold intent. These metaphors, expressing sectional conflict in familial paradigms, present the opportunity to examine a formally related constellation of metaphors. Their linguistic kinship expresses a perceived conceptual kinship. Taken together, they express the rhetorical recognition that the conflicts described in these related metaphors bear a family resemblance to one another.

Each of these metaphoric conflicts presents, in the second instance, an opportunity to examine both the conflict which serves as signifier and the conflict signified. The temporal coincidence of the revision of national and familial structures, and the consequent employment of the latter as metaphoric of the former, produced a situation in which each influenced popular understanding of the meaning of the other. This same reciprocity is evident in the changing significance of particular metaphors and conflicts they symbolize. Sex roles in the family, and as metaphorically representative of the contending sections, illustrate this reciprocity most clearly.

The most popular interpretation of the "house divided" metaphor is that of fraternal conflict. The Civil War was a "war of brother against brother." This metaphor emphasizes the natural and indissoluble kinship of the two parties. It is appropriate, therefore, that it should have currency in the postwar Union. Similarly, it admits no disparity between the brothers, and thus none between the sections.

The metaphor of fraternal conflict did not have the same dominance in the Civil War period that it has in our time. Although descriptions of the Rebellion as a "war of brother against brother" were current in the war years, the paradigm of fraternal conflict was more frequently expressed in biblical terms, which stressed a fundamental disparity in the participants. The archetypal fraternal conflicts of Scripture are those of Cain and Abel and Jacob and Esau. The North was regularly associated with the former and the South with the latter brother in each case. The first was much used by the South; its perceived applicability derived from Abel's innocence. The latter story had been earlier and more frequently employed to describe conflict with the Indians. It suggested the divine approbation of the victor, the superior right of the vanquished, and the victor's superior intelligence and duplicity. The common association of the South with the Indian enhanced the applicability of the metaphor by conflating a historical application with the current one.

Michael Rogin, in his examination of American views of the annihilation of the Indian as fratricidal, observes that Americans tended to transfer repudiated characteristics onto the Indians they annihilated. By projecting related aspects of the collective character onto the enemy Indian, they could effectively excise these traits from themselves. The same mechanism operated in sectional conflict. Characterizations of the South as lawless (Lincoln), disorderly, sexual (Weld), miscegenate (Garrison), proud, intemperate, and violent enabled Northerners to repudiate these characteristics. The defeat of the South ritually excised them from the national character. This aspect of fratricidal conflict illustrates the interplay of personal identity and allegiance. There is also a notable correspondence between the traits which Americans collectively repudiated in the annihilation of the Indian and in the conquest of the South. Each of the defeated was associated with nature and with traits ascribed to men in the natural state: individuality, independence, lawlessness, violence, sexuality, and godlessness. Each victory thus effected a constriction of individual and collective identity. Each was an exercise of collective repression. The success of each enterprise is shown in the increasingly repressive culture of the succeeding period.

In the Jacksonian period, American ideology had distanced itself dramatically from the revolutionary ideology of the Founding and the Revolution of 1801. Whigs and Democrats likewise deprecated the right of revolution. Whig historians attempted to repudiate the Revolution altogether, giving all to the Pilgrims. Increasingly restrictive notions of appropriate conduct were promulgated; class divisions widened; social hierarchies flourished; personal and cultural diversity were deprecated. After the Civil War, class divisions and capitalist exploitation were praised rather than merely tolerated. Public demonstrations, strikes, and riots were put down with increasing severity, and became infrequent. Embryonic labor unions died out altogether. When they emerged again, it was in a far more conservative form, divested of the intent and ideology of revolution. Cultural repression was even more dramatic, with feminine roles strictly delineated, sexuality regulated, and social forms complex and discriminatory. Application of the fratricidal metaphor thus indicates the perception of a collective attempt to repress traits regarded as natural by the political culture.

John Quincy Adams, in his apology for Indian annihilation, cast the Indian and the white man as brothers warring for the mother's breast. Southern political rhetoric emphasized maternal indulgence: Northern rhetoric, conversely, complained of the section's deprivation—of influence in the government, of resources in nature. The fraternal metaphor could thus be related to metaphors of mother and child relations. Southern political culture employed the maternal metaphor to describe political development. In this scheme, fraternal disparity was the natural and expected consequence of maturation. This symbolic paradigm was foreign to Northern political culture. There, maternal indulgence was marked as the source of intemperance, passion, and willfulness, the lack of self-control and self-restraint. These traits were equated in Northern political culture with man's natural, instinctive condition. Maternal indulgence was thus equated with less repressive—and less civilized—cultures.

This articulation was congruent with enduring Puritan conceptions of the proper function and organization of the family. Paternal authority was the source of familial order. The father, as the divine agent, subordinated the child's will to his own, and hence to the will of God.

Because Puritan family structure stressed the father's role as the agent of God, Puritan rhetoric invested metaphoric paternity with similar attributes. The notion that the elders of the community, especially those with executive authority, were charged with responsibility for the moral duties as well as the rights of individuals in the community had shaped paradigms for good governance in New England's political culture. This understanding of moral stewardship in the executive was most important to those most closely akin to the Puritans. It dominated the political actions of the New England Whigs. The archetypal leaders in that region—Winthrop, Bradford, Mather, the later and secular Adamses—accorded to this idea of moral stewardship and paternal authority.

The archetype of presidential paternity was of course George Washington, the Father of his Country. Washington, however, did not lay claim to a paternal character in his official pronouncements, believing that it smacked too much of the monarchy he had refused. He also evinced a restraint in the exercise of executive authority that went unheeded by his imitators.

The two presidents who most vigorously laid claim to a paternal character were those who most vigorously pursued the subordination of the South. Jackson's Force Bill was promulgated in order to compel Southern acquiescence to the tariff, a measure designed to aid the North's development of those industries which would enable them to overcome the hardships of its niggardly natural endowment. Abolitionists protested that the South had too long been indulged in the exercise of its passions and demanded that it be forced to submit to executive authority. Presidential authority thus acquired a paternal character, and proponents of executive primacy, like Jackson and Lincoln, were wont to present themselves as patriarchs.

Each of those presidents—Washington, Jackson, and Lincoln— who were ascribed a paternal character in the exercise of their presidential office, was personally associated with the establishment and maintenance of the nation through force. This reflects prevailing notions of the character of paternal authority, in both familial and religious contexts.

This interpretation casts Lincoln in the role of the stern but righteous father, restoring the family through the forceful exercise of paternal authority. Like Jackson against the Indians, Lincoln waged war against his recalcitrant "sons" only to show them mercy afterwards. The Second Inaugural Address marks the restoration of the family and begins its reconstruction under the aegis of paternal authority.

Many commentators have read in Lincoln's Lyceum Speech envy and emulation of the Founding Fathers. In refounding a purportedly purer America, cleansed of the sin of slavery, Lincoln at once reenacted and replaced the achievement of the Founders. He was Father Abraham before the war was out. The recruiting song "We Are Coming, Father Abraham, Three Hundred Thousand Strong" expressed both Lincoln's successful replacement of Washington and popular approbation of the notion of executive as paternal authority. This also enhanced by reiteration the association of paternal authority with the exercise of force.[74]

It is to the North, then, rather than to the South, that Hartz should have looked for the forces of Filmerian reaction. The pose of the Old Testament patriarch and the accompanying assertion of the primacy of the executive, which had—as Hartz acknowledges—no political reality in the South, achieved both legitimacy and archetypal significance in the North. There it accorded to prevailing social institutions and constitutive myths of both the American Revolution and the Puritan theocracy. It occupied a position of unparalleled importance in that region for it reconciled these conflicting mythologies and provided a pattern of legitimate governance which could be reconciled to each. Lincoln, by according himself to this pattern and enhancing its rhetorical power with simultaneous appeals to both traditions, achieved a mythic status which surpassed that of Washington.

For the North, the paternal Lincoln was the temporal vicar of God; his authority, like that of the Puritan father, was divinely sanctioned. Subordination to his authority would secure the nation in conformity to the divine will. Soldiers and citizens in referring to Lincoln as their father expressed their loyalty to God and their adherence to compact. In this paradigm, the consequence and product of loyalty is obedience. It emphasizes the virtues of submission—to God, to fathers, and to conventional authority.

The virtues of submission were not firmly established in the South. The absence of Puritan familial structures and theology excpeted this paradigm from Southern political culture. Indeed, one of the most common familial paradigms employed in the antebellum South was that of the fatherless family, the mother and her children. This endured into the war years. The absent fathers were typically engaged in Revolution. This paradigm gave rise to two Southern variants of the father/son model.

In the first, the conduct of the living generation, the sons, is likened to their fathers' conduct in the Revolution. This is replacement. The oedipal wish implicit in the mother/child paradigm is satisfied here. This variant is particularly symbolic of the process of maturation: the son becomes the father. The South, developed and mature, aims at an appropriate independence. Because the fathers had been engaged in the process of revolution and founding which the establishment of Southern independence would demand of the sons, this metaphoric replacement was particularly descriptive.

In the second variant, which is conjoined to the figure of the "Southern Hamlet," there are two fathers, the quick and the dead, the false and the true. This metaphor expressed loyalty to the dead father, figuratively to the defunct Constitution or the old regime, and hostility to its illegitimate and undeserving successor. This spoke to Northern metaphors which would invest the executive with paternal authority. Like the first, this variant stressed the implicit instruction that a legitimate and appropriate emulation of the fathers involved a like involvement in these same activities.

Both of the Southern variants of the father/son metaphoric paradigm stressed emulation rather than obedience. They expressed that view of politics as dynamic and developing which pervaded Southern political culture. From Jefferson to the romantic reactionaries, Southerners emphasized the authority of the present generation and protested against the heavy hand of the dead. The evident absence of distant generations from the temporal world to which politics was properly confined invalidated their rule. The Puritans and their Northern heirs, however, regarded the community as properly inclusive of the past and of posterity. They were encompassed in a community together with their predecessors. Southerners saw themselves, the living, as having an open field in the present. Northerners, whose polity was more extensive, perceived rival claimants in previous generations. Lincoln's Lyceum Speech is a fine example of Northern ambivalence to their honored and envied predecessors. If this generation was to establish its preeminence, it was obliged to surpass the accomplishments of those past, to build upon rather than merely enjoy its inheritance. Only material evidence of national development—territorial expansion, constitutional change, victorious war—could evince political maturity.

This perception of a rivalry with the previous generation expresses collectively the oedipal anxieties of individual men. In both national and personal cases, maturation requires subordination to the father. That these anxieties did not manifest themselves in the political culture of the South as they did in that of the North speaks not to the superior stability of separate Southern psyches, but rather to that Enlightenment tradition which affirmed the natural independence of the existing generation. Southerners exhibited less hostility to their fathers, mythic and historic, because they entertained fewer doubts about their political independence of them.

The metaphor of father/son relations reveals how partisans of the opposed section thought of themselves with regard to the previous generation. Metaphors which cast these partisans as man and woman, husband and wife, elucidate relations in the societies themselves. Prior to the war, references to the impending schism as the dissolution of the Union marriage were commonplace. This metaphor recognized the disparate character of the two sections, and their joining in contract. It attempted to attach to the South's secession and the consequent dissolution of the Union something of the shame and tragedy which were popularly associated with divorce.

North and South were not always cast as husband and wife, in metaphors of sexual conflict in the house divided, but they were invariably cast as man and woman. The sexual typing of the two sections was acknowledged and employed consistently, North and South. The South's femininity, especially as expressed by Southerners, took a multitude of forms: mother, virgin, wife, daughter, amazon. The masculinity of the North was, however, expressed almost exclusively in patriarchal forms.

Lincoln's paternal character became representative of the section as a whole. This contained, given existing social relations, an implicit assertion of the propriety of the South's subordination. The importance of paternal domination in the Puritan family, and the unhappy consequences of maternal indulgence, were recalled to Northern minds by Southern references to the South as mother.

Conceptions of maternal and paternal roles common throughout the Union in the antebellum period associated the father with order, the conventional, contractual worlds worlds of god and politics, and the mother with nature, home, and instinct. These associations influenced sectional typing. The industrialization of the North had removed men from the home and separated men and women in their daily activities. Women had been confined increasingly to domestic activities. These developments had increased the political significance of this sectional typing by evoking the increasing economic disparity of the two sections and the corresponding difference in their mores and institutions. The rapid decline in the status of women in the North similarly increased the significance of the metaphor, exacerbating Southern suspicions of Northern ambition and arrogance.

The association of women with nature and men with culture in these metaphors indicates that the terms of sexual conflict, like those of fraternal conflict, signify perceptions of the war as fundamentally repressive.

Five
THE REFORMATION

The men of this closing trinity of chapters are the mythmakers of modern America. From the shards of a nationality splintered in civil war they refashioned an American identity. In the ruins of a rejected heritage they refounded the American regime. Each of these mythic representations of a renascent America is embedded in the nation we know. Yet they are profoundly different.

Melville belongs to the nation of the Founding. He recorded that nation's death: he revealed the meaning of its successor. Melville was mindful of the Revolutionary faith in nature and in man, and of the Puritan tradition that buried these in its resurgence. He saw ancient conflicts in this opposition: God and Lucifer, the giver of order and the founder of rebellion, Jew and Sabaean, white man and Indian. His vision of an altered America looks backwards to its antecedents.

Lincoln, no less than Melville and Whitman, was engaged in creating for a nation altered by civil war altered standards for the regime's legitimacy, and an amended national identity. He was, however, the only one of the three who was an essential component of the myth.

Lincoln made war. In putting down the Rebellion he reclaimed a province unpersuaded of its wrong and a disenfranchised but unrepentant people. The Union he preserved was a union in law. It could no longer claim the identity conferred by common sentiment or interest. Despite the frailty of this repaired foundation, the Union endured. Lincoln preserved it not through the war but through the peace he made. Before the war ended, he had begun the mythic reconstruction of the nation.

I end with Whitman. Whitman begins a new America. The spirit of rebellion, the boundless faith in man, the celebration of nature, of the body, that the Union had conquered and cast away was recaptured and restored by Whitman. His mythic nation reunited the contradictory sentiments, interests, myths, and ideologies of the warring sections. He created an American identity great enough to embrace the defeated with the victorious. He laid the foundations for a regime that would be built not merely on conquest, but on consent.

10 Melville and the Conquest of Nature

In a supplement to his *Battle Pieces*, written at the war's close and urging reconciliation, Melville describes himself as "one who never was a blind adherent."[1] That he adhered, with all the fervor of the most ardent partisan, to the North's cause is amply demonstrated by the poems that preceded his assertion. He adds, then, only that he was not blind.

Melville saw much in the war. Transmuted into poetry, the second sight, sight, second hands, and hindsight became the chronicle of an apocalyptic conflict. The contending nations—so Melville recognized them—were identified with contending forces in still greater struggles, mythic and historic.[2]

The South's alienation and secession, and the internecine strife that it occasioned, bespoke the failure of the Founding. That halcyon time when the separate states would be united not by arms and the law but by a confluence of interest, sentiment, and ideology had clearly passed. Melville's *Battle Pieces* mark its passage. They mark not the opening but the closing of an age. They are, therefore, imbued with an appropriate melancholy.

Melville wrote:

> Who looks at Lee must think of Washington
> In pain must think and hide the thought
> So deep with grevious meaning is it fraught.[3]

The South's secession implied a betrayal of the Union: it was a willful withdrawal from the nation of the Founders. Those whose ancestors, like Lee's, had had so great a hand in nation building were to become the instruments of its undoing. A painful thought, this, but there were others worse.

Lee had been Washington's descendant in more than blood. The recollection of the patrician provincial leading the dissident provinces out of empire was uncomfortably applicable. Who was it, then, who had renounced the Founding? The constitutional dispute, Melville asserted in his supplement, might arguably have been awarded to the South. His identification of the contending communities with Right and Wrong moved the dispute beyond the power of Constitution to determine. Like Seward he had recourse to a Higher Law:

> In this strife of brothers
> God, hear their country call
> However it be, whatever betide
> Let not the just one fall.[4]

The cataclysmic collision of the North and South, ending in a Northern victory, provided the foundation "whereon the throes of ages rear / The final empire and the happier world." It was this, and the justice of the Northern cause, that transformed the Civil War from a crisis of legitimacy to a conflict of unparalleled eschatological significance. In setting aside the Constitution and the ideology that bottomed the regime as the standards whereby the opponents were to be judged, Melville at once aligns himself with the North and reveals the political significance of the Northern victory. The inauguration of that final empire was an act of irrefragable righteousness. Melville was not blind, however, to the violence it did the Founding, or to the revolutionary reconstitution of the regime that would of necessity accompany it.

> The Founders' dream shall flee
> Age after age shall be
> What age after age has been
> From man's changeless heart their way they win.

That providential predestination which determined the course of history and sanctified the Union enterprise took precedence, morally and actually, over the Constitution. In a concise and elegant abbreviation of the Hegelian formula, Melville pronounced:

> Yea and Nay each hath its say
> But God he keeps the middle way.

The Union victory, though it evinced divine approval of the cause, was nonetheless an imperfect indicator of the national destiny.[5]

Laurence Thompson, in his provocative study *Melville's Quarrel with God*, argues that Melville's novels evince a heretical kicking against the pricks and an intemperate resistance to the rule of an indifferent and omnipotent deity. Melville, Thompson argues, coyly dissociating himself from the heresy, acceded to the errors of the Manichaeans, holding that an omnipotent God must answer for the wrongs occasioned by disinterest or malevolence. Flirting with the Ophites, who looked to Genesis and saw more truth in the promises of the serpent than beneficence in the proscriptions of the deity, Melville engaged in an esoteric indictment of God. Attempting to dissociate himself from the flunkeyism which characterized the Christian, he seeded his stories with satirical stories and blasphemous imagery.[6] All this is absent in the *Battle Pieces*. There Melville is on the side of the angels.

The nine silent years which had preceded their publication had wrought some change in Melville. He had not become a convert to orthodoxy, he had merely changed heresies. In the novels and *Battle Pieces* Melville's presentation of nature remains constant. Indifferent to man, seductively alluring, fatal, powerful, beautiful, chaotic, and amoral, nature represents a force and fortune on which men were dependent. In the novels, Melville, numbering omnipotence among God's attributes, attributed to that deity the creation and control of nature. The injuries men suffered in nature were thus the consequences of a criminal neglect. In the *Battle Pieces*, Melville separated nature from God. God, no longer omnipotent, may now be innocent. Melville's new faith in divine right contains, however, no surety for men. There is no longer the certainty of God's triumph. There can be no perfect confidence in the efficacy of divine action or benevolence. Nor can men be sure that the good for God is the good for men. Thus the *Battle Pieces*, divested and defiant, retain the melancholy aspect of the novels, and Melville continues in them the chronicle of apocalyptic contests. He asks:

> Can no final good be wrought?
> Over and over and over again
> Must the fight for the Right be fought?[7]

The outcome of the Civil War was but one moment in a long struggle, a battle in a longer war. This, the ultimate confrontation, provided the eschatological significance of the temporal enmity of North and South. Southerners were "the zealots of the Wrong,"[8] ignorant of their role in this final war. Deriving their convictions from the Constitution, they were seduced into violation of a higher law, "Such brave ones, foully ensnared / By Belial's wily plea."[9] They were to be "Martyrs for the Wrong."[10] The North, conversely, marched with God.

> So God appears in apt events
> The Lord is a man of war.[11]

Like Julia Ward Howe, Melville believed that God participated vicariously in the Union's triumph. He suggested too that the victory came in consequence not merely of divine predestination, but of divine intervention:

> Heaven lent strength, the Right strove well
> And emerged from the Wilderness.[12]

In his account of "The Conflict of Convictions," Melville indicates the significance of his identifications. The North is not merely right but Right, the South Wrong. When the North takes up arms he will

> Mark a twinkling in the tent
> Of Michael the warrior one.[13]

The South's Rebellion is a surrogate for a greater:

> Satan's old age is strong and hale
> A disciplined captain gray in skill.[14]

Their Lookout Mountain is "the fastness of the Anarch"; their defeat is "the Anarch's plunging flight."[15]

The Southerners, like that great Rebel Lucifer, were Sons of the Morning. They shone in the nation's dawn, but in opposing themselves to that Union ordained by history, and thus by God, they too rebelled. The wilderness was the South's home ground. The South was associated with the Anarch and Rebellion, with the Founding and the Revolution. That chaos which characterized anarchy and rebellion, national genesis and revolution, was the province of nature:

> The fight for the city is fought
> In Nature's old domain.[16]

Melville conflates the conflict of Wrong and Right with that of nature and culture. Of the defeated Southerners, he says, "Tis Nature's wrong they rue."[17]

The rights they claimed were those of nature, and of nature's God. In the agnostic humanity of the Founding, Melville saw the old enemy of the Jews resurgent:

> None can relate that strife in the pines
> A seal is on it, Sabaean lore.[18]

The South's defeat recalled an earlier defeat, by God through his chosen people, of a pagan polity. The American regime was founded by men within the memory of men. When asked to invoke the blessing of God upon the enterprise, one of the Founders had replied, "We need no foreign aid."

Washed like the North in the waves of revivalism that spread over the nation, the South had nonetheless clung intrepidly to the notion that governments should insist upon the rights of the people and not upon their moral duties, securing their lives in this world rather than fitting them for life in the next. The central figures of the Southern Revolutionary pantheon had a distinctly deistical smell about them: Washington, who refused to kneel in public, Jefferson, who regarded the divinity of Jesus as a myth, and Patrick Henry, whose religious views were both heretical and rudimentary.

Stonewall Jackson, in the poem "ascribed to a Virginian," had "a Roman heart"; he was "a stoic."

> A Modern lived who sleeps in death
> Calm as the marble Ancients are.[19]

The South, in Melville's articulation, had remained "True as John Brown"[20] to a pagan tradition. Stonewall Jackson had been, his Northern eulogist observed, a man "whose sword and prayer were long," yet he had "stoutly stood for Wrong."[21] He had prayed, it appears, to the wrong gods. Melville elaborates the comparison in *Clarel*, where he likens the Confederate veteran Ungar to Varus's legions searching for their lost eagles. The image of the lost eagle suggests that the Confederates were loyal to an older, classical America. The eagle belonged both to America and to the Romans. Varus's legions were the archetype of unswerving fidelity and Roman virtue. Melville has Ungar "sharing with infidels a home,"[22] fighting in company with the pagan

Muslims. He calls the Rebel "an armed man in the Druid grove"[23] and "the Parsee of a sun gone out."[24] He is another of the pagan partisans of nature.

In describing the growing fissure between North and South, culminating in the South's rebellion, Melville employs a network of images which liken the South's rebellion to a natural disaster; "ocean clouds over inland hills sweep storming in late autumn brown . . . And the spire falls in upon the town." In this confrontation of nature and culture, the church is the first target. In the South's rebellion, "nature's dark side is heeded now." So profound is the force of that rebellious nature that it goes to the heart of culture's constructs: "The hemlock shakes in the rafter, the oak in the driving keel."[25]

They, like the American regime, are shaken by this recollection of their origins. Lee, asked in Melville's interrogative account for the reason for the South's rebellion, attributes it to her allegiance to an earlier and natural authority. His analogy likens the South to a Christian convert who will renounce her faith before she will prove faithless to her natural bonds. Apostasy is the South's crime.

So in the South, vain every plea
'Gainst Nature's strong fidelity.
True to the home and to the heart,
Throngs cast their lot with kith and kin,
Forboding, cleaved to the natural part
Was this the unforgivable sin?[26]

The Rebellion was the South's recurrence to nature, not solely because with it the people in the states went out of the regime, seized that authority which came in consequences of their natural rights, and sought to reconstitute themselves. Rather it represented, to Melville, a collective choice of nature over culture, an election which entailed apostasy and rebellion against that God whose earthly progress was marked by the increase and extension of civilization.

The South had revived the threat of the Indian:

The Indian has creeped away
But creeping comes another.[27]

Melville's Ungar, unreconciled to the North and the new order, is the offspring of Catholic and Indian, "An Anglo brain and an Indian heart,"[28] very much as Paulding had described Randolph.

The Southerners owed nature their first allegiance. Nature granted them the same protection God was thought to afford the North. "Blessings on the friendly screen—I'm for the South: says the leafage green."[29] Melville had linked the Rebels to Indians, in a long-standing poetic tradition, but when he described Mosby's guerrillas, fighting in their natural environment, he enrolled nature itself into the rebel ranks:

> The Pleiads, as from ambush sly,
> Peep out—Mosby's men in the sky!
> Maple and hemlock, beech and lime
> Are Mosby's confederates, share the crime.[30]

Mosby himself seems "a satyr's child."[31] Ungar is described as "the officer with the forest eyes."[32] With the South's defeat, that forest is changed: "Sad woods they be where wild things sleep."[33]

The playfulness of Mosby's men, their courage and their easy grace, are freely contrasted with the stern sobriety of "Captain Cloud." Mosby's men revive the pagan rites, singing of fertility, and when the moon comes up,

> Oh we multiply merrily in the May
> The birds and Mosby's men we say.[34]

The captain responds, "Four walls will end that saucy mood."[35] The constructions of civilization restrain both internal and external nature.

Melville argues for the necessity of repression. The political repression of the South was accompanied by a repudiation of the playfulness, hedonism, self-display, and exuberant self-satisfaction, which were marked as characteristic of Southern life. Repression, Freud contended, provides the foundations of civilization. Marcuse and others have observed that repression accompanies bourgeois society. The establishment of legal-rational authority, of a regime in which objectivity is the primary value, necessarily entails the denigration of the subjective and the self-indulgent. Playfulness then becomes an attribute of outlawry.

Mosby recalled, no less to the Northern than to the Southern mind, Robin Hood and his Merry Men, a band of outlaws hidden in the forest, outside the polity, in enmity to the state. They represented an enduring alternative for civilized men. the escape to nature.

The Ancient of Days forever is young
Forever the scheme of Nature thrives.[36]

Youth, gaiety and fearlessness were the attributes of men in that natural state. They have an intrinsic charm, and even Captain Cloud is drawn to sing with the captured Confederates. But Melville is distrustful. In "The Scout Towards Aldie," as in *White-Jacket*, the charms of nature lure men to forgetfulness of death. Aeschylus thought, with his pagan Greek compatriots, that this forgetfulness of death was the beginning of greatness. Melville is distrustful. He adopts the character of that symbol dear to the religious, the skeleton engraved on gravestones who utters dampening reminders of our imminent demise. Behind the charms of nature is a certain death, the wilderness is a trap for men. Melville's poem, for all its playful tone and pastoral interludes, ends with death. The reader, like those of whom he reads, is lured within the wilderness, lulled there, and ambushed. "To Mosby-land the dirges cling,"[37] Melville's account concludes. Civilization, sanctioned by Providence, the guarantor of eternal life, offers the only alternative to annihilation.

"I have pretty much made up my mind to be annihilated," Melville told Hawthorne in 1857. But, Hawthorne wrote, "he does not seem to rest in the anticipation," and speculated that Melville "will never rest until he gets hold of a definite belief." Mosby's homily, according to Melville, was "Man must die."[38] This natural injunction and the consequent implication of the futility of human endeavor proved a good deal to Melville. His poem recording the bravery of McClellan's men at Malvern Hill marks nature's indifference to the righteousness of the men he honors:

> We elms of Malvern Hill
> Remember every thing.
> But sap the twig will fill,
> Wag the world how it will,
> Leaves must be green in spring.[39]

He is impelled not to the conquest, but to the denial and the destruction of nature.

Melville's poem about Sherman's march to Atlanta is moved by this spirit. Explicitly an acclamation, this poem recounts the desolation of the South. The living die, the growing are cut down.

> The grand pines waving over them
> Bowed to axes keen and cool.
> The grain of endless acres
> Was threshed as in the East
> By the trampling of the Takers
> Strong march of man and beast
> The flails of those earth-shakers
> Left a havoc where they ceased.

It was "glorious glad marching, that marching to the sea." Sherman's men are Takers, foragers, despoilers. This poem, more than any of Melville's poems of the war, is imbued with the spirit of the liminal. "Fighting was but frolic" for Sherman's men. "Cocks crowed from the cannon," the regiments "laughed in Plenty's glee." Joined by slaves and animals, the army marched unhindered to the sea. This was the army of destruction. Like the urban rioters of a generation previous, they saw themselves as "world-destroyers," rejecting what they endeavored to destroy. Melville endorses and acclaims them.[40]

This riotous destruction was not directed towards the "liberation" of hoarded foodstuffs, the destruction of money, or the annihilation of machines, customary objects of riot. Indeed, Melville makes little of the slaves they freed. Nor was it spontaneous and disorganized. Rather it represented the victory of civilization over nature. The objects of attack are natural commodities, foodstuffs, plants growing in the field, neither hoarded nor withheld. The marchers were an army organized and uniformed, not impelled by private will, but drafted and ordered.

> It was glorious glad marching
> But ah, the stern decree.

Melville can endorse this liminal effusion because it is on behalf of, rather than against, the state. Unlike most revolutionary moments of destruction and renewal, it rejected nature for culture, directing its anger against the symbols of the natural rather than the artificial. It was the revenge of civilization on its apostates.

> For they left behind a wailing
> A terror and a ban
> And blazing cinders sailing
> And houseless households wan

> Wide zones of counties paling,
> And towns where maniacs ran.[41]

Melville consistently marks the Union's victory over the Confederacy with symbols of the victory of civilization over nature. In "Lee in the Capitol," the association is explicit. In "Donelson," the announcement of victory is followed by the words:

> In Dover hut and house are full
> Of rebels dead or dying.
> The National flag is flying
> From the crammed courthouse pinnacle.[42]

Even in death and defeat, the Rebels retain their claim to house and hearth. The flag flies from the courthouse. It was, as Melville notes, a "winter victory." When the final battle and the war were won, Melville wrote of the defeated Rebel:

> Home, home his heart is full of it,
> But home he shall never see.
> Even should he stand upon the spot:
> 'Tis gone! where his brothers be.[43]

His memories are likened to the foliage of his region, his eyes to "a mountain pool," but he is in "the City of the Foe." The revolutionary recourse to destruction that marked the ending of the first regime had ended in the city's triumph.

> The fight for the city is fought
> In Nature's old Domain
> Man goes out in the wilds
> And Orpheus's charm is vain.[44]

Melville considered the Union's victory a victory for reason. Urbanization, law and industry, the offspring and allies of rationalization, were also named victors in the contest. Melville, no less than the Southerners he opposed, was convinced that the war would secure or destroy a peculiarly Southern way of life. That this way of life entailed proximity to nature, agriculture, and an opposition to mechanization, neither party disputed. The North's had been "the fight for the city." The Union victory was "a victory of LAW."[45]

The war had placed war "where War belongs—among the trades and artisans." The same process of abstraction and rationalization that hastened the development and domination of capitalism proceeded in war. In this new manner of war, "all went by crank, pivot, screw, and calculations of caloric." Officers were specialists; "warriors are now but operatives." In fact, the same types of men who filled the ranks at the factory filled them at the front: immigrants and the poor.[46]

Each soldier and each operative in this civil scheme had an assigned place and attendant duties. This resulted in civil order and in the selflessness of separate men. Melville in his gnostic way recognized that the selflessness he praised resulted in a substantial loss to the selfless:

> It is not that leg is lost,
> It is not that an arm is maimed
> It is not that the fever has wracked
> Self he has long disclaimed.[47]

For Melville, self and the innate individuality of corporeality were inextricably entangled. Selflessness was a civil virtue, not a natural one. Attendance to the duties it enjoined secured not individual welfare, but the welfare of the state. The common attendance of each operative, soldier, and citizen to this singular end results in an invincible and enduring state. Good, Melville believed, belongs to the determinate.

> Evolving rhyme and stars divine
> Have rules and they endure."[48]

Order, no less for Melville than the Puritans, was an attribute of divinity. The ordering of the state in law was thus an effort to assimilate it to God.

That "Canticle" with which Melville celebrates the "national exaltation of enthusiasm at the close of the war," and the victory of the Union, honors both God and the state. In the Union triumph, Melville declares, "Thou Lord of Hosts victorious / Fulfill the end designed." The South's defeat marked a decisive moment in the providential progress of history.

> The generations pouring
> From times of endless date

In their going, in their flowing,
Ever form the steadfast State
And Humanity is growing
Toward the fullness of her fate.[49]

The state, in this articulation, is the end God intended for man. It is, moreover, the culmination of a long historical progress. In this canticle, alternating paeans to God and to the state, Melville conflates history and the will of God, evincing the ability of the Puritan notion of America as God's chosen nation to accommodate the innovations of Continental philosophy. The culmination of history in the ascendancy of the state was not merely inevitable, but right.

Certain of Melville's expressions suggest that he withdrew from a complete identification of the inevitable and the good. The celebratory canticle intimates the extent of the unknown—"the foamy Deep unsounded" lies before them, into it has swept the multitudinous national throng. They go unknowing forward. Melville refrains from pronouncing good the end of humanity in the state. His condition, it appears, is very likely that which he commends to the South. "It is enough, for all practical purposes, if the South has been taught by the terrors of civil war to feel that Secession, like Slavery, is against Destiny . . . and that together we comprise the Nation."[50]

The nation "moved in power," power created it. Its law was to be ratified not by consent, but by coercion. Having conquered, Melville's soldiers returned with "vindicated laws."[51] The acquiescence rather than the deliberate consent of the ruled was now the measure of the regime's legitimacy. This Civil War, and the Union thereby preserved, were forced by men forced into soldiery upon an unwilling people. This Melville saw, and grimly commended.

His poem "The House Top" recapitulates the conflict on a smaller scale. Here the forced soldiery resisting represents those on whom the Union would be forced. The draft resisters, like that South for whom they stand surrogate, are in defiance of God. Theirs is "the Atheist roar of riot." They likewise reject "all civil charms, and priestly spells which late held hearts in awe." Religion and the law, Melville recognized, held men "fear-bound." Freed of those bonds which had held them "subjected to a better sway than sway of self," they rebounded, "whole aeons back in nature." Nature, then, was the province of the self and the individual. Religion and civility held men in subjection to God. These ruled through fear; behind the fear was "Black artillery."[52]

The recourse to arms which quells "the Atheist roar of riot," and forces rebellious citizens to a reluctant submission, comes "corroborating Calvin's creed." Calvin, and "the cynic tyranny of honest kings" stand in opposition to the faith of the Republic. Melville recognized that democracy depended on the inviolable right to revolution, on that creed "which holds that man is naturally good, / And—more is Nature's Roman, never to be scourged."[53] The towns' redemption—so Melville terms it—corroborates Calvin and denies the ideology of the American regime. Melville saw not only the Founding's fall, but what would replace it. The redeemed townspeople—bourgeois citizens indeed—were, he observes, heedless of the coup, but he gives his allegiance mindfully. Better God than Man; for Melville, the former has more to give. Better Calvin than Jefferson, better the self subjected to a better rule than man with rights inviolable and free to err.

The vindication of law in the city and the nation was likewise accomplished through coercion. Melville's Lee, brought to the capitol, speaks there for the old regime: "From reason who can urge the plea / Freemen conquerors of the free?"[54] Lee's American was "Nature's Roman." Tyranny against such men would "confirm the curse, infix the hate. / In Union's name forever alienate."[55] In Lee's old regime, the now-defunct democracy, it was their allegiance, not their surrender, which had to be won. But "they dismissed him." Consent no longer ratified the law. Sovereignty had moved from the people to Providence. Power was the stuff of Providence: "The Lord is a man of war." The nation had been, like the town, redeemed. Being so redeemed, the men within had lost their freedom and their sovereignty. They had preferred, like Melville and Milton before him, to serve in Heaven rather than rule in Hell.

This denigration of personal liberty—the rights of man—in favor of selfless service to an objective and disinterested God, bears the features of its Puritan progenitors. It retains the Calvinist uncertainty of individual salvation, the Puritan preoccupation with covenant and community. This selfless devotion to the common good is accompanied, as Melville recognized, by an abjuration of one's natural rights. The nation animated by this impulse

> Moves in power not in pride
> And is deep in her devotion
> As Humanity is wide.[56]

The national victory thus represented the triumph of the objective. Melville's poems, reflecting what they record, are of forces rather than individuals. Unlike the novels, in which individuals predominate, the poems record the contests of abstract forces and collectivities. Southerners, and a woman formerly a slave, retain their individuality. Of the Northerners there are three who do also: Lincoln, who is ascribed the character of comprehensive divinity; a returning soldier now "selfless"; and the Union generals. Of the last group, Melville said, "when of a free country we name the soldiers we thereby name the people."[57] S. E. Finer has observed that it is less the people who are named in this fashion than the state. Soldiers in their uniformity and their capacity for coercion represent legal-rational authority. Their commonality is abstracted from their individuality; they are rendered uniform without being made equal. Like the operatives with whom Melville grouped them, they are disciplined and arranged in ordered hierarchies conducive to the operation of the whole.

Melville was aware, as his poems on the riots demonstrates, that the army was formed from the drafted and destitute; in short, not of free men, but of those the state compelled. Neither state nor people, in Melville's articulation, was an aggregate of free individuals. Each represented a collective, comprehensive identity in which men, transcending their natural individuality, could participate in a common devotion to right. Despite this doctrinal similarity to what David Greenstone calls the substantive standards tradition, Melville held to the heterodox view that the North's victory represented a revolutionary rejection of the earlier Revolution, an abridgment rather than a continuance of the American regime. While he acceded to, indeed acclaimed, the alteration of the regime, he was not among those who in their gratitude for the city's salvation ignored the slur on the Republic's faith. Rather he recognized in the victory of the Union the repudiation of the democracy, preferring a coercive order to a chaotic liberty. He became, in a personal recapitulation of Protestant history, an opponent of private and subjective authority, and an advocate of law.

Melville's novels and his poems are distinguished by a marked attention to structure, a formal order. He himself identifies this aspect of his artistry with the advocacy of law. In "Dupont's Round Fight," a divine and orderly creation, rhyme, the order of battle, and the victory of law are likened and allied. This poem provides a poetic exemplum of Weber's articulations of legal-rational authority. The primacy of the written word, the sanctity of order, the impulse to universality, which Weber marked as characteristic of legal-rational authority, are demonstrated in Melville's account of the battle. Both Melville and Weber acknowledged the dependence of this type of authority on the military. The forms of bureaucracy were derived from military discipline; unquestioning obedience to authority bottomed each system. Melville had granted to the army the title of savior. The army had preserved the nation. It is an assertion we have heard often enough in our time. Those revolutionaries who founded the regime regarded the army as an improbable savior, but as a certain enemy. They had endeavored to limit its tenure, restrict its jurisdiction, and in all ways subordinate it to popular authority and republican legislation. They had feared that a standing army, always the servant of the state, might be employed by the government against the people. The best answer to their fears, if answer it be, is that given by Melville at the fall of Richmond:

> God is in Heaven and Grant is in the Town
> And Right through Might makes Law
> God's way adore.[58]

11   Lincoln, The Great Emancipator

Lincoln was in his time, and remains in ours, the central figure of the Civil War. Richard Hofstadter has called him a "self-made myth."[1] He created in that myth, as in his addresses and proclamations, the pattern for a reconstructed Union. He provided, no less in his person than his policies, the parameters of a now constricted culture, and the tenets of an amended ideology. With the legitimacy of the regime, indeed the legitimacy of the restored nation, very much in question, Lincoln culled those myths and paradigms which retained their meaning in the altered circumstances of the Union and created, on his own authority, a new paradigm for legitimate governance. In the revised American myth he was, as his secretary called him, "the greatest character since Christ," an American avatar of a universal deity.[2] In examining Lincoln, as with all charismatic leaders, one is obliged to consider the man with the president, the speaker with the words.

Weber distinguished charisma as a species of authority in which the leader's title to rule is independent, and often in defiance, of objective law and traditionally validated modes of authority. The charismatic leader establishes new standards for legitimation, and a new paradigm for legitimate governance. While, as Weber asserted, the charismatic leader's possession of authority is credited to no one but himself, the decisive moment in the establishment of charismatic leadership is not the leader's private reception of grace, but the people's validation of his authority.[3]

This process is immediate and subjective, and hence occurs outside the objective, public procedures offered in law and custom. The individual recognition of charismatic authority is exercised in the same fashion and on the same plane of political relations as subjective allegiance. As in allegiance, the individual's recognition of charismatic authority acknowledges a consonance between his private identity and that collective identity represented by the polity.

293

The perception, expression, and validation of charismatic authority, though procedurally free of the structures contained in law and custom, are nevertheless governed by the dominant paradigms of the political culture. Indeed, because the charismatic leader's authority must be validated collectively and immediately, without the mediation of specified procedures, it must conform to standards for legitimate governance recognizable to all within the political culture.

It is for this reason, charismatic leaders commonly refer to canonical scriptures or documents, and to historical figures who exemplify ideal governance within the mythology of the political culture. Jesus' presentation of himself as satisfying prophecies contained in accepted scriptures and Nasser's identification of himself with Salah-ad-din are examples of this.

Abraham Lincoln established new standards for legitimate political action and a new paradigm for legitimate governance in American political culture. His extraordinary status in American political myth and the amended standards for good governance which his personal authority secured, were, however, established only with his death. The assassination was a circumstance of such symbolic import in the context of American political culture that it conferred on his actions, his speeches, and the model of governance he exemplified an authority they had hitherto lacked. It was, however, only because his death was mythically consonant with the paradigms and metaphors that Lincoln had employed in his creation of his political identity that it could confer on that identity a posthumous charismatic authority.

Latter-day inquirers after Lincoln are thus faced with a great paradox: Lincoln the sectional president, faced with rebellion in the Confederacy, and dissension in the states he held, criticized, caricatured, and suspected of stealing elections; and Lincoln the national martyr, universally revered. This paradox itself evinces the great transformation in the ideal character of the nation effected in the Civil War.

Like all charismatic leaders, Lincoln's speeches and actions were replete with symbols, metaphors, and historical references. Conscious of his own historical significance, he placed himself, in his public speeches and actions, within a well-delineated historical context. His manner of governance accorded with the paternal pattern of political authority. This paradigm, and the scriptural and historic references Lincoln most often employed, were, however, confined to the North and were insignificant or negative models in the political culture of the South. It was only after the cultural constriction effected in the Civil War that they could acquire constitutive authority in the nation.

The North's success in the war assured the national promulgation of the formerly sectional political culture within which Lincoln had constructed his political identity. Lincoln's death sped its acceptance by changing the principal mythic referent of his identity from that of patriarchy and Puritan magistracy to the Christian myth of incarnation, sacrifice, and redemption, which was far more generally recognized as a model for legitimate authority.

Lincoln's speeches, actions, and the paradigm for leadership which he represented are thus expressive of that narrow sectional culture which gained primacy in the official histories and dominance in the determination of institutional structures through the Union's military success. This sectional culture was intimately related to industrialization and the political structures that attended it. It had provided the cultural underpinnings for industrial capitalism and had itself been altered in response to the experience of industrialization.

Lincoln's mythic persona, because it was developed within, and as a representation of, that political culture, was distinguished by the same preoccupations, metaphors, and paradigms. He derived from his culture a symbolic vocabulary, paradigms for political action, and a designated set of historically significant experiences. Within this cultural context, certain of his private circumstances and personal traits acquired political significance. His method of resolving the problems they presented thus acquired political salience, providing him with presumably reliable strategies for effective political action.

Lincoln's enthusiasm for legal-rational authority, for objective law and rationalization, and his rejection of the family as the principal unit of social organization were representative of a politically dominant strain of Northern culture in the period. They were consonant with industrialization and an understanding of political development which regarded it as characterized by an increasing degree of abstraction, rationality, and universality.

The private circumstances which encouraged Lincoln to verify the policies and objectives of the Whigs and align himself with them are significant because they attached particular associations to the policies and the political circumstances that were thought to demand them. They can thus clarify the conception of the South that guided Lincoln's response to Southern secession and the experientially derived associations of issues that guided his conduct of the war and governed his construction of the peace.

Edmund Wilson, in an otherwise astute study of Lincoln, asserted that Lincoln was "not unsympathetic to the South" because his

maternal grandfather had been Southern.[4] Certainly it is not too cred-
ulous to take war as evidence of an attitude in which sympathy does not
predominate. Moreover, Lincoln was moved by other than familial
sentiments. He appears to have been indifferent, where he was not
hostile, to almost all his familial ties. His rare and cursory mentions of
mother and stepmother, his evident contempt for his father, and his
indifference to his kinsmen scarcely suggest a man who might be
moved to sentiment by the memory of an unacknowledged ancestor a
generation distant. On the contrary, this figure firmly associated the
South with illegitimacy in Lincoln's personal history.

Lincoln's mother, so he believed, was the daughter of a Southern
planter who had fathered her outside the bonds of matrimony. Thus
the South, for Lincoln, was the mother's province, and the province of
lawless sexuality. Throughout his career, Lincoln's speeches would
contrast reason with passion, passion with law, and "the order-loving
citizens of the land of steady habits" with "the pleasure-hunting masters of Southern slaves."[5] The conjunction of his family history with his
characterizations of North and South suggests a deeper personal meaning in Lincoln's continued reiterations of the South's disdain for law.
Lincoln's capacity to appeal to and to recreate Northern sectional, and
ultimately national, identity grew in part out of this consonance between his private experience and his political culture.

Lincoln endowed the law with sacred significance. It was, he affirmed, properly perpetual and inviolable. Florid paeans to the law
marked his early speeches. In later years he was to insist that the rebellion he so strenuously opposed was unlawful, in the face of his own
expressed conviction that the lawful right of revolution might be exercised with equal legitimacy by a portion, as by a whole of a people. The
South, as Lincoln presented and perceived it, was the province of "disorder," "lawlessness," "passion," and "pleasure." The North was the
province of "order," "steady habits," "reason," and "reverence for
law."[6] This suggests that Lincoln's understanding of the South and
Southern defects was derived from his family history. It also clarifies
his early allegiance to the Whigs.

The Whigs, heavily influenced by, and occasionally identical to,
the Moral Reform movement, had promulgated a similar association of
Southern lawlessness, intemperance, and passion. This was attractive
to Lincoln. They were also popularly regarded as the party of the rich.

Harry Jaffa makes much of Lincoln's identification with the poor
to belittle his connection with the rich and socially prominent Whig
elite.[7] Lincoln did emphasize, throughout his career, his obscure and

impoverished origins. Nor do I regard this as merely an act of political expediency. Lincoln's early attraction to the Whigs, his profitable marriage, and his efforts to advance himself politically, socially, and economically indicate another intention. This becomes clearest in Lincoln's refusal to furnish materials on his youth and upbringing. These years, he told the biographer, were adequately described by the phrase, "the short and simple annals of the poor."[8] He did not regard either his family or his early situation as deserving of pride, loyalty, or sentiment. Each was something to be escaped.

Herndon described Lincoln's ambition as the greatest force in him, "a little engine which knew no rest."[9] In his early career, most of his ambition was directed at distancing himself from his humble origins. He worked tirelessly to acquire that education, wealth, and political influence which had been so markedly absent from his childhood home. He joined not the party which went to some lengths to glorify poverty and simplicity, but the party associated with the rich and educated.

Lincoln regarded equality as producing social mobility rather than as the absence of class or a political indifference to class. His most famous praise of equality in the American economic sphere praises a situation which enables those who were themselves hirelings to become the employers of hirelings. He objected not to the existence of classes or class interests, but to classes defined and continued by birth, to familial influence and authority. He thus ran directly counter to that prevailing Southern view which affirmed familial authority even as it rejected the explicit advancement of class interests. Lincoln knew that he owed his own success and reformation to his escape from the influence and authority of his own family. He could therefore predict with confidence that the extirpation of these nationally would prove a blessing to individuals.

In matters economic, Lincoln regularly explained his principles by his experience. In this he evinced the conviction both that he was profoundly representative of America and that his accomplishment provided an instructive political model. He also revealed the derivation of his economic opinions. For white men as for black, Lincoln's dedication to the principles of freedom and equality was entirely divorced from the achievement or advocacy of social and economic equality for individuals.

Lincoln thus associated equality, in both personal and political contexts, with the absence or diminution of familial authority. This made him resistant to Southern arguments that slavery was a species of familial authority. Had he accepted these arguments, he would have opposed slavery all the more. As he said, he would not wish it for himself. Abolitionist arguments that slavery produced intemperance and excessive sexuality in the Southerner had, however, a powerful corollary in his own experience.

I do not argue that Lincoln derived either his principles or his policies solely from his familial situation. I contend rather that his familial experience inclined him to validate one set of arguments and reject the other. His antipathy to his family would then be transferred to the South when it appeared to exhibit those traits he had rejected. Because the law came to occupy a central position in his successful effort to distance himself from his Southern family, Southern lawlessness became an object of particular enmity.

Lincoln was a lawyer, a man of the law, trained in it, sworn to it. His personal advancement, education, and fame were owed to this. He had made a steadfast adherence to the law the first principle of his public pronouncements. His actual indifference to legal niceties in matters of state is all the more revealing for this.

For Lincoln, the object of preserving the Union, and therein the fundamental law of the land, was an adequate apology for the suspension of habeas corpus and censorship of the press. The nation was nonetheless lawful for being under martial law. The Rebellion, conversely, was "against the law," which rendered the greater scrupulousness of the Confederacy in maintaining freedom of the press entirely insignificant. Lawfulness had become an abstract principle for Lincoln, and as such was inextricably entangled with phenomenally related but inherently distinct concepts: Union, freedom, and the North. The North was defined by Lincoln as "the land of steady habits and inhabited by good men; men who love tranquillity and desire to abide by the laws."[10] Loyalty to this trinity demonstrated the legitimacy of Lincoln's actions and his personal reverence for law, thus absolving him of any imputation of illegality attached to particular acts.

Lincoln's role as defender of the Union is intimately related to this. As opposition to the lawless had evinced his own legitimacy, so the preservation of the Union absolved him of the imputation of infidelity to the Founders. Lincoln's warning of an ambitious genius who would challenge the work of the Founders has often been discussed. It had been observed nearly as often that Lincoln spoke, unselfconsciously perhaps, of himself. George Forgie has argued persuasively that the greater part of Lincoln's political career was spent in the search for an object onto which he might displace the impulse to patricide that he could not acknowledge in himself.[11] Forgie has marked Douglas as Lincoln's patricidal scapegoat. I believe that Douglas was merely the forerunner of a greater foe.

Both North and South, before and since, described the Civil War as a fratricidal conflict. The North endeavored to present itself as the righteous brother, selflessly defending the paternal legacy; the South endeavored to mark the North with the brand of Cain. Each contended that the other was engaged in undoing the work of the Founding Fathers.

For some men, notably the radical abolitionists, the charge that they were altering the work of the Revolution was not unwelcome. The Constitution, they contended, was marred by the perpetuation of slavery. Their fathers had acquiesced to the slaveholders. They would not. Lincoln came finally to accept this view. In the Second Inaugural Address he numbered the consequences of this national sin. He culled from Scripture the saying "Woe unto the world because of offenses; for it must needs be that offenses come, but woe unto that man by whom the offense cometh."[12] The passage Lincoln chose contains an acknowledgment, hidden in the speech itself, of the manner of this reformation. It left the nation deformed. "If thy hand or thy foot offend thee, cut them off and cast them from thee; it is better for thee to enter into life halt or maimed rather than having two hands or two feet to be cast into everlasting fire. And if thine eye offend thee, pluck it out."[13] The hand that caused the sin had been cut off and cast away. The conquest of the South excised the sin of slavery. In separating itself from the sin of the South, the Union separated itself, as Melville recognized, from the culture and ideology of the Founding. The preservation of the territorial integrity of the Union disguised a fundamental maiming.

The reformed Union, however, continued to claim the Revolution and the Founding as its own. In doing so the Union took upon itself the guilt that history occasioned. This assumption of the Founders' sin gave to the present generation a singularly Christlike character. Having freed themselves from sin, they through their own sufferings and sacrifice chose to make retribution for the sins of others. They "died that the nation might live."[14] The analogy becomes still more apt when it is remembered that Lincoln's nation was ideal rather than phenomenal, a temporally infinite form of community. The essence of that community was the simultaneous transcendence and apotheosis of the individual in the community. Lincoln was to become the primary exemplar of this Christ-like justification of the state. When he died it was as the people's representative. Lincoln had taken the *imitatio christi* and made it the task no longer of separate men, but of the community. He had purged the automachia of its self-regarding and self-interested character, thus solving the dilemma which had so vexed the Puritans.

In the Second Inaugural Address, Lincoln affirmed the willingness of the present generation to take upon itself the sins of the fathers. Lincoln had intimated something of the Founders' defects as early as the Lyceum Speech. There he observed that their extraordinary accomplishment had been motivated by ambition and accomplished in part through "the basest principles of our nature." From an object of veneration, the Founding had declined to an object of emulation, a benchmark to be surpassed, and finally to a legacy of sin. The refounding was thus freed from the imputation of filial impiety. Lincoln's generation was blessed by an attendant transformation. Rather than patricides, they became collectively an avatar of Christ, the source of America's salvation. In this way, Lincoln had secured not only absolution, but apotheosis to the unrepentant patricides, the new founders of the reformed Union.

Lincoln confirmed the South's claim that the North was engaged in undoing the regime of the Founders. The Founders, however, being both dead and immortal, could not be immediately attacked. Nor could Lincoln bring himself to acknowledge his patricidal hostility directly. Instead he himself assumed a patriarchal character. His accession to the presidency had put him in the Fathers' place. After his election, he grew a beard and with it assumed a more paternal persona. He was notably successful in this. Songs and poems from the war years refer to Lincoln almost invariably as "Abraham," recalling the archetypal patriarch, or—yet more pointedly—as "Father Abraham."[15] Citizens were reduced to children. One of the most famous songs of the war responded to Lincoln's call for recruit with the promise, "We are coming, Father Abraham, 100,000 more." This song, attributed to several authors, spawned versions giving the requested recruitment in denominations of 300 and 600 thousand, and at least one parody which made the singers those greenbacks which the mint was assiduously producing.[16] In the North, Lincoln's paternal authority went unquestioned, even by dissenters. The "Daily Song of the 100 Day Soldier," ran "I'm sick of the fife, more sick of the drum. / Kind Father Abraham, let me go home."[17]

Popular acceptance, in the North, of Lincoln's patriarchal authority may have eased his imposition of martial law, for it suggested an authority superior to, and independent of, the people. Paternity entailed an absolute and arbitrary authority throughout the culture.

Those who named Lincoln 'father' were therefore likely to accept, and even to expect, such authority in him. A particularly telling expression of Lincoln's patriarchy occurs in a popular song published in Philadelphia at the outbreak of the war, "all about a volunteer who's goin' to fight for glory":

> We're goin' down to Washington to fight for Abraham's daughter.
> Oh should you ask me who she am, Columbia is her name, sir.
> She is the child of Abraham, or Uncle Sam, the same, sir.[18]

Here Lincoln is explicitly granted the status of the Founders, who were, with greater justice, credited with fathering the nation. He is simultaneously identified with the personification of the government (Uncle Sam). With the boundaries of Lincoln's identity so blurred in popular political culture, it became difficult to distinguish Lincoln's personal arrogations of authority from the legitimate exercise of a delegated power in the performance of the duties of the executive.

Lincoln, however, appears to have entertained some doubts about the legitimacy of his title. Forgie, in suggesting Lincoln's guilt over his fratricidal defeat of Douglas, has drawn attention to Lincoln's preoccupation with three Shakespearean speeches. Each of these—Claudius's speech in *Hamlet*, Richard III's at the opening of the play, and Macbeth's after the murder of Duncan—expresses the guilt and ambition of the murderer. Each character has gained a throne through the murder of a brother or kinsman. Forgie asks, "How could Lincoln have identified with the mentality of a man consumed with fratricidal guilt?" He answers, Douglas.[19] By the time of the recorded recitals, however, Lincoln had engaged in a fratricidal conflict far greater than his debates with Douglas. Douglas had indeed been defeated, and died shortly after Lincoln's triumph, but men died daily in the Civil War. Lincoln's office, if not his own ambition, obliged him to identify himself with those he represented. He personified one brother in that war of brothers.

It is, of course, a commonplace for contending parties to be identified with their respective leaders. This becomes more marked when a leader's personal, charismatic authority eclipses other claims to the allegiance of his partisans, or when the conflict is itself denigrated as insignificant. Thus a song protesting the Union draft of 1863 advised:

> Oh, should he meet a rebel a pointin' with his gun
> I hope he'll have the courage to take care of number one

If I were him I'd offer the fellow but a dram
For what's the use of fighting just for Jeff or Abraham?[20]

Lincoln's conquest of the South, and his consequent restoration of the Union, would assure him a glory far surpassing mere election. The defeat of the South confirmed Lincoln's role as national father and thus enabled him to transcend fratricidal strife. While the war continued, and the outcome remained doubtful, Lincoln's patriarchal character encompassed only the North.

Lincoln's preoccupation with *Hamlet* is particularly interesting in this regard. The soliloquy which Lincoln named "One of the finest touches of nature in the world" was that of Claudius. Claudius had murdered Hamlet's father, the king of Denmark, and assumed his place. He was thus both father and fratricide. For Hamlet, he was his father's murderer. The character of Hamlet had been for some decades associated with Southerners, no less in the North than the South. He expressed the Southern sentiment that they alone had remained faithful to the fathers. When Hamlet undertakes the murder of the man who claims paternal authority over him, it is at the instigation of his father's ghost, a poetic situation manifestly expressive of the Southern sentiment that their opposition to the government—and to Lincoln—was loyalty to the memory of the Founding Fathers. It is noteworthy that the respective identifications of Lincoln and his Southern foes are so exactly consonant.

Lincoln's identification with Richard III, his unconscious assumption of that role, recalls the prophecy of the Lyceum Speech. Richard, like the "towering genius" of the speech, regrets the "weak, piping time of peace" and is "determined to prove a villain" if it will gratify his ambition.

In each play, the accession of the king—Richard, Claudius, Macbeth—is secured by the death of the legitimate heirs. This would answer to the Southern protest that they were the true heirs of the Founding. The speeches, then, appear to express Lincoln's subconscious anxiety over their claim.

For a man of the law, the imputation of illegitimacy was serious indeed. The law was Lincoln's vocation in both a sacred and a profane sense. It had been his occupation, he had raised himself to social prominence through it. He had pledged himself to its defense; this became his mission. The question of his own legitimacy thus challenged the fundamental constructs of his identity.

If the resolution of this conflict was necessary for Lincoln's psychic constitution, it was equally necessary to the Union. The partisans of the Union claimed that it was constitutionally indissoluble, yet they were obliged to recall that the nation had been formed by revolution, and the Constitution by "the people in the states." The legitimacy of secession was thus at least plausible, when judged by the standards of legitimacy established in the nation's founding. Lincoln's successful amendment of these standards, and the national refounding which this entailed, thus resolved both Lincoln's personal and the Union's political dilemma.

The personal authority which Lincoln was granted and which Weber termed "charismatic" comes in consequence of the people's recognition of their collective identity in the experiences and ideology of the leader. The identification of Lincoln as the father of Columbia, and as Uncle Sam, expressed the popular perception that he personified the nation. They recognized in his character, sentiments, and circumstances aspects of their collective identity. The deification which followed his death was not merely a sentimental effusion prompted by an unprecedented tragedy. Rather it indicated a profound increase in the resemblance of Lincoln's personal experience to that of the nation. He had come truly to represent them.

The words "represent" and "recognize" describe this process with precision. The representative is at once the proxy (the representative) of an existing commonalty—an aggregation of persons sharing a common allegiance—and the archetype for an amended identity (one who represents it). Each reiteration of a collective identity enriches it with additional mythic and historical associations, permitting the further development of particular aspects of the identity and constraining or precluding the development of other aspects. The recognition of charismatic leaders thus expresses both popular ratification of their claim to legitimacy and a rethinking of private allegiance and the standards of legitimacy.

Lincoln had been recognized in his lifetime as father and exemplar. Hofstadter's term "self-made myth" need not be dismissed as mere condemnation. More than many men, Lincoln perceived the points of coincidence between his personal experience and that of the nation. He willingly brought forward those aspects of his character and circumstances which would cause his compatriots to choose him as their representative. The poverty of his origins likened him to many of his fellows; more importantly, it recapitulated the nation's relative insignificance in the world order and gave promise of a similar rise to power. This enabled men of few resources and less influence to identify their circumstances with Lincoln's, and Lincoln's with the state of the nation. They were thus spared the ignominy and alienation which threatens to overwhelm citizens who see themselves as lost and impotent in the grandeur of their great republic. His speeches, and that campaign literature in which he noted that his father could do little more than "bunglingly write his own name," reflect an ambivalence toward the Founding Fathers that was characteristic of his entire generation. Similarly wavering between praise for their accomplishment and ambition to undo or to surpass it, Lincoln expressed the dilemma which troubled at least a portion of the nation, and provided them with the pattern for its resolution. His reverence for law and lawfulness, his affirmation of the virtue of hard work and enterprise and his liberal employment of biblical phrases and imagery associated him with long-established Northern cultural paradigms. These ties to tradition enabled him to accord the nation's "new birth of freedom" to existing patterns of legitimate governance, thus making the refounding a continuation rather than a breach of the nation's earlier and honored history.

The Gettysburg Address and the Second Inaugural Address made Lincoln's peace with the past and inaugurated a new era. The former demonstrated Lincoln's fulfillment of the duties of Puritan magistracy. In it, Lincoln vindicated the justice of his actions as he promulgated an alternative set of standards for the determination of legitimacy. His actions and intentions, and the character of the evidently altered nation, were accorded to the understanding of history propounded by the Puritans. He made recent events intelligible within that history. Thus he simultaneously enhanced the historical significance of recent events by embedding them in an articulation of history which claimed to reveal the nation's true and divine mission and enhanced the political significance and cultural importance of that Puritan history. This recourse to the Puritans profited from their earlier rehabilitation at the hands of the Whigs and the Protestant crusaders. These parties had praised the Puritans as models of orderliness, sobriety, and submission to authority. Lincoln, whose regime was threatened by disorder and rebellion, was ready to commend those traits to the divided Americans. In identifying his cause with the Puritans he made, however, a wholly sectional appeal. The Gettysburg Address reveals the narrowing cultural boundaries of America.

The fears awakened by the evident cultural divergence of the South, and by the influx of foreign immigrants, had produced men dedicated to "Americanization." The cultural ideal propogated by educators, historians, and politicians of this assimilative bent, came (as they had) from the North and West. They had created their ideal American from the myths, cultural constructs, and patterns of behavior which prevailed in their respective sections.

The Puritan understanding of American history, American mission, and the American character had been both altered and enhanced by territorial expansion. Migrant Yankees had carried the notion of America as God's chosen with them westward. There it became confounded with the idea of America as a vigorous and primitive Eden, the source of a new civilization. Settlers and the pious found common cause in the conquest of nature, a project in which they were equally engaged. Henry Clay, Daniel Webster, Thomas Hart Benton, and Timothy Dwight shared an enthusiasm for commerce, progress, and capitalism. For them, and for the constituencies which they represented, law had a sanctity it was denied in the South. It represented both the establishment of morality and the triumph of civilization over undifferentiated nature. Lincoln was the product and synthesis of this strange alliance. He combined Puritan rhetoric with Western manners. He had a firm faith in capitalism and the intellectual progress of mankind. He revered the law. He had that respect and unswerving dedication to order which likewise distinguished the Puritan and the settler.

One Western editor, naming Lincoln the example of "the Western type of Americans," declared with satisfaction that "the White House has never been occupied by a representative of the bourgeoisie or the citizen class of people" before Lincoln's election.[21] Lincoln's rhetorical apotheosis of law proved him a firm adherent to that legal-rational authority with which Weber associated the bourgeoisie. With that class he professed faith in the virtues of hard work and the principle that the market would reward the deserving. The erudition, sobriety, and rhetorical piety which likened Lincoln to the Puritans were alloyed with the plain manner and folk humor of the West. His public character, in common with his political thought, culled elements from those two cultures and made them the pattern for an altered America.

The Gettysburg Address became one of the canonical documents of the American nation. This speech, awesome for its brevity, elegant in its phrasing, was given over to generations of school children, myself among them, to recite as a sort of republican catechism. It carries the burden of the past and promise of the future. It was the inaugural address of the refounding. With it the boundaries of the nation were drawn again, not in space but, after the Puritan fashion, in time.

The address begins in the past, "four score and seven years ago." It proceeds to an account of the present crisis. This culminates in an exhortation. The people are enjoined to continue the work of the dead in the interests of the unborn. The speech closes with the promise of the nation's continuance.

Thus the address presents in small the history of the nation. Like that nation, it has its beginning in a documented past, and extends to an unforeseeable future. The Puritan conception of the temporal expansion of the nation has primacy in the matter of the speech, and the Puritan mode of instruction and exhortation governs its mode. The speech thus exhibits Lincoln's conformity to the Puritan pattern for legitimate and virtuous governance.

The temporal continuance of the nation was, Lincoln affirmed, the principal object of the war. The battles tested "whether that nation, or any nation so conceived and dedicated, can long endure." The destruction of the American nation would promise a rapid and certain end to nations similarly conceived and dedicated only if that conception and dedication were themselves the cause of the nation's demise.

It was not uncommon, in the early years of the republic, for men to forecast the imminent end of that happy state. The notion that democracies were doomed to a short tenure had a long and respectable standing in the annals of history and philosophy. The authors of *The Federalist* had confronted it in several of their papers. As Napoloen brought the French Revolution to an unworthy and unhappy close, congressmen aired their apprehensions that the events in France intimated their expected peril. Federalists, and certain of their Whig successors, arguing that democracy was an explosive substance with a short half-life, advised the restraint and diminution of popular authority—that is, a decrease in the democratic component of "mixed government"—as a remedy for this threatened instability. Lincoln was to aid this process by expanding the powers of the executive and enhancing the prestige of the military. He asserted, however, that he acted as he did for the extension rather than the diminution of democracy.

By Lincoln's time, democracy had acquired the patina proper to established authority. The defense of democracy was synonymous with the defense of the status quo. Those who challenged the Union's claim saw in Lincoln's resistance to secession and declaration of martial law the death rather than the defense of democracy. Like Napoleon he claimed to liberate those he conquered, contriving simultaneously to reduce the liberties of those at home in response to the demands of war.

Southerners had characteristically inveighed against standing armies and executive authority rather than popular authority. Lincoln's threat of coercion on the eve of the war merely confirmed long-standing suspicions that the aggrandizement of federal, and most particularly executive, authority had made the army a threat to the American people. When Lee wrote on the eve of secession, "It has been evident for years that the country was doomed to run the full length of democracy,"[22] he reminded his correspondent of a characteristically Southern strain of political criticism. Suspicion of executive arrogation of military power had marked all Southern politicians. Even Calhoun's early hawkery was forgotten in favor of his later repentance. The Southern secessionist literati, Simms, Tucker, and the like, had given these fears a literary as well as an overtly political expression. Van Buren, in Tucker's *Partisan Leader*, conforms to the archetype of the executive whose despotic ambitions culminate in the invasion of the South by federal troops.

Because Lincoln identified the preservation of free government with the maintenance of constituted authority, he and his supporters with him could excuse the evidently undemocratic suppression of the Rebellion. As Robert Frost was to observe, "Some say the world will end in fire, some say in ice." Northern political tradition marked anarchy as the nemesis of democracy. Southern political tradition held military despotism as democracy's expected end, recalling the Romans and the more recent French Imperium. The imposition of martial law by Lincoln was perceived in the South as the death kneel of Northern democracy. In the North such fears were more subdued. Lincoln's imposition of martial law was commonly adjudged an attack upon democratic institutions rather than, as Southerners regarded it, evidence of failure of democracy in the North.

Lincoln's assertion in the Gettysburg Address that the outcome of the war would prove the durability of democracy evinces his embeddedness in Northern political culture. The condemnation of secession which Lincoln delivered in the First Inaugural Address exhibited the traditional Northern view that anarchy rather than despotism threatened the republic: "Plainly, the central idea of secession is anarchy." The diffusion of authority which secession represented augured a consequent diffusion, from a loose confederation of independent states to state sovereignty simply and hence until each man was his own ruler, and anarchy triumphed. Some Southerners, Jefferson among them, might have regarded this as an idyllic rather than apocalyptic scenario. For Melville, for Whitman, for Sherman, and for those who supported the war in the North, it was "a crime against the Almighty and against humanity, wholly without parallel for enormity in the world's history."[23] The world's history had been marked, Northern political tradition held, by a steady progress toward ever more comprehensive states. The increasing ability of men to see in others an abstracted and universal humanity, to alter, incorporate, use, and hence possess an ever-greater variety of the world's resources, was reflected in the capacity of their states to become more increasingly expansive and consolidated. The action of the South threatened to prevent the continuance of the historical progress. It was, therefore, the greatest crime in the world's history, and a crime against the Almighty.

Lincoln's assertion in the Gettysburg Address that the outcome of the war would determine the fate of republican government also reflects this same sense of the Union's world historical significance. He too believed that the Union (rather than the United States) had a divinely determined object. He divided the partisans of the present crisis into two camps: the living and the dead. The latter "gave their lives that the nation might live." They are advanced as exemplars of that selfless devotion to community which Lincoln enjoins upon the living. The living are to "take increased devotion to that cause for which they gave the last full measure of devotion."

Only in death, and only in a death on behalf of the community, is that virtuous condition of selflessness finally achieved. The living are exhorted to an emulation of that selflessness, subordinating their welfare and their will to the dead and to the unborn, to the past and to posterity.

It has been often said that Lincoln in this speech revised the ideals of Jefferson's Declaration. Jefferson had counseled posterity to be wary of the dead. Nowhere does the dead hand of the past lie so heavily on our shoulders as in the Gettysburg Address. Lincoln said "the world will little note nor long remember what we say here, but it can never forget what they did here." Few men could know better than Lincoln knew how easily men were killed, how readily they were replaced, the numbers of the dead, and the ease with which the world forgot them. A moment before he had recalled some words which had survived their maker. His would do likewise. He had suited his speech to the circumstances. This speech, given in a graveyard, proved the spoken word superior to the unspeaking dead. Yet these dead and their predecessors were to exercise a moral authority over their living compatriots.

The address begins and ends with the mention of American liberties. These go unspoken in the body of the speech. This likens it further to the nation it describes, which had the memory of the past and the hope of future freedom, though it was at present under martial law. The initial mention of freedom, as Jaffa has observed, transforms Jefferson's self-evident truths to an inheritance. Already Lincoln has removed his audience one generation from their liberties. Nor are the promised freedoms with which the speech closes those of the present; they belong to posterity. These invocations of American freedom have a formal, ritual character; they have declined from rights to legacy, from the exhortations of the insurgent to the liturgy of a civil religion.

The speech ends with an oath: "that we here highly resolve that these dead shall not have died in vain; that this nation, under God, shall have a new birth of freedom; that government of the people, by the people, for the people, shall not perish from the earth." The living thus give their allegiance, or rather have it given for them, to the nation reformed.

Here Lincoln, following the form of the jeremiad, finds in present affliction evidence of past and future greatness. He exhorts Americans not to seize their rights but to shoulder their duties. He articulates the vision of a temporally infinite nation, accomplishing a great task in the fullness of time. This is a Puritan speech. But there is something Western in it as well. The national reformation, this "new birth of freedom," is achieved through battle and death. It exemplifies that "regeneration through violence" that Slotkin marked as the central mythic construction of the West.[24]

Lincoln merged the histories and the paradigms of the North and West to provide the cultural foundations of the refounded and reformed republic. The address on the field at Gettysburg had seen in the violence of Civil War the throes of a "new birth of freedom," a national reformation. In the Second Inaugural Address, he proposed an altered understanding of the war which would accord with the altered character of the regime.

On the occasion of his second inauguration, with the nation nearing the close of the war, Lincoln said "little that is new could be presented." Upon the occasion of his first inauguration, "a statement somewhat in detail of a course to be pursued seemed fitting and proper." With four years past, and a cataclysmic event nearly over, Lincoln paused for a reprise. There would, he said, be little new in it. Yet in this recollection and remembrance of the war, Lincoln radically altered the place and character of the conflict in American mythology.

In the beginning, it had been a war for the Union. One party,

Lincoln recalled, "would make war rather than let the nation survive, and the other would accept war rather than let it perish." This is a piece of Lincoln's characteristically delicate phrasing. Generations of readers, moved by the grandeur of Lincoln's rhetoric, have praised its beauty at the expense of its precision. More than many men, he said what he meant. He could convey not merely facts but sentiments and he had a lawyer's feel for the prejudicial phrase. Union was not to be the subject of Lincoln's discourse. He might have said with justice, as he had said throughout the war, that the North fought for Union in perpetuity, the South for its dissolution and diminution. He did not but ended instead with the phrase "the war came." The words closed the subject of the Union.

Slavery, not Union, was to be marked the cause of the war. "To strengthen, perpetuate, and extend" the slave interest was, Lincoln affirmed, "the object for which the insurgents would rend the Union."

The First Inaugural Address, while claiming that slavery was "the only substantial dispute," addressed itself at length to the prevailing Southern interpretation of the Constitution and the rights of the states. Then, Lincoln had not been ready to reduce the grounds of the war to a conflict over slavery.

In the Second Inaugural Address, however, he would affirm that "all knew that this interest," that of the slaveholders, "was somehow the cause of the war." This statement, inviting agreement, is deceptively generous in latitude. In one sense it merely stated the obvious. The debates over the extension of slavery, fugitive slaves, the mails, and the gag rule, had demonstrated as they increased the extent of sectional animosity. Yet few on either side, when it came to war, claimed to war either for or against slavery. Slavery was less the cause than the occasion for war. In it the long-standing points of cultural divergence were made manifest, while allied political controversies acquired a new meaning and significance from their association with the slavery issue.

The Northerners had named their army for their cause: the Union. Lincoln, in a much publicized letter to Horace Greeley, wrote, "My paramount object in this struggle is to save the Union and is not either to save or destroy slavery." He and the army with him had fought for a Union "in perpetuity."

The Emancipation Proclamation had radically altered the character of the war. Lincoln observed, in his recollection of the war, "Neither anticipated that the cause of the conflict might cease with or even before the conflict itself." Four years before, he had stated, "I have no purpose, either directly or indirectly, to interfere with the institution of slavery in the states where it exists."[25] But the times had changed, needs had altered, and the slaves—at least the Southern slaves—were free. The London *Spectator* observed of the Emancipation Proclamation, "The principle is not that one man may not own another, but that he may not own him unless he is loyal to the United States." It was this act, avowedly the product of desperate military necessity, that won Lincoln the title "the Great Emancipator."

The proclamation did not acknowledge that the slaves possessed those rights common to all men. Rather it pretended to bestow them. Lincoln, in issuing the proclamation, acted as commander in chief. It was issued in response to military exigency; not justice but necessity was said to promote it. Already American blacks were condemned to the mere semblance of citizenship and equality. The natural rights of white men were self-evident, but those of black men came by executive fiat. It was a poor sort of emancipation, as succeeding years would witness, but it was a fine sort of strategem. Lincoln kept the border states, placated abolitionists, and affirmed a principle fundamental to his policies and ideology: that liberty was dependent upon the prior establishment of law.

In the years that followed the proclamation, and in that portion of the Second Inaugural Address that follows its recollection, Lincoln transformed the meaning of the war. The Southerners, he stated, had fought for the privilege of "wringing their bread from the sweat of other men's faces." If this were the true character of their offense, it was one they held in common with the capitalists of the North. The denial of natural rights was not the sin for which Lincoln chose to rebuke them, though they could claim no innocence on that score. "Let us judge not," Lincoln says of the Southerners, "lest we be judged," but he ignores his counsel. This speech is a speech of judgment. North and South were punished, with appropriate severity, for participation in a national sin. This, Lincoln avers, is the Lord's judgment on the nation. Having left judgment to God, and then described God's judgment, Lincoln proceeds to judge for himself the justice of the Lord. "Still it must be said," he concluded, "the judgments of the Lord are true and righteous altogether."

The final paragraph of Lincoln's speech is among the most quoted of his well-remembered utterances: "With malice toward none, with charity for all, with firmness in the right as God gives us to see the right, let us strive on to finish the work we are in, to bind up the nation's wounds, to care for him who shall have borne the battle and for his widow and his orphan, to do all which may achieve and cherish a just and lasting peace among ourselves and with all nations." Carved in stone on his memorial in Washington, this passage has become the literary evocation of Lincoln's character. In it we see a compassionate provision, a comprehensive and tolerant forgiveness, a devotion to the right, a pacific intent. It is forgotten in the beauty of the language, that the character of the work they were in was neither tolerant nor pacific. The penultimate paragraph had promised a bloody and unrelenting retribution. Four years had been spent in exacting it. The mythic image of Lincoln as compassionate and forgiving was not a recollection of traits he evinced in the conduct of the war. Rather it expressed his character as a Christian avatar and attached to him those traits associated with the image of Christ.

Lincoln's work, like that of the men buried at Gettysburg, was finished by another's hand. He had reformed the Union. He had made himself the Great Emancipator and the father of his country. John Wilkes Booth made him an avatar of Christ. He could scarcely have chosen a better day "Good Friday was the day / Of the prodigy and crime."[26] Lincoln was already regarded, as leaders often are, as representative of the people in a personal as well as an official sense. His assassination enhanced this representative character. He became the symbol of the Union dead, "those who gave their lives that the nation might live." He was thus, like Christ, both Representative and Redeemer, the scapegoat for the people's sins, at once the Saviour and the Son of Man.

Melville's martial requiem, which names Lincoln "martyr" and "Forgiver," suggests the multiple dimensions of Lincoln's identification with Christ. Recalling the traditional view of the clement and compassionate Christ, Melville wrote of Lincoln, "With yearning he was filled / To redeem the evil-willed," a passage which suggest Calvin's unflattering animadversions on human nature, as well as Christian redemption. Thus likened to the Son, he is also identified with the Father. "He lieth in his blood / The Father in his face," a seeming contradiction which the doctrine of the Trinity demands.[27]

The recollection of Lincoln's paternal character deepens the meaning of his martyrdom. Melville's use of Good Friday and the simple circumstances of the case show that Lincoln died as the nation's representative. His paternal character enabled his death to serve as symbol and substitute for the political patricide he had already wrought. Grief over the Father's death could disguise and displace guilt over the impiety of the Refounding.[28]

The frequency with which the assassinated Lincoln was likened to Christ indictates that the metaphor was sufficiently apt to override any suggestion of excess or blasphemy. Although Lincoln had been revered in some quarters in his lifetime, he had not yet reached the status of avatar. His assassination radically altered his mythic character. The principle elements of the Christian myth are the Redemption and the Incarnation. Each effects in its way the identification of the people with God. In the former, the Savior serves as compensatory sacrifice for the people; in the latter, he becomes manifest by assuming their characteristic corporeal form. He is the Word made flesh, the materialization of mind. The explicit identification of Lincoln with Christ reveals the increasing political significance of this myth.

Many have observed that partisans of the Union frequently identified the Union's triumph with the inauguration of the millennium. In the "Battle Hymn of the Republic," the temporal cause of the Union is explicitly the cause of God. The soldiers actively engaged in "trampling out the vintage where the grapes of wrath are stored" achieve a collective apotheosis. The Union has become the political manifestation of God. Lincoln's death provided a mythic recapitulation of this national epiphany. In reenacting the redeeming death of Jesus Christ on Good Friday, Lincoln reproduced the national imitation of Christ. "As he died to make men holy let us live to make men free." His death was thus the culmination of the Puritan idea of America. He had achieved a selfless imitation of Christ by making that imitation collective. The nation had become the temporal expression of divinity. The disparity between the individual and God, between the material and the ideal, was resolved in a great assimilation. Lincoln's death made him the exemplar of the national incarnation and redemption. The mythic persona which his assassination completed gave a dimension of tragic grandeur to the process of rationalization.

The idea of incarnation had thus far acquired a present and material expression only in the legal documentation of corporations. Lincoln's reenactment of the Incarnation in his official capacity as the people's representative gave this idea a more sublime expression. Thus, Lincoln's support for capitalism, for industry, for rationalization, and for law was far more profound than the support he gave it in policy. The mythic persona which he in part created integrated it within the structure of American myth. It served to make the idea of the materialization of the mind and the social constructs with which it was associated in antebellum America more intelligible and to embed them deeply in American culture. Lincoln's recapitulation of the Christian myth placed the war and the victory of the Union within the oldest and most powerful form of political discourse in Northern culture. The cycle of Incarnation and Redemption was important, however, not only because it fell within a form of political discourse which was both readily intelligible and independently legitimating, but because it resolved contradictions within the political culture which employed that form of discourse. The collapse of the distinction between the individual and the community, and the community and its deity, was effected in Lincoln's simultaneous representation of deity and people. Lincoln's personification of Incarnation and Redemption and his account of the meaning of the war also resolved the persistent tension between the partisans of industry and the romantic followers of the Transcendentalists. It removed the stigma of sterile utilitarianism from the industrial era the war ushered in.

The postwar nation boasted an invigorated industry, an expanded bureaucracy, the rudiments of a vast—and now legitimate—military-industrial complex, imperial ambitions abroad, and an aggrandized executive at home. The promised new birth of freedom, begun with the disenfranchisement of the rebels, would be lost to blacks with the continuance of social, economic, and political discrimination. Workers, whose cause had been lost in the furor, suffered increasing exploitation in the burgeoning industrial system. Southerners, purportedly gathered back into the covenanted community, became in fact the residents of a disdained colonial possession. The preservation of the Union and the promised new birth of freedom were thus, like the Emancipation Proclamation, partial and defective.

12 Whitman and the Race of the Conquering March

So great a schism, so profound a rupture is a civil war, that victor and vanquished are likewise altered. Each has subscribed to an understanding of the nation manifestly insufficient to cover all. The alienation that culminated in secession, the enmity that ended in conquest have created an irrefragable division. If arms could indeed effect a legal resolution of the conflict, then the resulting lawful union would be nonetheless insufficient and defective.

> States! Were you looking to be held together by lawyers?
> Or by an agreement on paper? Or by arms?
> Nay, nor the world, nor any living thing will so cohere.[1]

Once rent, the fabric of national identity must be rewoven if it is to be remade.

> But now, ah, now, to learn from the crisis of anguish, advancing,
> Grappling with direst fate and recoiling not,
> And now to conceive and show the world what your
> Children en-masse really are.[2]

For who but I, who but myself, Walt Whitman asked introspectively, parenthetically, "who except myself has conceived what your children en-masse really are?"[3]

Whitman's project was the construction of a comprehensive national character, an identity sufficient to embrace the evident disparity that empire occasions. Whitman was a Union man, unwilling to relinquish the South, willing indeed to expand the borders to encompass many more. The long lists of states and sections, sexes, circumstances, occupations that lend to Whitman's poetry a grand, progressive meter illustrate the grandeur of what he had conceived. "Only the poet begets,"[3] Whitman wrote. He named himself a mother and caught Walt Whitman in the act of parturition. "Walt, you contain enough, why don't you let it out then?"[4]

"Kanada," the South, Manhattan, Virginia, Ohio, and the West; Yankee tradesmen, the planter "hospitable and nonchalant," ancient eidolons and an imagined future are numbered in their diversity. All this was comprehended in Whitman's vision of the whole. Liminal Walt Whitman, man and woman, old and young, slave and freeman, worker and poet, bureaucrat and homosexual, stood on the boundaries of the state and looked within it. From his vantage position on the frontier he had a field of vision which could include the nation in its entirety.

> Of all races and eras these states with veins full of poetical stuff, most need
> poets, and are to have the greatest, and use them the greatest,
> Their presidents shall not be their common referee so much as their poets
> shall.[5]

The reconstruction of the Union, purportedly begun in the reiteration of old borders, required the propagation of new standards of legitimacy. In a democracy, consent bottoms the regime. A great and manifest dissent shakes the foundation of the state. Reconciliation requires a common referee:

> He is the arbiter of the diverse, he is the key,
> He is the equalizer of his age and land,
> He supplies what wants supplying, he checks what wants checking,
> In peace out of him speaks the spirit of peace . . .
> He is no arguer, he is judgment.[6]

The boundaries which determine men's allegiance, and the standards whereby they judge the legitimacy of the regime which rules them, were to be supplied by Whitman "to define America, her athletic democracy."[7] He would present a new national identity woven from the threads of earlier myths and recent conflict, and in so doing construct a history in which Americans could recognize their common character.

> I have charged myself, heeded or unheeded to compose a free march for
> these states
> To be exhilarating music to them, years, centuries hence.[8]

Whitman recognized that these eidolons in the new myths of national identity which he propagated among a divided and inchoate people would prove determinative of their future conduct. Indeed, it was only in years, centuries hence that Whitman's conception of nationality would come to fruition, and emerge as a material reality. The accomplishment of that period of gestation would be secured by popular acceptance of Whitman's vision. As his understanding of what American identity comprised became common, it became the standard whereby the propriety of actions, laws, and customs were determined. This agreement of what was American would inspire policy, giving to the operation of government, the political ambitions of separate men, and men's relations in society a common direction. Myth engenders national integration. Thus Whitman asked "States! Were you looking to be held together by lawyers?" and answered:

> Away! I arrive bringing these, beyond all the forces of courts and arms.
> These! to hold you together as firmly as the earth itself is held together.[9]

That Union which Whitman evokes is of the living rather than the made. It is held together as the earth is held together, it will cohere in the manner of living things. Whitman's Union is natural, represented by sexual union, by the indissoluble combination of atoms in conception and gestation. All its attributes are illustrated by the natural; his leaves of grass are "a uniform hieroglyphic"[10] for equal individuals; which means "sprouting alike in broad zones and narrow zones." As Whitman wrote, imagined, and envisioned, it moved from construction to conception, from a poetic eidolon, a poesis, to a song and a sensation. Whitman by his account, discovered America through the senses; he heard, saw, smelled, tasted, and touched America. Melville had seen it made.

This accounts perhaps for Melville's doubt and Whitman's surety. That sense of tragedy and loss which pervades Melville's poems of the victory is absent even in Whitman's poems of the war. Likewise assured of the progress of history, Melville saw the passing of the former age. Whitman was of the latter-day saints. Melville's nationality was of the old era in which the South had had so great a part. Thus he made the South the realm of nature, the North the province of law. The new order was created, for Melville, in the imposition of order on nature. This, he asserted, was the work of arms and the law. Whitman's nationality followed the refounding. He denied that law or arms had any hand in it. He was the proof of that refounding. He was himself evidence that the victory of the Union effected a change in the American constitution, in what it was to be American. This change corresponded to a change in the nation's territorial boundaries.

For Melville, it was the South which was liminal and in the wilderness. For Whitman, the wilderness was in the West, and the West was on the boundary, liminal, definitive, and determinative. This disparity reveals the kinship of the material and the metaphoric. Melville used the South, Whitman the West, as a sign for the cultural traits of the liminal. Each is the realm of nature. Here law is not determinative. It is at this juncture that nations are made and unmade. Melville's South is the realm of dissolution, Whitman's West the womb of nationality. Melville associated the South with Washington and the Revolution, the great events of national genesis. That nation ends. The region associated with the prepolitical became the wilderness. Whitman's wilderness was the West. This region, equally prepolitical, provided the rudiments of a new form of national identity which incorporated elements of the old nation in an extended whole.

The territoral expansion of the United States, with the consequent alteration of the nation's history, the introduction of hitherto-unknown customs and ways of life, altered the composition of the nation. Neither the citizens nor their culture were adequately described by the culture of the previous generation. The extension of the territorial boundaries demanded an attendant extension of the cultural boundaries. Melville saw the demise of the old order but could not see through it to the new. The affirmation of the providential progress of history with which he closed the conflict between nature and civilization was an act of faith. When Melville wrote, "we march with Providence cheery still" he was among those blessed who do not see, and yet believe.

While Melville's war was apocalyptic, Whitman included the war in a vision of America that extended back from the present to the primordial without a breach. His description of the nation as organic, his employment of natural metaphors, and his conception of America as at once a discovery and a creation, a sensation and an imagining, all indicate that Whitman's America was to him not merely what ought to be, but what is. His project was thus, as he perceived, exactly analogous to parturition. He was to be the person who brought forth something already conceived, shaped, and nourished; "I am the most venerable mother."[11]

Whitman's employment of the maternal metaphor, like that of the Southern poets and orators, marked maternity as prior to politics: "Underneath all, Nativity."[12] Northern poets of the war charac-

teristically associated the North with the masculine, leaving the feminine to the South. Southerners, seeing in secession a new nativity,
praised their several states as mothers. Whitman, unlike his compatriots, saw in the prelude to war a nascent nationality. It is Virginia,
in his poetry, who raised "the insane knife towards the Mother of
All."[13] Whitman's employment of metaphor speaks to its universality.
Like his opponent Southerners, he sees in maternity that comprehensive being common to nationality. Like them he employed maternity
as a metaphor for that subjective nationality which precedes and legiti-
mates constitutions and regimes. Like them he saw the English as
mother to the Americans:

Great is the English brood—what brood has so vast a destiny as the English?
It is the mother of the brood that must rule the earth with the new rule.[14]

Whitman's "Mother of All" was, however, the bearer of a new
order, a new form of nationality. She rose out of the West.

Beautiful world of new birth that rises to my eyes
Like a limitless golden cloud filling the western sky
Emblem of a general maternity lifted above all.[15]

Whitman describes this "Mother with Thy Equal Brood" as a comprehensive union, encompassing past and future, thought and fact, the
human and the divine, "thou transcendental Union!"[16] Carrying "a
varied chain of different States, yet one identity only,"[17] it represented
an alteration of an earlier nationality, less extensive, yet equally maternal in its transcendence of personal boundaries. The significant ideological change is clearly marked: "Mother! with subtle sense severe,
with the naked sword in your hand, I saw you at last refuse to treat but
directly with individuals."[18] Whitman indicates here and in the names
"Mother of All" and "Mother with Thy Equal Brood" that American
nationality had become primary, it was no longer a consequence of
allegiance to a confederate state. Equality and community were the
distinguishing attributes of this nationality. Like those of the Southern
states, Whitman's mother is a woman armed.

This enhanced maternity was unequaled in its fecundity. Whitman speaks of "its endless gestations of new States," thus reducing the
states to the status of offspring. "I'd sow," Whitman promises, "a seed
for thee of endless nationality,"[19] and warns "I am jetting the stuff of
far more arrogant republics."[20]

Whitman was to be mother and father to a universal nationality.

His was a comprehensive capacity for conception. He claimed the attributes of male and female in conception, of the mother in parturition, the father in dissemination. In each case the germ of nationality was contained within himself. In bringing it forth he identified himself with the "Mother of All." The distinction between the personal and the political was collapsed. The liminality of woman and mother attached to both Whitman and the nascent state. The comprehensive character of maternity was presented in each. As is proper to an evocation of allegiance, Whitman's entire corpus denies the distinction between the state and the self. The state was drawn from himself, yet he was the creature and creation of the state.

Knowing himself American, he derived his vision of the whole from himself, his conception of citizenship from an understanding of his own allegiance. It was all one long "Song of Myself."

> I celebrate myself and sing myself,
> And what I assume you shall assume.

Whitman was the "clean haired Yankee girl," "the man who knows how it stings to be slighted," the trapper, the half-breed, and the runaway slave.[21] He recorded a shameless narcissism and an unbounded capacity for comprehension, a universal embrace. (In our time it has been the spirit of the all-tolerant and entirely idiosyncratic Sixties). Whitman affirmed that he held within him the identity of all he names and more. His notion of nationality is sufficient to embrace all this diversity. This single identification would assimilate them. Yet never was an appeal made to something outside the self. If man was, as Whitman claimed, "a summons and a challenge," the challenge was to self-knowledge, the summons to a recognition of commonality in private experience.

Whitman disdained the Puritan preoccupation, much worried at in his time, between the soul and self. The self, in Whitman's articulation, was the moment of participation in the transcendent soul. He kept enough of the Puritan tradition to deny intermediaries, but he committed an unparalleled heresy: he enjoined man to an unqualified self-love. In a larger sense, he was the culmination of the Incarnation; he resolved its dilemmas by bringing it full circle. He collapsed the distinction between body and soul, and the distinction between God and man.

"I am the poet of the Body and I am the poet of the Soul,"[22] Whitman wrote; "O I say these are not the parts and poem of the body only, but of the soul."23 Whitman's reconciliation was effected not merely by simultaneously affirming the separate and distinct value of both the body and the soul. Rather he collapsed them: "And if the body were not the soul, what is the soul?"24 He dealt similarly with the division between the self and transcendent divinity. Divinity was an attribute, in Whitman's articulation, of citizenship, of the wide open, other-embracing self. Thus he ejaculated, "O yourself! O god! O divine average!"25 and affirmed, "In the faces of men and women I see God, and in my own face in the glass."26

In Whitman's articulation, the affirmation of citizenship, of common participation in a comprehensive being, revealed the immanent human divinity. The political expression of this universal communion was democracy. In such regimes, the individual attains apotheosis, becoming at once abandoned and exalted.

> One's self I sing a simple separate person
> But utter the word Democracy
> The word En-Masse.27

Whitman's political ideal, like those of the Puritans, was achieved as the self was subsumed in community.

Whitman's nation, like that of the Puritans, extended through time. He believed with them that the future was to justify the past

> In the name of these states shall I scorn the antique?
> Why these are the children of the antique to justify it.28

In "Antecedents," he follows the making of America in history, its providential creation. The poem follows history itself, each enumerated age following in linear progression ending with America. This listing, like a litany, is less information than invocation. He exclaims in the similarly constructed "Apostroph," "O vast preparations for these states! O years!"29 In "Roaming in Thought," subtitled "After Reading Hegel," Whitman revealed his own synthesis with Puritan providentialism and German historicism.

> Roaming in thought over the Universe I saw the little that is
> Good hasten toward immortality.30

Confidence of the direction and end of history invested Whitman with a sense at once of his peculiar moment of history, and with a vision of its eschatological significance:

Endless unfolding of words of ages!
And mine a word of the modern, the word En-Masse.[31]

Whitman's enthusiastic embrace of sexuality, indeed all aspects of things corporeal, and his explicit acceptance of evil have prompted many to regard him as entirely secular. He asserted, however, that his was "A word of the faith that never balks."[32] His preoccupation with the divine, his invocations of the deity, and a pervasive mysticism indicate that his heterodoxy was the consequence of too much rather than too little faith. His conviction of immanent divinity in the corporeal harks back to the Incarnation; his unqualified affirmation of the One appears as the culmination of monotheism. He was himself convinced that his evocation of the sacred came in direct descent from earlier religious traditions. Thus he employed such concepts as the Puritan concept of justification, consciously, endeavoring not to secularize the sacred, but to reveal the immanent divinity of the putatively profane.

Whitman's Puritan antecedents are also evinced in his praise of death. He and his predecessors were similarly impelled by a confidence in the temporal continuity of community and in the community's comprehension of individuals, to an indifference to individual death. This was transmuted in him, as it had been in them, to an acclamation of death. Whether it represented a return to God, a decisive collapse of past, present, and future into one infinity, or a dissolution of the atomic individual in the comprehensive material or spiritual whole, it represented the destruction of personal boundaries, and an irrevocable end. Whitman's praises to death have, however, other cultural antecedents. It is beautiful, he wrote,

that the hands of the sisters Death and Night incessantly
softly wash again, and ever again, this soil'd world.[33]

The poem in which these lines occur is titled "Reconciliation." In common with his Western forebears Whitman possessed a sense of the regenerative capacities of violence. He was able, therefore, to give unqualified praise to soldiers, and to conquest.

Whitman's style is in keeping with his intention. As he endeavored to forge a single national identity from states, regions, occupations, and allegiances, he evoked that comprehensive American identity poetically through the ritualistic enumeration of the names of its component parts. His longest poems are no more than litanies of diversity, lists of the names of states, of races, times, jobs, and descriptions of small moments of each. The poem thus became the prototype for the transcendental union, *e pluribus unum:*

> A song I make of the One formed out of all
> The fang'd and glittering One whose head is over all,
> Resolute warlike One including and over all.[34]

Whitman's nationality was a comprehensive One encompassing the South, he claimed, no less than the North, yet it was conceived in the preparations for war, and it showed the marks of the North's triumph. Despite Whitman's protestations that the regenerate Union was to be secured in "love, the life long love of comrades,"[35] he did not question the legitimacy of a victory gained by arms. Nor, with the war behind him, did he urge his "Democratic Individual" to enjoy the fruits of peace. When he conceived that One, he was, as he proclaimed, "jetting the stuff of far more arrogant republics."

Union had been, in Whitman's epic history, the principal object of the war. Though Whitman was opposed to slavery, it figures infrequently in his poems of the war. The crime with which the South is charged is sundering the Union, "the foulest crime in history known in any land or age."[36] Whitman's ejaculation "O Union impossible to dissever!"[37] indicates that the gravity of the South's crime lay rather in its intent than its likelihood of accomplishment. America's continuance was ordained; the vast preparations, the ancient antecedents of the states had made union inevitable. "O sacred Union!" Whitman named it and proclaimed, "O all, all inseparable—ages, ages, ages! / O a curse on him that would dissolve this Union for any reason whatever!"[38] A lack of success was not sufficient punishment for so impious a defiance. The South's assault on the historically hallowed Union was tantamount in Whitman's theology to Lucifer's revolt against the deity. In each case, the opposed One was omnipotent, the crime impossible yet undiminished. Whitman's war was not for Libertad, but for the One. Freedom does not even figure in the trinity:

> With Victory on thy left, and at thy right hand Law;
> Thou Union holding all, fusing, absorbing, tolerating all,
> Thee, ever thee, I sing.[39]

Whitman looked for the triumph of liberty in the completion of the One. In a fashion antithetical to that of Locke, but entirely consonant with the tenets of the Pilgrims, Whitman identified the achievement of liberty with the selfless participation in community. The Puritans had claimed that men were free when they surrendered will and intellect to God. Webster saw the secular applications of the thought and gave it its canonical formulation in antebellum political culture: "Liberty and Union! now and forever! One and inseparable." In Whitman the thought retained the undiminished grandeur of the Puritan dogma. Whitman's Democratic Individual was entirely comprehensive.

> One's self I sing, a simple, separate person
> But utter the word Democracy, the word En-Masse.[40]

Like Lincoln encompassed by the Puritan tradition, Whitman had so succeeded in abstracting individuality that there were no more individuals in it. Purified of the particular, liberty had become a sign for the sovereignty of law, an attribute of abstract community. For Whitman, as for the Puritans, the achievement of liberty was a consequence of participation in divinity. Freedom was an attribute of God, attained by men in their communion with God, and advanced in the world by the providential march of mind. Divorced from the self in its particularity, it existed only in a comprehensive, universally valid form of life. Liberty had thus become the creature and creation of law. Natural had given way to civil liberties. Community, union, was the prerequisite for freedom. Freedom was to be, Whitman wrote, a star "set in the sky of law."[41]

Whitman revered Lincoln for Lincoln's own reasons, not as the Emancipator, but as the man who saved the Union, the steward and servant of Whitman's One:

> The dust was once the man
> Gentle, plain, just and resolute, under whose cautious hand,
> Against the foulest crime in history known in any land or age,
> Was saved the Union of these states.[42]

Lincoln was less a statesman than a soldier for Whitman. The laws and ideology of the regime were less to him than the nation's union and continuance. Lincoln had held the Union by force. It is appropriate, therefore, that in Whitman's poems to him, he is hailed as captain and commander. In the laments, soldiers mourn for him. He retains the patriarchal character that popular songs assigned him, mingled with his martial rank. "O father!"[43] Whitman cries. Like the early archetypal heroes of the West, Lincoln is preeminently masculine. His mother is dead, his wife insane, and he has only sons. The Civil War, Whitman wrote to Grant, was the triumph and the vindication of the West. In it, "those prairie sovereigns of the West, Kansas, Missouri, Illinois— were all so justified."[44] Lincoln, when dead, was a "powerful, western fallen star,"[45] living "a western orb sailing the heaven."[46]

Whitman's professions of kinship with Lincoln were not merely a recognition of his patriarchal character. Rather they recognize an essential likeness. Each was of the West, a partisan of the Union, a proponent of expansion, a defender of law, and a maker of abstractions. After Lincoln's death, Whitman described the Mississippi as a "Abrahamic river."[47] Though he recalled the patriarch, it was Lincoln he evoked, rather than the prophet, for this stream, as he described its course, took all the smaller rivers with it, rather than releasing them as its offspring. Lincoln represented comprehensive nationality. His mythic persona offered a model which could reconcile and resolve myriad aspects of American nationality. Like Whitman, he presented in himself the boundaries of a new national identity, into which others might feed. Each was both advocate and exemplar. Whitman identified the war with Lincoln, assigning common attributes to each. The war was the justification of the West, Lincoln a Western star. The war and Lincoln were dedicated to the Union. Lincoln was masculine according to the Western paradigm. Whitman heard the outbreak of the war in 1861, "Your masculine voice, O year, as rising amid the great cities." Lincoln, as Whitman knew, was a partisan of industry, a latter-day adherent of Henry Clay, praising the invention of new machines, new processes of manufacturing, increases in production, and the spread of industrial capitalism across the land. Whitman too could wax enthusiastic over a prophetic vision of Gary, and apotheosize the transcendent Yankee:

> His daring foot is on land and sea everywhere, he colonizes the Pacific, the archipelagoes,
> With the steamship, the electric telepage, the newspaper, the wholesale engines of war.[48]

In this man, "average man,"[49] Whitman calls him, war and capitalism are allied. He is peddler and colonist, tinker and conqueror. He is to effect the universal union "with these and the world-spreading factories he interlinks all geography, all lands."[50] This prediction of American world dominance, effected by arms and the multinational corporation, speaks well for Whitman's claimed capacity to prophesy.

Whitman's intimations of the future, in their unqualified praise of industrial progress, their appetite for conquest, and their passion for the uniform, show the extent of the Northern victory. His delineation of the Union's future indicate that the South had not been excused but merely excised. The main shapes of the future are "shapes of turbulent manly cities."[51] Whitman's Union, had, as he had himself, its origins in urbanization. "Walt Whitman, a kosmos, of Manhattan the son."[52] He asked, "Give me solitude, give me Nature, give me again O Nature your primal sanities."[53] But even in asking he observes, "While yet incessantly asking still I adhere to my city."[54] The progress of democracy which he forecast was entangled with the progress of industry. Commonly impelled by an inexhaustible passion for consumption, incorporation, and aggrandizement, the soldier and the capitalist, allied in the Union, would absorb, fuse, and assimilate the world. In this fashion, Whitman prophesied, humanity would come within the Union, and thereafter commonly enjoy the civil liberties to which Amerians were entitled.

In "Starting From Paumanok," Whitman articulates this vision of an imperial America:

> Americanos! conquerors! marches humanitarian!
> Foremost! century marches! Libertad! masses!
> For you a programme of chants.[55]

After the war, Whitman's Americans were "no more credulity's race, abiding-temper'd race," they were the "race of the conquering march."[56] The universal human validity Whitman claimed for American nationality impelled its partisans to marches humanitarian. That evangelical enthusiasm for democratic conquest which had been characteristic of the political culture for the American West for half a century was made the rudder for Whitman's ship of state.

"I chant of the dilation or of pride," Whitman wrote, in the true Western fashion.

> We have had ducking and deprecating long enough,
> I show that size is only development.[57]

Here in this song of himself, the prototype of American identity, Whitman adopts the Eastern passion for consumption, incorporation, aggrandizement. He eats all he encounters, incorporates it within himself; he grows, he expands. Like the archetypical Westerner, he endows himself with superhuman capacities. He becomes the culmination of that type, "Walt Whitman a kosmos." Those central myths of Western political culture—the conquest of nature, the militant extension of liberty, the great appetites, the unbounded ambition, the ever-ambiguous, ever-expanding boundaries of the frontier, and hence the promise of future greatness—are themselves extended by Whitman to encompass the nation, past, present, and future. Seizing Lincoln's tenet that the nation was "founded in liberty," Whitman argued that the extension of liberty through conquest was not merely excused but entailed upon Americans. All men, Lincoln had affirmed, "are created equal." The blessings of that egalitarian nationality which was American were therefore universal. If equality could be extended by arms and the law to the blacks, no cause could be found for denying the same to the remaining masses.

> You plague swarms in Madras, Nankin, Kaubul, Cairo!
> You benighted roamer in Amazonia! You Patagonian! you Feejeeman!
> I do not prefer others so much before you either.[58]

America, Whitman proclaimed, was "not a nation, but a teeming Nation of nations,"[59] the idea, the universal archetype of nationality. Here, he asserted, "the doings of men correspond with the broadest doings of the day and night."[60] American laws, American customs, corresponded to universal laws. It was, therefore, both right and inevitable that Americans would be "masters of the world under a new powers."[61] That vast, all-encompassing America, full grown, would be "a world primal again, with vistas of glory incessant and branching."[62] Whitman's America was to be nature's nation, sanctioned by the irrefragable law of nature, primal and vigorous, universal: "I chant the world on my Western sea."[63] Yet that universal regeneration was not yet accomplished. All the world was not yet America.

To those "human forms with the fathomless, ever-impressive countenances of brutes," Whitman promised not an immediate but an eventual equality. For the "Austral negro, naked, red, sooty, with protrusive lip, groveling" no less than the American black "so blear, so hardly human," emancipation was to promise only a future equality. "You will come forward in due time to my side," he predicted, from "away back there where you stand."[64] In the meantime, they were to curtsy to the regiments.[65] America's marches humanitarian, like Sherman's march to the sea, were to elicit the deferential gratitude of an emancipated inferior.

> I chant the new empire, grander than any before, as in a vision it comes to
>   me,
> I chant America the mistress, I chant a greater supremacy.[66]

When Whitman wrote of the aging black woman paying homage to Sherman's armies, he named her Ethiopia, and made the Union army the model for an imperial America. Such was the mission of poets.

> The rapid arming and the march
> The flag of peace quick-folded, and instead, the flag we know,
> Warlike flag of the great idea."[67]

This "thick-sprinkled bunting! flag of stars!" would bring the world liberty through conquest, equality through subordination. Whitman retained a great lucidity regarding the course he advocated.

> Long yet your road, fatal flag—long yet your road and lined with bloody
>   death,
> For the prize I see at issue is the world.[68]

There would be in this uniform Union, in the single triumphant law of the American Imperium, small place for

> Those who have never been master'd
> For men and women whose tempers have never been master'd,
> For those whom laws, theories, conventions can never master.[69]

Yet Whitman says, "I am for those." He claims, "I confront peace, security, and all the settled laws, to unsettle them."[70] He praises "the American contempt for statutes and ceremonies, the boundless impatience of restraint."[71] The good city, Whitman affirms, is "where the men and women think lightly of the laws."[72] It was this strain of Whitman, appropriate to his spontaneity, his embrace of the impotent and disenfranchised, his disdain for sexual taboos and social conventions, that caused the people in the Sixties to regard him as kin. Though they adjured his ideal of imperial America and sought to stop his juggernaut at midcareer, they found in him the current of their own resistance. Whitman had drawn on the defeated as well as the victorious. It was

"To the States" that he addressed the exhortation, "Resist much, obey little."[73] Heeding this, and carrying within themselves that current of American resistance to the American uniformity that Whitman advocated, they praised as they opposed him. They preserved in the reformed Union the spirit of those the Union had excluded.

> Still though the one I sing
> (One yet of contradictions made,) I dedicate to Nationality,
> I leave in him revolt, (O latent right of insurrection! O quenchless,
>   indispensable fire!)[74]

It was the hot sun of the South that would fully ripen his songs.

Notes

INTRODUCTION

1. John Locke, *Two Treatises on Government*, ed. Peter Laslett (Cambridge: Cambridge University Press, 1960).

2. "Starting from Paumanok," in *Complete Poems of Walt Whitman*, ed. Francis Murphy (Harmondsworth, England: Penguin, 1975), p. 61.

3. Ibid.

4. *The Life and Major Works of Thomas Paine*, ed. Philip S. Foner (Secaucus, N.J.: Citadel Press, 1974), p. 3.

5. Benjamin Franklin, *The Political Theory of Benjamin Franklin*, ed. Ralph Ketcham (New York: Bobbs-Merrill Co., 1965), p. 303.

6. Alexis de Tocqueville, *Democracy in America*, trans. George Lawrence, ed. J. P. Meyer (New York: Doubleday and Co., 1969), 1:18–19.

7. Abraham Lincoln, Gettysburg Address.

8. Whitman, "Song of Myself," in *Complete Poems*, p. 123.

10. J. David Greenstone, "The Transient and the Permanent," in *Public Values and Private Power in American Politics*, ed. J. David Greenstone (Chicago: University of Chicago Press, 1982). My understanding of this period has been the gift of a consensual conflict with David Greenstone that mirrors the bipolarity he describes. Being so indebted, it is his theory I am most likely to do injustice to.

11. Gen. 6:2–4.

12. Stephen Vincent Benet, *John Brown's Body* (New York: Holt, Rinehart and Winston, 1928), p. 5. The poem continues:

> I think that I have seen you, not as one
> But clad in diverse semblances and powers
> Always the same, as light falls from the sun
> And always different as the differing hours.

13. Allen Ginsberg, "America," in *Howl*. (San Francisco: City Lights Books, 1956), p. 31.

14. Whitman, "Song of the Broad-Axe," in *Complete Poems*, p. 219.

15. Hartz, *Liberal Tradition in America*, pp. 8, 143.

16. Whitman, "Still Though the One I Sing," in *Complete Poems*, p. 48.

17. For a perceptive account of the affinities between Marxists and Puritans, see Michael Walzer's reflections on his own experience in the introduction to *Revolution of the Saints* (Cambridge: Harvard University Press, 1965).

18. Sacvan Bercovitch, *American Jeremiad* (Madison: University of Wisconsin Press, 1979).

19. Victor Turner, *The Ritual Process* (Ithaca, N.Y.: Cornell University Press, 1969).

20. Ibid., p. 106.

CHAPTER ONE

1. See Gen. 9:8–17. This is the first place at which God says, "I establish my Covenant with you." An earlier example of the inscribed covenant, and an important one, is at Gen. 4:13–15.

2. Quoted in Bercovitch, "The Biblical Basis of American Myth," in *The Bible and American Letters*, ed. Giles Gunn (Philadelphia: Fortress Press, 1983). It is ironic that Irving puts this speech in the mouth of a Muslim, for Islam itself was created in the command "Recite!"

3. I was led to this understanding by William Harris' fine essay "Bonding Word and Polity," in the *American Political Science Review* 76 (March 1982): 34–46.

4. See Paul Ricoeur's essay on inscription, "The Model of the Text: Meaningful Action Considered as a Text," in *Interpretive Social Science: A Reader*, ed. Paul Rabinow and William Sullivan (Berkeley and Los Angeles: University of California Press, 1979), pp. 73–102.

5. John Greenleaf Whittier, *Songs of Labor* (Boston: Ticknor, Reed, and Fields, 1850), p. 47.

6. Ibid., p. 14.

7. See, for example, sectional characterizations in the debates over war with England, in *Annals of Congress*, November 30, 1808 (Josiah Quincy in the House) and in Thomas Hart Benton, *Abridgements of the Debates in Congress*, 16 vols. (New York: D. Appleton and Co., 1857–61), p. 645 (Harmanus Bleeker in the House). Sectional characterizations occur frequently in the debates from the first Congress to secession.

8. Harding of Kentucky to Cushing of Massachusetts, quoted in "The New England Character," *Southern Literary Messenger*, July 1837, p. 414 (hereafter cited as *SLM*). This article is a satiric response to an article of the same name in the *North American Review* January 1837.

9. "The New England Character," in *SLM*, July 1837, p. 414.

10. *The New Songbook* (Hartford, Conn.: S. Andrus and Sons, 1848), p. 109.

11. Peleg Sprague, "The New England Character," *North American Review* 94 (January 1837): 259.

12. E. G. Squier, *The Workingman's Miscellany: Lecture on the Constitution and True Interest of the Laboring Class in America* (New York: New York Tribune, 1843), p. 11.

13. Whittier, *The Stranger in Lowell* (Boston: Waite, Pierce, and Co., 1845), pp. 2–3, 10–11, 12.

14. Ibid., pp. 10–11.

15. William Ellery Channing, *Lectures on the Elevation of the Laboring Classes* (Boston: Wm. Ticknor, 1840), p. 57.

16. Quoted in Daniel Walker Howe, *Political Culture of the American Whigs* (Chicago: University of Chicago Press, 1979), p. 229.

17. Sprague, *Dr. Sprague's Sermon Occasioned by the Late Tragical Deed at Washington* (Albany, N.Y.: Joel Munsell, 1848), p. 10.

18. J. V. Matthews, "Whig History: The New England Whigs and the Search for a Usable Past," *New England Quarterly* (June 1978): 195.

19. Howe, *American Whigs*, p. 229.

20. Ibid., p. 71. Not all, however, would regard this progress as equally praiseworthy.

21. Ibid., pp. 70–71.

22. Ibid., pp. 27, 82. See also Bercovitch, *American Jeremiad*.

23. Quoted in ibid., p. 34.

24. Ibid.

25. Quoted in Fred Somkin, *Unquiet Eagle* (Ithaca, N.Y.: Cornell University Press, 1967), pp. 110–11. This recognition of the power of words, and the consequent attempt to rule by naming are characteristic of Northern sectional culture. Such attempts, predicated by the primacy of the Logos in scriptural religion, reveal the inevitable ascendance of legal rational authority in the Union.

26. *Collected Works of Henry Clay*, ed. Calvin Colton, 6 vols. (New York: G. P. Putnam's Sons, 1904), 3:563. Clay's metaphor constructs masculine sexuality as a form of inscription, an imposition of the image of the self on the world. This inscription permits individuals to transcend the temporal limits imposed by their corporeality, but it is effective only insofar as they renounce individuality and see themselves perpetuated in the collective.

27. Rufus Choate quoted in Howe, *American Whigs*, p. 229.

28. For example, the punctilious prescription of the Muslims for disposing of all written and printed matter, in order to express reverence for Scripture.

29. Differences of opinion on this matter gave rise to the Yazoo land scandals and the Nullification and Secession controversies.

30. Herman Melville, *Clarel*, 2 vols. (New York: G. P. Putnam's Sons, 1876), 2:246.

CHAPTER TWO

1. Walton Felch, *The Cotton Mill Moralized* (Medway, Mass.: Privately printed, 1816), p. 14.

2. "English traits," in *Collected Works of Ralph Waldo Emerson*, ed. Edward Emerson, 12 vols. (Cambridge, Mass.: Houghton, Mifflin, and Co., 1903), vol. 5.

3. Emerson, "The Poet," in *Collected Works* 3:19.

4. Emerson, note to "The Young American," in *Collected Works* 1:453.

5. See chapter 6 for incidences of this metaphor in Southern rhetoric.

6. Emerson, "The Young American," in *Collected Works* 1:364.

7. Ferdinand Kurnberger, *Picture of American Culture*, quoted in Max Weber, *The Protestant Ethic and the Spirit of Capitalism*, trans. Talcott Parsons (New York: Charles Scribner's Sons, 1958), p. 51.

8. Jean Jacques Rousseau, *Emile*, trans. Allan Bloom (New York: Basic Books, 1979), p. 37.

9. Emerson, "English Traits," p. 98.

10. Weber, *From Max Weber*, trans. and ed. H. H. Gerth and C. Wright Mills (New York: Oxford University Press, 1946), p. 261.

11. Michel Chevalier, *Society, Manners, and Politics in the United States* (Boston: William Ticknor, 1839), p. 361.

12. Lucy Larcom, *A New England Girlhood* (Boston: Houghton and Mifflin, 1889).

13. Quoted in Herbert Gutman, *Work, Culture and Society in Industrializing America* (New York: Random House, 1977), p. 28.

14. Ibid., p. 4.

15. Quoted in ibid., p. 24.

16. Theodore Parker, *Social Classes in a Republic*, centenary ed. (Boston: American Unitarian Association, n.d.), p. 47.

17. John Taylor, *Arator* (Indianapolis: Liberty Classics, 1977), pp. 79–80.

18. Sarah Bagley, "Speech to the New England Workingmen's Association," May 27, 1845, in Philip Foner, *Factory Girls* (Urbana: University of Illinois Press, 1977), p. 109.

19. The agent of Manchester Mill No. 1, quoted in Foner, *Factory Girls*, p. 6.

20. Henry Miles, *Lowell as It Was and Is* (Lowell, Mass.: Powers and Bagley, 1845), pp. 128–30.

21. Ibid. For a critical reflection on rationalization, and a subtle and poignant account of the restructuring of gender roles under industrialization, see Herman Melville's pair of stories, "The Paradise of Bachelors" and "The Tartarus of Maids," in *The Complete Stories of Herman Melville*, ed. Jay Leyda (New York: Random House, 1949), pp. 185–95.

22. Quoted in Gutman, *Work, Culture and Society*, p. 5.

23. The idea of self-improvement is intimately related to the American tendencies explored by Tocqueville in "How Equality Suggests to Americans the Idea of the Indefinite Perfectibility of Man," in *Democracy in America*.

24. Quoted in Diane Ravitch, *The Great School Wars* (New York: Basic Books, 1974), p. 12.

25. Horace Mann *The Republic and the School,* Classics in Education (New York: Columbia Teachers' College, 1947), p. 79.

26. Ibid., p. 80.

27. Horace Mann, *Lecture on Education* (Boston: Marsh, Capen, Lyon and Webb, 1840), p. 53.

28. In contrast to maternal authority, which served as the privileged paradigm in the South. See chapter 4.

29. See Ira Katznelson, *City Trenches* (Chicago: University of Chicago Press, 1981) for an account of this development and a lucid exposition of its political consequences.

30. David Brion Davis, *Homicide in American Fiction* (Ithaca, N.Y.: Cornell University Press, 1957), p. 259.

31. Michael Katz, *The Irony of Early School Reform* (Cambridge: Harvard University Press, 1968), p. 174.

32. Ibid., p. 188.

33. Quoted in ibid.

34. Quoted in ibid., pp. 174, 187.

35. Elizabeth Geffen, "Violence in Philadelphia," *Pennsylvania History,* October 1969, p. 403.

36. *Workingman's Gazette,* November 11, 1830, p. 52; and January 12, 1831, p. 132.

37. Ibid., October 21, 1830, p. 30.

38. Geffen, "Violence in Philadelphia," p. 92.

39. Foner, *Factory Girls,* p. 138.

40. Quoted in ibid., p. 78.

41. *The Voice of Industry,* May 8, 1846.

42. Ibid., September 8, 1845.

43. David Grimsted, "Rioting in Its Jacksonian Setting," *American Historical Review,* April 1972, p. 382.

44. Leonard Richards, *Gentlemen of Property and Standing* (New York: Oxford University Press, 1970), p. 45.

45. "A Lowell Factory Girl," *Voice of Industry,* April 17, 1846.

46. *Workingman's Gazette,* November 4, 1830, p. 44.

47. Stephen Simpson, *The Workingman's Manual* (Philadelphia: Thomas Bonsal, 1831), p. 19.

48. Ibid., p. 13.

49. Ibid., p. 8.

50. *Workingman's Gazette,* November 4, 1830, p. 44.

51. Ibid., October 21, 1830, p. 29.

52. Ibid., January 12, 1831, p. 132.

53. Parker, "The Mercantile Class," in *Social Classes in a Republic,* pp. 10, 8, 37.

54. Channing, *Lectures on the Elevation of the Laboring Classes,* (Boston: W. M. Ticknor, 1840), p. 10.

55. Ibid., p. 49.

336

56. Channing, *The Ministry for the Poor* (Boston: Russell, Odiorne, and Metcalf, 1835), p. 3.
57. Ibid., pp. 2–4.
58. Ibid., pp. 9–12.
59. Channing, *Elevation of the Laboring Classes*, p. 4.
60. *Recollections of Samuel Breck* (Philadelphia: Porter and Coates, 1877), p. 301.
61. Foner, *Factory Girls*, p. 163.
62. Simpson, *Workingman's Manual*, p. 127.
63. Foner, *Factory Girls*, p. 24.
64. *Young America*, November 15, 1845, p. 1.
65. John Taylor, *Arator*, pp. 79–80.
66. Huldah Stone, *Voice of Industry*, July 2, 1847.
67. Foner, *Factory Girls*, p. 175.
68. Bagley, "Speech to New England Workingmen's Association," quoted in ibid., p. 109.
69. Foner, p. 297.
70. Quoted in Thomas Dublin, "Women, Work and Protest in the Early Lowell Mills," *Labor History*, Winter 1975, p. 115.
71. Quoted in William Alcott, *The Young Husband* (New York: J. C. Derby, 1835), pp. 228–29.
72. Michael Paul Rogin, *Fathers and Children: Andrew Jackson and the Subjugation of the American Indian* (New York: Alfred A. Knopf, 1975), p. 6.
73. Quoted in Alcott, *Young Husband*, p. 342. See chapter 6 below.
74. Ibid., pp. 345–46.
75. Chicago Workingman's Advocate, quoted in Gutman, pp. 7–8.
76. See Thomas Dew on women, in chapter 6.
77. See chapter 6.
78. See Katherine Kish Sklar, *Catherine Beecher: A Study in Domesticity* (New Haven: Yale University Press, 1973); Julie A. Mattaei, *An Economic History of Women in America* (New York: Schocken Books, 1982), and Carroll Smith Rosenberg, "Women's World of Love and Ritual," *Signs*, 1977, no. 1.
79. Noah Webster, *First American Dictionary*, s.v. "mother." This definition is maintained through the Civil War.
80. See Catherine Beecher, *A Treatise on Domestic Economy* (New York: Harper and Bros., 1849), and *Letters to the People on Health and Happiness* (New York: Harper and Bros., 1855); Eliza Ware (Mrs. John) Farrar, *The Young Lady's Friend* (New York: Samuel S. and William Wood, 1857); Sara Josepha Hale, *Housekeeping and Keeping House* (New York: Harper and Bros., 1845); and Lydia Sigourney, *Letters to Mothers* (New York: Harper and Bros., 1846). See also Sklar, *Catherine Beecher*; and Carl Degler, *At Odds* (New York: Oxford University Press, 1980).
81. "Authority" here designates both a preponderance of male authors in

the genre and male dominion of the fields of knowledge and technology developed.

82. Grimsted, "Rioting in Its Jacksonian Setting," p. 393.

83. Sprague, *Sermon*, p. 12.

84. Quoted in Geffen, "Violence in Philadelphia," p. 403.

85. *The Portable Thomas Jefferson*, ed. Merrill Peterson (New York: Viking Press, 1975), p. 417.

86. Grimsted, "Rioting in Its Jacksonian Setting," p. 366.

87. Quoted in John Runcie, "'Hunting the Nigs' in Philadelphia," *Pennsylvania History*, April 1972, p. 209.

88. Quoted in Somkin, *Unquiet Eagle*, p. 45.

89. Quoted in Grimsted, "Rioting in Its Jacksonian Setting," pp. 384, 385.

90. Quoted in ibid., pp. 385–87.

91. Quoted in ibid.

92. Ibid., p. 367.

93. Harriet Robinson, *Loom and Spindle* (New York: T. Y. Crowell and Co., 1898), p. 88.

94. Simpson, *Workingman's Manual*, p. 138.

CHAPTER THREE

1. I am especially indebted to Aristide Zolberg, who is presently producing a study of immigration, for insights into cross-continental patterns of immigration, and legislative responses to immigration in early nineteenth-century America.

2. *The Life of Rev. Herman Norton* (New York: American and Foreign Christian Union, 1854), p. 8.

3. John Noble, *Noble's Instructions to Emigrants* (Boston: Privately published, 1819).

4. See Turner, *The Ritual Process*. pp. 94–130.

5. Anthony Gavin, *The Great Red Dragon, or the Master Key to Popery* (Cincinnati: Rulison and Co., 1856), pp. 36–37.

6. *Pope or President?* (New York: R. L. Delisser, 1859), pp. 46, 113, 295, 337–39.

7. Robert Breckenridge, *Papism in the Nineteenth Century* (Baltimore: David Owen and Son, 1841).

8. Edward Beecher, *The Papal Conspiracy Exposed* (New York: Dodd, 1855), pp. 394–96.

9. William Hogan, *Popery! As It Was and As It Is* (Hartford, Conn.: S. Andrus and Sons, 1859), p. 126.

10. Breckenridge, *Papism in the Nineteenth Century*, p. 29.

11. Hogan, *Popery!* pp. 126, 246.

12. Gavin, *Red Dragon*, p. 43. Compare abolitionist pamphlets on the South, discussed in chapter 6.

13. *Pope or President?* p. 122.

14. Ibid., pp. 60, 274.

15. Sexuality itself was thought to distinguish Catholic from Protestant. "The weapons of this Union, unlike those of Romanism," wrote the author of *The Life of Rev. Herman Norton,* "are not carnal, but are mighty through God" (p. 6).

16. *Pope or President?* p. 48–58.

17. Gavin, *Red Dragon,* pp. 285–86, 387–92, 52–55, 58. An interesting sidelight on this metaphoric use of gender in the definition of religious identity is offered by Ann Douglas in *The Feminization of American Culture* (New York: Alfred A. Knopf, 1971), p. 34. Douglas focuses on the anxieties of Protestant clerics concerning their masculinity. Those doubtful of their masculinity contrast their "effeminate" weakness to the vigorous masculinity of such violent anti-Catholics as Lyman Beecher.

18. *Pope or President?* pp. 241, 243, 244, 247.

19. *Life of Rev. Herman Norton,* p. 34.

20. Amy Bridges, *A City in the Republic: Antebellum New York and the Origins of Machine* Politics (Cambridge: Cambridge University Press, 1984), p. 10.

21. Joseph Gusfield, *Symbolic Crusade* (Urbana: University of Illinois Press, 1963; Illini Books, 1972), pp. 40–43.

22. Lyman Beecher, *Six Sermons on Intemperance (New York: American Tract Society, 1827), p. 57.*

23. *Ibid.*

24. Robert Beverley, *History and Present State of Virginia,* ed. David Freeman Hawke (1705, New York: Bobbs-Merrill Co., 1971) p. 96.

25. Gusfield, *Symbolic Crusade,* p. 41.

26. This is by no means peculiar to America. Compare the behavior of rioting peasants in late Tokuugawa, Japan, or accounts of the French Revolution.

27. Lincoln, "Temperance Address," February 22, 1842.

28. Lyman Beecher, *A Plea for the West* (Cincinnati: Truman and Smith, 1835; New York: Arno Press, 1977), pp. 67, 143, 163.

29. Ibid., p. 49.

30. Breckinridge, *Papism in the Nineteenth Century,* p. 25.

31. Gavin, *Red Dragon,* p. 410.

32. Lyman Beecher, *Plea for the West,* p. 128.

33. Gavin, *Red Dragon,* p. 389.

34. Ibid., p. 388.

35. Lyman Beecher, *Plea for the West,* p. 53.

36. Quoted in *Life of Rev. Herman Norton,* pp. 46–47.

37. Diane Ravitch, *Great School Wars,* p. 37.

38. Quoted in Stanley K. Schultz, *The Culture Factory* (New York: Oxford University Press, 1973), pp. 230, 232.

39. Mann, *Lecture on Education,* p. 9.

40. Quoted in Schultz, *Culture Factory*, p. 231.

41. Ibid., p. 258.

42. Lyman Beecher, *Plea for the West*, p. 169.

43. Quoted in Michael Katz, ed., *School Reform Past and Present* (Boston: Little, Brown and Co., 1971).

44. Lyman Beecher, *Plea for the West*, pp. 48, 52, 58.

45. Quoted in Schultz, *Culture Factory*, pp. 232, 233, 306.

46. Quoted in ibid., p. 253.

47. Richard Rollins, "Words as Social Control," *American Quarterly*, Fall, 1976.

48. Quoted in Schultz, *Culture Factory*, 253.

49. Quoted in ibid., p. 307.

50. *Life of Rev. Herman Norton*, p. 46.

51. Ibid., p. 50.

52. Edward Beecher, *Papal Conspiracy*, p. 49.

53. Ravitch, *Great School Wars*, p. 35.

54. *Pope or President?* p. 247.

55. Ibid., p. 249.

56. Edward Beecher, *Papal Conspiracy*, p. 49.

57. *Life of Rev. Herman Norton*, p. 21.

58. Breckinridge, *Papism in the Nineteenth Century*, p. 20.

59. *Pope or President?* p. 259.

60. Jefferson, although friendly to French democratic immigration, retained some reservations on the issue of immigration generally, fearing that men accustomed to European decadence, and unaccustomed to free institutions, would prove poor citizens.

61. Hogan, *Popery!* pp. 121–22.

62. Ibid., p. 119.

63. *Pope or President?*, p. 263.

64. J. Walter Coleman, *The Molly Macguire Riots* (Richmond, Va.: Grant and Massie, 1936), p. 19.

65. Wayne Broehl, *The Molly Maguires* (Cambridge: Harvard University Press, 1964), p. 87.

66. Turner, *Ritual Process*.

67. Quoted in Broehl, *The Molly Maguires*, p. 27.

68. Parker, "The Dangerous Classes," in *Social Classes in a Republic*, p. 143.

69. Tocqueville, *Democracy in America* 2:278.

70. Douglas, *Feminization of American Culture*, p. 34.

71. Ibid.

72. Ibid.

73. Ibid.

74. Bertram Wyatt-Brown, *Lewis Tappan* (Cleveland: Case Western Reserve University Press, 1969), pp. 216–27.

75. Quoted in Rollins, "Words as Social Control," pp. 124, 146.

CHAPTER FOUR

1. Frank L. Owsley, "The Irrepressible Conflict," in *I'll Take My Stand: The South and the Agrarian Tradition*, ed. Donald Davidson (New York: Harper and Bros., 1930; Gloucester, Mass.: Peter Smith, 1976), p. 69.

2. Robert Redfield, *Peasant Society and Culture* (Chicago: University of Chicago Press, 1960), p. 19.

3. Davidson, *I'll Take My Stand*, p. xxxiv.

4. Owsley, in Davidson, *I'll Take My Stand*, p. 69.

5. "Economics" was derived, as nearly all educated Southerners knew, from the Greek for "household."

6. Howe, *American Whigs*, p. 239.

7. Francis Gaines, *The Southern Plantation* (New York: Columbia University Press, 1927), p. 227.

8. Quoted in Ronald Walters, *The Antislavery Appeal* (Baltimore: Johns Hopkins University Press, 1976), p. 77.

9. C. Van Woodward, "Southern Ethic in a Puritan World" in *Myth and Southern History*, ed. Patrick Gerster and Nicholas Cords (Chicago: Rand McNally, 1974), p. 3.

10. John Crowe Ransome, "Reconstructed but Unregenerate," in Davidson, *I'll Take My Stand*, p. 12.

11. W. J. Cash, *The Mind of the South* (New York: Alfred A. Knopf, 1941; New York: Vintage Book, 1960), p. 334.

12. Robert Dawidoff, *The Education of John Randolph* (New York: W. W. Norton and Co., 1979), p. 87. This is a remarkable biography, discerning, subtle, and just to its subject.

13. Philip Greven, *The Protestant Temperament* (New York: Alfred A. Knopf, 1977; Meridian, 1979).

14. Ibid., p. 269.

15. Daniel Blake Smith, *Inside the Great House* (Ithaca, N.Y.: Cornell University Press, 1980), p. 104.

16. N. Beverley Tucker, "Lecture on Government," *SLM*, April 1837, p. 210.

17. Calhoun, *Disquisition On Government* (New York: Bobbs-Merrill Co., 1953).

18. Tucker, p. 210.

19. Edmund Burke, *Speech on Conciliation with the Colonies* (New York: Bobbs-Merrill Co., 1966), pp. 59, 71, 72, 73, 78, 137, 141.

20. Backwoods, "America to England," *SLM*, June 1856, p. 424.

21. "1950," *SLM*, June 1856, p. 427.

22. Melville, "Lee in the Capitol," in *Battle Pieces* (New York: Harper and Bros., 1860; Amherst: University of Massachusetts Press, 1972), p. 232.

23. Edmund Wilson, *Patriotic Gore* (New York: Farrar, Straus and Giroux, 1977), p. 331.

24. "African Colonisation Society," *SLM*, January 1856, p. 11.

25. Ibid.
26. Ibid., p. 10.
27. *SLM*, November 1834, p. 83.
28. Richard Brown, "Missouri Crisis, Slavery, and the Politics of Jacksonianism," *South Atlantic Quarterly*, Winter 1966, p. 340.

CHAPTER FIVE

1. J. G. A. Pocock, *The Machiavellian Moment* (Princeton: Princeton University Press, 1975), p. 507.
2. Ibid.
3. Russell Kirk, *John Randolph of Roanoke* (Chicago: Henry Regnery, 1964) p. 163.
4. Lois G. Schwoerer, *No Standing Army!* (Baltimore: Johns Hopkins University Press, 1974) pp. 13–14, 2.
5. Ibid., p. 8.
6. See John Hope Franklin, *The Militant South* (Cambridge: Harvard University Press, 1956) and Bertram Wyatt-Brown, *Southern Honor* (New York: Oxford University Press, 1982) for the best examples of this argument. Wyatt-Brown's study presents an interesting an informative examination of Southern honor, considerably at variance with my own. He treats honor as a self-consciously conventional category, ignoring the parallels between Indians and duelists drawn by Southerners themselves. His account of his own Southern connections in the introduction to the work is subtle, perceptive, and charming.
7. Jefferson to James Madison, January 30, 1787, *The Portable Thomas Jefferson*.
8. Schwoerer, *No Standing Army!* p. 51,
9. John Taylor, *Arator*, p. 107.
10. Locke, *Two Treatises on Government*, p. 327. For a subtle and enlightening account of the self in Locke, see Uday Singh Mehta, "The Anxiety of Freedom: John Locke and the Emergence of Political Subjectivity," (Ph.D. diss., Princeton University, 1984).
11. Ibid., p. 55. See also Nathan Tarcov, *Locke's Education for Liberty* (Chicago: University of Chicago Press, 1984), pp. 35, 38, 55–56.
12. Ibid., p. 330.
13. John C. Calhoun, *A Disquisition on Government*, ed. C. Gordon Post (New York: Bobbs-Merrill Co., 1953), p. 34.
14. Ibid., pp. 53, 70, 86.
15. Ibid., p. 60.

CHAPTER SIX

1. Turner, *Ritual Process*, p. 95.
2. Ibid., pp. 106–7.

3. Ibid., p. 112.

4. Melville, "The Armies of the Wilderness," in *Battle Pieces,* p. 96.

5. Beverley, *History and Present State of Virginia,* pp. 3, 4, 88, 92, 101, 118.

6. Ibid., pp. 18–19.

7. Ibid., p. 101.

8. "A Review of *The Partisan Leader,*" *SLM,* January 1837, p. 73.

9. John Lyde Wilson, *The Code of Honor* (Charleston: James Phinney, 1858), p. 4.

10. Ibid., p. 35.

11. Ibid., p. 7. This interpretation of the political significance of dueling by those who practiced it is unfortunately, and misleadingly, neglected in Bertram Wyatt-Brown's otherwise admirable book *Southern Honor.* For another example see Randolph's remarks on dueling to Thomas Hart Benton, recounted in Benton's *Thirty Years in the Senate,* 2 vols. (New York: D. Appleton and Co., 1879), 1:475.

12. Timothy Dwight, *Sermon on Dueling* (New York: Collins, Perkins, and Co., 1805), p. 25.

13. *The Portable Thomas Jefferson,* p. 417.

14. Quoted in Norman Heard, *White into Red* (Oklahoma City: University of Oklahoma Press, 1970), p. 27.

15. Rogin, *Fathers and Children,* pp. 5–6.

16. Ibid., p. 6.

17. Ibid., p. 126.

18. Mrs. Mary Ware, "Song of Our Glorious Southland," in Simms, *War Poetry of the South,* ed. William Gilmore Simms (New York: Richardson and Co., 1866), p. 216.

19. Fawn Brodie, *Thomas Jefferson: An Intimate Biography* (New York: W. W. Norton and Co., 1974), pp. 232, 352.

20. Quoted in David Brion Davis, *Homicide in American Fiction,* p. 110.

21. Quoted in J. Merton England, "The Democratic Faith in American Schoolbooks," *American Quarterly,* Summer 1963, p. 193.

22. Tucker, "Lecture on Government," p. 210.

23. Elemire Zolla, *The Writer and the Shaman,* trans. Raymond Rosenthal (New York: Harcourt Brace Jovanovich, 1973), p. 14.

24. Quoted in Rogin, *Fathers and Children,* p. 5.

25. Quoted in Louise Barnett, *Ignoble Savage* (Westport, Conn.: Greenwood Press, 1975), p. 9.

26. Quoted in England, "Democratic Faith," p. 193.

27. Quoted in Zolla, *Writer and Shaman,* p. 50.

28. Quoted in Barnett, *Ignoble Savage,* p. 9.

29. Benton *Abridgement* 4:687.

30. Earl Endris Thorpe, *Eros and Freedom* (Durham, N.C.: Seeman Printery, 1967), p. 23.

31. Mary Young, "Reflections on Violence," *Reviews in American History,* March, 1975, p. 8.

32. Quoted in ibid.

33. Jefferson to John Holmes, April 22, 1820, *The Portable Thomas Jefferson*, p. 568.

34. Dawidoff, *Education of John Randolph*, pp. 49–50.

35. Frank Mathias, "John Randolph's Freedmen: The Thwarting of a Will," *Journal of Southern History*, May 1973.

36. Benton, *Thirty Years* 1:3.

37. Joel Williamson, *New People* (New York: Free Press, 1890).

38. Clement Eaton, *The Mind of the Old South* Baton Rouge: Louisiana State University Press, 1964), p. 241.

39. Thorpe, *Eros and Freedom*, p. 28.

40. This influence is happily receiving new attention, prompted by the work of such scholars as Albert Raboteau and Cheryl Gilkes.

41. C. G. Sellers, *The Southerner as American* (Chapel Hill: University of North Carolina Press, 1960), pp. 56–67.

42. Quoted in Eugene Genovese, *Roll, Jordan, Roll: The World the Slaves Made* (New York: Pantheon Books, 1974), p. 444.

43. *SLM*, January 1856, p. 12.

44. Genovese, *Roll, Jordan, Roll*, p. 446.

45. Frederick Law Olmsted, *Cotton Kingdom* (New York: Whitethorne, 1861), p. 46.

46. Ibid., p. 47.

47. Ibid.

48. "Review of A. M. Murray," *SLM*, June 1852, p. 428.

49. Olmsted, *Cotton Kingdom*, p. 47.

50. Ronald Walters, *The Antislavery Appeal: American Abolitionism after 1830* (Baltimore: Johns Hopkins University Press, 1976), p. 72.

51. Ibid., p. 74.

52. Sigmund Freud, *Civilization and Its Discontents*, trans. James Strachey (New York: W. W. Norton and Co., 1959), p. 14.

53. Quoted in Walters, "Erotic South," pp. 75, 74, 73.

54. Quoted in ibid., p. 74.

55. Quoted in ibid., p. 75.

56. Quoted in Walters, *Antislavery Appeal*, pp. 75–76.

57. Richard Grant White, ed., *Poetry Lyrical, Satirical, and Narrative of the Civil War* (New York: American New Co., 1866), p. 17.

58. Ibid., p. 108.

59. "Review of Harriet Martineau on Slavery," *SLM*, January 1856, p. 4.

60. Thorpe, *Eros and Freedom*, p. 35.

61. "Sketches of Southern Life," *SLM*, January 1856, p. 4. Much more could be said of this story. Observe the placement of women and blacks outside the house, the conflation of the black and the feminine in the dying slave, in the white women's knowledge of the slaves, and in the traits ascribed to both groups.

62. "A Memory of My Childhood," *SLM*, October 1856, p. 4.

63. Quoted in Walters, *Antislavery Appeal*, p. 105.

64. For examples of this type of response, see Leon Litwack, *Been in the Storm So Long* (New York: Random House, 1980).

65. Quoted in William Taylor, *Cavalier and Yankee* (Cambridge: Harvard University Press, 1979), p. 163.

66. Quoted in ibid. The association of women and nature across culture is interestingly discussed in Carol MacCormack and Marilyn Strathern, eds., *Nature, Culture, and Gender* (Cambridge: Cambridge University Press, 1981).

67. Simms, *War Poetry*, p. 46.

68. Quoted in William Taylor, *Cavalier and Yankee*, p. 163.

69. Thomas Dew, "On the Characteristic Differences between the Sexes and on Their Position and Influence in Society," *SLM*, August 1835, p. 679.

70. David Haberly, "Women and Indians," *American Quarterly*, Fall 1976, p. 436.

71. John Frost, *Daring and Heroic Deeds of American Women* (Philadelphia: J. W. Bradley, 1854), p. iv.

72. Dew, "The Sexes," p. 679.

73. Ibid., pp. 495–96.

74. Benton, *Thirty Years* 1:5.

75. See Maurice Agulhon, *Marianne into Combat* (New York: Cambridge University Press, 1981); and Neil Hertz, "Medusa's Head," *Representations*, November 1983.

76. Quoted in Taylor, *Cavalier and Yankee*, p. 158.

77. Quoted in Howe, *American Whigs*, p. 68.

78. Simms, *War Poetry*, and White, *Poetry*.

79. "Governor Wise's Oration," *SLM*, April 1858, p. 340.

80. "Rebels," in *Rebel Rhymes and Rhapsodies*, ed. Frank Moore (New York: George Putnam and Co., 1864), p. 39.

81. Adrian Beaufain, "Areytos V," *SLM*, February, 1858, p. 96. See also Simms, *War Poetry*, pp. 4, 98, 117; and An Ex-Confederate, *War Songs of the Confederacy* (Richmond, Va.: W. E. Scull and Co., 1904), pp. 246, 328, 364, 366, 372.

82. Simms, *War Poetry*, p. 84.

83. Beaufain, "Areytos III" *SLM*, December 1857, pp. 456–66.

84. Simms, *War Poetry*, p. 84.

85. Moore, *Rebel Rhymes*, p. 39.

86. Simms, *War Poetry*, p. 87.

87. Ibid., p. 128.

88. Moore, *Rebel Rhymes*, p. 78.

89. Simms, *War Poetry*, p. 180.

90. Ibid., p. 249.

91. Moore, *Rebel Rhymes*, p. 78.

92. Simms, *War Poetry*, p. 74.

93. Melville, "The Armies of the Wilderness," p. 101.

94. Julie Roy Jeffrey, *Frontier Women: The Trans-Mississippi West 1840–1880* (New York: Hill and Wang, 1979), p. 8.

95. Taylor, William, *Cavalier and Yankee*, p. 174.

96. Ibn Khaldun, *Muqaddimah*, trans. Franz Rosenthal, 3 vols. (New York: Pantheon Books, 1958).

97. See Rousseau, "A Discourse on Political Economy," in *The Social Contract and Discourses* (New York: E. P. Dutton and Co., 1950), and *Emile*.

98. Moore, *Rebel Rhymes*, pp. 16, 26, 29, 128, 133, 143, 158, 204, 207, 219, 226, 240, 241, 266.

99. Ibid., p. 29.

100. Frost, *Deeds of American Women*, p. 3.

101. Simms, *War Poetry*, p. 50.

102. Taylor, William, *Cavalier and Yankee*, p. 164.

103. Note that this is exactly the course recommended by Rousseau in *Emile*, and marked by him in his "Discourse on Political Economy," as the foundation of civility.

104. Quoted in William Taylor, *Cavalier and Yankee*, p. 170.

105. Quoted in Drew Faust, *A Sacred Circle* (Baltimore: Johns Hopkins University Press, 1977), p. 26.

106. "Editor's Table," *SLM*, May 1858, p. 396.

107. Hugh A. Garland, *Life of John Randolph of Roanoke*, 2 vols. (New York: D. Appleton and Co., 1850), 1:5.

108. Ibid. 1:141.

109. Ibid. 1:135.

110. Ibid. 1:133–34.

111. Ibid. 1:140.

112. Ibid. 1:1, 5.

113. Ibid. 1:10.

114. Ibid. 1:9.

115. Ibid. 1:2.

116. Ibid. 1:10.

117. Kirk, *Randolph*, p. 260.

118. "Two Manuscript Letters of John Randolph," *SLM*, November 1856.

119. "Review of Bancroft's History," *SLM*, April, 1837, p. 220.

120. Burke, *Speech on Conciliation*.

121. Randolph to Josiah Quincy, March 22, 1814, in Edmund Quincy, *Life of Josiah Quincy* (Boston: Ticknor and Fields, 1867), p. 350. This memoir contains some exceptionally charming anecdotes of Randolph.

122. Zolla, *The Writer and !he Shaman*, p. 34.

123. "Editor's Table," *SLM*, May 1858, p. 394.

124. Quoted in Dawidoff, *John Randolph*, p. 247.

125. Benton, *Thirty Years*, 1:474.

126. James Kirke Paulding, *Letters from the South* (New York: James Eastburn and Co., 1835), 1:14.

127. Bertram Wyatt-Brown remarks, in *Southern Honor*, that the adoption of eccentricities may have figured in Southern culture as a strategy for

making palatable intellectual preeminence. Note that this implies a high value on egalitarianism.

128. Benton, *Thirty Years* 1:4.

129. Dawidoff, *Education of John Randolph*, p. 26.

130. Randolph to Josiah Quincy, December 11, 1813, in Edmund Quincy, *Life of Josiah Quincy*, p. 340.

131. *Diary of John Quincy Adams*, ed. Allan Nevins (New York: Frederick Ungar Publishing Co., 1951), p. 229.

132. "On the Cumberland Road," *SLM*, April 1858, p. 271.

133. Whitman, "Song of Joys," in *Complete Poems*, p. 211.

134. Whitman, "Still Though the One I Sing," p. 48.

135. "Editor's Table," *SLM*, May 1858, p. 396.

136. Hugh Pleasants, "Sketches of the Virginia Convention of 1829–1830," *SLM*, May 1851, p. 303.

137. Henry Adams, *John Randolph* (Gloucester, Mass.: Peter Smith, 1969).

138. John Quincy Adams, *Diary*, p. 416. See also note 139 below.

139. Pleasants, "Sketches of the Virginia Convention," p. 303. For a perceptive account of the Gorgon metaphor, see Hertz, "Medusa's Head."

140. Pleasants, "Sketches of the Virginia Convention," p. 303.

141. John Taylor, *Arator*, p. 80.

142. For a thorough account of the land scandals, see C. Peter Magrath, *Yazoo* (New York: W. W. Norton and Co., 1966).

143. See particularly Randolph's speech in the House of Representatives of January 29, 1805. This speech is reprinted in Kirk, *Randolph.*

144. Garland, *Randolph* 1:205.

145. See Marcus Cunliffe, *Chattel Slavery and Wage Slavery* (Athens: University of Georgia Press, 1979).

146. Kirk, *Randolph*, pp. 128, 145.

147. See the letters in ibid., and Theodore Dudley, ed., *Letters to a Young Relative* (New York: D. Appleton and Co., 1834).

148. Whittier, "Randolph of Roanoke," in *Poems* (New York: Hurst and Co., 1847), pp. 193–94.

149. "Editor's Table," *SLM*, May 1858, p. 396. They meant, of course, that Randolph would not have tolerated abolitionists either.

150. Garland, *Randolph*, 151, 152.

151. Ibid.

152. Ibid. 1:11.

153. Taylor, William, *Cavalier and Yankee*, pp. 157–60.

154. Ibid., p. 160.

155. Ibid.

156. Garland, *Randolph* 1:11.

157. Quoted in Leon Harris, *The Fine Art of Political Wit* (New York: Bell Publishing, 1964), pp. 53–54.

CHAPTER SEVEN

1. Richard Slotkin, *Regeneration through Violence* (Middletown, Conn.: Wesleyan University Press, 1973).

2. Benton and Jackson, for example, began their friendship and political alliance in a violent brawl.

3. Richard Dorson, *Davy Crockett: American Comic Legend*, (New York: Rockland Editions, 1939), pp. 125, 34, 85, 4, 52, 55, 4, 51, 50–51.

4. Ibid., pp. 30, 32, 79.

5. Ibid., pp. 6, 48.

6. Dorson, *Crockett*, pp. 129, 126, 86, xx, 80, 90.

7. Quoted in Benton, *Abridgement*, p. 575.

8. Rogin, *Fathers and Children*, pp. 120, 122, 123.

9. Ibid., p. 9.

10. Langdon Cheeves, speech in the House of Representatives, January 17, 1812.

11. Rogin, *Fathers and Children*, p. 122.

12. See, for example, Burr Cartwright Brundage, *A Rain of Darts: The Mexica Aztecs* (Austin: University of Texas Press, 1972).

13. Quoted in Somkin, *Unquiet Eagle*.

14. Rogin, *Fathers and Children*, pp. 286–87, 291.

15. Erik Erikson, *Childhood and Society* (New York: W. W. Norton and Co., 1963); and Freud, *Civilization and Its Discontents*, p. 52.

16. Quoted in Rogin, *Fathers and Children*, p. 287.

17. Robert Bone, "Irving's Headless Horseman," *American Quarterly*, Spring 1963, p. 174.

18. Quoted in Rogin, *Fathers and Children*, p. 287.

19. Benton, *Abridgement*, 4:57, 62.

20. David Grimsted, *Notions of the Americans: 1820–1860* (New York: Goerge Braziller, 1970), p. 102, plate 3.

21. Slotkin, *Regeneration through Violence*, p. 413.

22. Ibid., p. 415.

23. Weber, *From Max Weber*.

CHAPTER EIGHT

1. Quoted in Chicago Campaign Document no. 1, pamphlet in the Lincoln Collection, University of Chicago Library, Special Collections.

2. Jefferson Davis, *The Rise and Fall of the Confederate Government* (New York: D. Appleton, 1881), 1:6, 2:160.

3. Ibid. 2:160.

4. *A Message From the Army of the Valley of Virginia to the General Assembly of Virginia and the Congress of the Confederacy, and the Richmond Newspapers*, pamphlet in the Lincoln Collection, University of Chicago Library.

5. *Address of E. C. Walthall,* pamphlet in the Lincoln Collection, University of Chicago Library.

6. These are rare and contain equally rare but nonetheless interesting accounts of the Haitian Revolution which portray it in (for the place and the period) an unusually favorable light. See George Stacy, *Abolition Hymns* (Hopedale, Mass.: Hopedale Community Press, 1834).

7. William MacKenzie, Chairman, *Report of the Committee of Merchants for the Relief of the Colored People Suffering from the Race Riots* (New York: Whitethorne, 1863).

8. Ibid., p. 21.

9. Ibid.

10. *Democrats' Reference Book* (Philadelphia: Democratic Party, 1848), pp. 1, 6, 7.

11. Howe, *American Whigs,* p. 96.

12. "Larry's Return from the War," in White, *Poetry,* pp. 144–46.

13. Thomas Drew, *Republican Songbook* (Boston: Thayer and Eldridge, 1860), p. 57.

14. Ibid., p. 32.

15. *Tony Pastor's Union Songster* (New York: Dick and Fitzgerald, 1864), p. 24.

16. Ibid., p. 20.

17. Civil War Songsheet no. 29, Special Collections Department, University of Chicago Library.

18. *The New Pantheon, or the Age of Black* (New York: Rollo, 1860), p. 26.

19. "Hoist up the Flag," Lincoln Sheet Music, Lincoln Collection, University of Chicago Library.

20. Charles Halpin, "Soldiers' Talk," in White, *Poetry,* p. 190.

21. Edgar McManus, *Black Bondage in the North* (Syracuse, N.Y.: Syracuse University Press, 1973), pp. 180–84.

22. Wyatt-Brown, *Tappan* p. 90.

23. Samuel Breck, *Recollections,* p. 302.

24. James Freeman Clarke *Slavery in the United States: A Sermon* (Boston: Benjamin H. Greene, 1843), p. 6.

25. Olmsted, *Cotton Kingdom,* p. 40.

26. Ibid., p. 48.

27. Ibid., p. 49.

28. Thomas Goodwin, *Natural History of Secession* (New York: John Bradburn, 1864), p. 60–62.

29. *Tony Pastor's Union Songster,* p. 10.

30. *Chicago Tribune* Campaign Document no. 1, Lincoln Collection, University of Chicago Library.

31. Rev. Henry Dexter, *What Ought to Be Done with the Freedmen and the Rebels* (Boston: Nichols and Noyes, 1865), p. 5.

32. Ibid., p. 14.

33. John Kasson, *Civilizing the Machine* (New York: Grossman Publishers, 1976), p. 122.

34. MacKenzie, *Report of the Committee of Merchants*, p. 37.

35. Here the term "men" may be properly confined to the gender. Women, who by 1850 were largely barred from industry and assigned to domestic labor, remained interested in this aspect of the evils of slavery. It is noteworthy that most of the accounts of the mistreatment of slaves were written by, or for, women.

36. Speech in the Senate *Annals of Congress* March 4, 1858,

37. *Voice of Industry*, Spetember 18, 1845.

38. Quoted in Foner, *Factory Girls*, p. 17.

39. *Nashua Gazette*, October 1, 1846.

40. Howe, *American Whigs*, p. 76.

41. *Fall River Mechanic*, October 5, 1845.

42. *The Man*, May 13, 1834.

CHAPTER NINE

1. "Rebel," in Moore, *Rebel Rhymes*, p. 39.

2. Ibid., p. 248.

3. *Congressional Globe*, Appendix, 1858, p. 271.

4. "Rebels," in Moore, *Rebel Rhymes*, p. 246.

5. John Munson, *Reminiscences of a Mosby Guerrilla* (New York: Moffat Yard and Co., 1906), p. 11.

6. "Song," in Moore, *Rebel Rhymes*, p. 222.

7. Michael C. C. Adams, *Our Masters the Rebels: A Speculation on Union Military Failure in the East* (Cambridge: Harvard University Press, 1978).

8. Henry Adams, *Democracy* (New York: Fawcett Publications, 1961), p. 79.

9. Melville, *Clarel* 2:230.

10. Henry Adams, *Democracy*, p. 126.

11. David Donald, "Died of Democracy," in David Donald, ed., *Why the North Won the Civil War* (London: Collier, Macmillan, 1960), p. 80.

12. Ibid.

13. John Hope Franklin's *The Militant South* and other works emphasizing the Southern relation to violence, and to the military, neglect the longstanding Southern resistance to a standing army, and the philosophy underlying the militia system, and collapse types of violence that should properly be distinguished.

14. Ibid., p. 85.

15. Ibid.

16. Lloyd Lewis, *Sherman, Fighting Prophet* (New York: Harcourt, Brace, 1932), p. 335.

17. Donald, "Died of Democracy," p. 81.

18. Ibid., p. 80.

19. Benton, *Thirty Years* 1:45.

20. Donald, "Died of Democracy," p. 81.

21. Ibid.

22. Melville, "Stonewall Jackson, attributed to a Virginian," in *Battle Pieces*, p. 83.

23. Munson, *Mosby Guerrilla*, p. 224.

24. Ibid., pp. 9–10.

25. Ibid., p. 41.

26. George Forgie, *Patricide and the House Divided* (New York: W. W. Norton and Co., 1979), pp. 208–10).

27. Munson, *Mosby Guerrilla*, p. 30.

28. Ibid., p. 22.

29. Sheridan to Bismarck, Quoted in Charles Francis Adams, *Message Addressed to the Virginia House of Delegates*, February 1928, pamphlet in the Lincoln Collection, University of Chicago Library.

30. Lewis, *Sherman*, p. 334.

31. Ibid., p. 187.

32. Ibid., pp. 334–35.

33. Ibid.

34. Richard Current, "God and the Strongest Battalions," in Donald, *Why the North Won the Civil War*, p. 30.

35. Moore, *Rebel Rhymes*, pp. 27, 29, 64, 99.

36. "We'll Be Free in Maryland," in Moore, Rebel Rhymes, p. 146.

37. "Battle of Bull Run," in Moore, Rebel Rhymes, p. 123.

38. "Southern War Song," in Moore, *Rebel Rhymes*, p. 144.

39. "Southrons" and "Southern Battle Song," in Moore, *Rebel Rhymes*, pp. 152, 228.

40. "Yankee Vandals" and "Nil Desperandum," in Moore, *Rebel Rhymes*, pp. 99, 154.

41. "Printers of Virginia to Old Abe," in Moore, Rebel Rhymes, p. 190.

42. "Song," in Moore, *Rebel Rhymes*, p. 223.

43. Eugene Murdock, *One Million Men: The Civil War Draft in the North* (Madison: Wisconsin State Historical Society, 1971), p. 51.

44. Adrian Cook, *The Armies of the Streets* (Lexington: University of Kentucky Press, 1974), p. 60.

45. Ibid., pp. 151–53.

46. Of these, eleven were black.

47. Murdock, *One Million Men*, pp. 34–35, 41, 55, 85–86.

48. Ibid., p. 199.

49. Cook, *Armies of the Street*, p. 121–22.

50. David Barnes, *The New York Draft Riots* (New York: Baker and Godwin, 1863).

51. Quoted in MacKenzie, *Report of the Committee of Merchants*.

52. David Brion Davis, *The Slave Power Conspiracy and the Paranoid Style* (Baton Rouge: Louisiana State University Press, 1969), p. 75.

53. White, *Poetry*, p. 66.

54. "The New England Character," *SLM*, July 1837, p. 413.

55. Quoted in "A Review of *The Partisan Leader*," *SLM*, January 1837, p. 84.

56. Sprague, "The New England Character," *North American Review*, January 1837, p. 260.

57. *SLM*, June 1835, pp. 587–88.

58. Ibid., p. 591.

59. In the House of Representatives, January 1811 (*Annals of Congress*, p. 541). For an earlier example, see Patrick Henry's speech in the Virginia State Ratifying Convention, collected in Herbert J. Storing, ed., *The Antifederalist* (Chicago: University of Chicago Press, 1981), pp. 296–97.

60. In the House of Representatives, January 6, 1813 (Benton, *Abridgement*, p. 645).

61. *SLM*, June 1835, p. 591.

62. *SLM*, January 1860, p. 39.

63. Jan Dawson, "The Puritan and the Cavalier," *Journal of Southern History* (November 1978): 598.

64. "Barney," "The Irish Picket," in White, *Poetry*, p. 94. Note that the South is also "down below" and associated with both the earth and sexuality as evoked by the phrase.

65. Lewis, *Sherman*, p. 335.

66. *SLM*, January 1858, p. 29.

67. "Cromwell," *SLM*, January 1858, p. 61.

68. St. George Tucker, "The Southern Cross," in Simms, *War Poetry*.

69. Melville's Miltonic imagery appears throughout the *Battle Pieces*, but is especially evident in "The Conflict of Convictions." For Whittier, see "Ein Feste Burg ist Unser Gott," in White, *Poems*, p. 404.

70. "The Flag," in White, *Poetry*, p. 110.

71. "The Fire of Freedom," in Simms, *War Poetry*, p. 55. The final line refers to Cromwell's Barebones Parliament, an assembly which acquired its name from the zeal of Praise God Barbon, an Anabaptist leatherseller and member of the parliament.

72. Ibid., p. 75.

73. Edward Lytton Bulwer, "Cromwell," *SLM*, September 1836, p. 607.

74. The connection between paternal authority, violence, and leadership is a central concern of Freud's *Group Psychology and the Analysis of the Ego* (New York: W. W. Norton and Co., 1959).

CHAPTER TEN

1. Melville, "Supplement," in *Battle Pieces*, p. 259.

2. For a rich and perceptive interpretation of *Battle Pieces*, which gives particular attention to the intersection of private and public, familial and national identity in Melville, see "The Iron Dome" in Michael Rogin, *Subversive*

Genealogy: The Politics and Art of Herman Melville (New York: Alfred A. Knopf, 1983), pp. 259–87.

3. Melville, "Lee in the Capitol," p. 232.

4. Melville, "The Armies of the Wilderness," p. 93.

5. Melville, "The Conflict of Convictions," pp. 17–18.

6. See, for example, the passage on spermaceti in *Moby Dick*. Melville, *Moby Dick* (New York: Bantam Books, 1981), p. 385. The chapter is entitled "A Squeeze of the Hand."

7. Melville, "The Armies of the Wilderness," p. 94.

8. Ibid., p. 91.

9. Ibid., p. 94.

10. Melville, "The Rebel Color-Bearers at Shiloh," p. 144.

11. Melville, "The Battle for the Mississippi," p. 64.

12. Melville, "The Armies of the Wilderness," p. 103.

13. Melville, "The Conflict of Convictions," p. 16.

14. Ibid., p. 14.

15. Melville, "Look-out Mountain," pp. 88–89.

16. Melville, "The Armies of the Wilderness," p. 101.

17. Melville, "The Released Rebel Prisoner," p. 150.

18. Melville, "The Armies of the Wilderness," p. 103. I am indebted to my teacher, Ralph Lerner, who enabled me to see the continued meaning of the Sabaeans.

19. Melville, "Stonewall Jackson (Ascribed to a Virginian)," p. 81.

20. Ibid., p. 79.

21. Ibid.

22. Melville, *Clarel* (London: Constable and Co., 1924) 2:176. John Randolph, whom Ungar markedly resembles, wrote that he had, in childhood, acquired a prejudice in favor of Mahometanism; "the crescent had a talismanic effect on my imagination, and I rejoiced in all its triumphs over the cross (which I despised)." Henry Adams commented acerbically on this taste in his *John Randolph*, p. 26.

23. Ibid. 2:230.

24. Ibid. 2:176.

25. Melville, "Misgivings," p. 13.

26. Melville, "Lee in the Capitol," p. 236. Here too the South is identified with Islam, and thus with Ishmael, the disowned seed of Abraham, the fatherless child. The children of Ishmael wander in the wilderness outside the city.

27. Melville, "The Armies of the Wilderness," p. 96.

28. Melville, *Clarel* 2:179.

29. Melville, "The Scout towards Aldie," p. 212.

30. Ibid., pp. 218–19.

31. Ibid., p. 188.

32. Melville, *Clarel* 2:175.

33. Ibid. 2:158.

34. Melville, "The Scout towards Aldie," p. 206.
35. Ibid.
36. Melville, "The Conflict of Conventions," p. 17.
37. Melville, "The Scout towards Aldie," p. 225.
38. Ibid., p. 224.
39. Melville, "Malvern Hill," p. 69.
40. Melville, "The March to the Sea," pp. 128–32.
41. Ibid.
42. Melville, "Donelson," p. 50.
43. Melville, "The Released Rebel Prisoner," p. 151.
44. Melville, "The Armies in the Wilderness," p. 101.
45. Melville, "Dupont's Round Fight," p. 30.
46. Melville, "A Utilitarian View of the Monitor's Fight," p. 61.
47. Melville, "The College Colonel," p. 121.
48. Melville, "Dupont's Round Fight," p. 30.
49. Melville, "A Canticle," pp. 138–40.
50. Melville, "Supplement," p. 260.
51. Melville, "Presentation to the Authorities," p. 182.
52. Melville, "The House Top," pp. 86–87.
53. Ibid.
54. Melville, "Lee in the Capitol," p. 237.
55. Ibid., p. 236.
56. Melville, "A Canticle," p. 138.
57. Melville, "Supplement," p. 261.
58. Melville, "The Fall of Richmond," p. 136.

CHAPTER ELEVEN

1. Richard Hofstadter, *The American Political Tradition and the Men Who Made It* (New York: Alfred A. Knopf, 1948), p. 92.
2. Ibid.
3. *From Max Weber*, ed. Hans Gerth and C. Wright Mills (New York: Oxford University Press, 1946), pp. 245–52.
4. Edmund Wilson, *Patriotic Gore*, p. 100.
5. Lincoln, Address to the Young Men's Lyceum of Springfield, Illinois.
6. As in the Lyceum and Temperance addresses.
7. Harry Jaffa, *The Crisis of the House Divided* (Garden City, N.Y.: Doubleday and Co., 1959).
8. J. L. Scripps to Herndon, Chicago, Illinois, June 24, 1865. Quoted in J. G. Randall, *Lincoln the President: From Springfield to Gettysburg* (New York: Dodd, Mead and Co., 1945) 1:4.
9. Quoted in Jaffa, *The Crisis*, p. 189.
10. Lincoln, Lyceum Address.
11. George Forgie, *Patricide and the House Divided*.
12. Matt. 18:7.

13. Matt. 18:8–9.

14. Lincoln, Gettysburg Address.

15. A Southerner also noted the propriety of the name, observing that Lincoln, however unwilling, was to become the "father of many nations" ("True to His Name," in Moore, *Rebel Rhymes*, p. 28).

16. See the Lincoln Sheet Music and Civil War Songsheets collections in the Department of Special Collections, University of Chicago Library.

17. "Daily Song of the 100 Day Soldier," Civil War Songsheet, no. 31, University of Chicago Library.

18. Sep Winner, "Abraham's Daughter" (Philadelphia: Sep Winner's Music Store, 1861), Lincoln Sheet Music Collection, University of Chicago Library.

19. Forgie, *Patricide*, pp. 244–47.

20. Lincoln Sheet Music no. 28, University of Chicago Library.

21. Hofstadter, *American Political Tradition*, p. 100.

22. Edmund Wilson, *Patriotic Gore*, pp. 334–35.

23. Lincoln, First Inaugural Address.

24. Slotkin, *Regeneration through Violence*.

25. Lincoln, First Inaugural Address.

26. Melville, "The Martyr," in *Battle Pieces*, p. 141.

27. Ibid., p. 142.

28. Note how closely this accords to Freud's description of the relation of Christianity to the killing of the father by the sons, in *Civilization and Its Discontents*.

CHAPTER TWELVE

1. Whitman, "Over the Carnage Rose Prophetic a Voice," in *Complete Poems*, p. 341. (All subsequent citations are from the *Complete Poems*.)

2. "Long, too Long, America," p. 336.

3. "Song of the Answerer," p. 199.

4. "Song of Myself," p. 89.

5. "By Blue Ontario's Shore," p. 368.

6. Ibid., pp. 368–69.

7. "To Foreign Lands," p. 39.

8. Ibid.

9. "States!" p. 620.

10. "Song of Myself," p. 68.

11. "A Song of Joys," p. 210.

12. "By Blue Ontario's Shore," p. 374.

13. "Virginia—the West," p. 319.

14. Ibid.

15. "Thou Mother with Thy Equal Brood," p. 470.

16. Ibid., p. 469.

17. Ibid., p. 468.

18. "By Blue Ontario's Shore," p. 374.
19. "Thou Mother with Thy Equal Blood," p. 468.
20. "Song of Myself," p. 109.
21. Ibid. pp. 109, 77, 69, 72, 101.
22. Ibid. p. 83.
23. "I Sing the Body Electric," p. 136.
24. Ibid., p. 128.
25. "Apostroph," p. 613.
26. "Song of Myself," p. 121.
27. "One's Self I Sing," p. 37.
28. "Starting From Paumanok," p. 52.
29. "Apostroph," p. 614.
30. "Roaming in Thought," p. 301.
31. "Song of Myself," p. 85.
32. Ibid.
33. "Reconciliation," p. 345.
34. "Starting From Paumanok," p. 53.
35. "For You O Democracy," p. 150.
36. "The Dust Was Once the Man," p. 361.
37. "Apostroph," p. 615.
38. Ibid.
39. "Song of the Exposition," p. 232.
40. "One's Self I Sing," p. 37.
41. "Thy Mother with Thy Equal Blood," p. 172.
42. "The Dust Was Once the Man," p. 361.
43. "O Captain! My Captain!" p. 360.
44. "What Best I See in Thee," p. 495.
45. "When Lilacs Last in the Dooryard Bloom'd," p. 351.
46. Ibid., p. 353.
47. Ibid.
48. "Years of the Modern," p. 499.
49. Ibid.
50. Ibid.
51. "Song of the Broad Axe," p. 225.
52. "Give Me the Silent Splendid Sun," p. 337.
53. Ibid.
54. Ibid.
55. "Starting From Paumanok," p. 51.
56. Whitman, "Race of Veterans," p. 344.
57. "Song of Myself," p. 83.
58. "Salut Au Monde!" p. 177.
59. "By Blue Ontario's Shores," p. 364.
60. Ibid.
61. "States!" p. 621.
62. "Starting From Paumanok," p. 61.

63. "A Broadway Pageant," p. 273.
64. "Salut Au Monde," p. 177.
65. "A Broadway Pageant," p. 273.
66. Ibid.
67. "By Blue Ontario's Shore," p. 369.
68. "Thick-sprinkled Bunting," p. 494.
69. "By Blue Ontario's Shore," p. 375.
70. "As I Lay with My Head in Your Lap, Comerado," p. 346.
71. "Song of the Broad Axe," p. 215.
72. Ibid., p. 219.
73. "To the States," p. 44.
74. "Still Though the One I Sing," p. 48.

Index